Bad Youth

STUDIES OF THE WEATHERHEAD EAST ASIAN INSTITUTE

Columbia University

Selected Titles
(Complete list at: *www.columbia.edu/cu/weai/publications/index.html*)

Bad Youth: Juvenile Delinquency and the Politics of Everyday Life in Modern Japan, by David R. Ambaras. University of California Press, 2005.

Rearranging the Landscape of the Gods: The Politics of a Pilgrimage Site in Japan, 1573–1912, by Sarah Thal. University of Chicago Press, 2005.

Takeuchi Yoshimi: Displacing the West, by Richard Calichman. Cornell University Press, 2004.

Gutenberg in Shanghai: Chinese Print Capitalism, 1876–1937, by Christopher A. Reed. UBC Press, 2004.

Japan's Colonization of Korea: Discourse and Power, by Alexis Dudden. University of Hawai'i Press, 2004.

Divorce in Japan: Family, Gender, and the State, 1600–2000, by Harald Fuess. Stanford University Press, 2004.

The Communist Takeover of Hangzhou: The Transformation of City and Cadre, 1949–1954, by James Gao. University of Hawai'i Press, 2004.

Taxation without Representation in Rural China, by Thomas P. Bernstein and Xiaobo Lü. Modern China Series, Cambridge University Press, 2003.

The Reluctant Dragon: Crisis Cycles in Chinese Foreign Economic Policy, by Lawrence Christopher Reardon. University of Washington Press, 2002.

Cadres and Corruption: The Organizational Involution of the Chinese Communist Party, by Xiaobo Lü. Stanford University Press, 2000.

Japan's Imperial Diplomacy: Consuls, Treaty Ports, and War with China, 1895–1938, by Barbara Brooks. University of Hawai'i Press, 2000.

China's Retreat from Equality: Income Distribution and Economic Transition, edited by Carl Riskin, Zhao Renwei, Li Shi. M.E. Sharpe, 2000.

Nation, Governance, and Modernity: Canton, 1900–1927, by Michael T.W. Tsin. Stanford University Press, 1999.

Assembled in Japan: Electrical Goods and the Making of the Japanese Consumer, by Simon Partner. University of California Press, 1999.

Civilization and Monsters: Spirits of Modernity in Meiji Japan, by Gerald Figal. Duke University Press, 1999.

The Logic of Japanese Politics: Leaders, Institutions, and the Limits of Change, by Gerald L. Curtis. Columbia University Press, 1999.

Contesting Citizenship in Urban China: Peasant Migrants, the State and Logic of the Market, by Dorothy Solinger. University of California Press, 1999.

Bicycle Citizens: The Political World of the Japanese Housewife, by Robin LeBlanc. University of California Press, 1999.

Alignment despite Antagonism: The United States, Japan, and Korea, by Victor Cha. Stanford University Press, 1999.

Bad Youth

Juvenile Delinquency and the Politics of Everyday Life in Modern Japan

David R. Ambaras

UNIVERSITY OF CALIFORNIA PRESS
Berkeley · Los Angeles · London

University of California Press
Berkeley and Los Angeles, California

University of California Press, Ltd.
London, England

© 2006 by The Regents of the University of California

Library of Congress Cataloging-in-Publication Data

Ambaras, David Richard, 1962–
 Bad youth : juvenile delinquency and the politics of
everyday life in modern Japan / David R. Ambaras.
    p.   cm. — (Studies of the Weatherhead East
Asian Institute, Columbia University)
 Includes bibliographical references and index.
 ISBN 0-520-24579-2 (cloth : alk. paper)
 1. Juvenile delinquency—Japan—Prevention—
History—20th century. 2. Problem youth—
Government policy—Japan—History—20th century.
3. Urban youth—Government policy—Japan—History—
20th century. 4. Social control—Japan—History—
20th century. 5. Social change—Japan. 6. Japan—
Social conditions—20th century. I. Title. II. Series.

HV9207.A5A56   2005
364.36′0952′09041—dc22   2005000432

Manufactured in the United States of America

15 14 13 12 11 10 09 08 07 06
10 9 8 7 6 5 4 3 2 1

To Misako, Allie, and Jeremy

Contents

Illustrations

Acknowledgments

During the too many years that have gone into the research and writing of this book, I have benefited greatly from ongoing conversations with Sheldon Garon and David Howell. I could not have wished for more generous, supportive teachers; each is a model of scholarship to which I can only aspire.

I would like to thank Andrew Gordon, Sally Hastings, Stephen Vlastos, Thomas Havens, Kären Wigen, Carol Gluck, Alexis Dudden, Jonathan Ocko, David Gilmartin, Akram Khater, Steven Levine, Ann Waltner, Alex De Grand, Steven Vincent, Donald Roden, and Martin Collcutt for their thoughtful comments regarding all or parts of various versions of this work. I have also gained many valuable insights from discussions with Dani Botsman, Sabine Frühstück, Greg Pflugfelder, Jan Bardsley, Miles Fletcher, Jordan Sand, Sumiko Otsubo, Mary Brinton, Peter Holquist, Umemori Naoyuki, Narita Ryūichi, and Yoshida Nobuyuki. For their ceaseless encouragement, thanks to Tony La Vopa, Barbara Brooks, Franziska Seraphim, Eika Tai, John Mertz, Richard Jaffe, Gennifer Weisenfeld, Kris Troost, Barbara Sato, Claudia Koonz, Arno Mayer, Jerry Surh, David Zonderman, Ken Vickery, John David Smith, and Tony Moyer.

The libraries and staffs of the following institutions provided invaluable assistance: the University of Tokyo, Hitotsubashi University, Waseda University, the Japan College of Social Work, the Kyōsei Kyōkai, the Ōhara Social Problems Research Institute, the National Diet Library, Taitō

Kuritsu Shitamachi Fūzoku Shiryōkan, the Taitō Ward Library, Princeton University (especially Yasuko Makino and her predecessor Soowon Kim), Duke University (especially Kris Troost), Harvard University, the Library of Congress, North Carolina State University, and the University of North Carolina at Chapel Hill. Thanks also to Toda Hiraku, Watanabe Yoshiyuki, and Yao-Hsiang Tsui for their help in securing newspaper materials and photographs. I would also like to express my gratitude to Nakamura Masanori, Ronald Toby, Okamoto Kōichi, Lee Hyang-Chul and Chon Chi-In, Kuroda Kinuyo, and the late Kikuchi Masanori for their hospitality and generosity during my several stays in Japan. And to Toda Keiko and Toda Shin'ichi, my heartfelt thanks for countless favors large and small.

I am deeply grateful to Carol Gluck for her ongoing interest in my work and her generous assistance in guiding it to publication. Madge Huntington at the Weatherhead East Asian Institute offered much-needed advice on preparing my manuscript. Reed Malcolm, my editor at the University of California Press, Jacqueline Volin, my production editor, and Harry Dolan, my copyeditor, have all made the publishing process as smooth and painless as possible.

The research and writing of this book were supported by funding from the National Endowment for the Humanities, the Fulbright Foundation, the Mrs. Giles Whiting Foundation, the Northeast Asia Council of the Association for Asian Studies, North Carolina State University and the NCSU College of Humanities and Social Sciences, and the North Carolina Japan Center. Parts of the introduction and chapters 2 and 3 have previously appeared in David R. Ambaras, "Social Knowledge, Cultural Capital, and the New Middle Class in Japan, 1895–1912," *The Journal of Japanese Studies* 24, no. 1 (1998). A slightly different version of chapter 6 appeared as David R. Ambaras, "Juvenile Delinquency and the National Defense State: Policing Young Workers in Wartime Japan, 1937–1945," *The Journal of Asian Studies* 63, no. 1 (2004, reprinted with permission of the Association for Asian Studies).

Finally, I want to thank my wife Misako Toda and our sons Alan and Jeremy—my "glad youth"—for their boundless patience and constant support. Without the love and joy they have brought me, none of this work would have been worthwhile. I dedicate this book to them.

Introduction

On the evening of August 1, 1927, a contingent of detectives from the Tokyo Metropolitan Police Department swept into the Ginza, the city's upscale amusement district, and, with auxiliary squads blocking escape routes, proceeded to arrest every young man in fashionable flared trousers they could find. In all, the police detained more than 150 "modern boys," ranging from affluent idlers in cafés to armed hoodlums who, in the company of "modern girls," accosted innocent promenaders and otherwise offended public morals. A few nights later in Asakusa, where crowds flocked to cinemas, cheap eateries, and other popular entertainments, police officers netted more than five hundred people in an all-out hunt for young pickpockets, shoplifters, muggers, kidnappers, prostitutes, vagrants, and other miscreants. Police actions targeted workplaces as well: two weeks earlier, officers had even raided Tokyo City Hall to crack down on groups like the Lightning Gang, violent office boys and the female typists and telephone operators with whom they associated.[1]

Such scenes were far from unusual in Tokyo and other cities in early-twentieth-century Japan. Indeed, as their country underwent a rapid, turbulent transition to modernity, not only the police but also a broad range of Japanese government officials and social reformers took aggressive, at times obsessive, steps to combat what they saw as the growing menace of crime and delinquency among young people. Whether or not such misbehavior was in fact increasing is far from clear, given the fragmentary nature of contemporary statistics and the subjective biases inherent in them. But dramatic changes in the economy, the educational system, and urban culture, along with the growth of a sensationalist mass media, combined to create the impression of widespread youth transgression and to inspire an animated discourse on the subject that often took on a life of its own. Moreover, to elites anxious to enhance Japan's status as a "civilized" nation and to concentrate the nation's energies on the struggle for survival in an imperialist world order, even the slightest youthful misdemeanor often appeared to be a sign of impending social chaos. If delinquency symbolized the dangers of uncontrolled social change and the defects of existing social arrangements, champions of juvenile reform and juvenile protection envisioned an orderly, productive Japan that could master the challenges of the modern era, from industrialization to imperialist expansion to total war. The ideas of these reformers, and the thick, intrusive network of socialization agencies that they constructed, have to this day played a critical role in shaping Japanese experiences of home, school, work, and play, and in fostering the culture of discipline and social vigilance for which contemporary Japan is internationally known.

This book treats the policing of urban youth as a crucial arena for the development of new state structures and new forms of social power, for the articulation of new class, gender, and family relations, and for the regulation of popular culture in modern Japan. Focusing on the years from 1895 to 1945, it examines the flows of knowledge, the ideological and institutional developments, and the strategic alliances that impelled the efforts of authorities to subject as much of the population as possible— not just children and adolescents but also young adults, parents, other family members, and even employers—to extended pedagogic treatment. The book analyzes the material conditions, cultural opportunities, and social tensions that shaped young people's behavior and the diversity of their responses to the reformers' interventions. Challenging widely held conceptions of a Japan that has only recently begun to experience youth problems, it offers new perspectives on the coarse texture of Japanese society and reconstructs a politics of everyday life that cannot be subsumed within available narratives of education, labor, welfare, and family history.

This study begins from the premise that "juvenile delinquency" is not an objective social fact but a phenomenon constructed through particular modes of representation, analysis, and treatment in relation to power structures that emerged in the modern era. Of course, young people's misbehavior, and official concern for it, were by no means new to Japan. During the Tokugawa era (1600–1868), for example, the shogunate and domain lords had at key moments treated violence, vagrancy, immorality, and petty crime committed by young men and children as serious threats to social order. Their responses, however, and the political rationality informing them, differed significantly from those that evolved in later years. The efforts of Tokugawa authorities to control unruly youth focused primarily on reinforcing the hierarchical power of self-regulating status groups—warriors, peasants, artisans, merchants, licensed beggars, outcastes, and others—over their members, thereby immobilizing the populace within those status positions and sustaining a political economy predicated upon "the production and delivery of tribute" to warrior rulers.[2] Early modern writers on childhood, meanwhile, provided no systematic analysis of juvenile deviance; nor, in an era when the age of fifteen marked the legal passage into adulthood, did the structures of socialization lend themselves to the production of a body of expertise concerning youth or adolescence (itself a modern term) as a developmental stage marked by particular problems.[3]

In contrast, the regime that emerged following the Meiji Restoration of 1868, responding to the incursion of Western imperialist power in East Asia with a drive to create a "rich nation and strong army," abolished the status system and took a much more direct, expansive role in administering, analyzing, and mobilizing the population and in regulating the environments that were believed to induce or impede desirable behavior.[4] In this new dispensation, children (jidō, shōnen, or, for girls, shōjo) and youths (seinen or, again for girls, shōjo) assumed a heightened prominence as Japan's future workers, soldiers, colonial settlers, administrators, and mothers—valuable human resources whose physical and moral training required new laws, new institutions, new educational theories, and the relentless attention of the entire national community. Moreover, just as authorities prescribed the norms to which these modern national subjects were to conform, they sought to identify the types of deviance against which conformity could be measured. It was in this context of industrial capitalist growth and imperialist competition that juvenile delinquency—a concept developed in contemporary Euro-American penological discourse to mark youthful offenders as dependent objects of pedagogy and therapy targeting both their environments and their individual characteristics—took shape as a salient social category. (In Japanese, delinquents were most commonly described after 1900 by terms employing the adjective furyō, meaning "no-good.")[5]

And to prevent young "treasures of the nation" from becoming delinquents, the state and its allies endeavored not simply to bolster existing
social structures but to radically transform social relationships and
reconfigure social space.[6]

Bad Youth follows this transformative project across three critical
junctures, highlighting both the long-term continuities in reformers'
approaches and the changes that each juncture made possible. First, it
locates the emergence of new Japanese discourses on and approaches to
juvenile delinquency at the turn of the twentieth century, when succes-
sive wars against China (1894–95) and Russia (1904–5) brought Japan
extensive colonial possessions, accelerated industrial development and
urbanization, and provoked widespread concerns over a variety of
social pathologies, from labor unrest to crime and disease. It then
focuses on the two decades following the end of World War I, when
juvenile protection programs formed a critical part of the state's efforts
to defuse rising social tensions by mobilizing a broad range of actors in
the name of society's collective responsibility to look after its least fortunate members, while simultaneously confronting a "radicalism of the
streets" brought about by continuing urban growth and the spread of
"modern" consumer culture.[7] Finally, it examines the elaboration of
new pedagogic and policing programs during the years from 1937 to
1945, when mobilization for total war in Asia and the Pacific exacerbated elite fears of delinquency and the crises of Japan's imperial modernity came to a head.

Throughout, this book emphasizes the leading role of new-middle-class
reformers, themselves products of Japan's modern social revolution, in
defining delinquency and related problems and developing appropriate
responses at the state and societal levels.[8] Experts in the transnational
disciplines of social work, education, penology, criminal justice, labor
management, psychology, and medicine, these moral and cultural entrepreneurs frequently invoked European and North American authorities
and statistics, which they eventually supplemented with the results of
their own surveys, to articulate new social categories and behavioral
standards, demand that Japanese subjects conform to them, and legitimate new forms of intervention to ensure that the subjects did.[9] Working within and on the periphery of the government, reformers promoted
their ideas in conferences and survey reports, professional journals and
books, the daily press, general-interest and women's magazines, parenting manuals, public lectures, and (later) radio broadcasts, and they gained
new prestige and power as their messages spread. Their prescriptions

included both "positive" programs of social integration and the more repressive forms of policing described earlier, and they occasionally clashed over political ideology, bureaucratic turf, or specific methods. But they shared a desire to create a Japan free from the dislocations, alienation, and moral confusion they saw afflicting modern industrial society.[10]

Complementing this focus is an examination of the ways in which discourses of class, race, and gender combined to shape reformers' views of the social body and their approaches to delinquency. While emphasizing the need to inculcate common values such as hygiene, diligence, thrift, and temperance in the Japanese people, new-middle-class experts also defined particular types of deviance that symbolized the deficiencies of the social formations against which they sought to establish their own superiority: the "lower class" or "the poor," symbolized by street urchins and disaffected working youths, and the "upper class," represented by violent or hedonistic students in secondary schools and colleges. Similarly, drawing on global discourses of empire and Japan's own encounters with newly subjugated peoples in Asia, reformers presented themselves as colonizing agents who could assimilate both "dark" urban slums and the "savage" minds of adolescent schoolboys to the norms of Japanese modernity.[11] As economic development and the expansion of the secondary education system fueled the growth of Japan's middle class, however, reformers strove to ensure that members of this class adhered to the behavioral codes that would sustain their primacy in discourses on social order and thus validate Japan's status as a world power. While young males constituted the overwhelming majority of those treated by reform agencies throughout the period under study (roughly 90 percent, in most reports), authorities proved remarkably sensitive to behavior by unlicensed prostitutes, "fallen" schoolgirls, café waitresses, and "modern girls" that allegedly endangered Japan's capacity to reproduce healthy subjects. Indeed, fears that young women were not simply victims of delinquent male predations but increasingly self-directed agents in the pursuit of illicit pleasure spurred authorities to intensify their crackdowns on alleged disruptions of public morality.[12]

This study also brings into focus the broad range of new programs that the juvenile protection movement deployed in its onslaught on the spaces and practices of everyday life. Institutional treatment took place in specialized reformatories, but policing measures also constituted a defining element in the daily operations of secondary schools for elite and middle-class children and elementary schools for slum children, which were designed to assimilate young people and their families to the norms of their respective social stations. Social workers, juvenile court officers, and educators also endeavored to turn homes *(katei)* into "a type of reformatory" by eliminating aspects of family life deemed conducive to delinquency and inculcating new forms of domesticity that responded to the demands of the capitalist economy and the imperial nation-state.[13] "Vocational guidance" experts attempted to manage working-class children's transition from elementary school to the workforce, thereby overcoming what they saw as parents' incompetence, employers' abusive practices, and the dangers that these portended. And as we have seen, the police and other reformers launched repeated campaigns to suppress autonomous youth cultures and restrict young people's access to the rapidly expanding sites of commercial pleasure, in the process treating virtually any unauthorized or unsupervised use of free time by young people as a transgressive act in need of correction.[14]

Compared to the glut of official sources, the voices of those targeted for reform are harder to recover, and the disparate sources that transmit them are not necessarily transparent windows into social reality. Nonetheless, this study "listens" to these voices by describing the complex forms of negotiation and contestation that each new reform project engendered. Reformatories, for example, became sites of constant, at times violent, struggle among inmates, staff, government officials, outside experts, and families, all pursuing their own self-defined interests.[15] Casework interventions into homes provoked both accommodation and resistance between families and external authorities; as significantly, such interventions exposed the conflicting interests that led family members to diverge in their responses to authorities' intrusions and at times to use those authorities as weapons in their internecine battles.[16] Programs to channel the workforce took root in a field that was also conditioned by young people's and families' immediate needs, by employers' own maneuvers for survival, and by powerful discourses on social mobility that often equated success and satisfaction with the achievement of middle-class careers that were tantalizingly beyond most aspirants' reach. Crackdowns on illicit play, meanwhile, offered no constructive responses to the desires and disaffections that young people of various classes experienced as they sought to define themselves in Japan's modern economy, educational system, and urban space. And in the heterogeneous sphere of public discourse, as representations by "reporters in disguise," novelists, and others revealed, young people's transgressive behavior constituted a form of entertainment as well as a social problem, even for those who denounced it vociferously.[17]

Finally, this study emphasizes the importance of total war as a catalyst for enduring changes in the position of youth and the structures of social discipline in Japan. The demands of wartime mobilization and fears of social disintegration led authorities to intensify their efforts to eliminate unauthorized forms of play and consumption and to establish new agencies to oversee the mass of working youths upon whom the state increasingly depended to expand munitions production. These projects formed part of a broader effort by Japan's wartime regime, like its counterparts in Nazi Germany, the United States, and elsewhere, to use policies of "enforced homogeneity" to foster national unity, overcome social conflict, and thus maximize social efficiency and productivity.[18] In the Japanese case, authorities pursued these goals through compulsory programs of rigorous training and assiduous "daily life guidance" that in effect turned the national defense state into a national reformatory. These were not simply aberrant practices that ended with Japan's military defeat, however. Many of these projects facilitated the development of a workforce capable of supporting postwar Japan's rapid economic growth and expanded middle class lifestyles, as well as a postwar society mobilized to "protect" young people and defend against delinquent behavior. Moreover, the imprint of prewar and wartime discourses on youth problems can still be seen in the Japanese people's responses to the changing economic challenges, cultural trends, and social problems of the twenty-first century.

While the concerns of this study are national, it stresses the urban character of the discourse and practice of juvenile protection. Urban areas consistently reported significantly higher numbers of juvenile delinquents than did more rural prefectures; indeed, in contemporary discourse, juvenile delinquency often appeared as one of many evils of the city that grew in tandem with the spread of modern, industrial, Westernized civilization.[19] Needless to say, rural society, as many scholars have shown, also had its own traditions of youthful misbehavior, and in the decades after the Meiji Restoration, local elites, state officials, and various ideologues all found cause for alarm in reports of undisciplined behavior among village youths. By the early twentieth century, however, the Education and Home ministries and the Imperial Army had successfully created a network of young men's associations *(seinendan)* and military reservist associations *(zaigō gunjinkai)*, later supplemented by youth training centers *(seinen kunrenjo)*, that mobilized teenagers and young men for community service, physical training, and military drill, while providing vocational and ethical education and heavy doses of nationalist indoctrination. Although these programs also operated in Japan's cities, urban enrollment rates remained strikingly low until the onset of total war mobilization in the late 1930s and 1940s. Hence, the state's inability to encompass urban youths within these pedagogic structures, combined with perceptions of the city as a morally and physically dangerous environment—to which, moreover, growing numbers of rural youths were drawn—led many government officials and social reformers to define delinquency as an urban problem.[20]

Bad Youth focuses primarily on developments in Tokyo. Formerly Edo, the seat of the Tokugawa shogunate, Tokyo became Japan's new imperial capital in 1868 and was its largest urban area: its population (in city wards and surrounding counties) reached 2 million at the turn of the century, 3.7 million at the time of the first national census in 1920, and added roughly one million people every five years after that, reaching 7.4 million, slightly over 10 percent of the national population, in 1940 (by which time the city had absorbed most of the counties).[21] Many of the immigrants driving this urban growth, like a good portion of the native population, were young people in search of work, education, new careers or lifestyles, or simply refuge from bleak realities and limited expectations. As important, Tokyo was the base of operations for many of the reformers and the site of many of the pioneering juvenile protection programs that will be discussed in this study. Of course, Tokyo's experience did not necessarily reflect that of Japan's other urban centers, such as Osaka or Nagoya, or of smaller provincial cities. Nonetheless, to contemporaries, Tokyo most starkly symbolized Japanese metropolitan modernity in its various manifestations. Like the antebellum New York described by Christine Stansell, Tokyo "was a historical stage writ large for encounters that reverberated across the rest of the nation."[22]

To set this stage, we begin with an examination of rough play and social disorder in the shogun's capital in the centuries prior to the Meiji Restoration.

CHAPTER I

Unruly Youth and the Early Modern Polity

Although late-nineteenth- and early-twentieth-century reformers treated juvenile delinquency as a problem of Japanese modernity, many of the behaviors they described had their roots in the social life of Tokugawa Japan. Indeed, not only had violent, larcenous, or dissolute youths been prominent fixtures in the early modern urban landscape, they had also spawned a repertoire of cultural practices and popular images upon which their modern successors drew freely. Moreover, they gave rise to a rhetoric of moral denunciation and an incipient set of disciplinary practices that informed subsequent efforts to police society.

This chapter highlights not only those elements of the early modern past that were to give a distinctive coloration to the politics and culture of juvenile delinquency in modern Japan, but also those that distinguished the treatment of youthful deviance in the Tokugawa era from that which followed. Focusing on Edo, the shogun's capital, it argues that young people's misbehavior challenged the state's efforts to contain the populace within a complex of status organizations, each with clearly defined responsibilities and internal hierarchies. In the early decades of Tokugawa rule, authorities contended with gangs of self-consciously outrageous youths struggling to negotiate the transition to a peacetime regime and a new urban labor market. Over time, commercialization and urban growth—by 1700, Edo's population had reached one million—exacerbated both stratification within status groups and official concern over violent outbursts by the young men of the lower classes.

Meanwhile, young men and children figured prominently among the growing numbers of people who, because of poverty or other factors, drifted into lives of vagrancy, mendicancy, or crime. In each case, the state's response centered on bolstering the legal, institutional, and ideological underpinnings of the status system; the increasing inviability of this system, combined with changes in Japan's geopolitical situation, foreshadowed the need for new approaches to the socialization of youth.

The social position of young people in Tokugawa Japan also differed from their position in the modern era. Shogunal laws such as the 1742 Rules for Determining Legal Matters *(Kujikata osadamegaki)* defined persons younger than fifteen as children, whose mental immaturity allowed for lenience in the application of punishments, but treated everyone fifteen and older as a fully responsible adult. (Because newborn children were assigned the age of one, a fifteen-year-old was actually, by modern reckoning, fourteen years of age and could be as young as thirteen.)[1] In customary terms, however, those who had graduated from childhood did not necessarily achieve full-fledged adult status. In commoner communities, these young people assumed a new identity as youths *(wakaishu, wakaimono,* or *wakamono)*, a category whose exit requirements and upper age limit also depended on local usage. Peasant village youth groups, for example, often defined members as men who had not attained the status of householders; in villages in eastern Japan, members could be as old as their early forties.[2] While some of the Edo sources on which the following discussion is based specifically identify deviant youths as being in their teens or twenties, others refer simply to the youths' membership in gangs, to their position within households—for example, as "tenants' sons"—or even to their "hot-blooded" characters as markers of youth.[3] Remarks about volatile temperaments, however, did not generate any sustained analyses of youth as a particular stage of psychological or moral development; this type of construction, and the social, economic, and political conditions that supported it, would emerge in a later period.

TRUE WARRIORS AND STREET KNIGHTS

In contrast to the period of bloody civil warfare that preceded it, the Tokugawa era came to be seen by many contemporaries as an era of "great peace." Building on approaches initiated by the powerful warlords who preceded them, the Tokugawa shoguns and domain lords *(daimyo)* presided over a polity that was organized into status groups, each bearing formal duties to the state as well as the responsibility for regulating the activities of its members. Principal status groups were defined according to occupation and residence, through measures including the compilation of cadastral surveys and registers of religious affiliation, the disarming of the peasantry, and the removal of the warriors to new castle towns, which they shared with communities of merchants and artisans. By the middle of the seventeenth century, the legal structure also encompassed groups such as court nobles, Buddhist clerics, outcastes, licensed beggars, and blind persons.[4] Detailed sumptuary regulations prescribed the appropriate hairstyles, clothes, and other physical markers for each status group, while teachings such as Neo-Confucianism provided an ideological gloss on the new power structure by positing natural, inviolable moral hierarchies (for example, of lord over retainer, parent over child, and husband over wife) and by prescribing what Mary Elizabeth Berry has termed "an embracing ethos of service and subordination to the collective, typically in the person of the lord."[5]

The establishment of this system, however, required the suppression of serious challenges in which youths figured prominently. During the first decades of the seventeenth century, shogunate and domain officials struggled to eradicate gangs of flamboyant young ruffians known as *kabukimono*. Like the popular theatrical form that emerged at this time, the term derives from the word *kabuku*, meaning to lean, to deviate, or to be outrageous. *Kabukimono* often wore short-hemmed kimonos with velvet collars, let their hair go long and untied or shaved their heads in unconventional ways, and grew thick sideburns or beards. Many carried extremely long swords, oversized sword guards, and crimson or gold-colored scabbards, some decorated with phrases such as "I am a man twenty-three years old! I have lived too long! I will never restrain myself!"[6]

Kabukimono were mainly warrior household servants or masterless samurai *(rōnin)* who vented their disaffection at a congealing sociopolitical order predicated on the cessation of armed conflicts and with it the closing of paths to upward social mobility through demonstrations of military prowess. In reaction to these changes, writes Kitajima Masamoto, *kabukimono* vigorously clung to the ethos of "inferiors overthrowing superiors" *(gekokujō)*, an idea that had legitimated conflict during the warring states era but which the new rulers sought to replace with the doctrine of unquestioning loyalty to one's lord and its corollary, resignation to one's position in the status hierarchy. Indeed, *kabukimono* explicitly prioritized horizontal loyalty to one another, through blood oaths and other rituals as well as through "fraternal allegiances" articulated in male-male sexual relationships *(shudō* or *nanshoku)*, over vertical obligations to lord or parents. Similarly, they clung to the traditional view that fighting to preserve one's honor, and the preparedness to unsheathe one's sword at the slightest provocation, constituted the most critical element of a warrior's manhood.[7]

The danger of the *kabukimono* manifested itself dramatically in 1612, when Shibayama Gonzaemon Masatsugu, a chief of the shogun's great guards, killed one of his servants after learning that he was such a deviant.[8] Although masters were legally permitted to kill servants who misbehaved, several other servants immediately rushed to the scene and killed Shibayama. When officials captured one of them several days later, he declared that he too was a *kabukimono,* a member of a large group led by a certain Ōtorii Ichibyōe, whose members had sworn to defend one another even at the cost of their own lives; a search of the culprit's lodgings uncovered a written oath bearing more than five hundred names, including those of several *daimyo*'s sons. Ōtorii was a former samurai servant who had been granted low-ranking samurai status, only to become a *rōnin.* One source described both his déclassé social position and his charisma in the following terms: "Not tied to a warrior, peasant, artisan, or merchant household, he led young warrior servants who adopted outlandish appearances, and spoke only of things related to praiseworthy and trustworthy manliness. Always relishing danger, he was neither of the townsmen nor of the samurai. . . . Hearing of him, young men exclaimed, 'Ichibyōe will help those who ask him, even if it costs his life.'"[9] Authorities soon arrested Ōtorii, interrogated him, and then executed him, as well as some three hundred young men associated with the gang, including a few sons of reputed Tokugawa vassals. Ōtorii himself was lionized for his determined refusal to give up the names of his followers, even as officials subjected him to increasingly cruel tortures.

Over the following decades, the *kabukimono* drew new members from the ranks of the urban lower class, many of them impoverished peasants who had run away to the city and who found employment as short-term contract servants in warrior households. Because of the tenuous nature of these service jobs, such laborers depended on employment agents called *hitoyado* not only to place them and act as guarantors but also to lodge them in between contracts.[10] The *hitoyado,* as Yoshida Nobuyuki has suggested, thus served as a means of integrating individuals who had fallen through the cracks of the status system into fictive "household" structures.[11] But patron-client ties between broker and dependent could easily take on the attributes of an outlaw organization, and in periods of high demand, brokers would provide *daimyo* and warrior households with servants of questionable character, some of them no different from vagrants.[12] The uncertainty of their situations, suggests Bitō Masahide, further spurred these low-ranking servants to assert themselves by adopting the exaggerated styles and attitudes they associated with the true way of the samurai or masculinity. Such toughs also came to be known as *yakko;* their stylized speech had its roots in the rough language of immigrants from the villages of the Kantō plain, Edo's hinterland.[13]

The *yakko* style soon spread to gangs of young Tokugawa bannermen *(hatamoto yakko)* who, bridling under the status restrictions and economic hardships that Tokugawa rule entailed and resentful of the prosperity of the urban merchant class, roamed the streets of Edo fighting one another and robbing and killing townsmen. Gangs of townsmen called *machi yakko* or *otokodate* (manly ones), with names like the Chinese Dogs, also appeared at this time; the 1657 murder of the townsman Banzuiin Chōbei by the bannerman Mizuno Jūrōzaemon, an event recounted in kabuki plays and stories, has been taken to symbolize the antagonism between the two types of gangs and the heroism of the commoners in defending against warrior predations.[14] Yet the fact that many prominent townsmen gangsters, including Chōbei, were labor brokers who enjoyed relatively easy access to warrior households, combined with the presence of *rōnin* in both types of gangs, confounds the image of strictly class- or status-based conflicts, illustrating instead the still unsettled nature of social roles and the widespread valorization of personal acts of violence in the rough-and-tumble urban centers of early-seventeenth-century Japan.[15]

The new state repeatedly cracked down on these deviant groups. In 1629, as the number of people cut down on the streets of Edo increased, the shogunate ordered the establishment of guardhouses in samurai residential areas across the city. By the end of the century, there were more than nine hundred such guardhouses, as well as guardhouses and gatehouses in each merchant and artisan residential quarter.[16] The shogunate also issued repeated prohibitions against the sartorial and tonsorial styles associated with the *kabukimono,* forbade the hiring or sheltering of such deviants, and revised the Rules Governing Warrior Houses to forbid the formation of "private groups" and engagement in private fights. In 1651, police inspectors carried out their first sweep through the city in search of *kabukimono;* the discovery later that year of a

planned uprising by a group of *rōnin* led by Yui Shōsetsu only amplified
the authorities' concerns. For each of the following six years, officers
conducted citywide roundups timed to coincide with the days of the
second month when warrior household servants were released from
their contracts and *kabukimono* were most vulnerable to discovery. The
shogunate also prohibited townsmen from wearing long swords; it
banned kite flying, popular dancing, and other forms of recreation that
attracted crowds and provided opportunities for brawling; and in 1652,
it ordered the cessation of *wakashu kabuki,* theatrical performances by
young male actors, in order to prevent outbreaks of violence over the
favors of the young thespians. From the 1650s to the 1680s, the shogunate executed prominent warrior and commoner gang leaders and
meted out harsh punishments to other gang members. The arrests in
1686 of two hundred members of the Greater and Lesser Gods, a warrior gang, followed by the execution of eleven leaders, marked the last
major action against the *kabukimono* and *yakko*.[17]

By this point, observers were criticizing the pointlessness of much
kabukimono violence. In 1682, the artist Hishikawa Moronobu, commenting on townsmen's gangs, lamented that the "many good men and
learned men among ... the *otokodate* of earlier days" had been
replaced by swaggering criminal upstarts—"former boatmen, green-
horn artisan punks, or former warrior servants and actors"—who committed evil acts "in the hot-bloodedness of youth."[18] Of course, the
delinquent or criminal side of these armed ruffians had always been evident in practice, but earlier generations had cloaked it in an idealized
language of samurai honor, true manhood, or responsibility to the
weak. And this "noble" image, what Nishiyama Matsunosuke has
called the aesthetic of the street knight *(kyōkaku* or *kyōsha),* took root
in kabuki theater through the *aragoto* style of acting developed by the
first Ichikawa Danjūrō (1660–1704), whose own father had belonged to
a townsmen's gang, as well as in other forms of popular entertainment
that would outlive the Tokugawa regime.[19]

Although the suppression of the *kabukimono* signified the elimination
of a significant threat to the Tokugawa order, it by no means marked the
end of the regime's struggles against violent youth subcultures. A century
later, for example, problems erupted in various castle towns as young
men from the warrior class aggressively pursued sexual relations with
younger boys. Gregory Pflugfelder notes that, although neither Tokugawa
nor domain laws criminalized male-male sexual relations per se, in some
domains, "the bureaucratic association of male-male erotic ties with

samurai conspiracy long outlasted the early era of domain consolidation," and that in many domains, officials took action against what they deemed egregious displays of "profitless" sexual contention that deviated from the way of loyalty and filial piety and led to "soured friendships, distressed parents, and strained community relations."[20] From the 1770s to the early 1800s, for example, officials in Wakamatsu, the castle town of the Aizu domain, contended with gangs of rowdy youths who accosted commoner boys or other samurai boys on the streets, dragged them back to their own homes, and raped them; in some cases, groups of youths appeared at the homes of the objects of their desire and pressed parents to hand them over. These aggressions became so serious that commoner families were afraid to send their sons to their lessons. Attacks on samurai boys could also escalate into vendettas: in one 1789 incident, when youths from the warrior neighborhood of Hanbei-chō raped a boy from the Shinmachi quarter, the young men of Shinmachi committed a similar outrage against a boy from Hanbei-chō. In all of these cases, domain officials responded with severe punishments that included house arrest, removal from the line of succession, expulsion from the castle town, banishment from the domain, and incarceration; punishments extended not only to the youths but also to their family members.[21] Clearly, the way of the warrior had still not been reduced to a single, universally accepted set of practices. And far from succumbing to official repression, this type of behavior, as we will see in chapter 3, would reemerge as a major social problem at the turn of the twentieth century.

A more general appetite for fighting also continued to shape the lives of many young samurai, as is evident in the memoirs of Katsu Kokichi (1802–50), a bannerman's son. Katsu, who grew up in Edo's Honjo district, took to street fighting with neighborhood children from an early age, and in his teens provoked brawls with lower-class workers at local shrine festivals. He then devoted himself to training as a swordsman, drawing followers as he won matches at various fencing schools in the city. Katsu recalled "ordering the swordsmen in the area as though they were my underlings" and "demolish[ing] every good-for-nothing in my own neighborhood of Honjo," while struggling to find the means to keep up appearances as a gang leader. "Challenging students from rival schools was getting to be a regular occupation. Night after night I roamed the streets with my followers in tow. . . . My foolishness was dragging me deeper into debt. I wouldn't stop, even then, and borrowed money with no prospect of being able to repay. I was twenty-one and penniless. . . . To take my mind off my woes, I went to the [licensed pleasure quarters at] Yoshiwara."[22] Katsu was also illiterate in his youth. He decided to run away from home to become an itinerant swordsman, but his relatives eventually lured him back and locked him in a cage in the sitting room, where he spent the next three years.[23] This form of confinement appears to have been widely practiced in the Tokugawa era, and continued at least into the early twentieth century. Harsh martial training may also have doubled as corporal punishment when applied to unruly warrior youths.

While many contemporaries viewed young men's peccadilloes as a form of hot bloodedness that they would eventually outgrow, families in the meantime had to struggle to keep their sons' misbehavior from reaching official notice, for, as the Aizu rape cases show, such publicity could entail severe consequences. Indeed, a young man's delinquency could seriously damage his father's, his siblings', or his own chances of obtaining an official post and increased income; in the worst case, unchecked juvenile misbehavior could prompt the authorities to terminate the family line, and with it the stipend and status that underpinned a household's position in the warrior class.[24] To prevent such catastrophes, warrior families may occasionally have disowned their problem sons, although the extent of this practice is not clear (more evidence exists concerning commoner households, as we will see below).

As in the case of the *hatamoto yakko*, Katsu's deviant career reflects the status and economic frustrations that continued to afflict Tokugawa bannermen and housemen *(gokenin)* during the eighteenth and nineteenth centuries. Many lived in poverty, with virtually no hope of obtaining official employment (which could entail great personal expenditures, including bribes to administrators); they and their families often supplemented their small stipends by making umbrellas or other items, or by working alongside commoners in construction and other trades.[25] Young warriors thus shared in the rough language and style of the plebeian quarters and amusement centers, and many developed reputations for lawlessness and behavior "worse than that of the lowly townsmen and idlers," as Buyō Inshi put it in his 1816 diatribe *Record of Things Seen and Heard (Seji kenmonroku)*.[26] Indeed, despite his declared intentions of reforming (and despite having learned to read and write), Katsu never obtained an official position. Instead, he earned a living as a sword dealer, moneylender, promoter of dubious religious sects and lotteries, and as a fixer or protection man for various samurai and commoner clients, including brothel keepers; he spent so much time in the Yoshiwara that by his mid-thirties he had become the leader of

"the roughnecks who prowled through the quarters."[27] Such individuals could also be found among hard-pressed retainers of the various
daimyo in the capital and in castle towns throughout the country. And
of course, a significant number of samurai remained *rōnin*, cut off from
ties to and stipends from any lords. It was hardly surprising that many
young warriors joined the ranks of the gamblers and outlaws who created so much trouble for the authorities in the closing decades of the
early modern era.

Warrior ruffianism, dissoluteness, and debt, combined with the
growing economic power of urban merchants and peasant entrepreneurs, clearly threatened to undercut the status hierarchy upon which
the Tokugawa regime was predicated. By the late eighteenth century,
however, it was the violent behavior of the lower classes that provoked
the greatest concern among both state officials and the commoner elites
whose positions depended upon the maintenance of social order. In
Edo, massive riots in the fifth month of 1787 led officials to step up
their efforts to control the young men of the plebeian quarters.

UNRULY YOUTH, 1780s–1860s

The Tenmei Riots of 1787 erupted in the midst of a four-year period of
famines that killed nearly two million people and provoked peasant
protests throughout Japan, and at a moment when the shogunate was
experiencing a leadership vacuum following the fall of senior councilor
Tanuma Okitsugu, whose policies were blamed for exacerbating popular hardships and official financial distress. In Edo, writes Anne
Walthall, popular disquiet mounted in response to "the state's inepti-
tude in responding to the crisis of subsistence." As rumors circulated
that merchants were hoarding foodstuffs in order to profit from the
crisis, city magistrates offered little assistance to townspeople other
than to order that prices be lowered and goods be put on the market;
contemporaries reported that government investigators actually took
bribes from merchants to help conceal their stocks. As a result, the city's
poor took matters into their own hands, attacking merchants' houses
and destroying their property. The rioters demonstrated remarkable discipline, punishing looters in their midst and taking no lives. Yet for five
days, the government had lost control of the capital.[28]

The riots facilitated the rise to power of senior councilor Matsudaira
Sadanobu, whose policies, known as the Kansei Reforms, were designed,
in Takeuchi Makoto's words, to "rebuild the structures governing

tax-assessed peasants, maintain social order in the cities, strengthen control over the *daimyo* and bannermen, and thus to suppress class struggles, restore the public authority of the shogunate, and, ultimately, restore its finances."[29] In their efforts to provide both relief and discipline to the urban poor, shogunal officials demonstrated a new sensitivity to acts of violence by young townsmen—in part because of rumors that children *(kodomo, warabe)* or youths *(wakamono, wakashu)*, aged somewhere from fourteen to eighteen, had been seen leading the rioters in 1787.[30]

In 1791, as part of a series of reforms of Edo's administration, officials issued the following edict:

> Commonly, there are difficult persons in every residential quarter who call themselves "youths" *(wakaimono)*, and they extort money from landlords during festivals. Moreover, they make unreasonable impositions on landlords, homeowners, and shop renters for so-called religious contributions during the All Souls' Festival *[bon]* in the seventh month. They put forth similar demands when sacred objects on loan from other temples are displayed in their own neighborhood temples; whenever believers meet; or when priests circulate subscription lists so as to gather pledges for a specific religious project. The youths harbor grudges against those who refuse to make contributions, and they take their revenge later.
>
> Such behavior is outrageous and inexcusable. When such individuals are found in a neighborhood, they are to be brought to the guardhouse along with a sealed statement explaining their activities. Their cases will then be adjudicated, appropriate punishments meted out, and care taken that they not seek revenge upon the plaintiffs.[31]

Edo's city magistrates had already sought to control young men's violent behavior in the first half of the eighteenth century, when they issued repeated edicts prohibiting "stone throwing" *(ishi uchi)*, a form of social sanction in which neighborhood youth groups inflicted damage on the property of those who married without their consent. As the record of one 1735 case suggests, the perpetrators were likely to be tenants' sons, while the victims were landlords or members of other affluent households who could afford to bring in brides from other neighborhoods. Although they prescribed punishments for "leaders" and "fellows," these laws had focused primarily on the act of stone throwing, without referring specifically to the social groups that initiated such actions.[32] The 1791 edict was thus the first shogunal law specifically identifying Edo's youths—defined by the social nomenclature they applied to themselves, rather than by a specific chronological age—as an object of regulation.[33]

As the edict indicates, local religious festivals provided a principal context for young men's unruly behavior. *Wakamono* who engaged in collective violence against wealthy householders at such moments could, explains Takeuchi, subsequently claim that their actions were the result of a spiritual frenzy, driven by the gods, and thus beyond adjudication by worldly authorities or claims for compensation.[34] Already in the 1770s, administrators at Asakusa's Sensōji temple noted that "many young people and children from the quarters before the gates" threatened merchants who refused to give money for festivals. By 1796, however, with memories of the Tenmei Riots still in everyone's mind, Sensōji officials wrote that local youths "frequent archery galleries and teahouses, strutting around haughtily. Moreover, they appear in front of saké shops [and] yell out for drinks and other favors. On top of that, those same young men carry the mikoshi during the Sanja Festival, when they mass in front of the houses of merchants who earlier have refused [their] demands. In revenge, the young men break into those shop-residences." Moreover, gangs of youths headed loosely by leaders called *wakamono-gashira* no longer limited their aggressions to these occasions, leading merchants across Edo to complain about these importunate trouble-makers. Writes Takeuchi: "Everywhere youths stood guilty of disrupting social harmony, and they became the objects of shogunal suppression."[35]

To check the spread of such troublemakers, the shogunate relied on neighborhood chiefs *(nanushi)* and "five-family groups" *(goningumi)* composed of homeowners, landlords, and their agents, who as Katō Takashi explains, "shared responsibility for ensuring that their own families, as well as the families who lived on their properties, knew every law and comported themselves as expected."[36] Yet contrary to the shogunate's expectations, local leaders often attempted to protect the *wakamono*. Young men's participation was essential to the successful performance of festivals and community rituals; moreover, gang leaders exercised a degree of control over their followers and often mediated local disputes, thereby maintaining community harmony. As Takeuchi notes, the state generally refused to become involved in adjudicating violent confrontations among commoners, treating them as private "cases of mutual harm" to be resolved by the conflicting parties. Conversely, the absence of effective mediation might lead to cases being referred for official judicial action. Commoner communities seeking to maximize their autonomy may thus have been willing to accept a measure of private violence as the price of avoiding "unwelcome intrusions of state power."[37]

Wakamono groups became even more prominent during the early nineteenth century, organizing along the intersecting geographical and occupational lines that formed the basic grid of Edo commoners' identity.[38] Firefighter companies, composed of roofers and construction workers who cultivated a distinctive rough style and a reputation for brawling, had their own *wakamono* groups, as did young men from the city's fish markets, one of the centers of the early modern commercial economy.[39] As entries in bookseller Fujiokaya Yoshizō's journal reveal, these young hotheads figured prominently in altercations over actual or perceived slights that frequently escalated into acts of destruction involving hundreds or even thousands of participants. In 1851, for example, during a festival in Kanda, the firefighters of Ha Company clashed with the *wakamono* from the fishermen's neighborhood of Koami-chō in a three-day battle that left several dead or injured. Mediation efforts by the young men from the nearby fish markets at Shinba and Odawara-chō failed, however, when the firefighters, rather than attending the conciliation banquet, took advantage of their enemies' absence to launch a sneak attack and tear down the popular theater *(yose)* in which they often congregated.[40] Two years earlier, Fujiokaya had reported that Ha Company firefighters on a pilgrimage to the sacred Mount Ōyama crossed through the Hon-Shiba fish market—"where the streets are narrow, the people bad, and the *wakamono* numerous"— without providing a customary gift to the local youths, and compounded the insult by declaring that the market and its environs were not really part of Edo but rather "in the country." In response, the *wakamono* jeered that the firefighters' ill manners stemmed from the fact that they were "not the Ha Company of Edo, but some Ha Company from the countryside." Over the following days, both sides and their sympathizers, their standing as true Edoites *(Edokko)* under attack, prepared for a massive battle, which was averted only when all of the city's fire company leaders agreed to intervene.[41]

The young men of Edo's laboring class saw themselves as the inheritors of the *otokodate* or *kyōkaku* style of street knight machismo. In their day, this style was symbolized not only by the heroes of popularized kabuki performances but also by the fire company chiefs and other labor bosses under whom these youths worked and who, often combining these public roles with illicit activities as gamblers, earned acclaim in plays, stories, or broadsides circulating in the city's thoroughfares and amusement areas.[42] Prohibitions against lower-class townsmen covering their bodies with tattoos, issued specifically because many *wakamono* used them as emblems of manliness, point to the continuing vibrancy of this outlaw style; as one 1834 description of Edo life remarked, during street fights these images of blue dragons seemed to come alive and join the fray.[43] Moreover, this culture spread rapidly beyond the city as rural *wakamono* groups—who also came under attack from state officials and local elites for acting to maintain community customs as they defined them—began organizing kabuki plays and other performances that brought them into contact with roving entertainers, gamblers, and other marginal elements.[44]

While *wakamono* groups claimed to represent their communities, youths with truly unmanageable outlaw tendencies could easily find themselves cut loose from their families and local ties. Commoner households, like those of the warrior class, relied on various private forms of confinement and corporal punishment, and in addition could apply to local authorities to have their "unfilial" children put in handcuffs for periods ranging from a few days to a few months. But many desperate parents, and especially those who feared that their children might commit crimes for which the entire household or five-family group would be held responsible, resorted to the more drastic step of formally disowning them (*kyūri*, or removal from the household register) and driving them away *(kandō)*. In 1650, Edo's city magistrates ordered that such disowned children be placed in jail; if they repented, they could be returned to their families. Five years later, the city magistrates added that disowned children who continued to harbor grudges against and inconvenience their parents were to be arrested and put to death.[45]

Families could informally drive out their children *(naishō kandō)* for a brief period in the hopes of teaching them a lesson, and this practice appears to have been widely used among wealthier commoner households. Many of Edo's prosperous merchants sent their dissolute sons to Chōshi and Kisarazu (across the Edo Bay, in present-day Chiba Prefecture), sometimes to work for the local fishing bosses, and welcomed them home when they had been properly chastened; some families had to repeat the process several times. Comic verses poked fun at pampered young hedonists forced to pawn their fine silk clothes and silver tobacco pipes, or those who sneaked back home to borrow money from their tearful mothers.[46] Similarly, in Santō Kyōden's 1787 satire *Playboy, Grilled Edo-Style (Edo umare uwaki no kabayaki)* a dim-witted merchant's son decides that he cannot earn a reputation as a true lover unless he has been disowned and begs his parents to put him out; thanks to his doting mother, the "punishment" includes an expense account.

Besides inspiring popular laughter, such young men-about-town provoked the ire (or envy) of warrior officials and moralizers struggling to
make do in an increasingly cash-driven economy.[47]

In contrast to wealthy townsmen, their tenants from the petty-
shopkeeper, artisan, and day-laboring strata appear to have opted quite
frequently for formal disownment, particularly as economic conditions
and social tensions worsened. In 1796, the rising number of such cases
prompted city magistrates to issue the following decree:

> Many townsmen submit requests to disown their children. Because parents
> neglect to teach their offspring of the proper relations between parents
> and children and between siblings, many young people grow up selfish
> from childhood, ultimately turning into ruffians who cannot be con-
> trolled by their families or others. At this point, they are disowned and
> removed from their families' registers. Many become vagrants and go
> hungry; some commit evil deeds and receive heavy punishments, while
> others become beggars and *hinin* [licensed beggars, to be discussed
> below]. Such results bring shame upon the families of these individuals.
> Disownment and removal from family registers are morally difficult
> actions. Not only families but also local officials must pay careful atten-
> tion to children and others with no assets, and must educate them so that
> they do not embark on the path of evil.[48]

Just as the 1791 edict was the first to target young people specifically,
this directive was, as Ishikawa Ken has noted, "the first law in Japanese
history to take up the issue of children's education, making it the obligation of parents, and linking it to parents' love for their offspring."[49]
But because the law was above all exhortatory, neither offering families
new resources to achieve the prescribed task nor specifying any sanctions should they fail, its effects were negligible. Over the following
decades, social critics continued to decry the activities of tenants' sons
who not only caused havoc during festivals and disrupted business in
the pleasure quarters but also blackmailed people over various indiscre-
tions, seduced women in order to extort money from their families or
force them into prostitution, and then drifted into the hinterland when
the authorities took notice of their activities. Meanwhile, many children
and teenagers joined the pickpocket gangs that roamed the thoroughfares of Edo and other cities, offering further signs of the regime's growing struggle to contain its floating population. Not only did households
continue to expunge such individuals from their registers; to avoid trouble, neighborhood elders appear to have encouraged them to do so.[50]

"Parental" disciplinary power also accrued to the masters with whom
many children and young people resided as servants and apprentices,

and in whose household registers they were listed. Notes Gary Leupp: "Ideal master-servant relationships were described in law codes and public notices, prescribed in sermons, household codes, and didactic tracts, and celebrated in popular fiction. All of these treated the service relationship as a component of the entire polity, hardly less essential to its smooth operation than correct parent-child relations."[51] The socialization process was often extremely rigorous. In Edo's large merchant houses, for example, apprentices came up from the provinces between the ages of ten and twelve and joined the ranks of "children" *(kodomo, kodomoshū)* who performed miscellaneous tasks while studying the skills necessary for their trades. After seven or eight years of service, they underwent a coming of age ceremony *(genbuku)* and graduated to the status of clerks *(tedai,* also called *wakaishu* to mark their youth), with responsibility for handling receipts and expenditures. Those who performed successfully at this rank might after another eight years graduate to the status of salesmen.[52] Not all apprentices could endure the strict regime and coarse diets that prevailed in such establishments, however. Hayashi Reiko's study of records compiled by Edo's Shirokiya dry goods store from 1839 to 1859, for example, shows that many boys stole shop goods, which they sold in order to purchase sushi, tempura, and sweets or, in the case of clerks, to pay for saké and visits to the theater or the licensed quarters. Often they relied on the help of kitchen hands and delivery boys *(daidokorokata, otokoshu),* young men hired on short-term contracts from among the urban day-laborer pool, who managers believed were a corrupting influence. Clerks, who spent much of the day in the company of customers, were known to skim receipts or to pretend that the items they had stolen had been sold to *daimyo* households, thereby taking advantage of merchants' inability to confront elite warrior clients over outstanding charges.[53]

Many apprentices absconded; in the worst cases, they became regular thieves. In 1846, for example, Nakamura Kasuke ran away during his eighth year at Shirokiya after having become infatuated with a prostitute named Tsuneura and having stolen more than thirty *ryō* worth of shop merchandise. After spending several months in his native village, he returned to Edo to seek work, but not finding any, he instead broke into his former employer's storerooms and made off with nearly five hundred *ryō* in cash as well as sundry items. Store employees managed to apprehend Kasuke, who had dallied at a brothel during his escape, and they recovered all but twenty-five *ryō* of the stolen money and goods. Shirokiya managers, like their counterparts in other establishments, conducted meticulous investigations of employees suspected of crimes, confining and interrogating them in the storehouse and tracing their visits to tea shops or brothels and their expenditures during the preceding three years. Many employers, like samurai masters, also used corporal punishment as one means of keeping their underlings in line.[54]

Despite the gravity of Kasuke's offenses, Shirokiya executives never reported him to the authorities. In this and other cases, managers confiscated their employees' belongings, attempted to exact compensation from their guarantors, and simply wrote off the amounts that were unrecoverable. Such internal settlements permitted merchants to avoid negative publicity and gossip about their excessive wealth. In the view of Buyō Inshi, on the other hand, this attitude essentially permitted apprentices to embezzle with impunity: "These types see no value in repaying their masters' benevolence through extended service. They believe it to their disadvantage not to embezzle, and generally end up as thieves."[55] Although the records leave no information concerning Kasuke's fate, Shirokiya frequently dismissed incorrigible employees, listing illness or similar circumstances as the cause. From 1837 to 1867, twenty-nine of 142 apprentices in their first nine years of service either absconded or were dismissed; when the cohort is extended to include those in their first sixteen years of service, the figure rises to fifty-one of 191.[56] Not all of those dismissed were delinquents, of course, but the figures nonetheless suggest how easy it was to stray from the ideal path of apprenticeship. And among those who ran away or were dismissed, the risk of marginalization, vagrancy, and further criminal behavior no doubt increased with age.

Masters' reluctance to involve the state in cases of absconding and theft also stemmed from the fact that Tokugawa law prescribed capital punishment for apprentices or servants aged fifteen or older who stole from their masters. When such offenses did draw official attention, moreover, masters often pleaded to have their employees' lives spared. In the absence of aggravating circumstances, authorities tended to grant such requests and reduce the sentences to banishment, which in the case of Edo usually meant expulsion from the area within a ten-league radius around the city. But both the act of absconding and the punishment it incurred led to the same result: an increase in the number of unattached persons and petty criminals drifting on the periphery of the city, often with little to keep them from returning.[57]

Vagrants (*mushuku* or *nobinin*) posed an increasingly serious challenge to public order, as shifts in the agrarian economy and periodic famines led many peasants to take to the roads, often with Edo or other cities as their destination. The shogunate constantly strove to return such uprooted persons to their original places of registration, but often to little avail; many, moreover, were no longer registered with a household or status group. By the early seventeenth century the shogunate adopted a policy of remanding all unregistered persons to the *hinin*, a status group of licensed beggars, and over the course of the century, many vagrants joined this organization. In return for a monopoly on alms rights, the *hinin* performed various policing and sanitation functions such as rounding up homeless persons, disposing of carcasses, and administering wards for sick prisoners; some also worked as entertainers or engaged in artisan labor such as repairing sandals. Organization rules were designed to prevent conflict among *hinin* and between *hinin* and townsmen; those who violated these rules were subjected to harsh punishments by their hut bosses, by the *hinin* headmen, or, in Edo, by Danzaemon, the outcaste headman. Remission to the *hinin*, like the establishment of quasi-household ties between immigrant day laborers and the city's labor brokers, thus permitted the state to resituate displaced persons within a defined status organization, to extend its capability to police the streets, and thus to demonstrate its "benevolence" *(jinsei)* toward the lower classes.[58]

Many children found their way into the ranks of the *hinin*. A certain Mantarō, for example, ran away from home after having nearly been murdered by his stepfather and then entered various service positions, from which he regularly absconded; he became a *hinin* in 1690, at the age of thirteen.[59] Beginning in 1742, Edo officials prescribed servitude in the *hinin* as a reduced form of punishment for vagrant children who also pilfered money or goods worth less than ten *ryō* (the punishment for adults was flogging). The case of Kashichi, who had run away from an abusive stepfather in outlying Kameido Village and had fallen in with a gang of pickpockets in the Ryōgokubashi thoroughfare only to be detained in a citywide sweep of vagrants, set the precedent for this approach; it was quickly incorporated into the legal code compiled by the shogunate in the same year.[60] Many adult *hinin*, of course, were in their late teens and twenties; interestingly, in Osaka, local *hinin* bosses under the authority of the city's four headmen were known as "the young men of the four localities" *(yokasho no wakaimono)*, although the origins of this term are unclear.[61]

But while the *hinin* organization constituted a valuable mechanism for maintaining the status structures of Tokugawa Japan, the organization offered few prospects for rehabilitating its members; nor did authorities desire that this group should absorb what seemed to be a limitless supply of displaced persons, to the detriment of agricultural and artisanal production. In the 1720s, shogunate officials had briefly deliberated constructing a facility where vagrants could be put to work until they were ready to be returned to their places of origin. In 1780, Edo's city magistrates opened such a facility, the vagrant care center (mushuku yōikusho), but they abandoned the project six years later following a rash of escapes.[62] The 1787 riots, however, combined with the fact that Edo's unregistered population had grown from 1,812 in 1777 to 6,975 in 1786, compelled officials to revisit the workhouse approach. Hence, in 1790, as part of the Kansei Reforms, senior councilor Matsudaira Sadanobu established a new facility, the Edo stockade (ninsoku yoseba), designed not only to remove idle, potentially dangerous elements from the city's streets but also to prepare them for renewed lives as productive, law-abiding commoners.[63]

The stockade was originally designed to hold so-called "innocent vagrants" (muzai no mushuku), a category that included both those who had committed no criminal offenses and petty criminals who had already been punished by beatings, tattooing, or handcuffing but could not be released for want of suitable guarantors. Inmates worked for wages, with one third held in compulsory savings and given to them upon their release. The shogunate also mobilized prominent preachers of Shingaku (a syncretic blend of Confucianism, Buddhism, and Shintō that emphasized the cultivation of morality by commoners) to deliver sermons to the inmates. Finally, officials provided reformed inmates with monetary assistance in setting themselves up as petty tradesmen or peasant farmers. On the other hand, regulations prescribed execution for those who attempted to escape and harsh punishments for other infractions. To Sadanobu, the stockade constituted another example of the benevolent rule of the Tokugawa shogunate.[64]

Stockade inmates were housed in wards according to age, sex, category of offense, and the type of work performed; limited evidence suggests that young people formed an important part of the inmate population. Some inmates were indeed very young, as may be seen in an early document concerning administrators' attempts to place children in the homes of trustworthy peasants or townsmen who might eventually adopt them. Shortly after it opened, the stockade also began taking in, for fixed terms, "incorrigible" servants in samurai households who had already been punished by beatings or handcuffing, as well as the delinquent children of townsmen who applied to have them confined. Indeed, the Osaka merchant scholars Nakai Riken and Nakai Chikuzan, whose proposals for a "long-term jail" *(nagarō)* influenced Sadanobu's decision to establish the stockade, had envisioned that such a facility would provide a positive alternative to the practice of disowning and expelling unruly sons. Many youths in their late teens and early twenties were sent to a branch stockade in Kamigō village, in present-day Ibaraki Prefecture, and were put to work on land reclamation projects. This group included younger outlaws *(akutō)* from the Kantō region around Edo who were deemed too dangerous to be returned to society after their punishments had been meted out; because of their youth, however, officials sought to avoid sending them to work as coolies in the mines at Sado, to which older outlaws were dispatched (and from which few returned). After the Kamigō facility closed in 1820, such young outlaws were sent to the Edo stockade, along with other criminals who had been sentenced to banishment but were deemed in need of preliminary discipline.[65]

By the 1840s, as yet another major famine exacerbated social dislocations and prompted a new round of shogunal reforms, city authorities advocated putting all dissolute and unfilial youths to work pressing oil in the Edo stockade, alongside vagrants and hardened criminals.[66] In 1846, the city magistrates, modifying their decrees of 1650 and 1655, ordered that disinherited vagrant youths who continued to make trouble for their families were to be placed in jail; if they repented and their relatives pleaded on their behalf, the youths would then be sent to the stockade for three years of rehabilitation. Those who "fail[ed] to understand the shogun's benevolence" and repeatedly importuned their relatives were to be banished from Edo.[67] A limited number of new stockades in other regions also took in youths upon their relatives' request. Beginning in 1861, for example, the Hakodate stockade, which dispatched inmates to mining operations in the Kushiro region of Ezo (modern-day Hokkaidō), admitted several such youths, including a young ruffian named Kinzō from Jizō-chō. Kinzō's desperate relatives, supported by the neighborhood headman, wrote that their efforts to prevent the boy from brawling had all failed, and pleaded with officials to "send him to the coal mines for a long, long time."[68]

The stockade did not represent a new regime of punishment, along the lines of the modern penitentiary, to replace earlier modes of discipline in the transition to a new type of social structure. It was designed, as recent scholarship suggests, to restore inmates to fixed positions within the existing status order, not to discipline "free" workers for a capitalist labor market. The effectiveness of this institution in reinforcing the status system is, however, far from clear. Officials in the early 1840s reported, for example, that many inmates in the Edo stockade had been committed on four or five previous occasions; their inability to secure guarantors or steady positions in society no doubt accounted for the high incidence of recidivism. Nonetheless, one can discern in the stockade's conception and implementation an increasing concern among shogunal officials to emphasize education and rehabilitation in the treatment of displaced persons. And by the closing years of Tokugawa rule, most of those targeted for such treatment were young: in 1869, one year after the fall of the shogunate, roughly 70 percent of the inmates in the former Edo stockade were aged twenty-five or younger. The stockade thus provided an indigenous precedent for approaches to socializing juvenile offenders after the Meiji Restoration, when the new government would place this project within the broader pursuit of "civilization and enlightenment."[69]

TOWARD RESTORATION

To Tokugawa authorities, young people's misbehavior challenged both the hierarchies essential to the operations of households and communities that comprised self-governing status groups and the regime's ability to encompass every subject of the realm within the status system. By the mid-nineteenth century, however, constantly expanding flows of cash, goods, ideas, and people had not only widened the cracks in the status edifice but also loosened its foundations, and the growing sense of crisis led intellectuals, local elites, other reformers, and the state itself to seek new modes of integrating society and ensuring that all subjects realized their productive potential.[70] Tokugawa rule, meanwhile, had also been predicated on what might be called a status system of limited diplomatic relations, in which the shogunate claimed to be the civilized center of a tribute system existing outside the system dominated by China. The foreign crisis of the mid-nineteenth century, a function of the expansion of Western imperialism into East Asia, undermined the shogunate's system, spurring the collapse of the Tokugawa regime and the establishment of a new state by a group of hotheaded young "men of high purpose" (shishi), a process known as the Meiji Restoration.[71]

Although the Meiji leaders lacked a clear agenda beyond toppling the Tokugawa and preserving Japan's sovereignty under the restored emperor, they quickly came to see the status system, with its intermediary layers of administration, as an obstacle to effective rule and economic development. Over the first decade of its existence, the new state thus abolished the status distinctions and permitted subjects to pursue occupations of their own choosing; it eliminated warrior stipends and sword-bearing privileges; it revised the tax system to legalize the alienation of land; and it "emancipated" the outcastes and *hinin,* stripping them of their occupational monopolies. In tandem with these acts of creative destruction, the Meiji leaders established a centralized state, a conscript army, universal compulsory elementary schooling, and a new police force and local governments as instruments for shaping, mobilizing, and directly administering the subjects of a newly conceived nation and empire.[72] Over time, these social revolutionary projects would produce new class relationships and subaltern categories, although the conceptual consciousness that had evolved under the early modern status order continued, in transmogrified form, to shape the ways in which Japanese people understood their identities.

Tokugawa traditions would also continue to inform young people's transgressive behavior in the Meiji period and beyond. The media image of the *kyōkaku* or *otokodate* as outlaw hero would prove remarkably resilient, as would the brawling and importunate activities of *wakamono*-type working youths in tenement neighborhoods, at festivals, and in the brothel and amusement districts. Warrior youths' traditions of violence, sexual and otherwise, also persisted, along with the customs of townsmen's sons who dissipated their family fortunes in the pleasure quarters and children who pinched purses in crowded thoroughfares. But while officials and reformers might denounce these activities, as well as newer types of transgression, in language that echoed the outrage of Edo's magistrates and moralizers, they would also adopt the discursive and practical instruments made available through intercourse with Europe, North America, and the colonial world in order to define and demand conformity to "modern" patterns of childhood and youth. In the new Japan, young people's misbehavior, and the responses it provoked, would once again lie at the center of efforts to construct and maintain the polity.

CHAPTER 2

Assimilating the Lower Classes

At the turn of the twentieth century, as Tokyo developed into the capital of a rising industrial, imperial power, children like ten-year-old "Naruse Kametarō" captured the public's attention as symbols of a different kind of urban space. Abandoned by his day-laborer stepfather shortly after their arrival in Tokyo in 1895, the boy spent a year as a beggar in the Shinbashi Station area, sleeping in horse sheds and befriending other vagrant children before he was picked up by the police and sent to the Tokyo City Poorhouse. Kametarō's tale of the juvenile underworld, peopled with characters named Shorty, Black Shorty, No Waist, and Granny, came to light in interviews conducted by poorhouse officers and was included in an 1896 exposé on the Tokyo poor in the newspaper *Jiji shinpō*. "They [beggar children] have indeed formed a hidden society, outside the law and undetected by the police," lamented the exposé's author. "In their dens, they dream easily and little by little learn the ways of evildoing."[1]

By the time it appeared in *Tokyo Manners and Customs (Tōkyō fūzokushi)*, Hirade Kojirō's 1899–1902 catalogue of life in the capital, Kametarō's story had become a well-known object of media consumption; meanwhile, other reporter-flaneurs set out to find similar "interesting materials" to satisfy public curiosity about the urban netherworld.[2] But such stories also symbolized the eruption of newly configured "social problems" into the national consciousness. Indeed, to turn-of-the-century reformers, children like Kametarō, whatever their actual number, stood for a much larger category: the lower classes of unskilled, casual laborers and others who, living in squalor and reproducing uncontrollably, threatened to infect society with the "virus" of crime and barbarity.[3]

In the Tokugawa era, Kametarō would most likely have been remanded to the *hinin* organization of licensed beggars, or possibly, after 1790, been placed in the Edo stockade for discipline and rehabilitation. But by the early Meiji years, the *hinin* organization, along with most of the Tokugawa status system, had been dismantled; and by the 1880s, institutions that supplanted the stockade had developed reputations as schools not of virtue but of crime. By the mid-1890s, however, following a victorious war against China, Japan had acquired Taiwan as a colony and jump-started its industrial revolution, and ideologues both within and outside the government argued heatedly for the need to cultivate a new generation of national subjects *(kokumin)* capable of supporting the empire both in times of war and in times of peace. Conflict with Russia in 1904–5, which brought new colonial possessions while severely straining the domestic economy, only strengthened this imperative.[4] To advocates of juvenile reform, Kametarō and those like him did not exist in the time-space of modern Japan: they had "no past, no present, and no future."[5] And if boys took to the streets to beg and steal, lower-class girls appeared susceptible to the lures of the unlicensed sex trade, another blight on the national body. These children had to be rescued from their environments, and those environments themselves had to be reformed so that the lower classes could be assimilated into the industrial capitalist economy, the nation-state, and the empire.

A cadre of new-middle-class social experts, armed with new, largely imported knowledge, emerged to spearhead this program of internal colonization.[6] From positions within and outside the government, they observed and analyzed lower-class life, developed institutions to transform the objects of their attention, and mobilized public opinion to support their agenda. Their efforts crystallized in the 1900 Reformatory Law (*Kanka hō,* revised in 1908) that empowered the state to take charge of delinquent or dependent children; in reformatories conceived as utopian models of diligence and domesticity; and, in Tokyo, in special elementary schools intended to extend the technologies of reform from slum children to their families.

Despite their humanitarian intentions, reformers tended to see the lower classes through the lens of their own prejudices. Moreover, the benefits they offered either paled before their clients' needs or appealed to a desire for (limited) upward mobility through education—a desire that as yet held little sway over most slum dwellers. Lower-class children and families often practiced a different kind of mobility, taking advantage of the opportunities that each day presented, whether or not they accorded with reformers' strategies for social improvement, national fortification, and middle-class empowerment.[7] By the same token, lower-class children proved particularly vulnerable to exploitation by employers and others who also cared little for reformers' initiatives. Institutions of assimilation and the ideologies that underpinned them thus reveal some of the main tensions at the core of urban social and economic change in late-nineteenth- and early-twentieth-century Japan.

SOCIAL PROBLEMS AND SOCIAL KNOWLEDGE AT THE TURN OF THE TWENTIETH CENTURY

The growth of the juvenile reform movement reflected the major changes that Japan was undergoing at the turn of the century. Since 1868, the Meiji state had promoted a series of far-reaching reforms aimed at constructing a modern nation that could thrive in an international capitalist economy and an imperialist diplomatic structure. In less than thirty years, Japan had developed a centralized state and a new constitution, a modern military that could wage and win foreign wars, an educational system based on the idea of compulsory elementary schooling, and a growing industrial sector.

As Japan entered the twentieth century, however, the pace of change intensified, and its effects filled contemporary observers with alarm. Japan's modern capitalist economy grew at an explosive pace in the last two decades of the Meiji era. The Sino-Japanese War of 1894–95, and the Russo-Japanese War that followed a decade later, massively stimulated this industrial revolution, and the urbanization it entailed.[8] From 1893 to 1914, the number of cities with more than 20,000 inhabitants doubled, from 59 to 122. The percentage of the population living in cities with more than 50,000 inhabitants also doubled from 7 percent in 1888 to 14 percent in 1913. The largest urban areas exploded. Tokyo Prefecture's population jumped from 1.8 million in 1893 to 2.9 million in 1915, while Osaka Prefecture's population climbed from 1.4 million to 2.3 million. Most of the new immigrants to the cities filled the ranks of the nascent industrial proletariat or the impoverished lower class of casual laborers, both groups remaining largely undifferentiated in terms of lifestyles and popular perceptions, and concentrated in rapidly expanding slum areas.[9]

Along with these changes came a new wave of reports of crime, poverty, and labor unrest. By 1899, many contemporary observers could agree with the investigative journalist Yokoyama Gennosuke when he wrote: "If one were to consider social problems in the broad sense, that is, as problems resulting from flaws in society, then Japan now has many social problems: conflicts between classes, conflicts between strong and weak, conflicts between wealthy and poor. Particularly since the war with China, the sudden rise of mechanized industries has provoked a labor problem, while massive price increases have generated problems of poverty. These problems are gradually assuming dimensions comparable to those in the West."[10]

While a few professional associations and magazines had begun to pay attention to social problems prior to the war with China, the conflict and its aftermath stimulated a heightened perception among urban middle-class intellectuals that society required them to act upon the problems they confronted. For example, the editors of *The Sociologist* (*Shakai zasshi*), the journal of the Sociological Society (Shakai Gakkai), expressed their "desire to awaken a sense of duty among the upper classes *(jōsō shakai)* and secure an appropriate livelihood for the lower classes *(kasō shakai)*" and to "raise the values of humanity and work for the progress of the Japanese people."[11] Society member Tomeoka Kōsuke espoused a similar view when he wrote in 1898 that a new group of philanthropists, armed with both compassion and scientific knowledge, should take the initiative in reforming not only the poor but also the upper classes, whose accumulated wealth brought moral corruption. Tomeoka and other champions of "Social Christianity," many of whom had traveled and studied in the West, helped pioneer the development of professions such as social work and urban administration. Indeed, the remarkable spread of Christianity, particularly Protestantism, among the educated urban middle class at the turn of the century decisively shaped the discourse on social structures and social problems. And despite the rise in the 1890s of polemical attacks on Christianity as a foreign creed incompatible with a nationalist public morality centered on Japan's imperial institution, Christian social reformers, because of their status as knowledge-bearing elites, actually assumed positions close to the center of the modern governing system.[12]

State agencies, needless to say, were highly sensitive to potential threats to social order, and sought to organize society and the economy to support rising military budgets and a colonial empire. The turn of the century saw the emergence of a new generation of what Kenneth Pyle has termed "bureaucrat-intellectuals" who "were convinced of the need for legislation to forestall social disintegration."[13] Home Ministry officials such as Ogawa Shigejirō, a specialist in penology, and Kubota Seitarō, an expert in public health and labor insurance, joined Tomeoka, Tokyo City Poorhouse manager Adachi Kenchū, and other private reformers in the Poverty Study Association (Hinmin Kenkyūkai, established in 1900), which combined academic exchanges with ground-level surveys of Tokyo slums.[14]

Fears of social disintegration mounted after 1905, when the burdens imposed by Japan's war with Russia threatened to devastate the economy. Heavy taxes and widespread out-migration brought many rural communities to the brink of collapse. Those who left their villages swelled the ranks of the urban poor, now called "lean people" *(saimin)*; but they could not escape conscription, taxes on basic consumer goods, and other financial impositions associated with the state's military programs. The 1905 Hibiya Riot, in which Tokyo crowds upset over the terms of the Portsmouth Treaty ending the Russo-Japanese War attacked police stations and other institutions affiliated with the government, raised fears among state leaders of the destructive potential of "the masses." The apparent spread of socialist ideas and the increase in the number of strikes—particularly violent eruptions like the 1907 Ashio Mine incident, in which the government sent in troops to suppress a labor dispute for the first time—further aggravated officials' concerns over "social destructionism."[15]

While the state employed measures such as the 1900 Peace Police Law to stifle labor organizers and socialists, government officials and their allies launched a new campaign, the Local Improvement Movement, that relied on youth and women's groups, agricultural cooperatives, and diligence and thrift promotion drives to secure the social and economic bases for imperial growth.[16] Assisted by Tomeoka and other private experts and Protestant activists, the Home Ministry in 1908 initiated a series of annual Reform and Relief Seminars to train social workers and local improvement leaders, and in the same year helped establish the Central Charities Association (Chūō Jizen Kyōkai), which provided information and guidance to local welfare programs.[17]

Juvenile crime figured prominently in the litany of mounting social evils. Officials observed, for example, that the number of minors sentenced to prison terms had more than tripled from some nine thousand cases in 1882 to more than twenty-seven thousand cases in 1894, and that these figures did not include youths detained or fined for misdemeanor infractions of police regulations, or those whose crimes were either undiscovered or unpunished for lack of evidence.[18] Experts agreed that poverty lay at the root of this phenomenon. In Tokyo, social workers such as poorhouse manager Adachi Kenchū and investigative reporters described in meticulous detail the various stages through which delinquent or dependent children like Naruse Kametarō evolved into either full-fledged criminals or poorhouse residents—in either case, parasites who destroyed the social body and had to be treated at public expense.[19]

STREET URCHINS AND THE PROBLEM OF LOWER-CLASS SOCIETY

Like Kametarō, most of the children whom investigators encountered had either run away from their homes or workplaces or been abandoned by relatives. Very small children might be taken in by adult slum dwellers and leased to adult beggars for a few *sen* each day; skinny, weak-looking children, who elicited sympathy from passersby, fetched a higher fee than plump ones. As they grew too old to be rented, girls were taught to play the shamisen or perform popular dances and were put out on the streets to beg. Boys were either sold to "lion dancer" *(kakubei shishi)* bosses, notoriously brutal men who forced them to dance all day while performing handstands, or simply thrown out to fend for themselves alongside other denizens of the streets.[20]

Many abandoned boys made their way to the crowded central fish market at Nihonbashi, where they scavenged fish guts, which could be sold as fertilizer, and slept huddled together under bridges or behind storage sheds. They shared their earnings with various bosses, most of whom were themselves in their teens or early twenties. Some boys paid a fixed daily sum to bosses who promised to care for them when they were ill; others handed over their entire daily takes in exchange for a few *sen* in spending money. Bullying, beatings, and expulsion from the market area awaited those who did not pay. Boys also acted as businessmen in their own right, bargaining hard with vagrant boys from neighboring districts who brought their own meager supplies of fish guts, scrounged from restaurants, inns, and garbage containers, to the market in search of cash.[21]

Many more children converged on Asakusa, the sprawling center of popular prayer and play along the Sumida River that regularly attracted huge throngs of visitors.[22] Rezoned as a park in 1885 as part of the new government's urban modernization schemes, Asakusa was home to the Sensōji temple complex and its vendors' shops, teahouses, and shadowy, wooded precincts (Okuyama); the Sixth District (Rokku) with its theaters, cinemas, amusement parks, carnival shows, and food shops; and the twelve-story tower (Ryōunkaku), a symbol of Tokyo's modernity, which overlooked the countless unlicensed brothels of the surrounding Senzoku-machi neighborhood. Asakusa was close to the Yoshiwara licensed quarters, and many men stopped there on their way to and from the brothels; it also bordered on notorious slums such as Mannenchō, from which street performers, beggars, and scavengers came in search of income. To concerned social investigators, Asakusa was, in journalist Matsubara Iwagorō's 1897 formulation, "a vast garbage dump" whose unhealthy elements contaminated the entire city.[23]

Begging and scavenging frequently blurred into fishing for coins in temple collection boxes, shoplifting, and petty theft. A "reporter in disguise" for the general interest magazine *New Review (Shin kōron)* reported in 1911 his nocturnal encounter in Asakusa's Luna Park amusement center with two "tricky" boys, aged twelve or thirteen: "Looking carefully, I saw that they had stuffed three or four dried bonito and some handkerchiefs into their clothes, and one had also stuffed in some new socks."[24] Local bosses either encouraged these activities or turned a blind eye to them. The recognized "overlord" of the scavengers in the fish market and in Asakusa, a woman known to all as Granny (Baaya), told a reporter in 1896 that she hoped to keep her own boys from becoming criminals, and provided them with special jackets that would set them apart from other, larcenous street children. Yet the same reporter noted that several of Granny's vassals were themselves convicted criminals, while another, Black Shorty, was a vicious triple murderer who died at the age of sixteen. Moreover, as Kametarō told Adachi, Granny's boys in fact took advantage of the jackets to pilfer with impunity, since the police treated them differently from other street children. And as the overlord, Granny appears to have received a share of whatever her boys brought in.[25] As in the Edo period, child beggars who showed promise were quickly taught to pick pockets. One of Adachi's informants, "Nakada Shinkichi," aged thirteen and abandoned by his father and older brother, met a boy in Asakusa Park who introduced him to a boss named Morikō in Honjo Ward. Morikō sent

Shinkichi out to beg, and then, after he had learned the tricks of the trade, to steal. The oldest boys in Morikō's group dressed well, sported gold watches, and were ready to join adult pickpocket gangs.[26]

Some children, like the boy who arrived at the Tokyo City Poorhouse in rags and covered with bruises from beatings he received in the fish market, accepted Adachi's offers of shelter and schooling as a welcome opportunity to leave the streets.[27] But others rejected these overtures. "I hate [the poorhouse]," declared Naruse Kametarō. "I want to run away and be a beggar, so I can walk around getting money from people."[28] Many children, moreover, earned a decent living. One eleven-year-old, born into an impoverished farm family and apprenticed to a textile mill from which he immediately escaped, told Adachi in 1906, "There is no life as easy as that of a beggar. If you only give five *sen* a day to the boss, no one bothers you. In fact, many people take pity on kids like us and give us not just food and drink but also money. We can eat sushi at the stand-up shops and have Imagawa-yaki sweets."[29] Even a boy who had been beaten repeatedly by a particularly cruel boss enjoyed life on the streets: he eventually escaped to the licensed quarter at Yoshiwara, where he worked selling fortunes at night, "made thirty to forty *sen* clean profit every day, . . . and lived as he pleased."[30] Given that factory workers and even some elementary school teachers made only about ten yen per month (one yen equaled one hundred *sen*), the boy could be said to have been doing quite well. Crime also paid. Writing in 1897, Matsubara Iwagorō described a gang of four or five boys, aged ten to thirteen, who entered a tea shop in the Okuyama section of Asakusa Park and ate sushi and tempura like adults. The oldest boy paid for the meal with a one yen note, collected his change, and left, unperturbed by the incredulous stares of the other customers. Following the boy, Matsubara confirmed that he was a pickpocket showering largesse on his followers.[31]

To Adachi, street children displayed an "aversion to disciplined life [that] makes one think of snakes or stinging insects."[32] At their worst, they could provoke disastrous conflagrations. Evidence of this problem came in 1897, when a fire destroyed a large section of Hongō Ward. The police arrested Hanamura Shinroku, a vagrant boy of not more than ten, for the crime, and found to their astonishment that he and other street children frequently set fires both for the pleasure of seeing the flames and in order to loot burned-out houses and shops.[33]

Like vagrancy and petty theft, arson by children was in fact far from a new phenomenon, and police officials in Edo had even developed particular ways of handling underage suspects.[34] Traces of the Edo social structure could also be seen in a figure such as Granny, who functioned as a late-Meiji analog of the Tokugawa-era *hinin* headman, overseeing ragpickers instead of beggars and street performers.[35] But whereas the Tokugawa rulers had deputized the *hinin* headmen as intermediaries in their policy to immobilize the populace in status organizations, the Meiji regime sought to mobilize subjects directly to meet the demands of a growing capitalist economy and a Darwinian world of fierce international rivalries. Despite her professed good intentions, Granny lacked any official authority to police her underlings, and she even facilitated, although perhaps unwittingly, their illegal practices. To reformers, she was part of the problem rather than its solution. Adachi and his peers thus sought new methods to turn delinquent and dependent children into dependable workers and subjects of the Japanese empire.

The actual size of Tokyo's street-child population cannot be ascertained. One 1896 news report put the number at fewer than five hundred; a police source two decades later suggested, without offering evidence, that there were two thousand street urchins and thieves in Asakusa, Shitaya, and nearby Nippori alone.[36] Regardless of their number, in public discourse these children symbolized all of the pathologies of urban lower-class life that threatened to drag down the nation. Observers such as Adachi and Yokoyama Gennosuke recognized that the root cause of many of the problems they described lay in the process of industrialization, and they wrote compassionately of poor people's daily struggle for survival.[37] But their arguments also revealed the prejudices of an emergent new middle class whose members deployed negative models of behavior in order to affirm their own "normality" and "superiority." For example, commenting on the rising number of abandoned children in Tokyo, Adachi wrote that the city's poor "know only lust, and their marriages and divorces are quick, easy affairs. To think of the offspring of these relationships and the kinds of upbringing they will receive makes one shudder with fright." Tomeoka Kōsuke, for his part, hypothesized in 1902 that the tendency among "lower humans" to have many children might be related to similar propensities among dogs and other "lower animals."[38]

Commentators graphically depicted slum dwellings as cramped, filthy tenement flats that lacked basic amenities and bred disease. In many cases, more than one family shared the same four- or six-mat flat, while some families did not even rent flats but lived in partitioned-off sections of flophouses whose clientele included a variety of day laborers, peddlers, and street entertainers. Many slum dwellers borrowed thin, soiled bedding from pawnshops at night and returned it in the morning; men and women had few if any clothes, and those they had were filthy. Describing the inhabitants of Shitaya Ward's notorious Mannenchō slum, a writer for the magazine *Illustrated Manners and Customs (Fūzoku gahō)* noted sardonically, "These are far from the naked bodies celebrated by Western artists as the extreme of beauty."[39]

These homes, emphasized reporter after reporter, provided not nurture but abuse and neglect. Parents fought ceaselessly, often taking out their anger on their children. In many cases, the children were stepchildren, and commentators repeatedly emphasized the connection between abusive stepparents and juvenile delinquency. Fathers drank heavily and gambled. Mothers worked all day, lacked basic domestic skills, and allowed children to roam the streets, where, Yokoyama wrote, they loitered around candy stores "enviously ogling the merchandise," played boisterously, and listened to the vulgar songs and tales of itinerant shamisen players and storytellers.[40] In Mannenchō, children played at temples in the hopes of encountering a funeral and receiving alms. And throughout the city, many children scavenged. A 1903 painting of the Samegahashi slum in Yotsuya Ward in *Illustrated Manners and Customs* shows boys romping in an alley where entertainers, peddlers, and others mingle; two boys rejoice upon having captured a mouse—to many contemporaries a symbol of epidemic disease, but in this case possibly a source of income—which one of them dangles by the tail. Slum parents, one investigator observed, praised children for bringing home stolen objects, such as used sandals, socks, or washbasins, that could be exchanged for cash.[41]

While boys scavenged and begged, girls allegedly adopted other means to earn money. Observers noted that few lower-class girls became vagrants or delinquents, possibly because they could find work more easily than boys and spent less time outdoors, but that many readily became unlicensed prostitutes, thus posing another danger to the social order.[42] One reason for this, suggested the authors of the 1916 book *Studies of Bad Children (Akudō kenkyū),* was to be found in girls' essential gender traits. Although they were not suited to committing "brazen crimes" to meet their economic needs, they could manage to get by in life "fairly painlessly" provided they were willing to accept their own degradation. But, the authors continued, the fault also lay in the particular conditions of the slums. In an environment where sexual precocity was

Figure 1. "Evening in the Samegahashi slum," 1903. Source: *Fūzoku gahō,*
CD-ROM version. ©1997, Yumani Shobō. Courtesy of Yumani Shobō.

the general rule, girls were especially precocious, and they offered their
bodies less out of carnal desire than as a means of exchange. Hence,
girls of ten or eleven, "who must struggle mightily to squeeze one *sen* in
spending money from their parents," could readily earn two or three
sen for brief encounters in vacant houses with young or middle-aged
men. Many eventually entered unlicensed brothels, known as "evil
dens," in the back streets of Asakusa. Even worse, when these girls visited their old neighborhoods "dressed in a different style," they were
welcomed as local kids-made-good who had risen in the world through
their labor.[43]

This appropriation of dominant ideological tropes of hard work,
success, and rising in the world to describe illicit and possibly autonomous
female sex workers must have irked Home Ministry officials to no end.
As many scholars have noted, the imperial Japanese state strove to
regulate sex through a network of licensed brothels that provided
hygienically controlled and spatially demarcated outlets for men while
discursively denying prostitutes' own sexual agency by treating them as
self-sacrificing, filial daughters of impoverished (and mainly rural)
families. Although the popular culture of the licensed quarters might

celebrate women who advanced in the trade, ideological orthodoxy precluded the possibility of sex work as an avenue of "success."[44] Middle-class social reformers, many of them Protestants who not only opposed all forms of sexual trafficking but also championed an Anglo-American model of feminine domesticity, must also have been horrified by the possibility that lower-class girls actively pursued sexual relations, whether for physical gratification or as a means of barter. And everyone concerned shared a fear of the venereal diseases that unlicensed prostitutes transmitted. Thus, whether they produced vagrant and criminal boys or sexually active, degenerate girls, the slums represented a clear danger on Japan's path to a healthy modernity.

Schools were supposed to mitigate the effects of this environment. The Meiji state had in 1872 established a system of public schools and compulsory elementary education, and historians generally point to the late-Meiji years as the time in which schooling in Japan became virtually universal. But these interpretations tend to overlook the fact that rising enrollment statistics covered only children defined as "having an obligation to attend" elementary school. In fact, the government's elementary school ordinances of 1886, 1890, and 1900 (the last of which remained in effect until 1941) all stipulated that poor children could be temporarily or permanently exempted from the obligation to attend; the number of exempted children nationwide climbed from 550,000 in 1897 to 880,000 in 1900, reached one million (15.7 percent of school-age children) in 1903, and stayed at comparable levels for years after. Moreover, many children whose births had never been officially registered remained invisible to educational authorities and absent from their statistics.[45] Hence, in densely populated cities such as Tokyo and Osaka, large numbers of working children either never attended school or left before completing the compulsory course (four years, extended to six years in 1907). Children's labor provided a necessary complement to parental earnings, while those who did not work were expected to care for their younger siblings or to scavenge fuel, food, or things that could be exchanged for cash—again, from where they obtained them was irrelevant. Many social investigators shared the opinion that, as one Tokyo educator put it, "The children of the slums are truly filial."[46] Needless to say, filial children offered a cheap source of labor to many employers in growing industries such as matches and textiles: at the turn of the century, elementary-school-age children accounted for roughly 15 percent of the factory workforce. The Ministry of Education, however, did not seek an end to child labor; in a 1900 directive, officials only called on employers to "provide education to the children in their hire through simple, convenient methods."[47]

Apprenticeships for boys in small commercial and manufacturing shops constituted a related problem. Many lower-class parents continued to rely on such apprenticeships (along with indenturing their daughters to weaving establishments north of Tokyo) to reduce the number of mouths they had to feed while preparing for their children's futures.[48] In theory, boys underwent several years of arduous, unpaid labor in exchange for education in a trade and possibly a share of the master's clientele, but changes in the economy had rendered the system increasingly dysfunctional. Some outraged commentators, echoing Buyō Inshi's 1816 lamentations, wrote that in an increasingly money-driven society, youths no longer appreciated the sanctity of the master-apprentice relationship. Social workers, however, reported that unscrupulous masters took advantage of young people's unpaid labor and then contrived pretexts to dismiss them just as their terms were about to expire, thus driving many to vagrancy.[49]

Moreover, harsh treatments that had traditionally been justified as a form of character-building now appeared in a different light. In an observation that applied equally to Tokyo and elsewhere, one critic of the Osaka apprenticeship system wrote in 1914 that local merchants "equate abuse and training." Filthy, slave-like conditions made apprentices "desperate, base, deceitful, and thieving." Excessive constraints led them to shoplift food, falsify ledgers, or abscond with goods or money, while long hours made them lose interest in labor and become slow and lazy. Meanwhile, reformers such as Home Ministry official Ogawa Shigejirō argued that child labor in any form constituted a serious impediment to much-needed schooling, while exposure to workplaces and older workers made children "precocious" and increased their potential for antisocial behavior.[50]

Ogawa and other reformers supported the government's proposed Factory Law, which would prohibit factory work for children under the age of eleven, as a first step in the process of eliminating child labor and promoting the development of a well-disciplined, productive workforce. Employers, however, mounted a fierce offensive against the bill. The watered-down version that the Diet finally approved in 1911—and which was not implemented until 1916—prohibited the employment of children under twelve, but allowed for exceptions so that children as young as ten could be hired for "simple" factory work. In addition, the law applied only to factories employing at least fifteen workers, and thus did not cover the small workshops where most children found jobs. Commercial establishments, moreover, remained free from government regulation. Reformers continued to advocate the prohibition of work by elementary-school-age children, and argued that the state and private agencies should find ways of helping families so that they did not need to send their children into the workforce.[51]

Although they often laced their commentaries with dehumanizing metaphors and disdainful phrases, late-Meiji reformers pointed to a number of realities of life among the poor. Urban infrastructures had not developed to support the massive population growth at the turn of the century, and slum crowding and concomitant problems were inevitable. Urban industry, furthermore, could not absorb new workers as quickly as they came. Many newcomers thus fell into the pool of laborers hired for poorly paid jobs in construction, road building, and hauling, while others took up odd jobs such as peddling and ragpicking. As in earlier periods of urban growth, an excess of males over females among urban immigrants delayed the spread of marriage among the poor; until the second decade of the twentieth century, writes historian Nakagawa Kiyoshi, Tokyo's lower classes replenished themselves more by immigration than by childbearing.[52] Those who did marry, moreover, often preferred common-law partnerships to the formal registration required by the state. This choice did not necessarily reflect a lack of commitment. For example, Yokoyama wrote in 1904 that couples living in flophouses were too ashamed of their conditions to have their family registers transferred from their place of origin to their flophouse address, and that this in part accounted for the high rates of illegitimate children among the poor.[53] The fact that mothers had to either take in piecework or commute to factories also prevented them from assuming the full-time domestic roles that middle-class wives were increasingly performing; to make time for money-earning activities, poor women often had to let their children play on the streets, where they learned their own ways of getting along.[54] Also, since employment in industries requiring an educated workforce was still far from standard for this group, parents could envision their children growing up without passing through a prolonged period of schooling. And even if parents did recognize the importance of education, lower-class household economies depended upon the contribution of every able member, including children, who were most vulnerable to exploitation by employers.

To many reformers, however, it appeared that the lower classes had yet to internalize the proper norms and objectives of family life. In reaction to these conditions, state agencies and private actors claimed the obligation to act *in loco parentis* to "protect" the neglected, dependent, and delinquent children of the lower class, and to prepare them to become the upstanding working class of the future.

THE REFORMATORY MOVEMENT
AND THE REFORMATORY LAW

The Meiji state had, from its inception, instituted new measures for the treatment of juvenile offenders. Early Meiji codes adopted prescriptions for lenience to children from both Tokugawa laws and Qing Chinese codes. The 1870 *Shinritsu kōryō*, an early criminal law code, stated that children seven or younger could not be held responsible for their actions, and provided for a system of fines to replace banishment, beatings, or tattooing for children aged eight to fifteen. Nonetheless, authorities in many localities continued to mete out corporal punishments to younger offenders.[55] To overcome this situation, and as part of its effort to create a new penal system, the government began to target children and young people for confinement in special correctional institutions. Officials such as Ohara Shigechika drew heavily on Western models of prisons in conceiving the new system, but they also built in part upon the precedents of the Edo stockade and shogunal decrees governing the confinement of unfilial sons. The 1872 Prison Regulations provided for the establishment of houses of correction *(chōjikan)*, which would be separated from regular prisons and would provide inmates with schooling and vocational training. The houses of correction were to hold prison convicts under the age of twenty who, having completed their prescribed sentences, still displayed criminal propensities or, because of their poverty, threatened to fall back into lives of crime; they were also to hold "delinquent" commoner youths committed at their parents' request. The notion that children should be educated as subjects of the emerging nation-state no doubt greatly influenced government officials' approach to the new institutions; indeed, the laws establishing the houses of correction appeared in the same year as the state's new ordinance on compulsory elementary education. Moreover, as the state took measures to break down the Tokugawa status system, the Justice Ministry in 1874 also permitted samurai families to have their children confined. The houses of correction, however, were not designed exclusively for juvenile inmates; they also held adult convicts who had completed their sentences but still showed "thoughts of rebelliousness or murder."[56] Furthermore, in April 1872, the government had enacted the Penal Servitude Law, which replaced corporal punishments with the generalized use of imprisonment. The extreme overcrowding that resulted from this reform stymied any efforts to separate juveniles from adults in the houses of correction.[57]

Western influences prompted further efforts to develop special programs for juvenile offenders. In 1876, the physician and Protestant missionary John C. Berry submitted to Home Minister Ōkubo Toshimichi a report on prison conditions in Japan, in which he called for the strict segregation of youths from adults, the elimination of cruel punishments, and greater emphasis on inmate education. Ōkubo had the report printed and distributed to officials in each prefecture. Three years later, Onoda Motohiro, a ranking police official, returned from a tour of Europe and published detailed reports on the systematic methods of classification and treatment employed in juvenile penitentiaries in France and Belgium.[58] In response to these recommendations, the state replaced the houses of correction with a new system of correctional centers (called, confusingly, chōjijō) for the rehabilitation of minors deemed not legally competent to be tried for their crimes. Under the new Penal Code of 1880, children under the age of twelve were not to be prosecuted for their offenses, but those aged eight or older could be placed in the correctional centers until they turned sixteen. Children aged twelve to fifteen at the time of their offense were to be prosecuted only if they understood the criminal nature of their acts; if not indicted, they could be placed in the correctional centers until they turned twenty. In addition, the Penal Code prescribed varying degrees of leniency for youths aged twelve to nineteen who were tried and found guilty. The new code thus established the possibility of official lenience for a wider age bracket than either Tokugawa or early Meiji laws had permitted. The state, meanwhile, continued to provide parents the option of having their "prodigal and delinquent" children—defined by one official as "lazy and selfish," "disobedient," and "wild"—confined for up to four consecutive six-month terms.[59]

As in the case of the earlier houses of correction, however, officials did not in practice devote much energy to developing a distinct sphere of juvenile corrections. Procurators tended to reason that even small children understood that to steal is wrong, thus vitiating the option of commission to the correctional centers. Furthermore, early Meiji procedural codes required procurators to indict anyone suspected of a criminal offense, and offered no alternatives to imprisonment, such as suspended sentencing, for those convicted. Judges thereby prescribed prison sentences for the overwhelming majority of children whose cases they tried, no matter how petty the crime (for example, stealing fruit from a neighbor's tree). Hence, in the early 1890s, whereas the number of minors in prison ranged from an astounding 20,000 to 28,000, the number of correctional center inmates never exceeded 275. Moreover, because most centers were barely separated from the prisons in which they had been established, even these inmates tended to be treated like regular prisoners.[60] In 1889, the government revised the Prison Regulations to eliminate the provision whereby parents could have their children committed to the correctional centers, but few parents had in fact been willing to stigmatize their wayward children by placing them in public correctional facilities alongside criminal elements (although some were willing to have their deaf, mute, or mentally handicapped children committed). Prefectural assemblies, meanwhile, tended to dismiss prison administrators' requests that they allot funds for special programs for the young.[61]

Under these circumstances, private activists and government officials, again drawing on Western models, promoted the establishment of specialized juvenile reformatories that were separate from the prison system. Information on juvenile reformatories in the West, particularly in England and the United States, had entered Japan since the late 1860s, and eventually attracted the attention of Japanese religious groups. In an 1880 article in the magazine The Universe (Rikugō zasshi), the Protestant minister Kozaki Hiromichi wrote that while the best method of preventing crime and social ills was to promote moral and religious instruction among the public, as Sunday schools did in the West, combating juvenile delinquency required the immediate establishment of private reformatories.[62] A group close to Kozaki failed in its attempt to open such an institution, but other private groups, many of them Buddhists responding to the challenge of Protestant philanthropy, started small-scale reformatories in Tokyo, Osaka, Kyoto, and elsewhere between 1884 and 1894, and organized to petition the government for recognition and subsidies.[63] The most widely noted of the new institutions was the Tokyo Reformatory (Tōkyō Kankain), established in 1885 by Takase Shinkyō, a former prison chaplain and an adherent of the syncretic Shingaku faith, who secured the support of Justice Ministry officials and their foreign legal advisers. After 1888, the newly established Greater Japan Prisons Association also promoted these efforts.[64]

Mounting concern for social problems after 1895 prompted more extensive public efforts to build a reformatory program. Adachi Kenchū, for example, proposed the establishment of a nationwide system of reformatories called victory houses, to be funded with the indemnity Japan received from China under the 1895 Treaty of Shimonoseki. This proposal never came to fruition, but Adachi and Shibusawa Eiichi, the prominent industrialist who oversaw the Tokyo City Poorhouse, gained permission from city officials to establish a reformatory division, which opened in 1900, using a charitable donation from the imperial household to commemorate the recent death of the empress dowager.[65] Within the government, Home Ministry official Ogawa Shigejirō emerged as the leading expert in the transnational discipline of penology and took the lead in calling for new, non-prison-centered approaches to the prevention of crime. In 1895, while in Paris, Ogawa attended the Fifth International Penal and Penitentiary Congress, where participants in a newly organized section on children and minors argued "that no boy or girl should be considered as criminal when educational discipline suffices for his reformation."[66] Back in Japan, Ogawa argued that juvenile delinquency was the most pressing social problem facing the nation, and that the state had a duty to take preventive measures: "Just as schools to teach the children of normal people to know right from wrong and become good citizens are public undertakings which the state and local governments are required to support, enterprises to take custody of and reform juvenile delinquents who have become criminals or are on the verge of doing so should also by their nature be the responsibility of the state and local governments."[67]

In February 1900, the government submitted to the Diet the draft of a Reformatory Law (Kanka hō), produced by Ogawa and his Home Ministry colleague Kubota Seitarō. The bill called for each prefecture to establish a reformatory, to be supervised by the prefectural governor and funded by the prefectures, although governors could choose to employ private reformatories as surrogate public facilities. Reformatories would hold "individuals between the ages of eight and fifteen who, in the determination of the prefectural governor, lack parents or guardians capable of exercising proper parental authority over them, and who engage in prodigality or mendicancy, or in bad relationships; [and] . . . juveniles sentenced to terms in the correctional centers [according to the Penal Code]." These youths could be kept until their twentieth birthday, or discharged if they were deemed to have reformed. Reformatories could also hold youths whose parents, in accordance with the provisions of the 1898 Civil Code, had secured court approval to have them confined for six-month terms in special "houses of discipline" *(chōkaijō)*, none of which had in fact been constructed; youths in this category could be kept beyond the age of majority.[68]

In theory, the Reformatory Law empowered state officials to penetrate family relationships in a radically new way. Ogawa admitted that the law's lack of specific definitions of "prodigality"—it included but was not limited to vagrancy, idleness, and debauchery—afforded prefectural governors wide berth in determining who should be committed to a reformatory. But Ogawa also told members of the House of Peers that respectable families did not have to fear state intrusions into their homes. It was in the "very lower class," he explained, that one found parents who exploited their children as beggars and pickpockets and subjected them to other forms of abuse. Similarly, Ogawa anticipated that very few parents (especially members of the propertied classes) would actually seek to have their children committed to reformatories under the Civil Code provisions.[69]

Legislators had no problems with the thrust of the bill, but they did worry about the costs of establishing reformatories. With little debate, the Diet passed an amended version that made implementation contingent upon approval by prefectural assemblies (which were generally averse to spending on social welfare). Between 1900 and 1908, only five prefectures implemented the Reformatory Law. Even Tokyo Prefecture waited until 1906, when officials designated the Tokyo City Poorhouse reformatory division as a surrogate facility.[70]

Concern for the apparent weakening of the social order after the 1904–5 Russo-Japanese War, however, led to a greater willingness to label young people as delinquent, and to a perceived need for more reformatories. Whereas Ogawa in 1900 had estimated that there were roughly five thousand juvenile delinquents to whom the Reformatory Law would apply, a 1907 Home Ministry survey reported that there were now fifty thousand delinquent youths throughout Japan.[71] The judicial framework for dealing with juveniles was also changing. In 1907, the government revised the Penal Code to prohibit the trial of children under the age of fourteen (up from twelve in the 1880 code); but the government also eliminated the correctional centers, to which children not competent to be tried had been committed. The 1908 Prisons Law *(Kangoku hō)* established juvenile penitentiaries or segregated prison sections for youths aged fourteen to eighteen, but contained no provisions for the treatment of those under fourteen. Meanwhile, judiciary officials began regularly suspending indictments for minors and petty offenders, while new legislation enabled judges to impose suspended sentences, especially in cases involving minors.[72] In response to these conditions, the government in 1908 revised the Reformatory Law to mandate that each prefecture either establish a reformatory or operate one jointly with other prefectures. The new law provided for national subsidies and declared that a national reformatory would eventually be opened to assist local efforts. Home Ministry officials also raised the upper age limit for referral to reformatories to seventeen, and replaced the already vague reference to youths "who engage in prodigality or mendicancy, or in bad relationships" in the 1900 text with language that included youths "who present a threat of" delinquency. The revised law also permitted parents or guardians to apply directly to the prefectural governor, rather than to the courts, to have their children committed to reformatories.[73]

Not everyone approved of these revisions, which greatly extended Home Ministry officials' discretionary power over purportedly delinquent youths. In a series of pointed interrogations on the Diet floor, Representative Hanai Takuzō attacked the law's authors for seeking to shift judicial authority to the administrative branch, noting that no Western nation employed such a system. In response, Local Affairs Bureau Chief Tokonami Takejirō argued that social order took priority over due process: "There is no need to rely on a court to ascertain guilt in each case. If it is determined [by the prefectural governor] that such youths present a threat to society if left untreated, it is necessary to take custody of them and educate them. One need not examine each case in terms of the presence or absence of a crime." Tokonami also claimed that the government's bill was actually "more progressive" than Western due process requirements, since it stemmed not from a desire to establish innocence or guilt, but from a "warm, kindly" motivation to lead children in the right direction.[74] In the name of "protection," the state and its allies sought to save youths from evil influences, while saving society from those youths. This ideology of governmental benevolence legitimated a system in which "delinquent" minors could be confined in institutions, although no precise definitions of delinquency had been established.

REFORMATORIES IN THEORY

By 1910, fifty-three reformatories—called "schools" or "academies" to avoid stigmatizing their pupils—accommodated 1,021 youths across Japan; 325 of these youths were held in facilities in Tokyo, 138 in Osaka, and 133 in the Yokohama area.[75] Inmates were overwhelmingly male. Parliamentarians did not discuss female juvenile delinquency during debates on the Reformatory Law and its revision, and reformers found little support for the idea of public facilities for girls. In fact, only a small number of girls were officially classified as juvenile delinquents: as late as 1917, one Tokyo social welfare official remarked that the entire prefecture had been producing ten delinquent girls each year![76] Girls were detained primarily for vagrancy or petty theft. Police officials in Tokyo evidently did not categorize underage unlicensed prostitutes (shishō or mitsuinbai) as juvenile delinquents, even though a 1908 survey of 1,565 female sex workers on the streets and in archery halls, "saké shops," and "newspaper reading rooms" revealed that forty-four were under fifteen while 634 were aged fifteen to nineteen (a good number would thus have come within the scope of the revised Reformatory Law). Not that the police had any effective means of dealing with such cases: until an aggressive campaign to suppress unlicensed prostitution in 1916, officers had tended to tolerate the trade in their precincts.[77] But the difference in administrative channels may have mitigated the perceived need for specialized institutions for delinquent girls. Public reformatories such as the one run by the Tokyo City Poorhouse did take in a handful of girls, and a few more went to a small, private Protestant-run institution for girls, the Yokohama Family School (Katei Gakuen), which was designated as a surrogate public reformatory by both Kanagawa and Tokyo prefectures after it opened in 1909. (As Japan's only reformatory for girls, it also accepted cases from across the country.) Police and the media publicized lurid tales of prostitution and sexual degeneracy among students in elite girls' high schools, but most authorities no doubt felt that families, not facilities run at the public's expense, should handle such cases.

Reformatory personnel had to deal with a range of individuals, from dependent waifs like Naruse Kametarō to grown young men whose presence seriously challenged the authority of reformatory staffs. Indeed, given that many lower-class children were not registered until several years after birth, if at all, some inmates may well have been over twenty, the legal age of majority. Yet whatever their charges' ages, reformatory administrators offered them a regime of fresh air, physical training, schooling, moral guidance, love, and work.

In developing their programs, reformatories relied heavily on the theoretical and practical expertise of Tomeoka Kōsuke. A Protestant minister and graduate of Dōshisha University who had served for several years as a prison chaplain in Hokkaidō, Tomeoka spent the period from 1894 to 1896 in the United States, where he studied the latest developments in penology and juvenile reform. Upon his return, Tomeoka published *The Development of Reformatory Operations (Kanka jigyō no hattatsu)*, the first comprehensive text on the subject to appear in Japanese, and in 1899, he established a private reformatory, the Family School (Katei Gakkō), in Sugamo, an outlying district in Tokyo Prefecture. From 1899 to 1904, Tomeoka also taught at the Home Ministry's new Police and Prisons School, introducing his ideas of social reform to over a thousand elite policemen who in turn served as instructors at prefectural police academies and in important positions throughout the empire. As a paid government consultant, Tomeoka also lectured regularly at the Home Ministry's Reform and Relief Seminars, the first of which, in 1908, focused primarily on juvenile delinquency.[78]

To Tomeoka, the first task in reforming delinquent youth was to get them away from the corrupting influences that surrounded them. He and other late-Meiji reformers did not deny the importance of heredity— particularly alcoholism or venereal disease among parents and other relatives—as a factor in delinquency. However, most rejected the view, associated with the Italian criminal anthropologist Cesare Lombroso, that criminals were "a distinct type of species," with physical traits reminiscent of apes and moral characters inferior to those of noncriminals. Rather, Tomeoka and his colleagues adopted the "eclectic, multifactor approach" of English criminologist William Douglas Morrison, who held that proper environmental controls could restrain or overcome unfavorable biological traits.[79] Thus, while some writers, including Ogawa, believed that youths had to be prepared to adapt successfully to city environments, the majority tended to follow Tomeoka, an anti-urban ideologue who recommended locating reformatories in the countryside, "where health, spirit, and vitality reside."[80]

Reformatories were to provide delinquents with the proper homes they had never known. Following the example of reformers like Enoch Wines in the United States and Mary Carpenter in England, Tomeoka advocated the adoption of the cottage system, in which a small number of youths lived, worked, and studied under the guidance of a strong father-figure and a compassionate matron. More than any other idea, the notion of a good home *(katei)*, frequently inspired by Anglo-American Protestant models, captured the imagination of new-middle-class reformers who presented it as the cornerstone of a sound social structure (even though most Japanese families at this time did not conform to the nuclear urban model). In particular, it was the middle-class mother, versed in home economics, hygiene, and "scientific" child-rearing, who protected the morality and well-being of her husband and children. Family life, domestic chores, and a woman's maternal love, Tomeoka stressed, would teach children obedience, discipline, cooperation, responsibility, affection, and religious feeling—all the requisite characteristics of decent members of society.[81] Tomeoka also emphasized the centrality of religious or moral instruction (but not proselytization), and called on reformatory personnel to embody "living religion," be it Christianity, Buddhism, or Shintō. Many reformatories combined religion with inspirational lectures and instruction in the articles of what Carol Gluck has called Japan's new "civil morality": the 1890 Imperial Rescript on Education and the 1908 Boshin Rescript on diligence and thrift.[82]

Tomeoka advocated rigorous training that began with cold baths and friction massages to combat the physical weakness and mental instability that were believed to afflict most reformatory inmates. This emphasis on physical cultivation formed part of a broader concern, spurred by wars with China and Russia, with preparing Japan's youth to participate in the nation's new imperialist enterprise. Play, music, and excursions to scenic or historic sites were all important, but regular schedules and exercise, particularly military drill, would instill discipline and overcome delinquents' weak-willed characters. As Tomeoka declared, cold baths at five o'clock each morning and drilling under the hot sun would prepare delinquent boys for uncomplaining service "if one day a national emergency arises."[83] Without such training, however, delinquents were a positive danger to Japanese sovereignty. In 1906, as Japan established a protectorate over Korea, one of Tomeoka's assistants wrote that his charges' lack of discipline and indifferent attitudes recalled the characteristics of Koreans, who, "while not all juvenile delinquents, are the people of a broken and defeated nation."[84]

Reformatories also had to teach their charges to become disciplined, productive workers. While some institutions offered the Ministry of Education's standard elementary course, experts such as Arima Shirōsuke, a Protestant prison and reformatory administrator in Kanagawa Prefecture, argued that schooling for delinquents could "not [be] like that for normal children from good homes, who can devote themselves entirely to studies." Youths under Arima's supervision had all been "independent" children, working as apprentices or in similar positions in the

Tokyo and Yokohama areas; they required "a type of vocational school" with a modified curriculum.[85] To its proponents, vocational education taught self-reliance and promoted balanced physical and mental development. It civilized the lower classes by inculcating virtues such as order, cleanliness, fastidiousness, trustworthiness, temperance, sexual propriety, and obedience. Together with moral instruction, training for work led delinquents to accept their status in life and, in the words of Protestant social worker Yatsuhama Tokusaburō, to "avoid the unhappiness and hardships that come from having desires that are not within their capabilities to achieve."[86]

Only occasionally was secondary education appropriate for lower-class delinquents. Tomeoka reported that children in his care "who used to live like beggars and then received middle school education immediately became argumentative and caused problems for others." To avoid such difficulties, Tomeoka put elementary-school graduates to work from morning to evening and provided them with two hours of nightly supplementary education. The results were "surprisingly good": children were less argumentative and more obedient, worked more, and improved their skills. "In general," he concluded, "one should place the main weight on training for work, and use whatever energy remains for school learning."[87] Indeed, Tomeoka also called for increased emphasis on work in regular elementary schools. "The [Ministry of Education's] current curriculum may be fine for children from the middle class or higher," he wrote in 1905, "but it is inappropriate for poor children." If schools did not increasingly provide vocational education, he warned, "the number of criminals will only continue to multiply."[88]

While some administrators adhered to what Ogawa Shigejirō called the mistaken belief in "farming as panacea" to children's and society's problems, others noted the importance of preparing reformatory youths for jobs that would help them exit the underclass.[89] However, given the problems posed by apprenticeships and factories, reformers' most pressing concern was no doubt simply to find employers who would promise to exercise responsibility for the boys they received. And despite discussions of specific job skills, reformers sought primarily to enlighten their charges to what one expert called "the sanctity, pleasure, beauty, and benefits of labor," just as they emphasized the sanctity of the home.[90] Rather than attempting to change the fundamental structural causes of the problems of the lower class, champions of the reformatory project strove above all to transform poor youths' attitudes.

REFORMATORIES IN PRACTICE

In practice, reformatories lacked the material resources to realize many of their objectives. Despite its ideological support, the Home Ministry provided only limited subsidies to public institutions, and restrictions by cost-conscious prefectures left reformatories unable to hire qualified instructors and matrons or to implement the cottage system, with its multiple buildings and high staff-to-inmate ratios. Private reformatories also scrambled for funds.[91]

Administrators also had to scramble to keep up with their charges, some of whom concocted false names and life stories, and many of whom saw escape from their rescuers as a more attractive goal than escape from lower-class life. In 1905, at ceremonies opening the Inokashira School (Inokashira Gakkō), the newly renamed and relocated reformatory division of the Tokyo City Poorhouse, administrator Yamamoto Tokushō solemnly apologized to assembled supporters and dignitaries for his facility's failure to stem the unauthorized exodus of inmates. Of 160 youths admitted since the reformatory opened its doors in 1900, 61 had run away. The situation only became worse: by 1908, 104 out of 245 inmates admitted had escaped.[92]

Tomeoka's Family School, a private institution, appears to have experienced a lower escape rate during its first decade of operation—only fifteen out of 107 boys admitted from 1899 to 1908 ran away—and staff in some cases succeeded in gaining the cooperation of lower-class parents who saw the reformatory as a place to have their children educated, or simply taken off their hands, while benefiting from tuition subsidies.[93] However, the struggles intensified once the school was designated a surrogate public reformatory and began admitting children referred by Tokyo Prefecture authorities in 1909. For example, in a December 1909 entry in his logbook, instructor Nishikikōri Chūji recorded that twelve of the twenty lower-class children in his cottage had run away at least once, and a few had run away as many as four times (several had already spent time in, and escaped from, the Inokashira School). While some boys fled to escape abuse by older inmates, others simply preferred life on the streets, and reformatory teachers made frequent trips to Asakusa and elsewhere to retrieve them. Escapes took various forms. In February 1910, Nishikikōri reported that two friends, Matsumoto and Kiriu, had used carpentry tools to cut a hole in the workshop floor: "This was no different from a prison breakout."[94] Small wonder, given that Tomeoka, who considered this group particularly hard to reform, kept them in a walled compound apart from the other boys in the school (some of whom were from affluent families)—except when he punished regular inmates by moving them into the street urchins' cottage. The street boys, Nishikikōri wrote sympathetically, understood how they were perceived and did not appreciate it.[95]

The following March, the school's staff decided to ship Matsumoto and Kiriu, who had been recaptured, off to the Bonin (Ogasawara) Islands, where officials had begun operating a reformatory and where local fishermen and farmers welcomed the influx of young laborers. However, Matsumoto, whose nickname "Fried Tōfu" derived from his nervous obsession with this foodstuff, again ran away from the Family School, and the staff ultimately decided to have him admitted to the Tokyo mental asylum. In his last appearance in Nishikikōri's logbook, Matsumoto escaped from the asylum through the toilet waste tank; teachers tracked him to Asakusa, but lost him there.[96]

Kiriu, on the other hand, does appear to have gone to the islands, and other difficult youths held in surrogate public reformatories followed when in the same year Tokyo Prefecture's own institution, the Shūsai Gakuen, opened there. Little is known about this reformatory, which combined historical traditions of island exile with Tokyo prefectural officials' plans for colonizing the islands. This facility—where, according to a 1913 report, boys worked at land reclamation, their bodies covered in muddy red volcanic soil—also experienced problems. To encourage colonization, authorities had decided to prevent inmates from returning to the mainland until they turned twenty; but the boys' despair at this prospect led them to set fires and to rob and vandalize islanders' homes in their attempts to escape. As relations between the reformatory and the islanders soured, Tokyo decided to close the reformatory in the early 1920s.[97] Tomeoka, meanwhile, came to realize that building walls around the boys sent to him by Tokyo authorities had been a mistake, and he began to integrate those inmates with the other youths at the Family School. But by 1914, in order to eliminate the baleful influences of urban life and let nature exercise its salutary influence, he had begun moving older, more difficult boys to a desolate part of inland Hokkaidō and younger ones to a new facility on the coast of Kanagawa Prefecture.[98]

Tokyo's reformatories were not the only ones to grapple with "unauthorized withdrawals." At a conference in late 1912, reformatory directors from across the country admitted that escape rates often ran over

30 percent; one even noted that he paid cash bounties to inmates who brought back runaways. By 1915, the problem had reached the point at which, remarked Home Ministry consultant Namae Takayuki, reformatories' reports of "good results" often meant simply that a youth had not run away.[99]

Hostile critics argued that reformatories coddled their charges instead of imposing proper discipline.[100] Justice Ministry officials expressed particular animosity toward Ogawa Shigejirō's progressive methods. In 1900, after he was transferred from the Home Ministry to the Justice Ministry, Ogawa assumed responsibility for administering the correctional centers, the wards for younger offenders constructed on prison premises according to the 1880 Penal Code. Under his guidance, progressive administrators converted several into reformatories (yōnenkan) that boasted the least punitive, most education-centered methods available—including instruction in Western dance, which one observer deemed "incomprehensible." Even Tomeoka, who praised these facilities as beacons of progress, had complained that it was inappropriate for instructors to address inmates using the polite suffix san and that children's clothes were too nice: "White kimono and hakama trousers seem too good for children of robbers, pickpockets, and beggars."[101] In 1908, the Justice Ministry purged Ogawa and his followers, and the following year the new director of one facility delivered to inmates a different message: "Punishment is pain. . . . [Y]ou are here to suffer that pain."[102]

Ogawa, who remained a leader in the reform movement, adamantly rejected criticisms of his educational approach and in 1914 advised reformatory administrators to treat escapes as "voluntary discharges." This was not mere lenience, for Ogawa reasoned that through "natural selection," escapees would eventually wind up in stricter facilities run by the Justice Ministry.[103] On the other hand, Ogawa also wrote that many reformatory inmates appeared to be mentally ill and required more specialized treatment than was currently available in prefectural facilities. The same view was held by influential psychiatrists such as Kure Shūzō, professor at Tokyo Imperial University and director of the Tokyo mental asylum, and Miyake Kōichi, his university colleague who served as a consultant to the Home and Justice ministries. Miyake, for example, called attention to delinquents' "inherent degeneracy" and "abnormal characters," and argued that up to two-thirds of delinquent children were feebleminded, hysterical, or afflicted with other mental disorders.[104] While mental illness may well have been a factor in some cases, these experts, in their zeal, appear to have found symptoms wherever they looked. Miyake and his colleagues at times relied on reformatory staff members' subjective characterizations of their charges—easily angered, inattentive, careless, lazy, wily, likes to fight, unclean, vulgar, selfish, rough, etc.—to ascertain the presence of abnormal characters.[105] For reformatory personnel, meanwhile, labeling individuals as mentally ill may have been a convenient means to avoid responsibility for the inability to treat them, and thus to shift the burden to another agency. In 1919, the Home Ministry did open a national reformatory near Tokyo, the Musashino Gakuin, to receive the most difficult psychiatric cases and to serve as a research center for new modes of therapeutic education. Over the following years, Miyake and others would continue to lobby for across-the-board institutional reforms.[106]

If boys were hard to reform, girls, most experts agreed, were even harder. At the Yokohama Family School, Principal Mimura Haruyo devised a curriculum that combined work (sewing, laundering, and some farming), schooling, and the inculcation of domesticity in a manner similar to that at Tomeoka's Family School, where she had previously taught. In addition to Christian prayer, moral instruction for younger girls centered on fables, while instruction for girls fifteen or older included *The Greater Learning for Women (Onna daigaku)*, a Tokugawa-era Confucian tract which, noting that women's inferiority derived from their "indocility, discontent, slander, jealousy, and silliness," exhorted them to submit to their parents, husbands, and in-laws: "The only qualities that befit a woman are gentle obedience, chastity, mercy, and quietness."[107] Middle- and upper-class Protestant women in Japan may have been at the vanguard of reform movements and actively promoted new roles for women, but their first priority in this case was to inculcate docility.

Meanwhile, observers reported that delinquent girls were often already sexually corrupted, and many contemporary observers no doubt accepted the view of "one prominent Tokyo reformatory director" who was quoted in 1915 as explaining: "Once a girl has known a man, there is no way to reform or improve her. Although she may get much better for a while and lead one to think that she is on the path back to decency, she will again go bad should the occasion arise. Based on our experience, this cannot be doubted."[108] In contrast, while reformers such as Tomeoka prescribed cold baths and busy schedules to control boys' sexual urges, few experts suggested that sexually experienced young males were beyond redemption.[109] Indeed, as the system of licensed brothels shows, the state and a broad segment of public discourse treated adult men's (hetero)sexual release as an innate, irrepressible need. Boys thus had to learn to defer their desire for gratification until adulthood and pursue it within legally sanctioned channels (even if many reformers hoped eventually to create a society free of prostitution and concubinage). Girls had to deny their sexuality, and even those who were victims of sexual exploitation had to endure the unforgiving ministrations and stigmatization imposed by authorities who claimed to protect them.

In practice, given the lack of reformatories, local officials sought whatever means they could find to handle delinquent girls, including placing them in geisha houses or other establishments widely recognized as sources of corruption. In 1917 and the years that followed, Tokyo authorities also placed a few delinquent girls in shelters run by the Salvation Army and the Japan branch of the Women's Christian Temperance Union, but some officials objected, fearing that contact with former prostitutes in these facilities would only lead the girls further astray.[110] Meanwhile, the relatively small number of girls processed as delinquents and concerns about female incorrigibility—not to mention budgetary constraints—frustrated efforts to establish girls' reformatories. Supervision by relatives, domestic service, or marriage thus constituted the main means to deal with wayward girls.

If reformatories represented a reactive approach to delinquency, late-Meiji authorities also called for new preventive measures. In a May 1901 directive, for example, Home Ministry officials pressed local authorities to "go to the root of the problem" and take "measures to educate the children of the poor to become decent people."[111] While governments across the country launched efforts to enroll these children in elementary schools, officials in Tokyo created an entirely new type of school to address the challenge.

ASSIMILATION AT THE LOCAL LEVEL: TOKYO'S SPECIAL ELEMENTARY SCHOOLS

Tokyo had for years struggled with low elementary-school enrollments, prompting one writer in 1898 to lament, "Our Tokyo is the capital of the empire and should serve as a model for all things. . . . But with regard to the spread of education, only Okinawa and ten other prefectures trail behind us in enrollment rates."[112] While Tokyo Prefecture (the city and outlying counties) lagged behind the national enrollment rate, within the fifteen wards of Tokyo City, those wards with the highest concentrations of poverty lagged behind the rest. Moreover, as noted earlier, enrollment figures included neither the large numbers of school-age children exempted from the compulsory education requirement nor those who appeared nowhere in the civil registers.[113] During the late 1880s, private reformers, mainly Buddhist and Christian groups, had established numerous small charity schools, but this movement had sharply declined by the mid-1890s. Public school construction had also failed to keep pace with the school-age population; and whereas after 1900 the Ministry of Education encouraged elementary schools to stop collecting tuition, Tokyo's schools continued to charge up to twenty *sen* per month, a prohibitive sum for most poor families.[114]

In 1901, the Tokyo City Council, in response to pressure from education boosters and the Home Ministry, passed a proposal for a unique system of municipal special elementary schools *(Tōkyō-shi tokushu jinjō shōgakkō)* to be located in the poorest districts, with the initial capital derived from a gift of imperial funds on the occasion of the crown prince's wedding. The first of these schools opened in 1903 in Shitaya Ward's Mannenchō, the home of many casual laborers, street entertainers, and ragpickers like Granny and her boys.[115] The special schools functioned as settlements among the poor, with principals residing on the premises. Rather than admit only residents of precisely delineated districts, teachers actively sought out poor households in distant neighborhoods and encouraged them to enroll their children. School staff also helped parents enter their illegitimate children in the civil registers: of those enrolled at Mannen Elementary in its first year, for example, 92 percent were not listed in any official documents. The schools, which operated two half-day shifts, waived tuition and provided pupils not only with basic supplies but also with items such as soap, washcloths, indoor footwear, laundry supplies, umbrellas, and smocks. They provided free haircuts, medical treatment, and baths; dedicated teachers apparently bathed with their pupils, risking exposure to skin ailments and other diseases in order to remove lice from their hair (although official photos from 1907 showed fully clothed instructors overseeing naked children in the tub). At least one school, Mikasa Special Elementary in Honjo Ward, provided lunch to children whose families could not afford to do so, collected donations of rice and sold it to families at discount prices, and established an installment purchase plan for mosquito netting.[116]

To those involved, the special schools were "a kind of reformatory" for pupils who were not fit for regular schooling.[117] "These children have grown up without being told fairy tales by their relatives," wrote Mannen principal Sakamoto Ryūnosuke in 1911. "They have been exposed to lewd things, and thus developed rough characters." Pupils, he wrote, could not keep still, fought frequently, and screamed at the top of their lungs when admonished about their bad habits. Other traits he noted included uncleanness, skill at lying, and "the strength to endure hardships to obtain food."[118] Perhaps the key element in civilizing these wild beings, in addition to baths and haircuts, was the provision of on-site wage work as a complement to regular classroom lessons. Teachers generally reported that the work programs mollified parents who viewed schooling as a disruption to the family economy; reduced the time children spent in their bad homes; and helped them cultivate a work ethic and savings habits (because schools withheld part of the children's wages for this purpose).[119] School staff also endeavored to provide ongoing supervision to working graduates. Mannen Elementary, for example, organized assemblies and other activities on apprentices' days off, both to promote desirable behavior and to keep children away from the temptations of theaters, shops, and parks. Most important, in 1905 the schools established night classes for working children; these also attracted older adolescents and a smattering of adults.[120]

Venturing beyond the school premises, staff members also surveyed pupils' home conditions and parents' employments, income, and spending habits, and encouraged parents to "think even a little about the future" by saving part of their earnings. From 1913 to 1918, teachers at Mikasa Elementary ran a program to collect leftover food and distribute it to pupils' parents, on condition that they join a savings plan so as not to develop a spirit of dependency.[121] The schools also benefited from the support of a fundraising committee of city notables who, among other activities, built affordable, well-equipped row-house apartments for pupils' families, complete with day care and vocational training facilities. Prominent supporters such as Tagawa Daikichirō, the Christian journalist, parliamentarian, and city official, celebrated the schools as unique symbols of Japanese metropolitan modernity. Western cities like London might have highly developed programs for the lower classes, he declared, but "I have yet to see anything like our special elementary schools."[122] By 1913, when ten such schools had opened throughout the city, day enrollments surpassed 7,000, and continued to rise until they peaked in 1919 at 9,254. (There were eventually eleven schools and one branch school.)[123]

Slum dwellers did not necessarily share the enthusiasm of elites. A good number of families certainly recognized the opportunities the schools offered and cooperated with teachers, who appear to have dedicated themselves to their mission. But school staff often had to struggle to persuade parents to enroll their children; more than the promise of character-building or literacy, it was the wage work programs that proved most effective in this respect. And even with this enticement, many parents refused to be involved with what were colloquially denigrated as "paupers' schools" or "free schools." Many children, taunted by pupils in the regular schools, refused to attend, and those who did may well have resented instructors' persistent attention to their bodies and behavior.[124] The stigmatization may have been doubly cruel for those placed in classes for the feeble-minded (teinōji); according to one visitor's 1911 report, such a class at Mannen Elementary contained pupils who had been deemed unrestrained or sexually precocious.[125]

Perhaps the most striking evidence of the tensions engendered by the special schools, and more broadly by Tokyo elites' efforts to educate the lower classes, can be seen in the lecture programs for adults sponsored by the Tokyo City Education Committee. At one such program at Mannen Elementary in 1910, roughly one thousand slum dwellers heard talks by educator and Diet member Ehara Soroku (whose lecture was titled "On the Home") and by Viscount Gotō Morimitsu ("On Family Registers"). According to a report in the newspaper Miyako shinbun, uniformed and plainclothes police officers were on hand to keep order while city and Home Ministry officials, who introduced the speakers as "great men," looked down from an imposing dais. This haughty approach, complained the reporter, would not impress the poor, who "curse the strong, but don't respect them." Moreover, although the audience appears to have enjoyed some of the popular entertainments included in the program, they began to exit the hall once a photographer attempted to record their presence. Attendees wished to avoid the humiliation of being known as so poor that they had been targeted for the lectures, and they did not want to be used as props to celebrate the good works of the city elites.[126] Slum dwellers may also have resented the substance of some lectures, such as Home Ministry consultant Tanaka Tarō's advice not to grumble about their conditions or envy others: "If you think that society was made for your sake, you're mistaken." Tanaka urged them instead to become "indispensable people" by working hard at their daily tasks. "Even if one's status is low and one lacks property or education," he offered, "to be needed by many people makes life worthwhile."[127] And one can only imagine the response of an audience at the Shibaura Special Elementary School to Tagawa Daikichirō's suggestion in 1911 that since the Rothschilds and Mitsuis had built their wealth through their honesty, "[p]eople who are poor today will, by living honestly, certainly see their fortunes turn for the better."[128]

As education historian Betchaku Atsuko notes, it must have been difficult for the poor to accept institutions premised on their own negation. In the case of Mannen Elementary, the negation was physical as well as rhetorical, for the city had razed a block of slum flats and displaced several hundred families to build the modern school edifice. It is not surprising that, as Sakamoto Ryūnosuke later recalled, many parents refused to let their children maintain contact with the schools after they graduated.[129] Yet despite these tensions, the special elementary schools reported success in producing employable graduates. Limited evidence suggests that a good number of boys and girls found jobs in Tokyo's growing industrial sector; many other boys continued to help in their parents' trades or found work as apprentices in small commercial shops, while large numbers of girls took on some form of domestic work. But not everyone graduated. In fact, consistently high dropout rates, due to families' urgent need for their children's labor as well as to deep-seated resistance to the schools' presence, constituted the greatest single challenge to the special schools' mission; according to one report, of the nearly 34,000 pupils enrolled from the schools' inception until 1921, 45 percent had withdrawn.[130]

Tokyo City eventually eliminated the municipal special elementary schools in 1925, turning them into regular schools. City officials explained that the number of poor children in many of the districts served by the special schools had decreased, as urban reorganization pushed inhabitants of the city's older slums to newer, outlying districts—"just as the Ainu of Hokkaidō are being driven into the mountains by settlers from the home islands," observed one Mannen Elementary teacher in 1921, juxtaposing two subaltern groups to reveal the colonizer's perspective infusing many of the state's social programs. Officials also argued that eliminating the schools would both eliminate the stigma attached to their pupils and reduce the dangers of delinquency posed by grouping large numbers of poor children in the same institutions. The city then shifted to an expanded program of night classes for poor and working children, but the former special schools, as well as many other schools in the expanding metropolis—and in other cities—continued to apply social-work methods to at-risk children and families.[131]

During the two decades after the Sino-Japanese War, social reformers produced studies of lower-class delinquency and slum conditions that invariably affirmed the desirability and superiority of middle-class norms of hygiene, diligence, frugality, domesticity, and temperance. Indeed, regardless of the actual numbers of delinquents involved, the discourse on reforming the poor constituted a crucial channel through which new-middle-class activists sought to establish themselves as arbiters of national health and progress. Many of these activists, led by Tomeoka Kōsuke, deployed a language shaped by Western social scientific categories, a heavily Anglo-American, Protestant-inflected moral vision, and a colonialist mentality that treated the lower classes as objects of ethnographic inquiry, pacification, and enlightenment or assimilation. As literary scholar Maeda Ai noted, Japanese reports on "Darkest Tokyo" consciously echoed both William Booth's *Darkest England and the Way Out* (a study of London's East End) and Henry Morton Stanley's *In Darkest Africa*.[132] For investigative journalists and social workers alike, the exploration of the urban netherworld, however repugnant it might be, offered a certain thrill akin to that reported by European writers such as Stanley. But as is revealed by reformers' equation of juvenile delinquents with "broken, defeated" Koreans and slum dwellers with the Ainu, local projects also took shape within the specific context of Japan's own colonial relationships; Tomeoka himself envisioned using reformed (i.e., civilized) delinquents as settlers in Hokkaidō and Korea.[133] The construction of social problems in Japan at the turn of the twentieth century thus signals the country's integration in a global network of power and knowledge organized around multiple imperial and industrial centers.

Reformatories were to be key instruments for civilizing the lower classes, and served above all as discursive blueprints for an ideal social order orbiting the three poles of home, school, and work. In practice, however, lower-class youths often refused to surrender their hearts and minds to the new regime. Try as they might to introduce new therapeutic techniques and acquire more funds, the institutions would continue to be plagued by the same basic problems and critiques that they experienced in their first decade of operation. But whereas reformatories remained points on the social map often isolated from their broader communities, the Tokyo special elementary schools constituted a pioneering effort to settle the slums. Responses to the special schools' intrusions ranged from forthcoming acceptance to outright resistance, but most slum dwellers probably greeted them with an ambivalent pragmatism that sought to derive the greatest material benefits under the least onerous terms, particularly with regard to engagement with the cultural values underlying the new programs. For while social investigators were not mistaken in describing the unsanitary, economically impoverished conditions under which the urban lower classes lived, the latter had little reason to embrace representations of their domestic and community lives as social and moral pathologies. The following observation of life in the Mannenchō slum, by a young boy from a nearby neighborhood, offers a tellingly different view from the reformist picture: "Mannenchō's a good place. My aunt lives there, so I often go play. And when there's no side dish for lunch, she goes to the flat next door and gets something from them. It's a mutual thing, so nobody minds. The lady next door comes to my aunt's place, says, 'I'm taking some pickles,' and just carries them out of the kitchen. It's like everybody's family."[134]

Sympathetic reporters such as Yokoyama Gennosuke also recognized the communal goodwill that made slum life bearable, but many reformers had greater difficulty striking this analytical balance.[135] In the same vein, state agents and their allies in the reform movement by and large failed to balance calls for improving the individual with programs to redress the economic disparities at the structural core of Japan's transition to modernity. Noting that morality could not flourish where food was lacking, Mannenchō Elementary principal Sakamoto Ryūnosuke even suggested in a 1914 article that the money used to finance his school might well have been better spent on more immediate forms of poor relief. Over the following decades, slum educators and other reformers would continue to struggle with both the economic conditions that impeded their mission and the cultural gap that lay between them and their clients.[136]

Just as efforts to assimilate the lower classes formed one part of a broader project to cultivate Japanese national subjects, lower-class youths constituted only one segment of the discourse on juvenile delinquency. As legal historian Toshitani Nobuyoshi has observed, mounting fears of social strife produced a spate of legislation designed to control all young people: this legislation included the 1898 Civil Code provisions that strengthened parental authority over minors; elementary- and middle-school regulations that clarified administrators' discretionary authority to impose "educational" punishments (but not corporal punishments); a 1900 law prohibiting smoking by minors; and the Reformatory Law.[137] And as observers of inmates in reformatories and juvenile penitentiaries reported that these inmates were characterized by, among other things, cruelty, egotism, uncontrolled anger, lying, and vanity, some writers noted that all children to a certain extent shared these traits. In a 1905 analysis of young vagrants in the journal *Child Studies (Jidō kenkyū)*, one social worker reminded his readers that one could easily detect sudden emotional shifts in "normal boys," and "particularly in spoiled, selfish boys who anger and rejoice easily."[138] It is to the "problem" of elite youth that we now turn.

CHAPTER 3

Civilizing "Degenerate Students"

Although turn-of-the-century reformers sought to control the children of the lower classes, they and the sensationalist press focused even greater attention on what they saw as the outrageous behavior of the nation's students, especially those attending secondary schools and private colleges. According to numerous reports, "ruffians" brawled, raped younger boys, and engaged in extortion, while "rakes" consorted with prostitutes and deviously seduced and exploited respectable female students. Of course, state officials and social critics had, since the Edo period, expressed alarm at the escapades of samurai and townsmen's wayward sons. But the new discourse on student degeneracy took the form of a moral panic about the dangers faced by Japan's incipient middle class, the backbone of the modern nation and empire, at a time when post-elementary schooling came to constitute the principal pathway to this social position. "Of all the things that poison society," wrote one observer of student life, "none is more frightful than a degenerate with a middle-school education."[1] In Tokyo, which had by far the highest concentration of students, public concerns prompted the Metropolitan Police Department (MPD) to establish a special student section in 1911 and to conduct its first citywide roundup of juvenile delinquents the following year.[2]

The overwrought rhetoric that often accompanied allegations of student misbehavior reflected reformers' concerns that the nation's future leaders were at risk and that its social institutions were still too fragile to meet the challenges of modern military and economic competition. Commentators attributed the presence of youthful deviants to a variety of causes: the decadence of the elite cliques who dominated the government; the relaxation of public morality and the spread of materialism and hedonism in the wake of victories over China and Russia; a crisis in the education system; and the deficiencies of "upper-class" *(jōryū)* homes. Underpinning all of these claims was a deep anxiety over the confusion of national identity in the midst of rapid industrialization and a dizzying influx of ideas from abroad.[3] It is thus not surprising that MPD Inspector Yamamoto Seikichi, author of a 1914 study on delinquent youth, began and ended his book with discussions of the special nature of Japanese society and located a cause of delinquency in the presence of "too many Japanese with Western hearts."[4]

Others saw the origin of the problem in the nature of childhood and youth itself. A new group of pediatric experts, espousing imported psychological theories of adolescence, argued that the development of the individual recapitulated the stages of social evolution from savagery to civilization. In this social Darwinist scheme, taming youths' unruly tendencies, like the assimilation of the lower classes, would demonstrate the nation's mastery of itself and, implicitly, its competence to master others in an imperialist world system. Indeed, as Japan emerged as an imperial power, Western writers distinguished it from the colonized "adolescent races" of China, India, Southeast Asia, Africa, and Latin America.[5] While some contemporary observers saw reformatories as a means to control wayward students, pediatric experts emphasized the need to turn mothers into agents of scientific child-rearing within modern homes, and zealous school administrators stressed the importance of strict regimentation and assiduous surveillance. In each case, authorities worked to define "student youth" as an extended period of economic dependence, moral tutelage, and limited autonomy. Student boys constituted the main object of this discourse, but student girls *(jogakusei),* who were expected to become the good wives and wise mothers of Japan's respectable classes, also figured as objects of both moral opprobrium and concupiscent curiosity. Popular songs, news articles, and informed experts tended to portray fallen *jogakusei* as frivolous, vain victims of predatory males, but some writers suggested that girls' dissolute behavior destabilized class, gender, and racial categories in ways that made these girls more frightening than delinquent boys.

The actual extent of the delinquency over which reformers and the media obsessed is far from clear and may not in fact have been very great. But as with the case of lower-class children, the power of the problem lay more in perceptions than in actual numbers. Students were a growing segment of the population, distinguished by their particular modes of dress—for boys, Western-style uniforms with stand-collared jackets and school caps, or, alternatively, pattern-dyed kimono and *hakama* trousers with school caps; for girls, pleated skirts (also called *hakama*) over kimono, sometimes with decorative hair ribbons.[6] Nationwide, the number of students enrolled in middle schools, which offered a liberal arts curriculum, grew from slightly over 10,000 in 1886 to nearly 129,000 in 1912, while enrollments in vocational schools, a less prestigious branch of the secondary school system, also rose to nearly 75,000. And whereas in 1895 secondary-school students accounted for only 1.1 percent of the twelve-to-seventeen age group, by 1910 that proportion had grown to 15.9 percent. (Secondary schools also continued to enroll a sizable number of students in their late teens and early twenties.) Enrollments in public and private technical schools and colleges *(senmon gakkō)* also climbed to roughly 34,000 in 1912. These institutions attracted middle-school graduates who could not enter the handful of public higher schools (gateways to the elite imperial universities), as well as youths who had passed middle-school equivalency tests; private schools also offered "special courses" with more relaxed admission requirements. The number of girl students also grew from a mere 838 in 1886 to over 75,000 in 1912, the largest number, as with boys, gathering in Tokyo.[7]

In general, these students came from families that could afford the high cost of tuition and board or at least attempt the sacrifices needed to pay it, sometimes in the hopes of reviving family fortunes. In 1898, for example, room and board in a private lodging house *(geshuku)* in Tokyo amounted to ten yen per month, as much as the average monthly salary of an elementary school teacher. This privileged group of students thus stood apart from both their less affluent peers who aspired to student status and the broader mass of youths who simply entered the workforce at an early age.[8] Keeping these privileged students away from the unauthorized popular cultural opportunities and alternative traditions of youth to which they nonetheless had access, and molding them into future pillars of modern society, lay at the core of the mission to civilize the student body.

ELEMENTS OF RUFFIANISM

If journalistic and official reports are to be believed, students in turn-of-the-century Tokyo displayed a penchant for public acts of violence on a par with that of Edo's *kabukimono*. Many carried short swords, cane swords, or knives, and "showdowns" among groups of students were, in one critic's words, "virtually a fashion."[9] According to a study by Inspector Sakaguchi Shizuo, who recalled being personally outraged at the activities of these hoodlums when he came to the capital as a student in 1903, some forty-five organized gangs flourished in the years between 1895 and 1912. Some of the earliest gangs claimed between one hundred and three hundred members (although the press often suggested even higher membership figures to amplify the menace these groups portended); subsequent gangs tended to count between thirty and fifty members.[10] Gangs such as the Tōhoku Righteous Young Men's Group, the Kagoshima Club, and the Ōita Club brought together students from the same regional background, thus constituting what Tomeoka Kōsuke called a "corrupted" offshoot of local-origin groups established by immigrants to Tokyo, often under the sponsorship of former domain lords.[11] These groups no doubt resembled those that the anarchist Ōsugi Sakae recalled in his memoirs of life in a provincial military academy, where he and his comrades were told to "never permit yourselves to be humiliated by those from other provinces."[12] Other groups, such as the Kyōbashi Gang, the Shinagawa Gang, and the Kanda Club took their names from Tokyo districts; still others, such as the Eastern Cherry Blossom Club, the White Hakama Brigade, or the Righteous Blue Dragons, bore no specific geographic references. Some gangs apparently included members who were not students, but the principal focus of concern was specifically on students.

Many of these groups fit into the category of "ruffians" *(kōha)*. The term *kōha* denoted a type of student who concentrated on physical activities like jūdō, adopted a swaggering, aggressive style, and rejected contact with women out of fear of becoming weak and effeminate—a view they held of those students, referred to as "rakes" *(nanpa)*, who dressed well and pursued the company of women.[13] These student types had been present since the 1870s, but in the decade after 1895, acts of forcible male-male eroticism and fights related to this behavior emerged as a defining feature of student degeneracy, as seen in the following complaint issued in 1898 by a group calling itself the Justice Club:

Look at the condition of Tokyo's students. While at first glance they
appear unsophisticated in their short *hakama* [trousers], there is, in this
day of rapid progress, an evil among them. What is it? Villainous youths
band together with others of similar character and seize young boys at
temple and shrine festivals, athletic events, boat races, and other places
where students congregate. In extreme cases, groups of three to five
prowl near middle school gates, accost pupils on their way home, take
them to deserted places and wantonly indulge their beastly desires for
[sodomy], thus plunging these pure, innocent boys into the world of
depraved lust. Such occurrences are nothing new, but these shameless
villains are now spreading their poison at such a rate that young boys
without a strong protector haven't the heart to walk outside their homes.
Having lost their liberty, these boys have also lost their fighting spirit.
Is this not deplorable?[14]

As the examples of the *kabukimono* and Aizu youths show, such
sexual violence was of course not new; it had also been part of the life
of many domain schools and the shogunate's academy in Edo.[15] Many
Meiji students were from samurai backgrounds, and, as Gregory
Pflugfelder has noted, readily adopted the homosocial, misogynous style
of masculinity inspired by samurai ideals and with it the male-male
sexual practice of *nanshoku*.[16] Nor was such behavior unique to Japanese schoolboys. "In English preparatory and public schools romance is
necessarily homosexual," wrote Robert Graves. "The opposite sex is
despised and treated as something obscene."[17] Yet in late-Meiji public
discourse, students' *nanshoku* predations appeared to derive particularly from the culture of the former domains of the southwest, especially
Satsuma, whose warriors had played leading roles in the Restoration
and in the Meiji government. *Nanshoku* practices were known as a
"Satsuma habit," and according to the novelist Shibusawa Seika, who
grew up "terrified by stories of such youths," marauding students were
commonly referred to as *Satsumappo*.[18]

Sociologist Furukawa Makoto has suggested that government leaders carried this culture from Satsuma to Tokyo, where it was promoted
with particular vigor in the nationalistic atmosphere of the decade from
the Sino-Japanese War to the Russo-Japanese War. To Furukawa, aggressive displays of *nanshoku* reflected students' desire to partake in the culture of the elites who dominated the government. In this context,
denunciations of such behavior, spearheaded by the crusading newspaper *Yorozu chōhō*, formed part of a broader attack on the Satsuma
clique's pernicious influence in national life (and by extension, on the
influence of the clique's Chōshū allies). As one *Yorozu* editorialist put it

in 1900, "The greatest inspiration that powerful men of the clique government have given to Tokyo youths is for *nanshoku* and dueling."[19] At
the same time, Pflugfelder notes, criticism of student *nanshoku* constituted part of an effort to impose new norms of "civilized morality" on
the discourse of the erotic. Within this discursive strategy, male-male
sexual relations represented a vestige of the barbaric past (and of a putatively particular regional past), a mode of behavior to be outgrown by
the individual adolescent and by the nation as a whole.[20]

Not all student gangs adopted *nanshoku* practices. Differences in
regional backgrounds may have been a factor in these varied approaches
to sexual behavior, just as regional rivalries may have fueled showdowns
over particular boys. *Nanshoku* traditions were probably weaker
among the sons of wealthy farmers, whose presence in the student body
increased greatly at the turn of the twentieth century, although the desire
to assimilate to a samurai-dominated student culture may have led some
to adopt this behavior. Whether or not the members of the Justice Club,
which was itself a major gang, in fact refrained from *nanshoku* acts is
hard to tell, but the authors of the manifesto quoted earlier consciously
manipulated public outrage for their own purposes.[21] Such ambiguities
aside, the Justice Club's posturing as defenders of the weak highlights a
second element in the ruffian cultural repertoire: many saw themselves
as heirs of a lineage of "Eastern heroes" *(Tōyōteki gōketsu)* who did not
hesitate to use violence in the pursuit of just causes.[22]

They were, of course, not the first generation to embrace this style.
Early Meiji students, for example, had sought to imitate the *shishi,* the
"men of high purpose" who had led the Restoration. In a description
that also conjures up images of the *kabukimono,* Donald Roden notes
that the new students "were unruly and free-wheeling. They delighted
in swaggering down congested streets, often in tattered kimonos and
with swords at their sides, boasting of themselves as prospective leaders
of the nation."[23] During the late 1870s and early 1880s, the heyday of
the Movement for Freedom and Popular Rights, many students entered
public space as activists or shock troops for the new political parties,
and many continued in this role in the years leading up to and following Japan's first parliamentary election in 1890. Basil Hall Chamberlain, writing at the turn of century, noted:

> Since 1888, there has sprung up a class of rowdy youths, called *sōshi* in
> Japanese,—juvenile agitators who have taken all politics to be their
> province, who obtrude their views and their presence on ministers of
> state, and waylay—bludgeon and knife in hand—those whose opinions

on matters of public interest happen to differ from their own. They are, in a strangely modern disguise, the representatives of the wandering swashbucklers [rōnin] of the old regime. Let us hope that anarchy never again visit Japan. If it does, it will find in this class of young men an instrument ready fitted to its hand.[24]

Sōshi distinguished themselves not by a specific political ideology but by a particular style. They wore torn clothes and high geta sandals, carried thick clubs or staffs, let their hair grow long, and hunched their shoulders in a menacing manner. They displayed a fondness for loud singing and recitation, sword dances, and Chinese-style verses that adopted a tone of indignation or outrage. To demonstrate their "fighting spirit" and physical prowess, they challenged others to duels (even if they never actually dueled), partook in brawls, and happily displayed their wounds. Many also composed and performed songs, called enka, as well as plays (sōshi shibai) that popularized social and political criticism.[25] They performed, suggests Jason Karlin, a rough (bankara) or "masculine" masculinity in opposition to the "high collar" (haikara) or "feminine" masculinity of the Meiji leaders, who were seen as having compromised the nation's integrity by adopting Western fashion in an effort to revise the unequal treaties imposed on Japan by the Western powers in the 1850s.[26] Just as the rough sōshi style overlapped with that of the kōha types, the sōshi critique of the haikara corresponded to the kōha view of nanpa as effeminate and effete.

But, as historian Kimura Naoe has suggested, in the waning phase of the Movement for Freedom and Popular Rights, sōshi also appeared in, and were in no small degree constructed through, public discourse as the antithesis of the seinen, a model of youth advanced by writers such as Tokutomi Sohō. Tokutomi, himself a young man, promoted the seinen in Youth of the New Japan (Shin Nihon no seinen), published in 1887, and in his magazine The Nation's Friend (Kokumin no tomo).[27] Drawing on (and modifying) the writings of Herbert Spencer, Tokutomi argued that Japan was following an inexorable, global pattern of evolution from a military society toward an industrial-commercial "commoner" society. He recognized that "student youth" had been principal agents in major historic events such as the Meiji Restoration, but warned that their energy was extremely dangerous. The sōshi represented this "destructive" political practice of the "old" Japan; in contrast, the new, constructive phase of Japanese history required that seinen educate and discipline themselves to become "youth of the nineteenth-century civilized world." For Japan's aspiring elites, in other

Figure 2. Drawing of a ruffian in the *sōshi* style, 1917. The soft hat is a late-
Meiji addition. Source: Sakaguchi Shizuo, *Furyō shōnen no kenkyū*.

words, youth was a period of preparation and the husbanding of one's
energies.[28]

To adherents of Tokutomi's view, such as the editors and contribu-
tors to the magazine *A Garden for Young People (Shōnen'en)*, youths
lacked the skills and economic resources necessary to assume the
responsibilities of mature citizens. As one of the magazine's readers

wrote to a friend who had quit school to join a political party, "Politics is necessary to society, but for inexperienced youth like ourselves, it is just not the thing to be debating."[29] According to Kimura, the appearance of *A Garden for Young People* in 1888 represents a new stage in the discursive depoliticization and neutralization of youth (in this case called *shōnen,* a term that would later denote a younger group than *seinen*). Published by a former Ministry of Education official, the magazine addressed itself first to teachers and fathers and second to middle-school students, fixing the latter as chronologically immature, socially dependent objects of education and adult care. In the new configuration, even apolitical *seinen* posed a problem because they continued to operate as subjects who organized peer associations, wrote and published magazines, and pursued other programs of cultivation on their own behalf. *Shōnen,* in contrast, were pure, innocent "subjects stripped of subjectivity."[30]

The *sōshi* style nonetheless continued to spread, with the radical Liberal Nakae Chōmin celebrating *sōshi* as "an element in the rise of the nation," but a growing part of public opinion, including many educated youths, tended to agree with the statement by a writer in the September 1891 issue of the journal *Japan (Nihon)* that *sōshi* were "a great poison in the realm."[31] Of course, the Meiji oligarchs, themselves former young "men of high purpose" who had achieved power through direct action, hardly welcomed the rise of a new generation of activists who might disturb the new political order, much as their Tokugawa predecessors had two centuries earlier feared the challenge from disaffected young ruffians espousing alternative views of political legitimacy. During the 1880s, the state initiated a series of directives prohibiting students from participating in politics, and by the early 1890s, following the promulgation of the Meiji constitution, officials had completely denied the political character of the *sōshi,* relegating them to the realm of delinquency. In 1892, the Tokyo Metropolitan Police Department defined *sōshi* as extortionists, while a police journal the following year treated them as "dissolute villains" in the same class as rickshaw drivers and gamblers.[32]

Such characterizations (like older commentaries on the *kabukimono*) were not necessarily wrong. For example, Soeda Tomomichi notes that by 1900, the Seinen Kurabu, a prominent group of *sōshi enka* performers, had degenerated into a nest of hooligans who frequented eating and drinking establishments without paying and burst out violently if confronted.[33] This behavioral shift can also be perceived in "I Was the

Guest of a Delinquent Youth Gang," a 1911 exposé in *New Review (Shin kōron)*, in which the author mentions his connection to "the Seinen Kurabu in Kanda" to demonstrate his delinquent credentials to the gang he is trying to infiltrate.[34] Turn-of-the-century gang names such as the Fraternity Society (Hakuai Kai), the Association of Patriotic Men of Purpose (Aikoku Risshi Kai), or the Liberal Party of the Realm (Tenka no Jiyūtō) also reveal the lingering influence of the *sōshi* model; and a 1911 report that delinquent gangs rented themselves out as "supporters" to individuals for fights at school field days *(undōkai)* suggests links to *sōshi* activities on behalf of their political patrons.[35] *Sōshi* had also held their own field days, which featured long, boisterous public marches followed by athletic contests such as capture the flag or tug of war, in which the opposing sides played the roles of the government and the opposition movement. (In some cases, the grueling contests would not end until the "opposition" had won.)[36] By the early twentieth century, however, education officials had established school field days, devoid of any symbols of political struggle, as the proper channel for promoting young men's physical cultivation and attachment to school and nation; any pretense of *sōshi* action (or patronage of such action) now appeared as nothing more than a disruptive element within this pedagogic matrix.[37] Similarly, the *bankara* or *sōshi* model might still be acceptable in boys' adventure magazines, which used stories of violent heroes to exhort young readers to train for future action on behalf of the nation and the empire, but it could not serve to legitimate students' claims to be heroes in the present.[38] The model of youth as a dependent, tutelary stage had thus established its primacy, and students who strayed too quickly into the adult world were marked as in need of correction.

The *shishi* and *sōshi* were not the only heroic models to influence late-Meiji student toughs. As ruffian groups settled into the Tokyo landscape and struggled to defend their turf and interests, they developed forms of organization inspired by those of gamblers, firefighters, and other subcultures in early modern commoner society.[39] In the process, some assimilated the ideal of masculine chivalry that these subcultures, along with popular theater, stories, and songs, had nourished—an ideal embodied in the street knight who defended weak townspeople against the predations of the powerful and corrupt.[40] Hamamoto Hiroshi (1890–1959), who came to Tokyo at the age of eighteen to write for the student magazine *Middle School World (Chūgaku sekai)*, recalled this ruffian demimonde in several short stories he published during the following decades. Hamamoto's protagonists are, despite their marginal status as dropouts, expellees, or student imposters, imbued with the spirit of heroism. In "The Youths beneath the Twelve-Story Tower" ("Jūnikai shita no shōnentachi," 1933), he writes: "I'm not bragging, but late-Meiji student toughs had soul. Our crowd burned with fighting spirit. We were poor, romantic, and on the side of justice." The protagonist in this story, "Crescent Moon" Ken, is described as follows: "Despite being a student hoodlum, Ken would never lift anything from night stalls or mug middle-school students. While he attracted many women with his good looks, he never had a relationship with a girl who wasn't a professional. Needless to say, he despised the evil idea of using his looks to squeeze a girl for spending money."[41] Indeed, a ubiquitous motif in Hamamoto's stories is the hero's rescuing, at the cost of his own life, innocent girls from predatory thugs who try to kidnap them and sell them to unlicensed brothels.

To Hamamoto, however, heroes like "Crescent Moon" Ken represented a fading brand of chivalry in a world marked by decadence and greed. By the period following the Russo-Japanese War, as social critics lamented the rise of materialism, individualism, and hedonism in society in general and in youth in particular, police agents and journalists observed a general shift in the nature of student delinquency.[42] In a 1912 article in *New Review,* one official contrasted the "extremely simple" delinquent students of previous years who brawled and "at most committed *nanshoku* acts" with present-day students who engaged in shoplifting, embezzlement, fraud, theft, robbery, and rape. "Not only are their wily ways no different from regular hoodlums on the street," he lamented, "but given that they have some knowledge, they actually tend to commit more complex crimes."[43] Students picked fights with innocent passers-by in order to extort "apology money" from them; they enlisted affluent younger boys in their activities, egging them on and then blackmailing them by threatening to expose them to parents and teachers. But the most alarming accounts of student delinquency to capture public attention now involved *nanpa* boys who seduced girls from good homes, ruthlessly exploited them, and then discarded them when they were of no more use.

RAKES AND THEIR VICTIMS

As noted earlier, the rakish type of student *(nanpa),* who focused on dressing well and pursuing erotic pleasure with women, had long coexisted with and rivaled the ruffian *(kōha);* and social reformers and critics who denounced the barbarism of *nanshoku* marauders had also lamented the degeneracy of students who engaged in illicit relations with the opposite sex.[44] Contemporaries reported that students visited popular amusement centers like archery galleries where dubious women drew in customers; students also frequented both the city's licensed quarters and the unlicensed brothels that cluttered the backstreets of Asakusa, and they occasionally committed rape.[45] As a popular song from 1905 put it: "The dapper student, looking smart in his sash, keeps flunking out of school; what he studies is buying whores, and between classes it's the geisha."[46] Another song offered the following image of a middle-school student: "Rather than spend his short life struggling with hard-to-read textbooks and hard-to-remember mathematics, he'd like to lay his head on the lap of a beauty; when he wakes, he wants to grab not a book but his love's hot hand—that's a pleasure that requires no tuition fees!"[47]

Many critics, both inside and outside the government, pointed to the popularity of allegedly erotic naturalist literature as a major cause of student licentiousness. They also cited the problem of students living unsupervised in private lodging houses, often run by unscrupulous individuals, with easy access to the city's theaters, vaudeville halls *(yose)*, movie houses, bars, and brothels, as well as to other degenerate students of both sexes.[48] In 1906, press reports of widespread venereal disease among middle-school and girls'-high-school students further exacerbated these fears, prompting various writers to call for the inclusion of tests for such ailments in school entrance requirements.[49] If *kōha* youths represented vestiges of barbarity, their *nanpa* counterparts embodied the afflictions and challenges of modern civilization.

Female students, of course, were seen as a major part of the problem. While the *jogakusei* occupied a special position in the early-twentieth-century social imagination as the symbol of modern education and new "high-collar" roles for women, she also constituted an object of social satire, moral outrage, and erotic fantasy.[50] The *enka* song "Jogakusei" (ca. 1900–1903), for example, depicts its subjects in the following terms: "Morning and evening they fuss with their makeup, putting roses in their hair; once in the classroom they prattle on endlessly, rating the men who teach them; more than the *Greater Learning for Women*, it's romance novels they go for." Such girls, the song continues, gathered in upstairs boarding house rooms, drinking and playing cards; they fantasized over photos of actors and went to Christian meetings not to discuss ideas of "fraternity and humanity" but to meet boys for

姿容の年少良不派軟

Figure 3. Drawing of a rake, attired in stylish kimono and student cap, 1917.
Source: Sakaguchi Shizuo, *Furyō shōnen no kenkyū.*

"free marriage."[51] And one of the most popular songs of the period,
Kaminaga Ryōgetsu's 1907 "Voice of the Pine" ("Matsu no koe," which
subsequently became the first *enka* phonographic record), tells of a girl
who, having come to Tokyo to study hard and bring honor to her family,
becomes sexually involved with a middle-school student: "Crazed by
the irrepressible feelings of first love, I fill my notebooks with drafts of

romantic letters, while my textbooks gather dust on the shelf." Yet as she loses her ability to focus on anything but her lover's kisses, her parents discover her behavior and cut off her funds. Distraught, she seeks the young man's advice, only to find that he has vanished without a trace.[52]

"Scientific" texts, meanwhile, differed little from popular songs in their treatment of female character. For example, Hara Masao's 1906 *Sexual Desire and Youth (Shikijō to seinen)*, a book ostensibly directed at students, explained: "Once [single women] begin [casual sexual] relationships with frivolous men, they focus exclusively on this, and have no mind for keeping matters secret or exercising self-control. Their shameless, rash, and rough behavior at times exceeds that of men; they abandon all honor and dignity, performing unsightly acts with no concern for others' opinions."[53] Writers also noted that girls who "played at husband and wife" risked unwanted pregnancies, and popular fiction such as Oguri Fūyō's serialized novel *Youth (Seishun)* included tales of botched abortions. One *enka* song, after asking "Why do today's *jogakusei* bear children so thoughtlessly?" suggested sardonically that it was only to be expected, since the three Chinese characters in the compound *jo-gaku-sei* could be read as "women learn and give birth."[54]

By the second decade of the twentieth century, media accounts of ruthless *nanpa* youths and their *jogakusei* victims had become increasingly graphic and sensational, designed to titillate as well as to "alert" readers. One particularly lurid representation appeared in an "exposé" of a group called the Kozakura Gumi (literally, the Little Cherry Gang) in the August 1915 issue of *New Review*.[55] Written ostensibly by a former member, the article purports to reveal the group's "insidious" methods and to warn fathers and elder brothers of the threats to their daughters and sisters. According to the article, what distinguished the Kozakura Gumi was its solid organization and adept manipulation of the "machinery of civilization," particularly "quick shot photography." The author provides the following plot as typical of the gang's operations: Members would photograph one of their own, dressed as a student, who had maneuvered his way under the parasol of a young woman out strolling, thus producing an image of the two of them as if in a lovers' meeting. Posing as a benevolent protector, another member would then send a letter to the girl (the gang having carefully researched their victim's background), offering to give her the photograph, which had happened to come into his possession. From this would ensue a meeting, at which time the young man would lure the girl to his house

Figure 4. Three typical girls'-high-school students, dressed in kimono and *hakama*, ca. 1907. The newness of their presence in public space and the distinctiveness of their clothing styles marked these young women as objects of both concern and fantasy. Source: The Mainichi Newspapers.

on the pretext of explaining his discovery of some evil plot against her. Once there, he would absent himself momentarily, inviting her in the meantime to look at a picture album, which she would find filled with lewd images that "physiologically stimulated her lust." When she was "tensed to the verge of release," he would reappear and "apply pressure, boldly and without compunction." At this moment, all was lost: the girl would abandon her virginity and sense of chastity, fall madly in love with her seducer, and provide him with whatever he desired, to the point of giving away even her clothes to support his lifestyle and the gang's operations. Unable to escape, she was like a "bug in a spider's snare."[56]

The author described the Kozakura Gumi's roughly one hundred members as "kinds of actors," assigned roles of student, factory worker, civil servant, company employee, store clerk, or wealthy merchant's son, according to their looks and personalities.[57] This distribution of roles suggests that while *nanpa* behavior tended to be associated with students, not all of the young men in question enjoyed this particular status; in fact, MPD Inspector Yamamoto Seikichi had written in 1914 that the *nanpa* category also included company employees as well as déclassé civil servants and schoolteachers who had fallen from their positions.[58] The analogy to a theater troupe also suggests a discursive link in the public eye between womanizing delinquents and professional actors, who had been associated since at least the Edo period with male prostitution. Indeed, the author located the delinquent youth gang within a broader genus of "male concubines," as well as in the category of "entertainers"—actors, geisha, prostitutes, barmaids, and Buddhist monks (another Tokugawa stereotype)—who "possess no fixed vocation and seek to lead lives of play, getting along by taking advantage of people's weak spots or their sexual desires."[59]

The reference to actors also highlights the connection between this story and the cinema, which, like still photography, engendered new forms of imagination and interaction. In the early 1910s, as film historian A. A. Gerow has observed, "any detective stories featuring chase scenes and criminal masterminds seemed to be a hit with Japanese movie audiences." In particular, *Zigomar,* a 1911 French film that depicted "the debonair criminal genius and master of disguise" of the title, proved wildly popular, spawning numerous sequels and imitations with titles such as *Japanese Zigomar* and *Woman Zigomar,* as well as new detective novels and *Zigomar*-inspired children's games. This sensation prompted the Home Ministry, which believed that the films stimulated viewers to commit criminal acts, to ban all films with "Zigomar" in their title and to promulgate new film-censorship regulations in 1912.[60] The story of the Kozakura Gumi, complete with the claim that gang members had carefully researched Tokyo's police force and could invariably outsmart its best detectives, clearly drew upon the cultural forms and narrative styles that drove the *Zigomar* sensation. Whether or not it actually occurred as described, the seduction scenario in this article was presented as public entertainment, conceived and staged for the mutual gratification of rakes and their audience.

Such stories in turn spawned accounts of *jogakusei* who became seductresses in their own right. For example, a January 1916 *New Review*

article, "The Truth about Gangs of High-Class Delinquent Girls Roaming the Yamanote," told of a disguised reporter's pursuit through
Kagurazaka, an amusement district in western Tokyo, of a group of fallen
jogakusei who attracted college boys by ogling them in movie theaters
and sending them perfumed love letters, which they had learned to com-
pose by reading "chocolaty" literature in school. (*Nanpa* boys, inciden-
tally, were also said to operate in movie theaters.) The search for a story
also permitted the reporter to indulge in, and share with his readers,
fantasies about the erotic mysteries of the nocturnal capital. To discover
his subjects, for example, the writer masqueraded (perhaps not very art-
fully) as a food-stall operator and as a "lecherous man visiting a shady
oden shop," engaging in innuendo-filled dialogues with local residents
before reverting in conclusion to his persona as an outraged member of
respectable society.[61] If rakes could use the streets as theater, so could
the urban reporter—and so could police detectives, who were reputed
for their arts of disguise. All of them entered a liminal world of play,
much like that of the festival at a Kagurazaka temple where, as
Hamamoto Hiroshi described it in a novella, "gentlemen of a respectable
age and lusty students enjoy being jostled by crowds of young geisha
[and] girls from the printing presses in their heavy makeup."[62] Like the
delinquent act itself, the investigation of delinquency afforded participants a pretext to transgress their "normal" identities and orthodox
social values.

Some transgressions, however, were not to be tolerated. This fear of
category blurring is most striking in Inspector Yamamoto's account of
the daughter of a prestigious military officer killed in the Russo-Japanese
War; the girl became the lover of a delinquent youth, spent her time and
money at plays, vaudeville halls, and festivals, stole from her family,
and drew her girlfriends into relationships with other delinquent boys.
Expelled from school for her immoral behavior, she used sex to support
herself, becoming a paid concubine for Chinese men. Eventually, she
established herself as the leader of a gang of delinquent male youths,
extorting money and "mediating" fights in the ruffian style. At this
point, writes Yamamoto, "her mind took a new turn" and, "transform-
ing her female nature," she had her body tattooed and assumed the style
of a "female street knight." By the age of twenty-five, "Tattooed
Otetsu" had again become the mistress of a Chinese man, moving from
place to place leading a bad life. Her behavior had destroyed her family:
its assets were gone, her siblings' honor and credit were damaged, and
her mother had died of illness brought on by these hardships.[63]

Tattooed Otetsu's story, as Yamamoto described it, calls to mind Judith Walkowitz's observation, regarding late-Victorian English discourse, that dangerous female sexualities "not only seemed to 'unsex' women but also to render them déclassé and racially degenerate."[64] Indeed, Otetsu symbolized the subversion of virtually every normative basis of the Japanese nation-state and empire. She had betrayed her father's martial sacrifice, negating a hard-earned battlefield victory with her lack of discipline at home. At a time when the emperor's 1908 Boshin Rescript called on all subjects to practice diligence and thrift, she played, spent, and stole. She crossed gender and class lines, indelibly marking these transgressions on her body in a way that prevented her return to respectable society (tattooing also signified a violation of Confucian morality, the defacement of the body one had received from one's parents). And not only did she engage in illicit sexual relations, but by becoming the concubine of resident Chinese men she had subjected a Japanese body to exploitation by continental Asians over whom Japan's leaders sought increasingly to establish their hegemony.[65] Ultimately, Otetsu symbolized the destruction of the family that was widely proclaimed to be the core unit of the imperial social order, the "family state."

How widespread was student delinquency in Tokyo? In 1912, when there were fifteen thousand middle-school students and thousands more young men attending vocational schools and private colleges (or, lacking formal affiliations, simply living on the fringes of student society), the Metropolitan Police Department rounded up 347 students or erstwhile students as delinquents and included six hundred on their list of male youths warranting observation.[66] Figures for female student delinquency are harder to find, and appear to have been much lower than those for boys: according to one 1908 newspaper article, the MPD had received reports concerning forty girls who had been detained or marked for surveillance by police in the Kanda, Hongō, Ushigome, and Koishikawa precincts. Inspector Yamamoto suggested that relatively few girls became known as delinquents because their families' status allowed them to conceal their behavior from public view.[67]

Such fragmentary evidence is hardly a reliable indicator of the extent of deviant behavior, nor does it permit assessments of the actual nature of the behavior in question. However, any report of delinquency exacerbated elites' fears of their offspring's assertions of autonomy and explorations of new relationships and new forms of play in a morally questionable but mysteriously seductive urban environment. These fears,

Figure 5. Four middle-school students pose for the camera, 1911. With their fashionable Western soft caps and cocky demeanor, these boys epitomize the kind of youth who tested their freedom in the urban environment, to the consternation of reformers, teachers, and parents. Source: The Mainichi Newspapers.

in turn, fueled a massive production of texts and images that assumed a life of their own in the popular imagination, just as they provided support to those who sought to use the "problem" of delinquency to pursue their own strategies of social change and self-empowerment. To these reformers, student youth had to be kept economically dependent, socially insulated, sexually abstinent, and physically fit in preparation for their future roles as middle-class men and women. In contrast, failure to conform to these prescribed status, class, gender, and sex roles threatened, in the view of many authorities, the utter disruption of the national body. "Nature," whether expressed in terms of male barbarity and predation or female frivolity and vanity, had to be overcome by nurture. Police reprimands alone could not achieve this goal. Instead, authorities looked to home and school.

POLICING HOME AND SCHOOL

Just as they responded to the street urchin problem by constructing a negative discourse on the lower class, reformers and experts often located the cause of the student problem in the licentious, decadent behavior of Japan's upper classes. Crusading journalists at the *Yorozu chōhō*, for example, published a series of articles exposing concubinage among the upper class, and another series that blamed student *nanshoku* practices and dueling on the example of influential members of the government.[68] As noted above, scholars have linked these campaigns to contemporary political struggles against the Satsuma-Chōshū oligarchy and to efforts to marginalize or repress *nanshoku* in the name of civilized, modern morality. Of equal significance is the way in which self-consciously middle-class activists sought to establish the superiority of their own values and models of social organization.

Among the upper classes, as with the lower classes, bad homes were thought to lie at the root of the problem. Writer after writer explained that upper-class men not only kept concubines but also were often absent on business and cared little for home life. When they were home, claimed Tomeoka Kōsuke, men from this class often slept with their housemaids, and the resultant offspring showed a remarkable tendency toward delinquency or feeble-mindedness. Mothers, on the other hand, were frequently former geisha, and were "crazy about actors."[69] They were deceitful, incompetent household managers who reigned as "queens" and allowed maids, houseboys, carriage men, live-in students, and visitors to spoil or pervert their children (or stepchildren, of whom, as in the lower classes, there were many). These people drank, threw lavish parties, and let their young acquire harmful tastes for money and the high life.[70] And while they might enjoy spending money, they disdained the effort to earn it: educator Hara Masao wrote in 1906 of the problem of enervated, feeble, urban students of both sexes who "look down on work as something for the lower classes," and "dream of lives of luxury and indolence."[71]

In practical terms, reformers argued that parents from more respectable segments of society had to learn how properly to care for their own young before they grew to be delinquent students. An emerging group of child-study experts were eager to help them. During the Tokugawa era, writers on childhood had tended to espouse the view that children were innately good but had to be molded by their environment into social beings, and these writers called upon parents to exercise care in this regard.[72] Late-Meiji experts in "educational pathology," however, codified a range of child-related problems, from "bad habits" to delinquency or other forms of deviance and abnormality (including mental illness or retardation). Ototake Iwazō, a professor at Tokyo Higher Normal School, emphasized in a 1910 book that the presence of one or more bad habits—such as "selfishness," which entailed willful unruliness; gang formation; pranks; bullying; and abuse of animals— did not necessarily lead to delinquency. But by describing delinquents as

pathological examples of traits that all children possessed, he and his
peers left the boundaries between these conditions ambiguous, and thus
stimulated parents' and others' anxieties.[73]

Social Darwinist ideas clearly structured the logic of the late-Meiji
child-study movement. Invoking the recapitulation theories of sociologist Herbert Spencer (whose writings had also deeply influenced Tokutomi
Sohō's writings on Japan's social development) and psychologist
G. Stanley Hall, the new experts explained that during their development children passed through the various stages of human biological
and moral evolution, and that their behavior thus derived partly from
hereditary vestiges of primitive social organization. Takashima Heizaburō,
for example, suggested that fighting and cruel behavior echoed primitive men's instincts for self-defense, while even the game of tag embodied
the premium placed on speed by savages in their harsh environments.
Parents, educators, and society at large thus needed to channel these
instincts so that, for example, possessive urges led not to theft but to
thrift.[74] Experts emphasized children's particularly powerful imitative
instinct as another factor in their socialization, and called upon adults
to exercise the utmost caution in screening out harmful examples.[75]
Explained Ototake: "[N]ormal children, when nurtured and educated,
see their bodies gradually develop into those of civilized people, while
their spirits follow suit."[76]

While they sought to minister to both fathers and mothers, pediatric
experts devoted far more attention to the latter.[77] At a time when government officials, social reformers, educators, and others worked to
institutionalize the "good wife, wise mother" (ryōsai kenbo) as the
model to which women should conform, members of the Child Study
Association (Jidō Kenkyūkai, established in 1898, later renamed Jidō
Gakkai) offered popularized lectures and texts on juvenile physiology,
psychology, and other child-related subjects including the prevention of
delinquency. Experts' lectures attracted many women whom Takashima
described as "making middle-class homes." (Indeed, as Kathleen Uno
notes, the model of a professional wife and mother would not have been
practicable in lower-class households that relied on the income from
women's full-time work.)[78] By the second decade of the twentieth century, concerns about their children's prospects for educational success
and social mobility in a fiercely competitive society led growing numbers of new-middle-class parents, especially mothers (who were increasingly graduates of girls' high schools), to apply the advice they read in
child-rearing manuals and newspaper advice columns.[79]

Just as they played to families' status anxieties, child-study experts emphasized the public significance of their work for Japan's survival in a harsh international environment. As the Child Study Association's Matsumoto Kōjirō explained during the Russo-Japanese War: "The state does not consist of just the present generation; in order to ensure the future development of the state, the family must awaken to its responsibility. Although it may seem thoughtless to discuss the home during this time of war, I do so solely out of my desire to achieve the final national victory."[80] Or as Takashima, contrasting the declining "countries of the Orient" with the advancing "Anglo-Saxon races," pointedly told a lecture audience in 1909: "In countries where civilization has not progressed, ignorant people abuse their children, deny them education, and view them as their personal possessions. In civilized countries, child protection activities are flourishing."[81] The government rewarded these experts with regular invitations to speak at venues such as the Home Ministry's Reform and Relief Seminars.

If society and the international arena were sites of struggle, so were the mind and body of the individual adolescent. Drawing heavily upon Hall's research, Takashima and his peers argued that adolescence (*seinenki, seishun,* or, more technically, *shunjō hatsudōki,* the stage of sexual awakening), with its physiological and psychological changes, was a period of "storm and stress" which, if not weathered properly, could ruin one's entire life. Takashima offered a rich catalogue of adolescent traits, which seemed primarily to reflect the situation of affluent students, especially in middle schools.[82] Adolescents had active imaginations; became easily agitated and were prone to fantasizing (which could lead to despair or skepticism); experienced numerous desires and passions; were impulsive, easily infatuated, and increasingly motivated by lust; agonized over the conflict between their fantasies and reality; developed strong interests in religion and philosophy; were potentially violent or aggressive; and were prone to hysteria and nervous exhaustion.[83] Adolescents had to be carefully and sympathetically guided in order to become able to guide themselves. Failure in this pedagogic enterprise, however, would signify a stunting or reversion of the evolutionary process, an inability to complete the transition from savagery to civilization. Such youths would remain, as an article in a leading education journal had put it in 1899, "barbarians with knowledge."[84] Japan's new educational institutions were no doubt creating environments conducive to a reconfiguration of young people's mentalities. However, experts' descriptions of adolescence clearly derived less from any empirical analysis of Japanese youths (although Takashima did work directly with a few families) than from the new experts' determination to make Japanese social reality conform to the logic of a global modernity that they, as cultural entrepreneurs and self-proclaimed arbiters of national progress, felt best suited to interpret.

While the "middle-class home" was the desired locus for leading children out of savagery, middle schools were supposed to be the central site for completing their transformation into civilized people. Yet to many critics, schools only fueled adolescent students' degenerate propensities. Not all writers used the delinquency issue to attack liberalism, constitutional theories that treated the emperor as a non-divine organ of the state, and ideas of popular sovereignty, as did Inspector Yamamoto, but many no doubt agreed with his view that imported educational models prioritized knowledge and the pursuit of selfish interests while neglecting the moral and spiritual education required by the Japanese people.[85] Like the increasingly dysfunctional apprenticeship system, which had traditionally served to socialize commoner youths within a purportedly family-like environment, schooling for the male offspring of the elite and elite-aspiring classes had in critics' eyes been reduced to a cold cash relationship stripped of any moral bonds. Schools had become impersonal institutions and "the way of the teacher" had declined. Instructors were merely salaried employees whose jobs depended upon their ability to spout empty theories; some held jobs at several schools and had no time for their students' questions. Students, on the other hand, saw teachers as hirelings who existed to help them pass exams and proceed to the next stage of schooling; they felt no obligation toward their instructors, nor could they find in them models to emulate.[86]

These criticisms reflected the changing conditions that governed post-elementary education at the turn of the century. By this time, the state had consolidated a hierarchical system of institutions through which students had to pass successfully if they were to reach the apex, the higher schools and then the imperial universities that guaranteed graduates elite careers in government agencies or other professions. Within this hierarchy, middle schools became the key institutions for both selecting the handful of elites and breeding the broader middle class (whose members, engaging in a wide range of occupations, would form the "brain and skeleton" of society).[87] For young people in a position to consider schooling beyond the compulsory elementary program, a middle-school education was the key to "success" in life.[88] It was thus no wonder that one contributor to the journal *Child Studies* in 1906 found that 80 percent of middle-school students were concerned only with exams and credentials. The worst of these students, he wrote, were "frivolous, indolent" types, while another 10 percent of middle-school boys were actually or on the verge of becoming "degenerate."[89]

A similar critique applied to girls' high schools. In 1899, Education Minister Kabayama Sukenori had explained that girls' high schools "exist for the nourishment of good wives and wise mothers [by] nourishing a warm and chaste character and the most beautiful and elevated temperament . . . [as well as] furnish[ing] the knowledge of arts and crafts necessary for middle to upper class life."[90] As we have seen, however, popular songs and other texts reveal that many critics complained that girls treated the schools simply as a means to polish their "high collar" credentials, focusing more on preening, gossip, and romance than on the substance of being a proper modern woman; other writers complained that male teachers in girls' schools lacked proper qualifications and were of dubious moral integrity.[91] In his 1914 study, Inspector Yamamoto also argued that the drive among less-affluent girls to attend girls' high schools and enter the middle class had left them vulnerable to numerous problems. Such girls had trouble finding marriage partners who satisfied their aspirations: they were too educated for men of their own status, but too lowly to qualify as spouses for the elite gentlemen they desired. Frustrated and prone to hysteria (another new subject of professional and popular interest), these young women took jobs as elementary school teachers, nurses, and office workers, positions in which they were vulnerable to seduction by delinquent youths and other lechers. Rather than go to secondary school, Yamamoto advised, these girls would be better off learning the skills appropriate for making homes of lower-middle-class or inferior standing.[92]

The solutions proposed for the various shortcomings of the education system varied in focus. Many writers called for a greater emphasis on moral instruction, others urged parents to keep their children in the provinces and enroll them in vocational schools instead of middle schools, and yet others proposed the introduction of sex education courses to help students grapple with their turbulent urges.[93] While these issues were debated in the media and in government circles, school administrators had to deal with the everyday management of the student population, a task made more challenging by the fact that the demand for schooling had led to exploding class sizes.[94] Drawing on the theories of European educator and philosopher Johann Herbart,

administrators such as Katsuura Tomoo, the influential principal of
Tokyo's First Prefectural Middle School, argued that male students in
the thirteen-to-eighteen age group needed strict discipline to temper
their bodies and minds to resist wild urges. Child-study experts such as
Takashima Heizaburō recognized the benefits of cold baths and physical training to strengthen adolescent boys' feeble nerves, but Katsuura
and his followers surpassed even reformatory administrators in their
emphasis on military drill, regimentation, and uniforms. As education
historian Saitō Toshihiko has shown, middle schools developed increasingly detailed regulations governing not only attendance and dress, but
even students' posture when seated or standing. To enforce these rules,
administrators and teachers conducted daily inspections and organized
"student oversight departments."[95]

Schools developed methods for ranking students according to the
degree to which they allegedly embodied certain moral norms, "such as
ardor, diligence, frugality, trustworthiness, and discipline."[96] Conduct
codes sought to isolate students from society's corrupting influences and
to protect their status as "student youth." Regulations at one Tokyo
public school, for example, included prohibitions on wasting time on
the way to or from school; lending or borrowing money without permission; smoking and drinking; reading novels; going to *yose;* and
entering eating or drinking establishments unless accompanied by an
adult relative. What's more, the regulations prohibited all behavior
unbecoming of students, "even if such behavior is not among the items
specifically enumerated in these guidelines."[97]

The Ministry of Education also pressed schools to establish student
surveillance programs, especially in the years after the Russo-Japanese
War, when elites fulminated against the evils of socialist ideas and
"erotic" naturalist literature. In June 1906, Education Minister Makino
Nobuaki, arguing that students' "indiscriminate reading" provoked
"unhealthy thoughts" that fostered decadence, suicidal despair, and
radicalism, issued a "directive on student morals" that urged teachers
and school officials to carefully monitor their charges' reading habits
and book purchases.[98] This directive provoked a wave of new efforts
not only in middle schools but also in girls' high schools, colleges, and
vocational schools. The ministry happily introduced a composite
overview of these practices in a 1907 report.[99]

Judging from this report, it appears that "student oversight departments" functioned like miniature police departments. They sent inspectors
to examine students' lodgings, interrogated boarding-house managers

and the guarantors who were required for commuting students, and provided principals with "secret reports" concerning the character of each student. Teachers patrolled parks, popular amusement districts, bookstores, and other places where students congregated, and paid particular attention to festivals and other entertainments. Some schools restricted the types of establishments in which students could board, monitored their mail, limited their ability to spend money, and tightly controlled when, for what purposes, and in what attire they could leave their lodgings. Girls were often prohibited from going out without an approved chaperone. Schools also strove to limit or prohibit coeducational recreational activities, and coordinated their vacation schedules so that boys and girls would not be able to travel on the same days. In some cases, students with "delinquent tendencies" were required to reside with teachers or were grouped together in a supervised lodging, "to correct their behavior and to prevent the spread of bad customs."[100] Schools also appointed students with good reputations to serve as monitors and relied on peer groups to impose social sanctions on rule-breakers (sanctions which, as Saitō mentions, were frequently arbitrary and violent).[101] The report also mentioned schools' attempts to overcome the distance between teachers and students through informal visits, and it noted that some teachers promoted "beneficial" reading matter, hiking trips, martial arts practice, and other forms of physical conditioning, as well as the cultivation of good taste. Yet the overall tone is one of surveillance rather than intimacy.

School principals, of course, were empowered to expel students whose behavior did not withstand their scrutiny, and many did so with little compunction, to the consternation of those who pointed out the lack of mechanisms to deal with expellees. To MPD Inspector Yamamoto, expulsion constituted an "academic death sentence" that stripped problem youths of their status as students and condemned them to a marginal existence.[102] Indeed, middle schools' rigorous policing—what one prominent educator called a virtually neurotic obsession with school purity—contributed as much to the creation of a group of student juvenile delinquents as did the various social evils to which reformers pointed in their analyses.[103]

Boys who had been expelled from or dropped out of other schools for reasons such as cheating on exams, forging attendance records, striking other students, or disrupting classes, often enrolled in various private middle schools in Tokyo, provided their families had the means to pay their tuition. In particular, many problem students from the provinces flowed into such institutions, which served as veritable dumping grounds for the maladjusted elite.[104] These schools, however, also expelled students in large numbers—in 1907 and 1909, roughly one in three expulsions was from a Tokyo private school. Boys who left private middle schools often entered vocational schools; Iwakura Railroad School, not far from Asakusa, gained particular notoriety as a nest of delinquents, particularly hard-to-handle *nanpa* types. Older boys who succeeded in completing middle school could be placed in private colleges such as Waseda, Keiō, Meiji, or Senshū, for which the principal admission requirement was ability to pay the tuition.[105] Others, like those in Hamamoto Hiroshi's novellas, simply stayed in the city, spending their parents' money or securing funds through a variety of licit and illicit means. The majority of students classified as "real" juvenile delinquents came from this segment of the student population.

FAMILIES' OTHER OPTIONS

Affluent families pursued various approaches to reforming their unruly offspring. Some hired private tutors or placed their children with relatives and acquaintances, while others appear to have shipped them abroad. As in the early modern period, confinement at home remained an option, and disownment remained the last resort. The Reformatory Law allowed parents to apply to have their children committed to public reformatories, but few in fact did so, out of fear that the children would be stigmatized and exposed to truly criminal elements.[106] In Osaka, the prefectural reformatory did house a handful of wealthy middle-school students, but the staff found them more difficult to manage than lower-class inmates and the principal noted that it was not possible to train "the nephew of a high-ranking bureaucrat" or "the son of a man worth several hundred thousand yen" to become a carpenter or a metal caster.[107] Although some observers suggested the need for a separate track of public reformatories that could provide elite children with middle-school education rather than vocational training, Home Ministry officials stressed that "good" parents should not see reformatories as a means to shirk their child-rearing obligations.[108] Moreover, public reformatories could not admit older boys.

In Tokyo, affluent parents concerned about discretion could turn to two private reformatories, Takase Shinkyō's Tokyo Reformatory (Tōkyō Kankain) and Tomeoka Kōsuke's Family School. An 1895 guide for parents applying to the Tokyo Reformatory stated: "The majority of our students are sons of men of status—nobles, gentlemen, and wealthy merchants and farmers. While there are some children of the poor here as subsidized students, they are kept in separate rooms."[109] According to another document from the same year, Takase also appears to have offered parents the option of confining their "dissolute and delinquent" *adult* sons aged twenty and over in private rooms, to be built at families' expense. The Tokyo Reformatory, however, promised only to oversee the young men's movements and assumed no responsibility for actually reforming them.[110] The overall results of this institution's programs are hard to ascertain: a 1903 report, for example, provides follow-up information on occupations for only 216 of the 424 students discharged between 1885 and 1902, and offers no details on their behavior.[111]

At the Family School, which admitted boys on either a full-tuition or a subsidized basis (as well as operating a segregated public ward), instructor Nishimura Shigeji recorded his frustrations in dealing with "degenerate students" in logbooks he kept from mid-1906 to early 1909.[112] Despite his numerous pronouncements about the virtues of cold baths, hard work, and military drill, Tomeoka appears to have adopted a more lenient approach to the sons of wealthy patrons whose tuition payments helped support his moral enterprise. In September 1906, for example, Nishimura wrote that a few boys had left the school at night to go drinking in Hongō, a student district, and appeared to have dallied in the licensed quarters at Itabashi. In other entries, he complained that boys avoided class and work; slept late and got up only to play baseball; styled and oiled their hair in "high collar" fashion; read novels and drew lewd pictures; masturbated day and night; and may have engaged in homosexual relations. Several of these boys apparently commuted to Waseda (most likely the middle-school division) and other schools, and Nishimura blamed them for introducing tobacco and other vices into the reformatory. Full-tuition boys also teased scholarship students, calling them the Family School's "domestic livestock" or "kept servants."[113]

Nishimura wrote repeatedly of one older boy, named Ōtani, whose relatives cared little for him and paid hefty fees to keep him in the reformatory. Tomeoka gave Ōtani special treatment, Nishimura lamented, and because the boy had numerous followers, it was impossible to maintain discipline in the school. "The only way to make him abandon his spoiled ways is to give him thirty frontal blows with a stick, but who will do this?"[114] At some point, Nishimura's complaints appear to have earned a sharp rebuke from Tomeoka, but after nearly two years, the principal asked school instructors to supervise Ōtani more strictly. In his own written comments, Tomeoka explained that he had tried to contact the boy's father, who was avoiding him, but that merely expelling Ōtani after several years was inhumane and an abdication of the school's pedagogic responsibility. In his next logbook entry, Nishimura recommended that Ōtani, who was roughly twenty years old, be given half his assets and sent to the United States, where he could learn to be independent.[115] As these examples show, reformers' proclaimed goals of training healthy national subjects and extending new pedagogic mechanisms into society appear to have taken a backseat to families' desires simply to warehouse their problems; the economics of the private reformatories (like the economics of private middle schools) further facilitated this inversion of priorities. Ōtani's subsequent history is not known, but for other youths turning twenty, compulsory military service (if they were not deemed physically unfit) may well have served as the ultimate disciplinary mechanism.

The options for parents of "degenerate" girls appear to have been even more limited. Takase Shinkyō took steps to establish a girls' reformatory in 1896, with funds raised through a women's charity association chaired by the wife of Navy Minister Saigō Tsugumichi, but it is not clear that this institution ever actually functioned.[116] The Yokohama Family School (Katei Gakuen), the Women's Christian Temperance Union's House of Benevolence (Jiaikan), and perhaps the Salvation Army's Women's Home also took in small numbers of "dissolute daughters" from good homes.[117] Ultimately, parents who did not disown their daughters (like those in the song "Voice of the Pine") no doubt simply waited anxiously for them to outgrow their "bad habits" and prayed that no rumors would prevent them from getting married. Once within this containing field, they would at least have the status of wives and (possibly) mothers, even if they were not necessarily as "good" and "wise" as society demanded they be.

The feverish public discourse on student delinquency, real or imagined, constituted a critical element in the development of new systems for reproducing Japan's respectable classes. At a moment when the Japanese state was consolidating a multitracked hierarchy of secondary and tertiary schools, commentaries on students' transgressions tied into debates over what types of education (and how much education) should be provided to those who were to become the mainstays of what one author emphatically termed "the progress of our advancing, expanding empire."[118] At issue was not only the moral and intellectual content of modern education but also the practical techniques of school administration required to concentrate students' energies on their prescribed missions. Many school officials and instructors believed ongoing, intrusive surveillance to be a core element of their pedagogic mission; the programs they developed provided a template upon which their successors drew for decades to come. Indeed, as the number of young people and families pursuing social mobility through post-elementary education continued to grow, so did the need to ensure that they were carefully molded to fit the behavioral norms of "student youth."

These concerns also contributed to the reconstitution of class-based standards of domesticity and to the empowerment of new forms of professional knowledge in society at large. Parents who feared for their children's futures and their families' social positions turned increasingly for advice to pediatric experts, who urged them, especially mothers, to carefully monitor and channel their children's potentially evil instincts and turbulent passions until they evolved into mature, well-adjusted people. For mothers, the ability to perform such oversight became a crucial measure of their competence as "women making middle-class homes" and exemplars of a healthy Japanese modernity. Of course, not all women conformed to these expectations, but in the decades to follow, reform agencies would increasingly count on them to do so and would attempt to mobilize them to bring proper maternal love and discipline to broader segments of the youth population.

Writers on student misbehavior used it as a vehicle through which to criticize a broad range of social, cultural, and political problems as they defined them. Yet stories of violent ruffians, devious rakes, and degenerate girls operated at more than one level in the social imagination, and reactions to them are difficult to assess. Exposés in daily newspapers such as *Yorozu chōhō* and more highbrow magazines such as *New Review* clearly provided readers racy entertainment along with moral outrage, while *enka* songs permitted the diffusion of images of Japanese student dissoluteness to an even broader audience that may well have thumbed their noses at elites' pretensions to moral superiority. Equally hard to gauge are the meanings that "degenerate" and "delinquent" students ascribed to their own behavior, and how they reacted to or sought to shape the emerging discourse. This chapter has attempted to trace some of the social contexts, cultural traditions, and emerging practices that informed students' play and the illegal activities into which it occasionally slipped, but the analysis of these students' subjectivities is constrained by the fact that few if any contemporary sources permitted the accused to speak for themselves.

By the second decade of the twentieth century, many of the basic elements of the modern Japanese discourse on juvenile delinquency had been put in place. During the following decades, new discursive elements, as well as new agencies of juvenile protection, would be added in response to the rapid growth of Japan's industrial economy and the unsettling complexity of modern social relations. The following chapters will examine the shifting strategies, disciplinary technologies, and social tensions that informed interwar efforts to treat "bad youth."

CHAPTER 4

Popularizing Protection

In a 1929 article, Miyagi Tamayo described to readers of the magazine *Women's Friend (Fujin no tomo)* how she had infused the home of "Saitō Shūji" (as I shall call him), a young teenage boy arrested for burglary, with maternal love. Shūji, who had a history of larceny going back to the age of eight, lived with his two sisters, his older brother, and their widowed father in a dark, dirty, cramped tenement flat that one entered through a stable. (The father and brother were cart pullers.) Upon her first visit in late 1924, Miyagi "shuddered" at the sight of soiled tatami mats, torn shōji screens, dirty clothes strewn about, and saké flasks littering the floor. But Miyagi rolled up her sleeves and set to work: she taught Shūji to enjoy diligent labor and saving money and taught his younger sisters to wash clothes and keep a tidy kitchen. Soon the mats and screens had been replaced, and after four months, Mr. Saitō, who had hit and railed at his children when drunk, had sworn off alcohol (except for two nights each month) and was setting aside the money he saved to purchase new clothes for his happy daughters. In this triumphal narrative of middle-class reformism, not only the individual delinquent but also his whole family had been rescued and a joyful domesticity constructed.[1]

Miyagi, a Protestant who had taught at Nara Women's Higher Normal School and studied social welfare at the progressive Ōhara Social Problems Research Institute, entered Shūji's life in her capacity as a staff probation officer for the Tokyo Juvenile Court. Established in 1923 by the

Justice Ministry, juvenile courts in Tokyo and Osaka adopted new methods of social diagnosis and casework to treat several thousand adolescents aged fourteen to eighteen each year. (A third court opened in
Nagoya in 1934.) These courts were not alone in this approach. Home
Ministry officials also developed new social policies and social work
programs to complement their reformatory operations. Education officials and school staffs, medical experts, private reformers, clerics, and
community notables also cooperated with the new projects, which, as in
the example of Shūji's family, often went beyond individual delinquents
to subject families, workplaces, and other aspects of everyday life to
external administration.[2]

This chapter focuses on the expansion of juvenile protection programs from 1918 to the mid-1930s, when Japan experienced the rise
and collapse of what is often referred to as "Taishō Democracy." World
War I stimulated the growth of Japan's commercial and heavy industrial
sectors, and with it an increase in labor unrest and consumer prices. In
1918, while the press reported that shipping magnates lit their cigars
with hundred-yen notes, people on the opposite end of the economic
spectrum rose in nationwide rice riots that exposed the weaknesses of
Japan's aging oligarchy and ushered in an era of governments led by
party politicians. Neither changes at the top nor the emergence of organized labor and leftist social movements offered much relief for Japan's
working masses, however, as the wartime boom gave way to a postwar
bust and what Hugh Patrick called the "economic muddle" of the
1920s.[3] In the Tokyo-Yokohama region, popular hardships were exacerbated by the Great Kantō Earthquake of September 1923, which
claimed nearly 100,000 lives and destroyed entire districts: Shūji's
family, for example, had lost everything (and this was the second
tragedy they suffered; only six years earlier, a major flood had washed
away their home and grocery store). Meanwhile, young people of various classes sought escape in cinemas, cafés, and other sites of "modern"
play, amplifying fears among conservatives and moral reformers that
the nation had been swept up in a wave of depravity. "The world trend
of self-centered democracy has filled the spirits of youth in general,"
wrote Tokyo social worker Kusama Yasoo in 1921, "and it is said that
this has caused the frequent appearance of juvenile delinquents."[4] Fears
of disorder and national weakness only escalated during the Great
Depression; when party governments collapsed in 1932 following the
army's occupation of Manchuria, Taishō Democracy gave way to
increasing authoritarianism at home and "go-fast imperialism" in

Asia—changes that further strengthened the desire of reformers to prevent youthful deviance and cultivate disciplined, productive Japanese subjects.[5]

Throughout this period, anxious observers pointed to a variety of statistics as evidence that the problem of juvenile crime and delinquency, especially among males, had reached massive proportions. Penal code violations by youths aged fourteen to nineteen nationwide rose from some 20,000 in 1914 to 30,000 by 1919; half of the offenders were younger than eighteen. These figures, noted one official, included neither violators of special laws such as police regulations or railway regulations nor "those who commit merely delinquent acts." Urban youth, again, figured most prominently in such reports. In Tokyo Prefecture, the police detained some 4,000 people under the age of twenty as delinquents in 1924 and more than 8,000 five years later; in 1928, the *Tōkyō Asahi shinbun* reported that "blacklists" compiled by Tokyo's police stations included some 30,000 names of young people warranting surveillance. In 1934, the director of the Tokyo Juvenile Court, using 1930 figures, estimated conservatively that there were 4.8 juvenile offenders per thousand members of the fourteen-to-seventeen age cohort in the city's thirty-six wards—a rate, he noted, that was much higher than in most American cities.[6]

Demographic trends no doubt accounted for much of this alleged increase. The population of Tokyo Prefecture, which included both the city wards and large industrial and commuter residential districts in the surrounding counties, reached 3.7 million in 1920, 5.4 million in 1930, and 6.4 million in 1935 (in 1932, the city incorporated five of the counties into new wards). During the same period, Osaka Prefecture's population went from 2.6 million to 4.3 million. The male populations of these prefectures grew at a particularly explosive rate, spearheaded by the immigration of young men in the fifteen-to-nineteen age bracket, followed by those in the twenty-to-twenty-four and ten-to-fourteen cohorts.[7] Young people's increased presence thus made them a natural object of concern and policing, while the emergence of new institutions such as the juvenile court created an incentive for police officers to produce case files on youths to whom they might earlier have administered harsh but informal reprimands. Such figures (which, furthermore, reveal little about the degree of the offenses involved) thus need not be taken as accurate reflections of increasing social disorder or moral collapse. But public interest in the problem of delinquency also grew, fed by hundreds of sensational articles in the daily press and general-interest magazines, book-length studies filled with warnings to parents, and novels and films that explored the darker side of urban popular culture. In 1933, the mass-circulation *Heibonsha Encyclopedia* departed from its short-entry format to devote an entire page to an article on juvenile delinquents.[8]

The growth of an interventionist system of juvenile protection was justified not only by fears of disorder but also by new civic ideologies. Children had the right, declared the prominent pediatrician and social worker Sandaya Hiraku in 1924, to be raised vigorously, to be educated wisely, and to be guided to the good.[9] While not everyone was comfortable with the discourse of rights, all embraced the language of duties. Social welfare experts drew on continental European ideas of "social solidarity" to argue that each member of society had an obligation to contribute to the progress of the whole and to maintain its most disadvantaged members. Protecting children from illness, deprivation, and delinquency—through day-care centers, infant health programs, settlements, special education, vocational counseling, reformatories, and other means—formed a key part of this agenda.[10] Justice Ministry officials also embraced what one jurist called "the supreme concept of collective social responsibility" as a critical element in the development of prophylactic criminal policies that underpinned the juvenile court approach.[11] But while protection agencies worked to build a popular movement and bring order into the lives of young people and their families, the latter's responses to this effort continued to be far from predictable.

THE SPREAD OF SOCIAL POLICY

The 1918 rice riots prompted the Home Ministry to implement a new series of social policy initiatives to stabilize the lives of the poor. Already in 1917, the ministry had established a small Relief Section within the Local Affairs Bureau. By 1922, this agency had grown into a separate Bureau of Social Affairs, or Social Bureau, with divisions covering labor issues, social welfare, and (after 1923) health insurance. Local governments, as well as governments-general in colonial Korea and Taiwan, established similar agencies. Under Governor Inoue Tomoichi, formerly head of the Home Ministry's Local Affairs Bureau and a key organizer of poor relief policy and the Reform and Relief Seminars, Tokyo Prefecture opened both a Social Section and a semiofficial Social Work Association; Tokyo City established its own Social Bureau in 1919.[12]

These agencies actively promoted new forms of social work. The government briefly operated a social work training center near Tokyo, but then shifted to providing subsidies to private programs such as the one at Japan Women's College, where the Protestant social reformer and government consultant Namae Takayuki (Tomeoka Kōsuke's protégé) introduced Japanese students to the latest theories of social diagnosis and casework pioneered by Americans such as Mary Richmond. Social work offered new career opportunities to middle-class Japanese women, and local governments came to rely on their expertise, particularly in areas dealing with children, female labor, and family life.[13]

Tokyo officials quickly took advantage of this new pool of experts. Staff at the Tokyo Children's Shelter, established in 1913 by the prefecture and eventually taken over and expanded by the city Social Bureau, handled vagrant or delinquent youth for up to fifty days, coordinated longer-term treatment for roughly five hundred youths each year, and provided counseling services to hundreds of families concerned about their children's behavior.[14] In April 1920, the prefecture's Social Section hired thirty full-time child-protection commissioners (jidō hogoin), most of them graduates of private colleges, to conduct casework in the poorest sections of the city and the outlying areas. Male commissioners patrolled working-class districts including Shitaya, Asakusa, Honjo, and Fukagawa. Female commissioners, who constituted roughly one-third of the staff, were posted to Social Section headquarters, police stations, schools, and the procurator's office. Commissioners investigated cases involving juvenile offenders, abandoned, neglected, or abused children, working children, and feeble-minded children. They attempted when possible to visit homes and compiled files on clients' domestic conditions, family and medical histories, school records, and work situations; commissioners also conducted numerous surveys of slum areas as a basis for policy formulation. Financial constraints, particularly after the 1923 earthquake, forced the prefecture to eliminate the program in 1927, but the Social Section then established a Children's Desk staffed by a director and eighteen full-time caseworkers. From 1920 to 1929, the prefecture's professional caseworkers handled roughly 5,000 children, of whom 2,144 (1,837 boys and 307 girls) were classified as delinquent and/or vagrant. Agents handled many fewer delinquents after 1923, when the new juvenile court assumed primary responsibility for youths aged fourteen or older.[15]

To minimize the costs of social work, Home Ministry officials in Tokyo, and throughout Japan, built a system of unpaid, volunteer district welfare commissioners *(hōmen iin)*, drawn largely from among local business owners and similar pillars of the community. By coordinating access to various social services, and even by providing funds from their own pockets, commissioners were to discourage the poor from applying for public assistance; they also helped to implement government campaigns to promote thrift, morality, and reverence for the emperor. Because they were respected community figures, it was believed that their interventions would provoke less resistance than those by public officials. As agents of juvenile welfare, wrote Ogawa Shigejirō, who devised the system in Osaka in 1918, district commissioners were the Japanese counterpart to the American system of supervision by probation officers, parole officers, and big brothers. Enthusiasm for the new system ran so high among government officials at the local and national levels that in 1928, the Home Minister declared the commissioners to be "the central institution of social work" in Japan.[16]

Meanwhile, the police, a branch of the Home Ministry with a reputation for arrogance and even brutality that belied their claims to act as "nursemaids" of the people, implemented new social work programs, including "personal counseling" services, as part of a concerted post-1918 effort to overcome popular hostility, cultivate popular cooperation, and prevent the spread of "dangerous thoughts" among society's less fortunate members.[17] Christian groups, which had pioneered social welfare efforts since the early Meiji years, joined in these efforts, as did Buddhist organizations: by the 1920s, major sects and temples had organized social departments with professionally trained staffs to provide welfare services to both parishioners and the broader community.

Caseworkers also endeavored to expose children and their families to the authority of experts in psychiatry and child psychology. In 1917, Tokyo officials appointed a committee including Ishii Ryōichi, a specialist in educating "feeble-minded" children, and Takashima Heizaburō, the prominent child-study expert, to study vagrant and delinquent youths in the children's shelter and in police holding facilities. Four years later, Ishii established a new, publicly subsidized facility, the Tokyo Prefecture Juvenile Research Institute, which examined children referred not only by the police and welfare agencies but also by schools and families. From 1921 to 1934, for example, institute staff classified roughly one in four of the nearly five thousand children they examined as delinquents and reported that the majority of these displayed signs of inferior intelligence or mental retardation, while those with normal intelligence revealed abnormal personalities. Local governments, universities, women's groups, temples, and various private experts also established counseling centers, most of them small-scale operations, in Tokyo and elsewhere.[18]

Education officials often cooperated with their Home Ministry counterparts on social policy issues. Beginning in the mid-1920s, the Education Ministry's Regular School Affairs Bureau and the Home Ministry's Social Bureau jointly promoted vocational guidance programs designed to prepare elementary-school pupils for productive, wholesome working lives free from the dissatisfaction and alienation that led to unemployment, crime, and delinquency. And in urban slums, elementary-school personnel continued to conduct surveys, visit homes, and impart messages of civilization and uplift through learning, diligence, frugality, and hygiene to impoverished children and their families. At least one school, Reigan Special Elementary School in Fukagawa Ward, operated its own social department that incorporated many of the programs, including personal counseling, vocational training, and infant and maternity protection, then being developed by Home Ministry experts at the national and local levels. Reigan and other schools also established mothers' associations (haha no kai) that offered both recreation and lectures on subjects such as the prevention of delinquency.[19]

Educators also expanded programs begun in the late-Meiji years to monitor children's behavior outside school. For example, in the mid-1920s, teachers from several Tokyo elementary schools participated in the Association for the Extracurricular Surveillance of Children (Kōgai Jidō Torishimarikai), which sought among other things to visit delinquent children in their homes. Secondary school teachers also used home visits to establish close ties with and gain detailed knowledge about families. Teachers' efforts achieved a new level of vitality after 1929, as a growing number of regions established "Educational Protection Federations" and lobbied the Ministry of Education to issue regulations and provide funds for their activities. The major political parties, the Seiyūkai and the Minseitō, also supported these projects as a means to cultivate upstanding national subjects. By 1934, sixty regions had established federations, whose members shared responsibility for monitoring the behavior of students in their precincts (some associations targeted only secondary-school students, while others included elementary-school pupils).[20] Tokyo Prefecture's Secondary School Guidance Association, according to a 1935 report, linked 7,000 teachers from roughly 250 middle schools, girls' high schools, and vocational schools with a combined student population of 140,000. Among other activities, association members worked to gain the release of students detained by the police, kept such incidents secret, and endeavored to guide these youths toward reform. Like other participants in the juvenile protection movement, educators often expressed their aspirations in the language of collective social responsibility. "Our highest ideal," wrote the Tokyo Prefecture school superintendent, "is to have people from all walks of life become good educators . . . [so that] through total social mobilization we can produce good, useful, subjects who are mainstays of the nation."[21]

THE JUVENILE COURT

Justice Ministry programs for dealing with delinquent youth also promoted new clinical approaches and expanded social participation. During the 1910s, procurators had begun combining suspended indictments or sentences for petty juvenile offenders with referrals to private agencies such as the Tokyo Prisoner Rehabilitation Association, run by the noted Protestant reformer Hara Taneaki. In 1917, district courts established special juvenile sections that further employed this practice; during the late 1910s and early 1920s, the Tokyo District Court's juvenile section handled on average more than two thousand cases per year, of which only 10 percent involved formal indictments. Justice officials also studied the juvenile court systems that had been run in the United States and Europe since the turn of the century and prepared to establish their own version.[22]

The details of a proposed juvenile court (shōnen shinpanjo) system emerged in the draft of a Juvenile Law (Shōnen hō), to apply to all youths under the age of eighteen, that the ministry submitted to the Diet in 1918. These courts could receive referrals from procurators, other authorities, or the general public, and would evaluate cases on an individual basis, beginning with a staff probation officer's investigation of both the youth and his or her family's background and living conditions. Court referees would then determine whether or not to open the case, and in those they did open, could select from a menu of "protective measures." One-time measures included reprimands, referral to school staff for guidance, requirements that youths sign oaths promising to reform, and remission to parents or guardians. Continuing measures, which could last until an individual turned twenty-three, included placement on probation and commission to private "protection associations" (hogo dantai), reformatories, or, for the most difficult cases, new juvenile training schools *(kyōseiin)* where strict discipline would prevail. Referees could combine protective measures, modify measures according to a youth's behavior, and refer cases deemed too severe to the criminal courts. The juvenile court, however, would not have automatic jurisdiction over juvenile offenders. For example, it could not hear cases involving criminal offenders aged sixteen or older or youths accused of crimes punishable by execution or prison terms of three years or longer, unless they were referred to the court by a procurator or criminal court judge. (The bill also provided for reduced sentencing of juvenile offenders in criminal courts.)[23]

Home Ministry officials and their allies in the reformatory movement such as Tomeoka Kōsuke and Ogawa Shigejirō (who a decade earlier had been driven from the Justice Ministry by proponents of a more punitive approach) fiercely opposed the bill, arguing that the central role of procurators and the inclusion of penal measures reflected an anachronistic, authoritarian approach more suited to abusing than reeducating troubled young people.[24] Needless to say, the Justice bill would have stripped the Home Ministry of its jurisdiction over juvenile delinquents. In 1919, Home Ministry officials submitted a rival bill that called for each village, town, or city to appoint a number of social workers, educators, doctors, midwives, clerics, police officers, or other suitable individuals to oversee a wide range of delinquent, dependent, neglected, or disabled children. This debate was only one front in a more extensive battle between the two ministries, which also clashed over responses to the 1918 rice riots and the mounting wave of labor disputes during and immediately after World War I. Whereas a rising generation of Home Ministry bureaucrats actively promoted new social policies and labor legislation to mitigate the excesses of capitalism and positively integrate the lower and working classes, the Justice Ministry remained under the sway of men such as Hiranuma Kiichirō and Suzuki Kisaburō, who defined their mission as the forceful suppression of any attempts, indigenous or foreign-inspired, to subvert the emperor-centered national polity *(kokutai)*.[25]

Yet this mutual animosity belied a common desire among officials in both ministries to build a system of protective agencies with deep, extensive roots in society. Yamaoka Mannosuke, a ranking Justice Ministry official who helped draft the juvenile bill, echoed his Home Ministry counterparts when he argued that juvenile protection was a form of social work that "must be performed in the spirit of social solidarity." He also stressed that court hearings would be held in family-like, intimate settings and noted that the juvenile court's probation officers would be modeled on the Tokyo juvenile protection commissioners— who in fact had, since their inception, cooperated closely with the Tokyo District Court.[26] Home Ministry consultant Namae Takayuki, while sharing some of Ogawa's concerns, observed in 1920 that the Justice Ministry draft provided for a range of nonpunitive measures that "fit with the desires of the Home Ministry," and that its incorporation of probation was "actually an improvement over the [existing] Reformatory Law." "Judging from the spirit of the law," he wrote, "the only difference is that the Justice Ministry submitted it."[27]

After several years of wrangling, the two ministries compromised. The Juvenile Law would apply only to youths aged fourteen to seventeen, while those under fourteen would continue to be covered by the Reformatory Law unless referred to a juvenile court by prefectural authorities. In addition, juvenile courts would be established only in Tokyo (with jurisdiction over Tokyo and Kanagawa Prefectures) and Osaka (with jurisdiction over Osaka, Hyogo, and Kyoto Prefectures). While this fell short of the Justice Ministry's ambitions, these regions reported the highest concentrations of delinquent or predelinquent youths. (The two courts would gradually expand their jurisdictions, and a third court was established in Nagoya in 1934.) The Home Ministry dropped its proposed legislation; the Juvenile Law was passed in 1922 and implemented on January 1, 1923.[28]

The number of cases taken in by the juvenile courts grew rapidly, while the criminal prosecution of juvenile offenders declined dramatically. From 1923 to 1937, the juvenile courts in Tokyo, Osaka, and (after 1934) Nagoya handled a total of 241,329 cases. The Tokyo court handled 112,485 cases during this period, an average of 7,499 per year, with intake rising to 10,000 cases by 1934. The Osaka court, which took in on average 7,857 cases per year during the same period, handled more cases than the Tokyo court from 1923 to 1930 but fewer after that. Court officials, however, chose not to open roughly two-thirds of the cases they received, mainly because the offenses were too minor to merit adjudication and protective measures—a fact which supports the impression that interwar statistics on rising delinquency were in no small part a function of intensified reporting rather than of significant social collapse. Of the cases they did open, the courts imposed milder one-time measures in 58 percent and ordered either probation or custodial treatment for the remainder. Working or unemployed boys constituted the primary pool of cases, most of which involved violations

Figure 6. Occupational breakdown of youths receiving protective measures from the Tokyo Juvenile Court, 1934. Among boys, shop clerks constitute the largest group, followed by unemployed youths, artisans and factory workers, students, and automobile assistants. Among girls, housemaids constitute the largest group, followed by those with no employment and café waitresses. The inset shows numbers of crimes committed by season. Source: *Tokufū* 6, no. 6 (1935).

of the Penal Code (especially theft, but also embezzlement, fraud, gambling, injury to persons, and extortion) or of special laws such as misdemeanor police regulations, railroad and automobile regulations, and firearms regulations (the latter in only a minuscule number of cases).[29]

The juvenile courts mobilized a staff whose backgrounds reflected the consensus among key elements of the state and the middle-class reform lobby—regardless of their primary bureaucratic allegiances—on the need for new agencies of intervention into the lives of delinquent adolescents. During its first years, for example, the Tokyo Juvenile Court employed several prefecture child-protection commissioners and medical experts affiliated with the Home Ministry to evaluate the physical and psychological condition of each youth. Protestants played a significant role in the court's early activities and in shaping its reputation as a progressive institution. Mitsui Hisaji, a district court judge and Sunday-school teacher, served as the court's first director. Women such as Fujii Koto, formerly a Tokyo Prefecture child-protection commissioner, and Ueda (later Miyagi) Tamayo also joined as staff probation officers. As one observer of the Tokyo court noted in 1925, "It is frequently believed that all of the court's personnel are Christians." Yet Buddhist clerics such as Tokunaga Kenjun, formerly a prison chaplain and director of a rehabilitation center for ex-convicts, and Shinbori Tetsugaku, who worked extensively with Tokyo's homeless children, also played a central role as staff probation officers, and Buddhist organizations conducted training sessions for juvenile protection workers.[30]

The courts drew on a growing network of ancillary agencies to implement protective measures. Commissioned probation officers *(shokutaku hogoshi)*, most of them community notables (many in their late forties or fifties), handled much of the court's casework. Buddhist clerics, recruited because of the traditionally strong ties between temples and their communities, constituted the largest group, followed by school principals and administrators. Others included Christian social reformers (even Tomeoka Kōsuke, who had vociferously opposed the Juvenile Law, accepted a commission), district welfare commissioners, settlement workers, representatives of Shintō sects and new religions, active or retired civil servants, local businessmen, midwives, and other new-middle-class professionals.[31] Commissioned probation officers formed neighborhood- or district-level associations, conducted research, investigated reports of delinquent behavior by local youths, and worked with both young people treated by the court and those whose cases were deemed too petty to be opened. This group thus complemented, and at times overlapped with, both the casework systems established under Home Ministry auspices and the extracurricular guidance federations administered by the Ministry of Education. The Justice Ministry also worked with various private associations that provided custodial care for delinquent youths; in addition to maintaining existing relationships with Christian groups such as Hara Taneaki's ex-convict rehabilitation center, officials pressed the Buddhist community, Shintō and new religious groups, as well as various secular groups, into service.

Like those officials who sought to "popularize the police," juvenile court and Justice Ministry officials also orchestrated various campaigns to elicit public cooperation. The court's main outreach group, the Japan Juvenile Protection Association, organized lectures, research, and public relations activities, and provided subsidies to juvenile protection programs and support to poor youths under the court's supervision. Beginning in 1928, the Justice Ministry organized national "Juvenile Protection Days" that featured public lectures, newspaper and magazine articles, radio broadcasts, and films. In Tokyo, publishing houses and leading department stores provided funds for leaflets with titles such as "The Rearing of Children," "To All Boys and Girls," "For Parents Worried about Their Children's Upbringing," and "Everyone's Juvenile Court," which were distributed by youth groups in Tokyo and Kanagawa. Noted women reformers including Patriotic Women's Association leader Motono Hisako, doctor and educator Yoshioka Yayoi, educator Hatoyama Haruko, and the Tokyo court's own Miyagi Tamayo occupied prominent places on the lecture circuit. In 1925, Motono, Yoshioka, and others founded the Juvenile Protection Women's Association to publicize delinquency-related issues and provide "maternal love" to delinquent youths who had lacked such affection during their upbringings. The association operated a small protective association for girls, and its Osaka branch established a counseling center for families with problem children. In Tokyo, juvenile court director Suzuki Kaichirō served as an adviser to the Secondary School Guidance Association, and some of the association's members also served as commissioned probation officers. These efforts—geared to what one official called the "socialization of protection"—constitute a defining characteristic of the Justice Ministry's anti-delinquency programs during the interwar years and beyond.[32]

The interwar years thus saw a rapid increase in the number of agencies surveying social conditions, identifying delinquency and other social problems, and implementing treatment programs that emphasized close contacts between reformers and their objects. These agencies operated through different administrative hierarchies, at times handled different populations (especially after the passage of the Juvenile Law), and often claimed distinct ideologies or orientations. Moreover, not everyone subscribed to the new paradigms of social welfare and protection: for example, many policemen continued to use heavy-handed tactics in their everyday dealings with young people, many schoolteachers relied on corporal punishment to discipline problem children, and many middle schools continued to expel delinquent students rather than try to reform them. Yet by the mid-1920s, social work agencies, juvenile courts, schools, and the police often cooperated in practice and sent representatives to round-table meetings where they agreed on the desirability of a holistic, integrated approach to the prevention and treatment of delinquency.[33]

The remainder of this chapter will examine the actual encounters between protection agencies in Tokyo and the young people and families they strove to treat. Rather than proceeding on an institution-by-institution basis, the study will endeavor to provide a composite view of these relationships, using reports by Tokyo social work agencies and the juvenile court, professional journals, books and articles written by reformers for the general public, newspaper reports, and contemporary fiction. These sources highlight both common strategies and contradictions in reformers' approaches, as well as the contingent nature of authorities' interventions and people's responses.

SOCIAL WORK AND PROBATION: FROM THE INDIVIDUAL TO THE FAMILY

Caseworkers employed a variety of approaches to treat delinquent or at-risk youths. Because many youths had either worked or drifted about the city on their own before coming to the authorities' attention, social workers or probation officers often endeavored to place them in suitable apprenticeships and follow up with visits, sometimes even on a daily basis. These relationships could require great perseverance. For example, prefecture social worker Gotō Fumio (not to be confused with the prominent Home Ministry official of the same name) struggled to keep one boy—I shall call him "Kuroda Takeo"—in apprenticeships from which he repeatedly escaped. Takeo had experienced poverty and a difficult family life. Bouncing between the capital and his hometown in Hokkaidō, he had changed jobs frequently, suffered the abuses of factory work, spent time in and escaped from a reformatory, and eventually joined a gang of high-living juvenile criminals in Asakusa whose boss blew his nose with five-yen notes (a delinquent analog to the parvenu industrialists who used money to light their cigars). After three arduous years of probation—including an initial period in which he played on Gotō's sympathies by lying about his age and passing himself off as an abandoned child at the city shelter before escaping to commit more burglaries—Takeo reported a change of heart and declared that he planned to return to his family. This case could have ended otherwise: many children, especially those who had been in custody at the city shelter, tended to run away from their employers after only a few days, and not all of them came to regret their ways.[34] Caseworkers generally proceeded by trial and error until they found an option that seemed to work or until the youth somehow passed beyond their jurisdiction.

When possible, caseworkers endeavored to work closely with parents and relatives, but the harsh realities of life among the urban poor often severely challenged their abilities. In general terms, the standards of living of the urban lower classes were improving steadily, as Naka-gawa Kiyoshi has shown in his studies of Tokyo. By the late 1920s, for example, most of the dense slum concentrations of the pre-earthquake era had given way to more dispersed and discrete patterns of residence among Tokyo's poor (although some newer outlying concentrations persisted). In households, legal marriages surpassed common-law rela-tionships by roughly nine to one; 74 percent of wives stayed home focusing primarily on domestic rather than income-earning activities; 90 percent of children attended school (70 percent if one excludes those attending special elementary or night elementary courses); and only 14 percent of children were employed.[35] Yet, conversely, these figures demonstrate that a significant minority had not attained this level. And by and large, the lower classes remained extremely vulnerable to eco-nomic dislocations and—like the majority of the population—were hit particularly hard by events such as the 1923 earthquake and the depres-sion of the late 1920s and early 1930s.

Statistics on general trends regarding standards of living, further-more, do not reflect the transitions and ruptures within individual households that could affect the socialization process. A 1926 report by Tokyo's child-protection commissioners noted, for example, that nearly 60 percent of the delinquent children handled since 1920 had been raised in "abnormal" family contexts—that is, in homes lacking one or both natural parents or in homes with stepparents, adoptive parents, or other adults. Tokyo Juvenile Court statistics from 1923 to 1932 also indicate that roughly half of the youths given protective measures came from such backgrounds.[36] In the cases mentioned thus far in this chap-ter, Saitō Shūji had lost his mother, but Kuroda Takeo's upbringing offers an even starker example of the instability of many children's domestic situations. The illegitimate child of a woman who bore him when she was fifteen, he was raised by his grandparents until he turned nine, then by his parents (whom he had not previously met), and, after his father died, by his mother and her new boyfriend. Sent away to work because his mother now found his presence inconvenient, Takeo later returned to an equally uncomfortable situation when he found "a different stepfather I'd never seen before, a construction worker, and a couple of his henchmen hanging around the house."[37]

Under these circumstances, "reorganizing" the home constituted a main goal of the protection movement.[38] Probation officer Miyagi Tamayo's work with Saitō Shūji and his family, discussed earlier, represents the ideal to which the casework system aspired. The fact that Miyagi was a woman made this kind of radical intervention possible, for she and her superiors believed that female social workers or probation officers could bring both maternal love and practical knowledge of home economics to their tasks. But despite their increasing prominence, women remained a minority among professional and volunteer caseworkers, each of whom generally handled only a few cases at a time. While protection agents might offer economic advice or the occasional small sum, most interventions focused above all on finding means to contain problem children and resolve immediate conflicts.

Many of these conflicts involved abusive family situations. In one 1922 incident, for example, a "Mr. and Mrs. Okada" bound, beat, and kicked their fifteen-year-old daughter "Kiku" because she spent her wages, as well as household money she pilfered, on personal items and excursions to the movies with her friends, sometimes staying out until late at night. A landmark 1904 Supreme Court decision had recognized parents' right to restrain, confine, or strike their children so long as such measures did not cause injury or death or violate common-sense standards of cruelty, but this case clearly exceeded such norms, for neighbors, concerned that the Okadas were treating Kiku "as harshly as a policeman handles a criminal," alerted the authorities.[39] A Tokyo child-protection commissioner stepped in to offer repeated advice and reminded the parents that their daughter's moral judgment was impaired by her low intelligence. Kiku had in fact dropped out of second grade and worked since the age of nine, first as a live-in nursemaid and then commuting to various factory jobs. Her parents no doubt counted on and expected to control her wages. Mr. Okada, a nominally literate sixty-four-year-old, reported an "irregular" income from renting bedding to inhabitants of the family's slum neighborhood; fifty-two-year-old Mrs. Okada, who helped around the house, had never attended school and earned no income. Kiku's brother also worked in a factory, and the family rented one of the four rooms in their "extremely unhygienic" tenement to a family of boarders. To show her remorse, Kiku had shorn off her hair, but this only exacerbated the problem, since her despair at her appearance caused her to stop going to work.

After eleven months, the caseworker reported that the Okadas showed a less draconian attitude toward Kiku, who had resumed work at a local factory and no longer misbehaved. This intervention achieved multiple ends: the commissioner had protected Kiku from parental abuse and returned her to productive labor, had reeducated the Okadas and rendered them compliant to his authority, and had strengthened the family's finances by restoring parental control over the girl's income and time. Kiku, however, no longer enjoyed the opportunity to partake of new leisure activities with her friends—indeed, her own agency and desires had no place in an analysis that emphasized her lack of intelligence and her susceptibility to temptation. Yet faced with similar choices, other girls, as well as boys, may have been less accommodating.[40]

Caseworkers might also remove children from abusive environments. In 1924, a child-protection commissioner confronted the family of nine-year-old "Suzuki Kinnosuke," following reports that they had chained the boy's legs and locked him in a room to keep him from stealing and staying out on the streets. Kinnosuke, the offspring of a common-law relationship, had been shunted among various relatives for five years after his father, a factory watchman, had separated from his mother, described in the report only as a "loose woman." When he was finally returned to his father's home, the boy had to confront the antipathy of a new stepmother and two stepsisters. Sensing the tensions and the father's inability to provide proper supervision, the caseworker placed Kinnosuke in an apprenticeship, where he struggled for three years punctuated by episodes of theft and vagrancy (at the time when the commissioner composed his report, the case remained open).[41]

On occasion, protecting children involved realigning power balances within families. In 1926, the juvenile court referred to the prefecture Social Section the case of fourteen-year-old "Kimura Shigeko," a live-in maid and errand girl who had repeatedly stolen money from her employer's wallet.[42] Shigeko's mother, forty-one-year-old "Kimura Yasue," claimed that the girl's employer provided her with neither adequate spending money nor proper clothing, thus driving her to theft. Caseworker "S," however, accepted a local police officer's report that the mother had urged Shigeko to steal in order to acquire money to purchase alcohol for the mother's common-law husband "Eiji," an unskilled day laborer. Shigeko's father, a miner in Fukushima Prefecture, had died when she was ten, at which time Yasue took her four children to Tokyo and began working in a textile mill. But Yasue gave up her job after remarrying and depended on Eiji to provide for her children, one of whom was bedridden with a heart ailment (this boy, who had brought in a decent wage as a factory worker, died while the case was in progress). Experts at the Tokyo Prefecture Child Research Institute reported that Shigeko had an I.Q. of 57 and—as they found in many cases—a limited understanding of right and wrong. After placing the girl in the employ of a couple who ran a large inn, where she was to be clothed and given a small allowance, S persuaded Yasue to cooperate in planning for her daughter's future. Eiji, however, repeatedly barged into the inn, loudly demanded that the owners lend him money to settle his drinking debts, and threatened to take away Shigeko should they refuse. S arranged for the innkeepers to provide part of the required sum, asked the local drinking-house owner to serve Eiji only when he had money, and, together with Yasue, reprimanded Eiji at length.

New disputes erupted a few months later when Eiji, against Yasue's wishes, attempted to relieve his financial hardships by selling Shigeko to another employer. S visited Eiji at his workplace and, after lecturing him on his mistaken ways, demanded that he not interfere in decisions concerning Shigeko's future. The caseworker then secretly gave Yasue twenty yen, which the innkeepers provided, for use in an emergency, and continued to keep a close eye on the family. But S was not willing to do whatever Yasue thought was in her and her children's best interest. When at one point Yasue attempted to leave Eiji in anger over his scheming, S "got her to go home, despite her aversion to it." Yasue had gained an important ally in restraining Eiji's abusive behavior (and Eiji did show signs of improvement), but her economic dependence on her husband and the paucity of support services available to single mothers meant that the balance of power had not truly shifted in her favor. After two years and eight months on the case, S reported that Shigeko, at the ripe age of seventeen, was working in a tea shop; Eiji still had designs on the girl, the couple continued to fight, and "the greatest problems are yet to come."

Like Yasue, some parents or guardians welcomed help from protection agencies as a means to discipline their children or to escape what they felt to be unbearable or shameful situations. One father, for example, "shed tears of joy" when the juvenile court prescribed custodial treatment for his "unfilial" seventeen-year-old daughter, who had abandoned her factory job to play at the movies and then had run away, slept on the streets, been accosted by a delinquent man, and finally (through the intercession of a police detective) begun working at a café where she drank and caroused with her customers.[43] But reformers and families could also clash over the desired mode of treatment, especially when families demanded that their children be institutionalized.[44] Already in 1921, a report by the Tokyo Prefecture Social Section noted, "Once we begin to research cases, families expect us to implement some special protective measures, and their sense of responsibility for their children diminishes. If we cannot implement such measures, or if the steps we take do not fulfill their expectations, they become resentful." While acknowledging that such reactions stemmed from "a natural human emotion," the author emphasized the need to "persuade citizens that the collective protection of children requires responsibility, perseverance, and courage."[45]

Protecting children also required money, and the presence of an unruly child could threaten already unstable economic situations. As Saitō Shūji's father grumbled to juvenile court officers, "Today I can't work because I have to answer this summons. This runt will make the whole family starve to death. I sometimes think I should just kill him."[46] As in the United States and elsewhere, some families may well have regarded placement in reformatories or other custodial facilities as a temporary expedient given their marginal economic situations. In 1925, an administrator of the Yokohama Family School, the reformatory for girls, described how parents who had long been out of touch suddenly reappeared when their daughters reached marrying age, cowed administrators into releasing the girls, and immediately sold them to brothels. Other parents had daughters with venereal disease committed in order to receive medical treatment and then withdrew them as soon as they appeared fit for marriage; when one such girl died, the parents forced the reformatory to pay for her funeral.[47] These were perhaps the most egregious examples, but they, along with other cases discussed earlier, highlight the fact that adult family members (however families were constituted) could treat children according to determinations of economic or social utility that bore little relation to reformers' visions of proper domestic behavior or personal responsibility. Still, social workers and juvenile court officers did have children removed from their homes, albeit reluctantly, if they deemed that families were too poor or ill suited to care for them.

Many families (or family members) resisted reformers' overtures, however, prompting Tokyo social workers, schoolteachers, and juvenile court officers at a 1927 round-table discussion to remark upon the general difficulty of penetrating working-class homes. Citing the example of a uniformed Red Cross nurse who was told, "We don't have any contagious patients here," and was shoved unceremoniously back onto the street, Tokyo Social Section official Asahara Umeichi warned that if visitors "go dressed in clothes that are too different from those of the people they visit, they will provoke bad results." When visiting working-class homes, Asahara explained, caseworkers should dress and act like members of the working class. Should they display "the attitudes of officials or patrolmen," they would no doubt provoke "instinctive caution."[48] In the early years of the juvenile court, probation officers had investigated in pairs because they were afraid to enter delinquents' homes by themselves; but juvenile court officials soon encountered repeated charges of arrogance among commissioned probation officers. According to Osaka court director Furuya Shintarō, many officers in both Osaka and Tokyo failed to investigate cases properly or—in a description that calls to mind Edo-period police agents drawn from the ranks of the underworld—left the work to their "underlings" while keeping any monetary benefits for themselves. (Unlike district welfare commissioners, commissioned probation officers received stipends.) Some probation officers used their status as mid-ranking (sōnin) civil servants to pick fights with local police officers; a few got drunk on the job, losing case files or allowing their charges to escape. By the early 1930s, both the Tokyo and Osaka courts had dismissed large numbers of unqualified probation officers and had taken steps to professionalize the system, but public doubts remained.[49]

While some parents looked to schoolteachers to discipline their children, teachers' interventions in household affairs could also provoke anger or resentment. In "The White Walls" ("Shiroi kabe"), the proletarian novelist Honjo Mutsuo's 1934 story based on his experiences as a teacher in a Fukagawa slum, one father, an unemployed rice shop worker whose traditional skills became obsolete when the industry adopted the metric system, bridles at an instructor's suggestion that he buy eyeglasses for his mentally impaired son Yoshio. "What, are you kidding? With that kind of money we could eat for three days. If you say he needs those fancy glasses at school, you buy them for him." In fact, the father has visited an optician's shop, but he will not allow the teacher to dictate his behavior. When the teacher says, "But that's too unfortunate for Yoshio," the father explodes. "I'm the one who's unfortunate, living so long even though there's no more use for my skills! I won't have you commenting on my boy as well!" Another father vents his anger because his son, seeking to avoid being removed from school and placed in an apprenticeship, has insisted on consulting his teacher and has taken refuge in the school building. Pointing out that putting the boy out to work would reduce the number of mouths he has to feed, the father states, "Anyway, you've got no right to interfere with my son." The boy's stepmother chimes in, addressing the teacher in sarcastic tones: "In today's hard times, *you* get by unscathed, and make a good living playing with kids. We can't even scrape by."[50]

Yet Honjo also described parents who saw learning as the road to a better life, and Reigan Elementary teacher Kondō Kenzō recalled the plaintive appeals of one mother who wanted her child to have "an education like everyone else gets." These desires—or simply the need to survive—led many parents to see slum teachers, social workers, and the services they offered as valuable resources.[51] Those who did seek access to such resources, however, often exposed themselves to new forms of scrutiny and acquiesced, however reluctantly, in the reproduction of specific, morally determined images of their condition. Like late-Meiji reformers, many participants in the interwar juvenile protection movement viewed the poor and the working classes with a mixture of compassion and disdain: while recognizing that economic pressures prevented the poor from realizing their moral potential, Kondō and others nonetheless reproduced the standard tropes ("unable to control their instincts," "ruled by their desires") that had filled the pages of turn-of-the-century exposés.[52]

Children also displayed complex reactions. As seen in the foregoing examples, some children concocted stories to elicit authorities' sympathy, while others saw schoolteachers, social workers, or probation officers as allies in their efforts to build new lives or escape unpleasant family situations.[53] Yet others defended their families. In either case, many certainly found official scrutiny hard to bear. In Honjo's story of children assigned to a program for the mentally retarded, one boy reacts angrily when his instructor, as part of an intelligence test, queries him about his father's occupation. The instructor inwardly rationalizes this intrusion by telling himself, "I ask this only because a parent's occupation directly determines the child's intelligence, and this is the first item on the examination." The boy, however, is defiantly proud of his father, a river boatman struggling through hard times, and shows little patience for the teacher's inquiries: "Why the hell do you keep asking me things like a cop?" he demands. Other test items reveal a similar gulf between examination and examinee. Asked what he must do if he breaks something that belongs to someone else, the boy responds, "What a pain in the butt. I'd throw it in the mud. . . . If I did that, nobody'd know who broke it." (The "correct" answer was, "Apologize immediately.") What if a friend accidentally stepped on his foot? "Hey, I'd knock him over." The dejected teacher, who is himself from a poor family, had hoped the examination would prove that the boy had been labeled as retarded simply because of his poverty and dirty appearance. The teacher realizes that the clever pupil has rejected the premises upon which the examination is based, but the man is nonetheless required to record the boy's score as one which, according to psychological authorities, marks him as "unable to become a useful member of this society."[54]

As this episode reveals, far from being neutral technical assessments, mental evaluations often served to reinforce class and status hierarchies and degrade people's self-esteem. Tokyo Prefecture Juvenile Research Institute experts' findings of high rates of retardation and personality disorders among the children they classified as delinquent were no doubt shaped by the fact that the overwhelming majority of these children came from the working and petty commercial classes and few, like their parents, had completed even the compulsory elementary school course. Indeed, a study commissioned by the Tokyo City Social Bureau in 1930 found that intelligence correlated directly to parents' employment, from an average intelligence quotient of 104.3 for children of professionals to an average of 89.8 for children of unskilled laborers. To be sure, some experts disputed these findings, or at least recognized that economic conditions and different degrees of access to education lay behind the results. Others, however, equated low intelligence with moral backwardness and used such reports to justify a paternalistic approach to teaching the children of the working classes what was in their best interests.[55] Physical examinations, in which children were paraded naked before school medical staff, could also provoke humiliating experiences, as malnutrition and various ailments led to disparaging commentaries on pupils' social backgrounds. Parents and children alike confronted a symbolic violence that negated the culture in which they had been reared.[56]

Tensions with protection agencies also affected families trying to send their children out of the lower classes via the path of secondary schooling. High rates of elementary-school enrollment by the end of the Meiji era led, as Ōkado Masakatsu has noted, to a "massification" of secondary education, particularly in urban areas, during the interwar years.[57] By 1935, as noted earlier, Tokyo was home to between 140,000 and 160,000 secondary-school students "from an extremely complex mix of social strata"; and such schooling imposed heavy burdens on many families.[58] Members of the Tokyo Prefecture Secondary School Guidance Association, established in the same year, attempted to counsel poor families struggling to keep their children in school, to arrange part-time jobs for such students, and to prevent them from straying into delinquency. But a number of educators, social policy experts, and juvenile court officers questioned "ordinary," "middling," or working-class families' attempts to send their children beyond elementary school. In a 1935 case, for example, probation officer Morikawa Yoshiaki told one working-class couple that their son, who shoplifted and spent his time playing in Asakusa, would be better off in an apprenticeship than at his current vocational school. To Morikawa, the family's vanity had prompted them to pursue an educational path for which they were not suited.[59]

Although Morikawa yielded to the family's pleas to permit the boy to complete his studies and reported that the boy had improved his behavior and studied diligently, such accommodating responses were far from guaranteed, and the dangers of expulsion and social humiliation loomed large. One couple struggled to send their son to middle school in the hope that he could then enter a government-funded military academy, a prime career path for sons from non-elite families. When the boy was expelled for delinquency, a juvenile court officer recorded their lamentation: "We had no business sending him to middle school like other people; after all, we are carpenter types. If we had brought our son up to be a workingman like his father, we wouldn't have had this sad, shameful experience. Education is for the rich and the elites, not for the poor." This officer criticized schools' continuing eagerness to expel delinquent students, and hoped that the activities of the new Secondary School Guidance Association would lead to a decrease in expulsions.[60] Yet while the Tokyo Prefecture superintendent of schools explained in a 1935 article that the association rejected a "school police attitude," many teachers at middle schools and girls' high schools continued to polish their skills as detectives. In a 1937 contribution to the journal *Child Protection (Jidō Hogo)*, for example, Watanabe Ikkō urged his peers to adopt "the natural science of criminology" and advised them on how secretly to inspect male students' bags, desks, and clothes for shreds of tobacco, letters from or photographs of girls, and even semen stains. Home visits, he added, provided a means not only to impress parents but also to "catch the enemy at his weakest point."[61]

As in earlier years, the "enemy" could also be found throughout society, even among the most respectable strata. At the inaugural meeting of the Juvenile Protection Women's Association, for example, Yoshioka Yayoi, a leading doctor and educator, called attention to the problem of "boys and girls of cultivation" who fell into delinquency due to flaws in home education.[62] The juvenile court and other agencies in fact handled far fewer such cases than they did children from the working classes, but reformers actively stimulated parents' fears. In a 1934 book for the general public, *To Cry for Children (Ko no tame ni naku)*, Tokyo Juvenile Court director Suzuki Kaichirō, echoing earlier writers such as Tomeoka Kōsuke, explained that families from the propertied classes, governed by the evils of modern material civilization, tended to treat their children's education and character cultivation as a question of money, leaving everything in the hands of nursemaids, tutors, and other hired helpers. Upper-class parents, Suzuki claimed, were rarely present to care for their children when they returned from school; as a result, the children began to stay out late and spend time in coffee shops, at first using money they took from home but eventually finding thrills in stealing from others. Middle-class parents also had to be more attentive, Suzuki emphasized, pointing to the example of a mother and father who believed their boy to be a model student even as he skipped school, played with delinquent friends, stole, and was detained by the police for carousing with a female typist several years his senior.[63]

Suzuki and his colleagues offered advice to fathers, warning in particular against excessive strictness, but like professional child-rearing experts, they focused mainly on women, urging them to be "understanding mothers" who studied and made every effort to become their children's "best confidantes."[64] Daily newspapers' "home" columns and middle-class women's journals such as *Women's Friend* and *Women's Review (Fujin kōron)* helped to spread this message. The court encouraged parents to consult about their children's problems, guaranteed absolute discretion, and promised that its treatments would not, as a *Tōkyō Asahi* newspaper article put it, harm a child's "body, spirit, or eligibility"—the latter term included to assuage families' fears that involvement with the court could lead to expulsion from school.[65]

Yet families' desires to keep their children in secondary schools could also complicate the efforts of reformers, particularly when the latter suggested that such education was not in every youth's best interests. In 1920, for example (before the establishment of the juvenile court), the procurator's office referred to a Tokyo child-protection commissioner the case of "Terasaki Hideo," a seventeen-year-old student dropout arrested after he stole a theatergoer's wallet in Asakusa. The student's father, a section chief in the Imperial Household Ministry, adamantly resisted demands that he place his son in a reformatory—he had inquired about such institutions and found none to his liking—and opted instead to hire tutors to help the boy study for private middle school entrance examinations, which he failed repeatedly. At one point, the caseworker used personal connections to have the boy admitted to a school, but he was eventually expelled for absenteeism. For three years, Hideo repeatedly stole valuable family items, slept out, and roamed the city with a group of delinquent friends; his case ended not in reform but with military conscription, an event that gave the commissioner an excuse to close the file.[66] The juvenile court's Suzuki Kaichirō also described to his readers in cautionary terms a case in which wealthy parents' demands that their delinquent son be allowed to resume his life as a middle-school student almost derailed a probation officer's efforts. Not only did student toughs welcome the boy back as a respected "big brother," they almost succeeded in shipping him off to Manchuria (a popular outlet for ne'er-do-wells) to help him escape the pressures of probation.[67]

In other cases as well, authorities wrangled with affluent parents over the terms of probation. Some—for example, a widow who ran her family's successful cotton goods store and whose son had been arrested for embezzlement—pretended to cooperate with probation officers while in fact keeping them from prying any further into private affairs and possibly damaging hard-won local reputations. Naturally, detective-like schoolteachers, or teachers perceived as soliciting bribes to ensure children's scholastic success, received less than warm welcomes.[68] And as in less privileged households, adult members could disagree over how or if to approach the agencies of juvenile protection.

Statistical information concerning the effectiveness of social work and probation is partial and open to various interpretations. For example, in a 1926 report, the Tokyo Prefecture Social Section reported that child-protection commissioners had used home visits in 551 of 985 cases closed between 1920 and 1925, and that after subtracting cases settled when the youths in question were returned to places of origin, placed with relatives, or died, probation had produced positive results in 254 of 357 cases. In other cases, social workers' efforts were impeded by the Great Kantō Earthquake of 1923, which destroyed much of the city's infrastructure and scattered children and their families to locations beyond the commissioners' reach. Children's ages and educational levels also affected the outcomes. Subsequent figures are not available.[69]

Justice Ministry reports also suggest that probation by juvenile court officers largely achieved its aims. Of 6,621 probation orders terminated by the Tokyo Juvenile Court between 1923 and 1937, 73.9 percent were listed as due to "acceptable" results, 8 percent as due to "bad" results, and 9.9 percent as "whereabouts unknown." (The remainder were listed as "moved beyond court jurisdiction" or "other.") Reports from the Osaka and (after 1934) Nagoya courts reveal similar percentages. Given the mild nature of many cases, a few short visits may often have been all that was needed to settle them to the satisfaction of the authorities. Of course, the juvenile court reports offer no detailed definitions of "acceptable results." Some agents were no doubt more lenient or less meticulous than others, and determinations of reform rested on subjective evaluations. Moreover, the absence of delinquent behavior may in some cases have represented only the absence of *reported* delinquent behavior. Information about informal casework by district welfare commissioners or elementary- and middle-school teachers remains even more limited.[70]

Such caveats aside, social workers, probation officers, and educators infused social space at the local level with power that was, in Yoshio Sugimoto's phrase, visible and tangible, thus constraining the potential for continued delinquent behavior.[71] As important, interventions that went beyond the individual youth into his or her household served to articulate broad norms for family life and its relationship to external authority. For some juvenile court officers, this issue became tied up with the nature of the "Japanese family system," an ideological construct denoting an organic unit that managed its members' activities, mediated between the state and individuals, and underpinned the patriarchal "family-state" headed by the emperor. In a 1932 training manual for juvenile protection workers, for example, staff probation officer Tokunaga Kenjun argued that this system produced in young people a sense of solidarity with parents and siblings that was unforgettable even during moments of conflict; the most effective technique for probation officers was thus to teach parents and guardians how to use their children's sense of obligation to lead them toward better behavior.[72] Yet Suzuki Kaichirō, while lauding the strengths of the Japanese family system, complained after years of adjudicating juvenile cases that the system also led family members to conceal their affairs from public scrutiny and treat problems solely through "effort and sacrifice." Without the intervention of experts, Suzuki warned, families' "makeshift" methods were likely to fail. Or as the court's medical expert Narita Katsurō argued in 1937, the tendency to keep delinquent children from treatment until it was too late threatened to degrade the entire family's mental hygiene and its capacity to function as a cohesive unit; this phenomenon, he warned, was more corrosive to national solidarity than any foreign ideology.[73]

Such ideological fixation on the "Japanese family" notwithstanding, the examples discussed in this section suggest that specific family conditions and personal relationships, class, gender, or generational dynamics, and contingent events no doubt proved more salient than putatively ingrained cultural dispositions in shaping encounters with authorities. Still, juvenile court officers and others strove to rescue the Japanese family system, or in the case of those families deemed too eager to unload their problem children, endeavored to instill truly healthy "Japanese" family solidarity. To do so, these agents of protection—continuing the project undertaken by Tomeoka Kōsuke and his peers—strove to embed the family *(kazoku)* within a home *(katei)* in which traditional forms of patriarchal authority were modulated by new modes of domesticity, scientific knowledge, and openness to external authority. Indeed, the home lay at the core of the authorities' project to render surveillance ubiquitous. Wrote Suzuki in 1934: "If parents not only fear delinquency but also take care to immunize their children against exposure to it, then we will come closer to no longer needing protection [programs]. The reform and protection of the home—this is the method that we truly desire."[74] But when the home could not be trusted or an acceptable alternative setting arranged, authorities turned to institutional treatment.

INSTITUTIONAL TREATMENT:
BENEVOLENT EXPLOITATION?

Custodial treatment, of course, presented its own challenges. Reformatories under Home Ministry auspices, for example, continued to struggle with many of the same problems that had plagued them since their inception, even as they restricted admission to children under fourteen following the establishment of the juvenile courts. During the 1920s and 1930s, some fifty-five reformatories handled between two thousand and three thousand youths (almost all boys) each year; although a handful of these reformatories boasted large-scale, modern facilities, most were small and lacked adequate funds, and nearly two in five were either purely private institutions or surrogate public facilities not run directly by prefectural governments. In 1930, the thirtieth anniversary of the passage of the Reformatory Law, even sympathetic critics argued that staffs were overworked and poorly qualified and that children lacked proper food and clothing, lodged in drab quarters, and led "stultifying" lives. As one respected former reformatory director wrote: "While reformatories hold aloft the ideal of family-style treatment, the staffs' lifestyles differ greatly from those of their charges, as if in fact a relationship between masters and servants existed. Clearly, this situation not only damages youths' self-esteem; it also leads them to hate reformatory life."[75] Proletarian writer Fujimori Seikichi also highlighted this upstairs-downstairs relationship in his widely noted 1927 play (and 1930 hit film) *What Made Her Do It? (Nani ga kanojo o sō saseta ka)*, which in its climactic sequence has a long-suffering waif set fire to a Christian reformatory for girls in response to unjust treatment by a hypocritical, self-righteous principal.[76]

Although Fujimori presented the girl's act as one of resistance by a virtuous proletariat to a degenerate bourgeoisie, many professionals would have viewed it as the act of a victim of mental illness. The government did in 1933 revise the Reformatory Law, now called the Juvenile Educational Protection Law *(Shōnen kyōgo hō)*, to provide subsidies for more specialized clinical observation centers (as well as for probation by unpaid commissioners), but these programs were a far cry from experts' visions of an extensive system of psychiatric social work, and criticisms of the institutions continued unabated. Moreover, while relatively few inmates in real life chose to take a match to their reformatories, many did continue to resort to "unauthorized discharges" (i.e., escapes).[77]

The establishment of the juvenile courts, meanwhile, led the Justice Ministry to build its own custodial system for older adolescents who "engage in vagrancy, cannot receive appropriate upbringings at home, or who demonstrate an advanced degree of delinquency."[78] The Tokyo and Osaka courts each sent roughly seventy of the most difficult cases, all boys, to government-run juvenile training schools each year from 1923 to 1937. Many more wound up in private protective associations run by Buddhist, Christian, or other religious groups or by other reform-minded individuals. In 1923, thirty organizations took in 580 youths nationwide; fifteen years later, 114 organizations handled more than 5,000, including youths held pending adjudication. A handful of groups focused on delinquent girls, training them in domestic duties, while a small number of groups formed especially to treat feeble-minded youths, Korean youths, or others deemed to have particular needs.[79] In contrast to reformatories and training schools, these facilities, according to Protection Section chief Miyagi Chōgorō, were to be styled upon the private academies *(juku)* and temple schools *(terakoya)* which had in the pre-Meiji era served as "cultivation centers for children who

could not be led to the good only by their families' love." They would
be ordered by "the bonds between master and student," with youths
ranked according to their level of skill and each helping those less able.
Besides providing close personal relationships and practical training,
Miyagi anticipated that such facilities could take in large numbers of
students without having to expand their staffing budgets.[80]

A prime example of the new associations was Tokyo's Fukugyō
Chisankai, a Buddhist organization that was one of the first to work
with the juvenile court and that took as its goal, according to a 1938
report, "to raise artisans and manufacturing workers for the Honjo and
Fukagawa areas" east of the Sumida River. According to director
Fujisono Kentetsu, youths who had grown up in the "dark world" of
these working-class districts bore many psychological scars and suffered emotional problems that severely impinged upon their efficiency
as laborers. The association's program centered on training in non-
mechanized household industries such as woodworking, leatherwork-
ing, painting, furniture making, and chopstick manufacture, combined
with regular religious instruction. Administrators also imposed strictly
regimented schedules and, to encourage "spontaneous effort," made
group leaders responsible for overseeing and improving the work efficiency and personal conduct of each member of their group.[81]

In their emphasis on long days of work—making "lazy, selfish" delinquents "apply their heretofore wasted energies, which had poisoned
both state and society, to developing the national destiny," as Tokunaga
Kenjun put it—the protective associations differed little from the model
of reformatories as "a sort of vocational school" propounded by late-
Meiji reformers such as Tomeoka Kōsuke and Arima Shirōsuke.[82] In
fact, both Tomeoka's Family School and the girls' reformatory established by Arima accepted referrals from the Tokyo Juvenile Court. But
the emphasis on work raised other, serious problems. Because the juvenile courts provided only a meager *per diem* subsidy for each youth,
most associations relied on income from inmates' labor to keep their
enterprises solvent; some appear to have used their connection to the
juvenile court simply as a cover for exploiting young people placed in
their charge. In 1930, for example, the Metropolitan Police Department
reported that some facilities employing from thirty to a hundred boys
provided only minimal wages (at times as little as five *sen* for a full day's
work), filthy lodgings, inadequate food, and "absolutely no attention to
moral training." Ordinarily, enterprises of this scale would have been
cited for violations of the Factory Act, but protective association

managers applied to the MPD for exemptions—which were denied—on the grounds that these facilities were benevolent institutions! In effect, such operations replicated the kinds of environments that were believed to have driven many young people to delinquency.[83]

Agencies trumpeting the virtues of religion, farming, and fresh air revealed similar problems. In 1931, ninety boys went on a rampage at the Rokutōen Ōshima Farm, run by the Tenrikyō sect on an island in Izu Bay, destroying the farm's buildings and furnishings, razing the crops, and seriously injuring several staff members. In letters they sent to the Tōkyō Asahi newspaper, the boys' representatives complained that staff reduced the number of meals on rainy days when the boys could not work, beat them with baseball bats "until half dead" for complaining or attempting to escape, and denied them proper clothing, medical treatment, or schooling. "Our work is all for [the farm's] profit and not for our cultivation; they dress us like beggars and drive us like animals."[84]

In a few instances, it was not clear who was in charge. In 1927, the newspaper Hōritsu shinbun reported that a dormitory supervisor at one Buddhist facility actually encouraged inmates to go out and steal from neighboring houses, stores, and temples, took a share of the proceeds, and led the youths on excursions to downtown cafés and cinemas. The inmates then began to go out on their own initiative, paying the instructor to overlook their activities. This case was certainly exceptional, but it highlighted widespread doubts concerning the qualifications of protective association personnel—all the more because the staff member in question had graduated from a private college's social work program.[85]

Justice Ministry officials did attempt to eliminate what one euphemistically called "inappropriate methods."[86] In 1938, under the provisions of a new Legal Protection Operations Act (Shihō hogo jigyō hō), the ministry accorded official recognition and increased subsidies to the private protective associations, in exchange subjecting them to new licensing requirements and operating guidelines. The following year, the Japan Juvenile Protection Association established a research center and annual training courses for juvenile protection workers.[87] But such measures appear to have done little to assuage the public's suspicions.

Statistics underscore the questionable nature of protective associations' performance. Of 5,164 orders for treatment in protective associations that were terminated by the Tokyo Juvenile Court from 1923 to 1937, roughly 53 percent were recorded as having yielded "acceptable" results and nearly 12 percent "bad" results. The low number of bad results may have been the product of some statistical sleight of hand, however. In 1928, record keepers began reporting as "whereabouts unknown" large numbers of youths who in the preceding five years would have been recorded as bad results; from 1928 to 1937, this category accounted for roughly 32 percent of the total in Tokyo. Results for the Osaka court mirrored these trends.[88] "Whereabouts unknown," of course, suggests a large number of escapes. Indeed, a separate Justice Ministry survey found the escape rate to be extremely high; in 1937, it reached 48 percent of the total number of youths placed in protective associations. Moreover, in 1942, the highly respected director of one association noted that many agencies failed either to properly evaluate their charges or to follow up on former inmates' activities and thus grossly inflated the number of "good" results they reported. The new facilities also spawned their own underlives, complete with sexual exploitation of younger inmates by older ones and the proliferation of subcultural practices such as tattooing.[89] To those who were determined to socialize productive workers and useful national subjects, such outcomes were hardly encouraging.

These developments, of course, in many ways replicated the pattern observed in Home Ministry–affiliated reformatories, which Justice officials had accused of coddling their charges. And like reformatory administrators and experts since the 1910s, juvenile court officers and protective association managers pointed to youths' mental defects as a key factor in the shortcomings of the new programs, and called for the application of new diagnostic methods and specialized facilities. By the mid-1930s, both Home Ministry consultants such as Namae Takayuki and juvenile court officers such as Suzuki Kaichirō stepped up their calls for a national observation center, based on the model of Boston's Judge Baker Foundation, where psychiatrists, psychologists, sociologists, and others could cooperate in comprehensive evaluations of problem children.[90] Various experts also concurred that radical measures might be required for the most extreme cases. In 1931, the Tokyo Juvenile Court referred one family to a clinic where they had their son, a recidivist sexual offender, castrated. This, however, was an informal referral made at the request of the parents and (ostensibly) their son, and the only case of its kind on record. (Sexual offenses constituted only a small fraction of juvenile court cases.) Suzuki explained that while such treatments might be desirable in a number of cases, the court was at a loss to act because of the absence of specific legal provisions.[91]

Others pushed for a more eugenics-oriented approach. In 1937, Narita Katsurō argued that protective measures should be defined as mental hygiene measures, and that an absolute "law of hygiene," rather than any penal code, should govern the court's operations.[92] Some went even further. Hashimoto Katsutarō, a retired army officer who employed prominent researchers at the juvenile protective agency he established with the backing of then–prime minister Tanaka Giichi, vigorously called for laws for the sterilization of and restriction of marriage among individuals with "pronounced abnormal hereditary characteristics." Medical officers at the national juvenile training schools, several prominent reformatory administrators, and other experts in the diagnosis of juvenile problems joined Hashimoto in this campaign.[93] Their arguments no doubt contributed significantly to the debates surrounding the passage of the National Eugenics Act in 1940. However, as Sumiko Otsubo has shown, the Japanese government's principal concern in appropriating the language of eugenics was not to prevent the birth of "undesirable" people through sterilizations but to pursue a vigorous pronatalist policy "by tightening its control over unauthorized abortions performed on healthy people." Juvenile reform sources also suggest that Japan's pre-1945 eugenics programs entailed little in the way of implementation.[94]

Interwar social, educational, and criminal policies permitted the mobilization of a broad range of actors, both professionals and volunteers, to intervene in the everyday lives of potentially or actually delinquent children and their families. The growth of these programs, in which new-middle-class experts played leading roles, contributed to the increasing interpenetration of state and society and the articulation of a modern Japanese form of "collective social responsibility." Juvenile protection thus formed part of what Henry D. Smith has called the "nonliberal" or "small d" dimension of Taishō Democracy: people's increasing participation in various agencies—not only labor or tenant unions but also youth groups, women's groups, farmers' cooperatives, and reform campaigns—that determined the shape of their lives and the life of the nation.[95]

Dream as they might of creating a totalized system of surveillance and socialization, however, reformers confronted a thorny set of realities. Protection agents varied in their reliability, and a good number joined in pursuit of their own advantage rather than from any idealized sense of social solidarity. Clients often accommodated authorities' interventions only insofar as they perceived an advantage in doing so; within families, not everyone gauged opportunities and risks according to the same register.

Most importantly, protection agencies continued to lack the means to address the fundamental economic instability of the lower and working classes, from which most juvenile delinquents brought before the authorities hailed. Home Ministry officials sought to limit public assistance outlays, preferring instead to rely on unpaid district welfare commissioners to coordinate "neighborly mutual assistance" networks and morally reform the nation's poor. Although these commissioners lobbied successfully in 1929 for the passage of a Relief and Protection Law to replace the stringent 1874 Poor Relief Regulations, the new law continued to exclude all adults deemed capable of working.[96] Juvenile court officials, for their part, do not appear to have engaged in any serious public discussions of the structural impediments to improving lower- and working-class economic conditions. As in other countries, the "scientific" casework approach, while producing vivid empirical data about those conditions, often served to restrict the focus of treatment to individual or family disorders.[97] Meanwhile, by relying on custodial facilities that often exploited young workers in the name of redeeming them, authorities may well have contributed to reproducing the poverty and alienation that elites feared could destabilize Japan's social and political order. Juvenile protection agencies sought first and foremost simply to contain such dangerous energies, or, given the difficulties of both effectively monitoring everyday behavior and preventing escapes from institutions, at least to make it appear on paper that they had done so.

Officials could, however, point to the incompleteness of their efforts to justify even more vigorous initiatives. Wrote Suzuki Kaichirō, "We will not be able to speak of the results of protection until every member of society sees himself as a probation officer."[98] As Japan entered a period of increased militarization and "national crisis" after the Manchurian Incident of 1931, this vision of social solidarity began to blend smoothly into campaigns for total national mobilization.

While interwar reformers concurred that the main causes of delinquency could be found within the home, they also worked to reshape schooling to conform better to what they perceived to be the demands of an industrial capitalist economy and society, and they continued to clamp down on young people's participation in the morally dangerous world of urban play. These endeavors, as the following chapter shows, led to even more contests over the form and substance of Japanese modernity.

CHAPTER 5

Preparing Modern Workers, Policing Modern Play

Like their turn-of-the-century predecessors, social workers, juvenile court officers, and other reformers in the 1920s and 1930s often argued that young people's presence in the workforce rendered them particularly susceptible to delinquency. Japan's urban economy continued to rely heavily on youth labor; as noted previously, waves of youth immigration propelled the growth of Tokyo, Osaka, and other cities. In 1929, the *Ōsaka Mainichi* newspaper observed: "These annual infusions ensure the smooth functioning of urban life. . . . Without their young clerks and apprentices, stores and small factories would not be able to operate for a single day."[1] Nor, for that matter, could middle- and upper-class households do without their housemaids, or restaurants and cafés without their waitresses. According to experts, both the haphazard manner in which young people obtained employment and the harsh, stultifying conditions that many young workers experienced could lead to job switching, unemployment, vagrancy, crime, or, in the most extreme cases, to a radical rejection of the social and political order.[2] Some forms of work, particularly café waitressing, appeared by their very eroticized nature to promote moral degeneracy.

Reformers also continued to fret over young workers' exposure to the world of popular play. The vast majority of apprentices and clerks looked forward above all to the one or two days each month when, allowances in hand, they could abandon themselves to the "cheap, plentiful" sensory pleasures offered by the movie houses, theaters, game arcades, food shops, and drinking establishments of districts such as Tokyo's Asakusa.[3] Not surprisingly, for some youths this liminal world, where subcultural traditions rooted in the Edo past intermingled with "modern" styles of deviance, supplanted the world of work and conventional morality as the principal locus of identity formation. Their activities constituted a persistent feature of urban street life, and were given widespread publicity in daily news reports, "behind-the-scenes" accounts by urban chroniclers, and popular novels.

The question of young people's proper relation to work and play also shaped approaches to the urban middle classes, whose numbers had expanded dramatically due to the economic stimulus of World War I. In particular, the emergence of new working women in clerical and other service-sector positions struck the popular imagination as symbolic of not only the rapidity of Japan's modernization but also the challenges of a modernity that questioned established gender roles and celebrated new forms of consumerism. For just as they stood out in the workplace, unmarried young middle-class women, regardless of the realities of their own lives, attracted an inordinate amount of attention from both outraged moralizers and an intrigued media, which viewed these women as impulsive pleasure seekers and sexual adventurers oblivious to the needs of family and society. "Modern boys" and "class-cutting students" also figured prominently in this discourse on middle-class decadence.

Official responses to these perceived problems proceeded along two main tracks. To combat working-class deviance, advocates of "vocational guidance" prescribed the use of new curricula, employment agencies, child guidance clinics, and other institutions to modernize children's transition from school to work. As in probation programs, however, experts often confronted a variety of obstacles, not least of which was young people's own expectations of what modern education and modern life should provide. Meanwhile, the police continued to lead the charge to restrict young people's access, whatever their social position or age, to the realm of play. Police agents, who since the Meiji era defined themselves as the "people's nursemaids," had adopted social work methods in dealing with the poor, but they did not hesitate to apply raw coercive power against youthful behavior that contravened dominant notions of work, morality, and gender, and the police proved especially harsh in their dealings with older youths beyond the purview of the Juvenile Law. Reform experts might recoil at some of their methods, but Inspector Iijima Mitsuyasu, head of the Metropolitan Police Department's juvenile delinquency section in the late 1920s, explained:

"If we give [these kids] a good working over *(koppidoku yattsukeru)*, most of them get better."[4] Training for work and "a good working over" thus rounded out the state's policies for protecting youth.

THE RIGHT PERSON IN THE RIGHT PLACE

The discourse on protecting young workers evolved in tandem with broad changes in Japan's educational system during and after World War I, in the context of rapid industrialization and the spread of new social and political discourses associated with Taishō Democracy. As Byron Marshall notes, "The Meiji vision—a massive elementary school base with only limited necessity for middle-level schooling and even smaller segments of society advancing to college—now slowly gave ground to the pressures for greater opportunity at the secondary and even tertiary levels."[5] From 1912 to 1926, for example, the number of middle-school students climbed from 128,973 to 316,759; the number of vocational-school students rose from 74,869 to 233,433; and the number of girls'-high-school students rose from 75,128 to 326,208. In any given year, moreover, the number of applicants far outstripped the number who actually enrolled. But while the secondary-school student cohort gradually incorporated young people from less affluent strata, economic hardship prevented many more children who wanted to continue in school from pursuing such tracks.[6] In 1926, the Protestant social work expert Namae Takayuki, a close ally of the Home Ministry's Social Bureau, lamented that while the government and society took great care to provide for the needs of the mainly middle-to-upper-class youths who could attend secondary or higher schools, they virtually ignored the needs of the vast number of "young daily life warriors" to whom the doors of "bourgeois education" remained closed.[7] While liberal educational reformers promoted the idea of "people's middle schools," even conservative political parties included promises to promote education or equalize educational opportunities in their platforms. Leading heavy-industrial firms, which focused increasingly on hiring fourteen- to sixteen-year-olds as trainees, also demanded a better-educated entry-level workforce.[8]

The government did not ignore these voices. Although proposals to extend compulsory education from six to eight years (through the age of fourteen) failed to gain sufficient support, the government in 1926 revised the curriculum at two-year higher elementary schools *(kōtō shōgakkō)*, an optional program that constituted a popular alternative for children who could not pursue secondary education. In 1914, some 410,000 children (45 percent of compulsory-school graduates) went on to such programs, but in 1924 this number had climbed to roughly 700,000 (58 percent). Under the 1926 revisions, required subjects included handicrafts, drafting, and more advanced mathematics, as well as vocational courses (industry, agriculture, or commerce, and, for girls, home economics), all to be taught by subject-specialized instructors rather than generalist teachers. These schools also began to provide more intensive instruction in civics *(kōmin kyōiku)* as a means of addressing the growing importance of the masses in political life and of ensuring the primacy of a discourse of duties and responsibilities over one of freedoms and rights—a matter of particular concern to government elites following the spread of democratic ideas and the adoption of universal male suffrage in 1925, as well as to employers confronting a more assertive workforce. By the 1930s, more than 60 percent of sixth graders went on to these programs.[9]

As importantly, education and social policy experts developed new programs to rationalize the transition from school to work. "Vocational guidance" *(shokugyō shidō)*, which emphasized "placing the right person in the right place" through preparatory courses, mental and physical aptitude tests, and other methods, emerged as a keyword of the elementary, especially the higher elementary, school agenda, as well as of the juvenile protection movement. In some formulations, this program fused social Darwinist ideas with an emerging technocratic discourse on efficiency. In 1918, a contributor to the journal *Urban Education (Toshi kyōiku)*, predicting a postwar economic downturn and intensified competition for jobs and markets, argued: "In today's extremely fierce struggle for survival, one must select an occupation that suits one's nature and be able to work even a little more efficiently than others; if one takes any job without considering his own talents and suitability, he will doubtless wind up a social failure." When all Japanese were able to apply their talents in occupations to which they were suited, the author continued, "We will see remarkable advances in science and industry, and will easily achieve our goal of national wealth and strength." This vision gained force in the 1920s as many Japanese in government, business, and professional circles embraced Taylorism, Fordism, and German ideas of industrial rationalization as the way to improve productivity, lower production costs, increase exports, and promote workers' welfare.[10]

Vocational guidance also reflected the influence of progressive educators and social workers who, inspired by the ideas of John Dewey and others, called for a shift from schooling based on abstract ideas of "general cultivation" to more practical methods reflecting the "modernization, industrialization, and socialization of education." According to one contributor to the journal *Social Work (Shakai jigyō),* vocational guidance would teach children that labor was a form of "social service," undertaken out of a belief in social solidarity and collective responsibility.[11] The new programs also included a nod to those liberal pedagogues for whom, as Mark Lincicome notes, "the ideal of education was the full development of every person's natural abilities . . . and the harmonious or balanced development of a person's innate faculties." The Ministry of Education, perhaps seeking to assuage concerns that vocational guidance would involve bureaucratically dictating careers to those who had left school, underscored this position in a 1927 directive on the importance of respecting the character of the individual child.[12] All of these positions, moreover, accorded with the emphasis on individualized treatments based on careful diagnosis that informed the ideology of interwar social work and the juvenile courts. But while proponents emphasized their project's modernizing, clinical functions, they also reasoned, as Home Ministry Social Bureau chief Moriya Shigeo explained, that it would preserve the ethos of the traditional apprenticeship system by providing young workers with both practical and moral education in the context of ongoing personal relationships.[13]

Achieving this end required modifying existing relationships and eliminating "common, traditional" approaches to selecting employment. Parents, experts argued, could not properly evaluate their children's capabilities, lacked crucial information about job opportunities, and tended to base decisions on their own limited experiences. Employers ignored proper methods of hiring and treating young workers, while schoolteachers provided lackadaisical advice to pupils entering the workforce. Only by applying professional expertise to the integration of schools and the labor market could society and the state prevent the creation of what Moriya called "vocational cripples" prone to marginalization and deviant careers.[14]

Japan's major cities took the first steps to develop employment programs for young workers in the early 1920s. In Tokyo, for example, the Municipal Employment Agency in 1921 hired psychologists, doctors, and other experts to run a Youth Efficiency Testing and Counseling Center, which eventually evolved into a full-fledged women's and young people's employment agency with branches across the city. The Tokyo Prefecture Employment Agency also opened a youth vocational counseling center in 1925. In conjunction with the new Tokyo Vocational Guid-ance Association, the employment agencies developed school courses that explained the concept of work, surveyed the history of various trades, and offered pupils hands-on experience, and they dispatched experts to conduct mental tests and other evaluations at hundreds of elementary schools.[15]

At the national level, the Ministry of Education's Regular School Affairs Bureau and the Home Ministry's Social Bureau in 1925 issued a joint directive calling upon elementary-school teachers, public employ-ment agencies, doctors, and other experts to cooperate by forming com-mittees, when possible, to evaluate pupils, identify potential employers and labor market trends, guide pupils' families through the job place-ment process, and conduct follow-up surveys of working youths.[16] In 1932, fifty-seven such committees had been formed nationwide. By the same year, 279 employment agencies handled juvenile workers, attracting over 250,000 applicants aged eighteen or younger (75,000 of these were in Tokyo and 50,000 in Osaka), and some 4,800 elementary schools had established formal ties with these agencies. These numbers continued to grow over the course of the 1930s. Other young people contacted quasi-public employment agencies such as those run by the YMCA or the Women's Patriotic Association; increasing numbers of male and female secondary-school graduates also applied to the public employment agencies for the educated classes (chishiki kaikyū).[17]

But despite their claims to scientific knowledge, vocational-guidance and employment-agency personnel faced numerous challenges in their efforts to "place the right person in the right job." On the one hand, agencies received job advertisements mainly from small commercial and manufacturing enterprises that sought live-in shop clerks or appren-tices, or from households in search of maids or nursemaids. Such jobs, the traditional forms of juvenile employment outside the home, required long hours in exchange for limited pay and few if any opportunities for leisure. On the other hand, many applicants to the agencies—both grad-uates of local schools and large numbers of young people up from the provinces—sought to commute to jobs in the new economy: boys as clerks (jimuin) or errand boys (kyūji) in government offices and private corporations, and girls in similar positions or as department store clerks, telephone operators, or bus and streetcar conductors. Such jobs promised relatively high salaries, regular hours, and free time for per-sonal pursuits and continuing education, and thus exerted an appeal to "struggling students" aspiring to move up the social ladder.[18] A 1932 survey of 1,532 students in evening secondary schools in Tokyo, for example, revealed that 70 percent worked in offices or department stores. In an employment guide for young women published the same year, educator and journalist Kawasaki Natsu wrote that "one hears numerous stories of women who passed vocational qualifying examinations or who became such-and-such while working as office girls." Indeed, continuing education appeared to be the special privilege of young people in these jobs.[19]

Popular media reinforced these images. For example, *Boys' Club (Shōnen kurabu)*, one of the magazines most widely read by children in the upper elementary grades and by younger adolescents, regularly featured a column by "Kyūbei," a fictitious errand boy who described life behind the scenes at the magazine's editorial offices and urged readers to identify with his (and the publisher's) objectives. Kōdansha, the magazine's publisher, in fact adopted a policy of hiring large numbers of young boys, many from the provinces, as junior employees in the editorial and sales departments and providing them with ongoing education and practical career experience. Moreover, *Boys' Club* published fiction, such as Satō Kōroku's wildly successful *Flower in a Jeweled Cup (Aa gyokuhai ni hana ukete,* 1927), that emphasized young adolescents' striving against adversity to obtain higher education.[20]

Even a deepening economic depression and widespread unemployment among the educated classes in the late 1920s and early 1930s did not necessarily deter young people from pursuing their ambitions. Of the 12,228 graduates of Tokyo elementary schools in March 1932 who applied for work through the prefectural and municipal employment agencies, for example, 36 percent desired office or transport and communications jobs although only 4 percent of the positions listed fit those categories. More than seven boys responded to each posting for an office errand boy and more than three for a clerk's position. In contrast, only twenty-one boys applied for every one hundred retail store jobs and thirty-four boys for every one hundred manufacturing jobs advertised. Similarly, more than ten girls applied for each errand girl's position, more than seven for each communications or transportation job, and four for each clerk's job. Girls applied for retail jobs at a much higher rate than did boys (2.3 applications per job), but the jobs they sought were primarily in department stores rather than in smaller shops. Domestic service jobs drew applications at a rate of only 30 percent. Similar trends could be seen among graduates of girls' high schools.[21] Young people who could not obtain desirable positions through the public agencies most likely did not remain jobless (few if any could afford prolonged unemployment), but the types of jobs they ultimately found, and the channels through which they found them, cannot be ascertained from the official statistics.

While the *Tōkyō Asahi* newspaper might point out that this situation reflected young people's "extremely clear understanding" of jobs and conditions—in theory, a successful result of the development of higher elementary schooling and vocational guidance programs—others saw it as the fault of an educational system that "still reveres the ruling class and denigrates the productive working class."[22] In a 1933 contribution to a Tokyo social work journal, Ishihara Yoshiharu of the Home Ministry's Tokyo Regional Employment Agency Bureau lamented that the lack of attention to vocational education since the Meiji Restoration had "led children of Japan's working classes to see commuting to school as the sole means to achieve social status," even though the prospects for success through night schooling were limited and employment as an office boy was a dead-end situation. "Readers cannot imagine," he noted, "how many of today's juvenile delinquents once made hasty, short-term employment decisions out of a fantastic desire for honor."[23] The press also suggested that most "notorious" delinquent students were in fact office boys who took classes at night and lived on their own in boarding houses.[24] Various commentators also voiced concerns that young women's pursuit of clerical and transport employment deprived both younger and adult male workers of needed jobs, thus driving them to crime and delinquency. (Such critics also saw female clerical workers themselves as prone to delinquency.)[25]

Public employment agencies, which required that applicants have personal guarantors, were also unable to assist the growing numbers of "struggling students" who had run away from their homes in the provinces in pursuit of their dreams. Such youths often answered newspaper advertisements marked "Struggling Students Welcome" and found themselves hawking newspapers, delivering milk, or peddling other goods on the streets and in cafés late into the night and early in the morning; even as their debts for room and board mounted, they were too exhausted to attend school or stay awake once they got there. These conditions, authorities reported, led easily to vagrancy or delinquent careers.[26] Already in 1930, the *Tōkyō Asahi,* declaring that "it is no longer the age of the struggling student," trumpeted the dangers to elementary-school graduates coming to the capital lured by advertisements from unscrupulous brokers.[27] Young women, cautioned reformers and the press, faced the added threat of rape, kidnapping, and sale into prostitution by delinquents or shady procurers known as *ponbiki*.[28]

Although issued by urban bureaucrats, reformers, and editorialists, these warnings overlapped with interwar agrarianist discourses on the plight of the countryside, the tyranny of the cities, and what Stephen Vlastos has called "a deep and pervasive fear of Japanese farmers: the out-migration of village youths."[29] In a 1931 *Tōkyō Asahi* column, for example, the Christian social activist Yamada Waka told a poor graduate of a rural girls' high school that answering a dubious newspaper ad for struggling students in the hopes of eventually becoming a professional working woman was no way to repay the parents who had sacrificed so much for her education. In the midst of a devastating agrarian depression, Yamada exhorted her correspondent, "For your sake and the nation's sake, a better way is to go home and help your parents in their work. . . . If educated young men and women do not stay in their villages, then there can be no rural revitalization."[30] Vocational guidance programs in provincial schools also sought to fortify local economies and keep children from leaving for the cities. Still, in their drive to encourage pupils to aim for self-improvement, they published essays by alumni who had successfully worked their way through school in the capital and urged others to do the same. These immigrants continued to exacerbate the imbalance between types of supply and demand for youth labor in Tokyo and other cities into the mid-1930s.[31]

Employment agencies also proved unable to place many applicants who did seek live-in manufacturing and commercial positions, and officials recognized that the main obstacle lay in the exploitative conditions that prevailed in most small, individually owned enterprises.[32] Proletarian novelist Tokunaga Sunao's semi-autobiographical account of life at a rice merchant's shop suggests that the burdensome nature of such work had changed little since the Tokugawa era:

> From the start, I didn't really know what my job was. I had to do any-thing I was told to. I delivered rice, firewood, and soy sauce; I helped out with the hulling and cleaned the shop and office. When the nursemaid was busy in the kitchen, I carried around the baby. I massaged the Mrs.'s shoulders. I ran secret errands for Tora, the head clerk. When it suddenly rained, I had to rush over to the girls' school to bring an umbrella to the master's daughter O-Chiyo. And I was playmate to the master's son Kenzō [a middle-school student].[33]

A growing number of prospective apprentices and clerks also desired free time for night or correspondence courses, but as the *Yomiuri* newspaper reported in 1929, "virtually no employers are willing to provide this opportunity any more."[34] More importantly, many small businesses attempted to ride out the economic crisis of the 1920s and early 1930s on the backs of young workers, who commanded lower wages and fewer benefits than did adults, and these businesses saw the youth employment agencies as potential accomplices in their efforts.[35]

Many other employers tended simply to distrust the "scientific" vocational guidance programs implemented in the cities. Isomura Eiichi, a social work specialist with Marxist leanings, wrote in 1929 that employers found graduates of such programs to be "too intelligent and advanced," and preferred to hire children from the countryside.[36] As if to corroborate Isomura's claim, the Tokyo Prefecture Social Section found in a 1935 survey of nearly five thousand male apprentices in factories employing fewer than ten workers, that 75 percent came from outside Tokyo, some from as far as Nagano and Niigata prefectures. These youths, roughly half of whom lived with their employers, worked ten or more hours per day for minimal wages, and were frequently required to put in evening hours for no additional pay.[37]

Primogeniture and poverty created an available pool of such workers. Many no doubt came from backgrounds like that of the fifteen-year-old protagonist of another Tokunaga short story, "Airplane Shopboy" ("Hikōki kozō," 1937), whose father, having indentured him to a small factory near Tokyo, told him, "I have to leave our tenanted fields to your older brother. It's not that I want to treat you differently, but it can't be helped. Your body is your only capital, so work hard and don't even think of home or parents until you've become a skilled worker."[38] Despite generally rising education levels, a significant number of children from needy families continued to enter the workforce immediately following the sixth grade or even earlier. In February 1931, for example, a Tokyo daily reported that some four thousand lower-class boys in the city were bound for small shops whose owners had given parents cash advances of 150 yen, under contracts that would pay the boys no more than one yen in spending money each month for the nine years until they reached the age of conscription. "At this level," wrote one observer of neighborhood factories, "aptitude tests are meaningless." At a time when social critics wrote with alarm of impoverished rural families forced to sell their daughters to brothels, the Tokyo papers carried stories of growing numbers of lower-class parents indenturing their daughters to geisha houses.[39] Many other girls simply answered newspaper advertisements or window signs for waitresses in cafés, bars, restaurants, and coffee shops—jobs that, while seen by reformers as morally dangerous, required no education or special qualifications, were easily obtained, and just as easily abandoned.

As in earlier decades, social reformers feared the impact on young workers of harsh labor conditions largely devoid of the economic and social guarantees that had—in theory—underpinned the traditional apprenticeship system or, for girls, domestic service in "good homes" (although abuse or rape of housemaids was a widely noted phenomenon).[40] Mistreatment by employers, wrote Ishihara Yoshiharu in 1932, led youths with rebellious spirits to delinquency and crime, those with weak wills to suicide, and those with normal temperaments to job switching and unemployment.[41] Sociologist Miyoshi Toyotarō's 1936 study of the life histories of reformatory and children's shelter inmates in Tokyo offered ample evidence to support these concerns. One boy, a printing press worker's son, recounted his experience as follows: "As soon as I got out of elementary school, I was apprenticed to a barber in Adachi Ward. Not only did I have to work from six in the morning till after ten at night, but because there were no other employees, I had to do all the cleaning myself. On top of that, I didn't get enough to eat, so it was really tough." Scolded for taking some of his master's money to buy a snack, the boy quit, only to take a job in a liquor store where "they made me pedal around on a bicycle running errands from early morning to late at night; it was unbearable." He then absconded with ten yen, but was eventually apprehended. "Since then, I've been an apprentice at a rice shop, a bookbinder's, a liquor shop, and another bookbinder's, but I've always hated working and never lasted more than a couple of days."[42] This boy switched jobs more frequently than some of the others in Miyoshi's study, but the nature of his experiences was by no means atypical.

Groups such as the quasi-official Central Social Work Association, which had commissioned Miyoshi's study, drew on these findings (and Miyoshi himself went on the radio) to press for new laws to regulate working conditions. In 1938, these lobbying efforts contributed to the passage of a Commercial Stores Law (Shōten hō) that included provisions limiting working hours and guaranteeing vacation days. However, because it contained numerous loopholes and provided for delays in implementation, this legislation offered no real solutions to the problem; nor did it address the needs of young apprentices in the multitude of small-scale manufacturing establishments which were beyond the purview of the 1911 Factory Law.[43] Legal codes, furthermore, were of little use in shaping workplace cultures and the uses of leisure time, and observers continued to argue that exposure to "nihilistic" older workers and the lure of the streets and amusement centers drove shop clerks and apprentices to ruin. Young workers, went the common refrain, drank and smoked, stole employers' money, skipped work to go to movies and cafés, stayed out at night, and filled their minds with "thoughts of only sex."[44]

Reformers also emphasized the need for continuing education programs to provide both practical training and moral guidance to working youths. At the turn of the century, the national government had passed legislation providing for the establishment of a system of practical continuation schools *(jitsugyō hoshūkō)* to serve the needs of elementary-school graduates. Tokyo City operated a number of these schools during the 1920s, but few were located in the districts where most manufacturing and commercial establishments operated, and attendance remained low even at schools that did serve those areas. In 1926, at the initiative of the army and the Ministry of Education, the government established a new national system of youth training centers *(seinen kunrenjo)* to provide military drill, civic and moral education, and some vocational training to youths aged sixteen to twenty. Again, Tokyo, like other urban areas, reported low attendance rates through the 1930s.[45] Others looked to state-sponsored youth groups *(seinen-dan)* as the solution, since the army and the Education and Home ministries had used these groups to great effect to promote patriotism and community service in the countryside. In Tokyo Prefecture, however, membership in such associations was frequently limited to graduates of specific elementary schools or to sons of local notables; in 1930, for example, only 12.7 percent of eligible youths had in fact joined. Other public and private efforts to organize recreation or cultural activities for working boys also reached only a limited audience. Working girls, meanwhile, fell largely outside of the scope of the few continuing education programs that did emerge, as did the many young people who remained unemployed.[46]

Working-class youths thus developed their own forms of getting by in popular neighborhoods and amusement centers, and many did indeed pursue desires, defined both positively and negatively, in ways that tested the boundaries of the legal and moral order. While official reports on delinquency highlight the statistical preponderance of individual acts of petty larceny by young workers, frequent articles in the press suggest that various groups of friends, influenced by older traditions of youth

Figure 7. Young shop clerks, dressed for their day off, on the streets of Asakusa, 1937. Kuwabara Kineo. Courtesy of Kuwabara Kineo.

and new technologies of play, could also metamorphose into gangs with the ability to disrupt urban life.

STREET TOUGHS AND PROFESSIONAL DELINQUENTS

Working-youth gang culture had received little media attention during the heyday of student ruffianism, even among those who wrote about the problems of the lower class, but despite the increasing influence of elementary schools and new ideas of youth, the traditions of the *waka-mono* had continued as a basic feature of urban life in many neighborhoods. "Growing Up" ("Takekurabe"), Higuchi Ichiyō's 1895–96 story of children coming of age in a tenement district near the Yoshiwara licensed quarters, described a world still in touch with its Edo roots, where rivalries between gangs from different streets led to destructive clashes during festivals, where artisans' apprentices drifted into the gambling underworld, and where groups of "stout young fellows, glib and swaggering at sixteen," loitered in front of brothels, begging tobacco, pinching the girls, and picking fights. According to MPD Inspector Sakaguchi Shizuo, moreover, the decline of student ruffians after the Russo-Japanese War had created the space for clashes among working youths to emerge as the predominant form of urban fighting.[47] By the 1920s, newspapers regularly featured reports of groups of working and unemployed youths, often armed, who took pleasure in harassing, picking fights with, or mugging people on the streets, or in wreaking havoc in eating and drinking establishments. Such youths were referred to as *yotamono* or *yota*, "locals" *(jimawari)*, or simply as "no-goods" *(furyō)*.

Yotamono groups were largely male, but included some girls, occasionally in leadership positions. They congregated in cafés, coffee shops, movie theaters, parks, temple and shrine grounds, or empty houses across the city. Some groups were loosely structured, while others claimed affiliation to broader gang associations with names such as the Kantō Blue Dragons, as well as distinct territories.[48] Like the Edo *waka-mono*, these toughs pieced together identities by drawing on images of Japanese outlaw heroes, now amplified through the cinema and popular historical novels, as well as on the organizational patterns, dress, and argot of street hawkers, actors, construction workers, gamblers, and other groups with whom they came in contact. Others added elements derived from Western films—for example, gang names such as the Indians and the Apaches, or the slang of Asakusa delinquents who in the early 1920s called fighting "Eddie Polo-ing," after a popular action hero. They carried Japanese swords or daggers in red or white sheaths, but also knuckle-dusters and similar implements, called "American sacks," made from bicycle chains or scrap metal.[49]

Many of these youths sought nothing more than to kill time and have fun, however ephemeral, in a world of limited everyday prospects. Some, however, actually attempted to transcend those constraints, and occasionally built their fantasies around images projected from the imperial frontier. The boys and girls of Shibuya's Horseshoe Gang, for example, embezzled from their employers, mugged women and children, and extorted from café customers in an effort to save up ten thousand yen to start new careers as mounted bandits in Manchuria.[50] Such dreams notwithstanding, delinquent gangs, like the working-class youth "cliques" of Weimar Germany studied by Eve Rosenhaft, "offered no alternative to the existing system of economic and power relations and no escape for their members."[51] Hence, although some gang members proved more committed to, or unable to extricate themselves from, delinquent or criminal careers, the majority no doubt gradually shed their affiliations, perhaps (in the case of males) at the time of their military service.[52]

Local toughs' interactions with other youths, particularly students who entered the city's amusement spaces, suggest the complexity of their attitudes toward the dominant social structures. In some cases, delinquent play facilitated the formation of peer groups across class and status boundaries: for example, "Terasaki Hideo," the government official's son discussed in the preceding chapter, described his friends as truant students, boys posing as students, and street hawkers; they roamed around Asakusa and the Ginza together and slept in flophouses on the city outskirts.[53] In other cases, gangs mirrored mainstream social hierarchies. In 1923, Suzuki Kaichirō reported that a few gangs of factory workers were led by college students, and in 1925 the MPD broke up a gang of students "from bad homes," factory workers, and day laborers in which the leader, a middle-school teacher's son, allegedly took pride in being a "Taishō-era Ishikawa Goemon" (the reference is to a famed sixteenth-century robber) who bestowed stolen clothing on his less fortunate friends.[54]

But hierarchies could be subverted as well: Ishizumi Harunosuke reported that prior to the Great Earthquake, street gangs in Asakusa often accosted students, dragged them back to their hideouts and confined them there before forcing them to serve as their underlings and

commit various crimes. According to Suzuki Kaichirō, one such gang of
factory workers and vagrants, the Rabbits, targeted Keiō College boys;
the leader sported a Keiō cap and Keiō Commercial School pin along
with his gang tattoo.[55] Lower-class gangs could thus simultaneously
mock and embrace the symbols of the dominant culture. Like the turn-
of-the-century Parisian Apaches studied by Michelle Perrot, "They mim-
icked existing society, reproducing its hierarchies and its appetites. This
desire to imitate was even one of the sources of their aggressiveness."[56]

In working-class districts with strong street-knight traditions, locals
organized in part to repel incursions by student groups. In one 1927
incident in the northeastern district of Kita Senjū, for example, members of the Jacks, led by a nineteen-year-old carpenter, accosted a group
of middle-school students out for a walk along the Arakawa River levee
and stabbed one of them. According to the gang's leader, the victim's
brother had folded the bill of his cap in a style that caused the Jacks to
think that the boys were delinquents trying to muscle in on their turf; to
another gang member, the victim was an "uppity student."[57] Police officers noted that students were no match for "pure" delinquents in the
entertainment districts. One Asakusa tough scoffed in an interview that
students roughhousing like "heroes" in coffee shops were merely
"affected"; and officials, as well as the novelist Kawabata Yasunari,
warned that schoolboys adopting delinquent styles (a rumpled cap or
unbuttoned jacket was apparently all it took) would invariably become
prime targets for mugging and extortion.[58] Indeed, for working-class
toughs, mugging students, whether they were "semi-delinquents" or
just boys on their way to school or a movie, constituted not only a
source of income but also a declaration, as Joan Neuberger has written
of St. Petersburg's pre-1917 hooligans, of "the power to define street
behavior and assert control over the streets."[59]

Some students, however, relished the opportunity for a scuffle with
the locals. In 1934, police in the amusement district of Ōtsuka, on the
city's northern fringe, struggled to control students from the preparatory
division at Takushoku College who, besides threatening customers in
coffee shops and bars, went out looking for fights with neighborhood
delinquents. With their long hair, faded *haori* jackets and worn-out
hakama trousers, wooden swords, and flasks of saké dangling from their
waists, these students drew inspiration less from the *yotamono* style than
from the traditions of the Meiji-era *sōshi, bankara,* or *kōha* ruffians
(although the press also treated them as imitators of contemporary

criminal gangs). And given that these young men were enrolled in the Chinese language program at an institution established to promote Japanese colonialism, they appeared to be headed toward careers as "continental adventurers," hoodlums who often worked under the patronage of the Imperial Army. For such youths, seizing urban territory could be a prelude to the adventure of colonial conquest, while fighting with working-class toughs offered training for dealing with recalcitrant Chinese or Koreans. But Japan's imperial enterprise had room for working-class punks as well, and those who got into too much trouble at home could find a ready outlet in Korea or Manchuria.[60] The *yotamono* milieu also provided recruits for groups of thugs, the descendants of the Meiji-era *sōshi,* in the service of political parties, and no doubt served as a recruiting ground for strikebreakers or ultranationalist groups. In contrast (and unlike, for example, the German Communist Party, which needed all the manpower it could find for its battles with Nazi thugs), the parties of the left and the labor movement undertook no discernible efforts to mobilize the disaffections of the segment of the working or unemployed population from which most street toughs hailed.[61]

Local gangs continued to form throughout the interwar period, but police crackdowns, like those targeting violent gangs of street hawkers or adult criminal organizations into which *yotamono* sometimes blended, led to a weakening of their ability to impose their will on the urban landscape.[62] In Asakusa, Ishizumi Harunosuke observed in 1929 that the days when delinquents brought down "showers of blood" in the streets were over; large groups with notorious leaders had given way to smaller clusters of youths who preferred to use intimidation rather than actual violence.[63] In 1934, an Asakusa *yota,* "Hayabusa Ryū II" (a.k.a. Saitō Hideaki), described the transformation as follows, in the process highlighting the desires for self-aggrandizement, shock value, and control of social space that had informed street toughs' behavior:

> Five or six years ago, you used to be able to go into a coffee shop or café and get money from the owners, who were afraid of you and didn't want you around. If they didn't give you anything, you'd sit there for half a day drinking only a glass of water and giving menacing looks to the other customers. That would damage the shop's business. But today, [*yotamono*] are ingratiating themselves with café owners, trying to get a little spending money. The police have changed, too. . . . In my neighborhood, you don't really hear stories of guys getting all bloodied in knife fights over their names and turf. Things have gotten really petty, with everybody playing up to detectives, calling them "Boss, boss" and hoping to get treated nicely.[64]

In the more upscale Ginza and at suburban beaches as well, the police hauled in "delinquent kingpins" with "vicious nicknames and tattoos" who allegedly terrorized innocent citizens.[65] According to one contributor to a Tokyo social work journal, "One used to be able to recognize [*yotamono*] by the glint in their eyes or the clothes they wore. But at some point they began to come into close contact with normal people, adjusted to fit their ways, and were thus 'massified.'" But the *yotamono* had also, the writer suggested, been "castrated."[66] Like late-Meiji commentators, police officers and reporters from the 1920s and 1930s wrote of the decline of the ruffian *(kōha)* and the predominance of the rake *(nanpa)* style of delinquency, often in tones of regret tinged with cultural and gender anxiety. In 1930, the writer Satō Hachirō, himself a former juvenile delinquent, observed that "[male] delinquents can't earn a living any more. . . . Their skills have decayed, and the latest trend is for gangs to take on a beautiful girl as their leader."[67]

As with fallen girl students (a few of whom continued to figure in police and press reports), the number of "professional" delinquent girls was most likely not very high, but a few occupied a particular place in urban lore: some for their masculine toughness, but others for their sexual wiles.[68] Perhaps the most famous of the latter was Karatachi Oshin, the leader of the Hayabusa girl gang in Fukagawa who, as Suzuki Kaichirō put it in his 1923 study, "had by the age of 16 slept with over 150 men, fleeced them of several thousand yen, and lived a life of extreme luxury."[69] In the years from 1918 to the 1923 earthquake, actresses from the Asakusa opera, which despite its high-art name offered mainly operetta and music-hall fare, emerged as the newest type of delinquent. Onstage, these working-class women kicked up their legs and "[took] care to ogle everyone in the audience, earning gratitude as saviors from men who hunger for flesh," from "pimple-faced students and clean-shaven office workers [to] printing-press workers and young carpenters." Offstage, many acquired reputations for selling their sexual favors and lording over boisterous claques of fans known as *peragoro* (a contraction of the words "opera" and "gigolo") who competed for their attention with gifts and backstage visits, and who sometimes paid for their pursuits by mugging young students or other pedestrians.[70]

To the popular novelist Hamamoto Hiroshi, a self-proclaimed *peragoro,* the opera girls were largely innocent victims of seamy procurers, street hoodlums, and other debauched men. Other observers, such as social worker Kusama Yasoo and urban ethnographer Ishizumi Harunosuke, focused on the women's low pay and materialistic desires as causes of their misbehavior.[71] One might also consider these women's "delinquency" as a form of active engagement with the customs of the theatrical demimonde, in which cultivating a vocal fan base was a legitimate means of advancing one's career and gaining immediate material benefits. But causative factors did not particularly concern the police, who, following an approach to regulating actors and the theater inherited from the Tokugawa shogunate's dealings with *kabuki,* simply treated the women as disrupters of morals and expelled several from the district.[72]

The post-earthquake years produced few "legendary" female delinquents, but journalists and other investigators in the 1920s and 1930s wrote of runaway girls who drifted into Asakusa Park and from there into prostitution; of girls (sometimes masquerading as daughters of wealthy families) who seduced men and then robbed them while they were asleep; or of young women who lured "soft-looking" men (often students) into compromising situations so that male gang members could burst in, shout things like "What have you done to my sister? Now she's damaged goods!" and extort money from them.[73] Kawabata Yasunari's reportage-novel *The Crimson Gang of Asakusa* (*Asakusa kurenaidan,* 1929–30) also depicted a delinquent street gang as a loose formation centered on two young women, whom he used to symbolize the transformations wrought by the Great Earthquake. In the story's first half, the author follows Yumiko, an androgynous, occasionally cross-dressing quick-change artist, as she seeks to exact vengeance on the man who seduced and then abandoned her older sister during the post-earthquake disorder, driving her to insanity. This vendetta signifies, as Maeda Ai has noted, an attempt at "world renewal" (*yonaoshi*) and a restoration of gender balance: having witnessed her sister's fate, Yumiko has never allowed herself to become a real woman. But when Yumiko gives the man a poisoned kiss and disappears from the narrative, she is abruptly replaced by Haruko, a girl from the provinces who, after having been lured to Tokyo and abducted by a delinquent youth, has evolved into an audacious "modern geisha," taking pleasure in kissing several men in succession on the roof of one of the district's new ferro-concrete towers.[74]

Kawabata's delinquents were thoroughly enmeshed in the subterranean network of rules and obligations that kept order in Asakusa; Haruko, for example, dismisses the narrator's suggestion that these codes resembled the old customs of remote islands or African villages as the naive view of a student interloper.[75] But Haruko's unabashed mode of comportment, the public character of her transgressions, as the author presented them, signaled a sort of "modernization" of female delinquency, and they too could be read as an underworld variant on a broader social trend. Indeed, in a 1931 article in the journal *Reconstruction (Kaizō)*, Satō Hachirō suggested that this type of behavior had shifted from the margins of society to the mainstream: "These days, when I walk down the street, every young woman I meet seems to be a juvenile delinquent. Every one of them just looks like she's going to give me a wink when we pass. This is not just a product of my lewd thoughts." To Satō, Japan had entered an era when young women embraced "the delinquent girl as fashion," performing brazen acts for their shock value and walking the streets essentially proclaiming that their chastity was available for the taking. Japan, Satō lamented, perhaps with tongue in cheek, "is in big trouble." Straight-faced police officials and moral reformers agreed. While they continued to crack down on petty thieves, street toughs, and professional girls, the authorities devoted increasing efforts to stamping out the erotic play of a mass of "modern" youths driven by an "ideology of hedonism."[76]

"DELINQUENCY IN THE FORM OF UP-TEMPO LOVE"

Satō Hachirō's observation echoed a long series of commentaries on a new type of woman, the modern girl (also known by the derisive contraction *moga*), who had appeared on the streets and in the media in the years after the Great Kantō Earthquake of 1923.[77] With her Western clothes and bobbed hair, the modern girl symbolized a radically new form of women's social and sexual agency—a middle-class consumerist dynamo who thrived in the department stores, dance halls, and thoroughfares of the city's more upscale districts, particularly the Ginza. The actual number of women fitting the modern-girl stereotype may have been rather limited, but the press, as Satō Takeshi has noted, latched onto the *moga*, or more broadly the "modern aspect" for which she stood, and turned it into a "pseudo-event" for popular consumption.[78] Novels such as Tanizaki Jun'ichirō's *Naomi* (*Chijin no ai*, 1924–25), which depicted the title character's evolution from a child waitress in an Asakusa café to a ruthless vamp who dominated her middle-class husband and played in dance halls and at beach resorts with delinquent college boys and foreigners, also fueled this interest.[79] While intellectuals struggled to understand the significance of the modern girl in the context of the evolution of Japanese capitalism and

Figure 8. Modern girls posing in front of a new-model automobile, ca. 1930.
Source: The Mainichi Newspapers.

society, the police and other guardians of morality like the Women's
Christian Temperance Union treated her—and her counterpart, the
modern boy *(mobo)*, with his flared trousers and brushed-back hair—
above all as a delinquent libertine in need of surveillance and discipline.
Media representations thus evolved in tandem with police crackdowns,
each inspiring the other.

The modern girl, as Barbara Sato has noted, was in many ways "an
imaginary by-product of modernization," a discursive construct that
lacked "a clear social referent."[80] In practice, most of those labeled as
modern girls were unmarried young women employed in new, mainly
service-sector occupations that had opened up in the course of Japan's
rapid economic development since the First World War. The term
"working woman" *(shokugyō fujin)* also appeared in the media in the
1920s to denote this group, with some contemporaries using it to refer
primarily to women in white-collar jobs such as office employees, teachers, nurses, or journalists, and others adopting a more expansive definition that also encompassed bus conductors, elevator girls, store clerks,
café, bar, and restaurant waitresses, usherettes, actresses, taxi dancers,
and cleaning women.[81]

Of these various occupational types, office workers—typists, clerks, and telephone operators—figured most prominently in the myriad reports of the modern girl as juvenile delinquent during the 1920s. The precise number of women in white-collar office jobs during the interwar years is not known, but it was clearly growing. In 1924, for example, 3,500 of the 30,000 office workers commuting to Tokyo's Marunouchi business district were women; some 700 of them worked in the Marunouchi Building, or Marubiru, the edifice that most symbolized Japan's corporate modernity. In 1931, a survey of 818 relatively large companies and factories in Tokyo City reported that they employed 9,797 working women (as opposed to female laborers), of whom 5,551 were clerks, typists, and operators; this was not an exhaustive survey.[82] Compared to farm laborers, factory workers, or domestics, office workers (along with other new working women) represented a relatively small segment of the female workforce, but their new prominence in public life in roles other than those of daughter, student, or wife and mother marked them as objects of erotic fetishization and moral concern.[83] Indeed, in the public eye, young women's very presence in offices appeared to confound the fundamental distinction between places of work and places of play, turning the former into the latter.

In their crudest and most common form, depictions of office girls as juvenile delinquents focused obsessively on their alleged irresponsibility, consumerism, and sexual avarice. In 1924, for example, a leading daily reported the arrest of nineteen-year-old typist Hayashi Kimiko, whose good looks and glamorous appearance had earned her a reputation as "the top-rated beauty" in the Marunouchi Building. Although Kimiko subsequently quit her job in the wake of loud rumors about her numerous relationships with male office workers, she continued to appear once or twice a week at the Marubiru in her flashy clothing. Also known as "Jeanne d'Arc no Okimi," she was the notorious leader of a group of delinquent office girls called the Yotsuya Heart Gang, whose other members included "Carmen no O-Toyo"; when the police apprehended her, Kimiko was in a restaurant in Hongō cavorting with a group of students.[84] Three years later, MPD detectives investigating rumors about female office workers in the Marunouchi district reported that these women and their male coworkers were using the Marubiru as a "love market," gathering in the basement dining room at lunchtime to flirt over cups of coffee and plan after-work dates that would take them to suburban inns or houses of assignation. In shock, Inspector Gotō of the MPD's juvenile delinquency section declared that these young women

"are all worse than those that Tanizaki Jun'ichirō depicts in his novels."
One of the women investigated, twenty-one-year-old typist "Unno Matsuko," was reported to be cohabiting with one company employee from
the Marubiru while selling her favors to at least ten other male office
workers for sums ranging from ten to fifty yen. To the police, the problem was not simply that Matsuko was prostituting herself, but also that
she rejected the accusation: she declared that she had no intention of
marrying, that she associated with all of the men in question as friends,
and that the money involved represented unsolicited gifts.[85]

Complementing these news reports were literary works such as Asahara
Rokurō's "Unfolding Emotions in the Marunouchi" ("Marunouchi no
tenjō," 1930), which portrayed the modern office building as a home to
skirt-chasers, secret sex clubs, and "really shrewd" typists who devoted
their energies to finding wealthy men.[86] And in his 1930 film *Walk
Cheerfully (Hogaraka ni ayume),* an homage to American cinema and
style, Ozu Yasujirō depicted the modern girl typist as an indolent degenerate who spent her working hours polishing her nails, reading magazines, and chewing gum—which she parked on her typewriter—and her
evenings in a jazzed-up, neon-lit billiard hall called the Avalon Club,
seducing and shaking down well-to-do young men with the help of her
boyfriend "Ken the Knife" and his gang.[87]

On the other hand, police officials and other reformers, echoing an
earlier generation, pointed to men's exploitation of women's vanity or
what one educator called their essential "seduceability" as a key problem.[88] During the 1927 Marubiru investigations, for example, Inspector
Gotō emphasized the need to crack down on executives and other ranking employees who enticed innocent female workers with allowances
and eventually lured them on trips where the men had their way with
them; indeed, in the case of Unno Matsuko, one might wonder how
many young salarymen, whose starting monthly wages tended to range
from fifty to eighty-five yen, would have been able to provide fifty-yen
"allowances" to their lovers.[89] Socially conscious filmmakers offered
similar critiques. Ozu's *Walk Cheerfully,* for example, features a lecherous employer who tries to ensnare a virtuous young employee with an
expensive ring and later, abetted by the aforementioned delinquent
typist, by luring her to a hotel. The modern girl, the film suggests, may
herself once have been such an innocent.[90] Mizoguchi Kenji offered perhaps the most sympathetic interpretation of the delinquent office
worker and the most pointed critique of male hypocrisy in his 1936 film
Osaka Elegy (Naniwa eregii). The protagonist, a young switchboard

operator, is an exemplar of filial piety: in order to pay back the money that her father has embezzled from his company and to put her siblings through school, she becomes the consort of her employer and his circle of predatory older men. Arrested by the police following an altercation with one patron, she is rejected by the young salaryman she truly loves and is ultimately thrown out by her ungrateful family (the cowardly father having concealed the real cause of her behavior from his other children). The film closes with her on a downtown bridge, having defiantly accepted the label of "delinquent girl" and turning to brave the winds of adversity.[91] Yet while reformers and social critics—as well as working women themselves—might complain about delinquent employers, the police never actively pursued them.

They did, however, go after "delinquent foreigners." From May to July 1927, MPD agents rounded up foreign nationals accused of seducing or raping modern girls—office workers, café waitresses, movie actresses, and daughters of the bourgeoisie. The foreigners in question cruised dance halls, cinemas, cafés, and the Ginza thoroughfares, dazzling their prey with offers of rides home. (One police agent observed that working girls, who had little experience with automobiles, were particularly susceptible to this approach.) Other foreigners attracted women by posting matrimonial or help-wanted ads in the newspapers. In some cases, the perpetrators forced the women to accept money to make it appear a matter of consensual prostitution. Of the victims, the press reported, one eighteen-year-old wound up as a drifter who answered ads for café or restaurant waitresses, robbed her employers and coworkers, and then moved on to the next establishment.[92]

Stories of Japanese women's "worship of foreigners" (which, in the 1927 case and later cases, included not only Europeans and Americans but also Chinese and Filipinos), and reports that foreigners saw Japanese women as easy pickings, no doubt generated a source of national outrage. A similar concern, tinged by fears of Japanese male inadequacy in the face of these threats, provided grist for literary works such as Tanizaki's *Naomi* and Asahara's "Unfolding Emotions," in which the narrator regrets not having had the courage to "conquer the body" of a young typist before she became the mistress of a wealthy American— although in both stories it was precisely the modern girl's contact with the foreign and concomitant transformation into a vamp that rendered her so erotically attractive to the narrator.[93] But with few actual delinquent foreigners to pursue (in the 1927 crackdowns, the police questioned some thirty men and deported a handful of them), most official attention focused on modern boys and other young Japanese men as corrupters of women. The MPD's first crackdown on modern boys, the August 1927 raid on the Ginza discussed in the introduction to this book, was reportedly planned in response to complaints from elite families that their sons and daughters had been accosted by such well-dressed hoodlums.[94]

While the foregoing reports and representations focused on the activities, real or alleged, of a relatively small number of female office workers, the discourse on delinquency does point to changing life-expectations and patterns of social interaction among youths in or aspiring to join the urban middle class, and to the authorities' fears of those changes. The large majority of working girls took jobs to help support their families during the tight economic conditions of the 1920s and early 1930s, or to save money for marriage (another form of reducing parents' financial burdens). Although only a small percentage sought lifelong careers or true economic independence, many did see work as a form of education or personal cultivation *(shūyō)* that would make them better individuals and partners in companionate marriages, an ideal discussed in the women's magazines they read.[95] For others, work offered the opportunity to experience a good time free (albeit temporarily) from the constraints of school or marriage, and these young women could justify going out to play because they were contributing to their family economies. (Of course, some no doubt hoped to find a desirable marital partner in the process.) Surveys that reported earnest working women's complaints about their coworkers' excessive concern with clothing, cosmetics, and gossip reveal the contrasting forms of desire that shaped women's responses to new types and places of employment—responses that were also shaped by male employers' and coworkers' views of office girls as aesthetic or erotic accoutrements rather than as legitimate workers.[96] But even those who thought in terms of cultivation and companionate marriage often sought their life partners among coworkers or other men they met in public spaces outside working hours. It was in this period that the word *avekku* or *abekku,* from the French *avec,* gained currency as a term for couples on dates (although many people continued to refer to dates as *mikkai,* or secret encounters), and a market soon grew for manuals and guidebooks geared to their needs.[97]

Moreover, given that women's magazines offered not only discussions of marriage but also romance fiction and articles and advertisements about sex and contraception (while not affirming premarital sex), it is not surprising that growing numbers of young people showed themselves to be open to experimentation. Even adolescent male students read and sometimes wrote to women's magazines for information on sexual matters, and the Women's Christian Temperance Union and fellow women reformers pressed the Home Ministry to prohibit publishers from printing material that "poisons the minds of young women and men."[98] The results of new sexual encounters, of course, ranged from "success" in achieving a love marriage to regrets at having being abandoned by a disingenuous partner, or, worse, to having to deal with an unwanted pregnancy. The above-mentioned Unno Matsuko was first detained on suspicion, later confirmed, of having had an abortion, and in May 1927, Tokyo District Court procurators uncovered what they called a secret abortion ring involving typists and other office women in the Marunouchi district, as well as women working in dance halls and cafés. One man, the head of a certain "Family Planning Promotion Society," was sentenced to eighteen months in prison for having performed the abortions (taking advantage of the women's plights to charge exorbitant fees), and a female dance-hall worker received a two-month suspended sentence for having helped to arrange them. The women who requested these services were not prosecuted, but they did have to suffer the ignominy of interrogations that called into question their sex lives, family backgrounds, economic circumstances, and general character.[99] And so did many other young women and men who, whether in search of true love, sexual experiences, or just a night on the town, found themselves in police custody as "delinquent *mobo* and *moga*," as in the August 1929 police roundups that netted forty to fifty people each evening in the Ginza, Shinjuku, Shibuya, and Yotsuya. By late 1932, even couples sitting on park benches after dark were hauled in for questioning during increasingly zealous anti-delinquency campaigns.[100]

The "problem" of young women and men playing together also provoked widespread concerns about another central institution of Japanese modernity, the café, and the waitresses who served not only drinks and food but also conversation and commodified eroticism to male customers.[101] Café and bar waitresses, most of whom were between the ages of seventeen and twenty-three, hailed mainly from urban and rural working-class backgrounds, and surveys showed that the majority, like office workers, took jobs above all to help support their families. A 1926 study of nearly three thousand waitresses in Tokyo and Osaka conducted by the Central Employment Agency Bureau, for example, found that 27 percent of respondents came from homes in which there was a mother but no father and 80 percent from homes with between three and nine siblings. Because waitressing required no training and appeared to pay better than other jobs, it also attracted large numbers of women who had previously worked elsewhere—not only maids and factory girls but also store clerks and even office workers.[102] While the overwhelming majority had not attended school beyond the elementary grades (94 percent, according to a 1929 MPD survey of 13,849 Tokyo waitresses), a growing number, primarily in the more upscale cafés, had attended girls' high schools. These "modern waitresses with new minds," suggested social worker Kusama Yasoo in 1930, were responsible for the gradual transformation of the pleasure trade away from the forms of interaction associated with the geisha.[103]

For many students and unmarried salarymen, as journalist Murashima Yoriyuki noted in 1929, going to a café was the only way to meet women. Although Murashima claimed that these youthful customers sought a "love feeling" more than the fulfillment of carnal desires and preferred the process of erotic negotiation to the actual consummation of a sexual relationship, many waitresses complained about importunate or repugnant customers of all ages. "I was off to buy me a prostitute, but I've taken a liking to you, so how about it?" says one man in Hayashi Fumiko's 1929 *Diary of a Vagabond (Hōrōki)*, a text inspired by her own work experiences. As Hayashi shows, some women devised humiliating ways to rebuff their pursuers.[104] On the other hand, a good number, like office workers, seized the opportunity to enjoy the pleasures of city life in the company of men of their own choosing.[105] From the perspective of reformers, however, the most serious problem surrounding café waitresses was the apparent tendency of many to move from seductive performance to casual prostitution.

The economics of the café combined with waitresses' own living conditions to encourage this trend. While waitresses aged thirteen to sixteen worked for a fixed wage, most aged seventeen and older worked for tips, and were thus under pressure to ingratiate themselves with their customers. In addition to purchasing their own clothing, cosmetics, and other necessities, these waitresses also had to pay café owners daily fees, called *desen* in Tokyo, to cover their evening meals and overhead costs such as cooks' and busboys' wages or replacing lost or damaged tableware. (Waitresses also had to pay fines if they were late, missed work, or left during their shifts to play with customers.) *Desen* generally ranged from fifty sen to one yen per day; some café owners also skimmed 10 to 15 percent of waitresses' tips, while others implemented compulsory savings systems designed above all to keep attractive waitresses from moving, which they nonetheless did quite frequently. While the roughly 2 percent of Tokyo waitresses (according to the 1926 survey cited earlier) who earned one hundred yen or more per month in first-class cafés could afford the fees, the 87 percent who earned less than sixty yen per month in second- or third-class establishments certainly saw them as an onerous burden.[106] And because tips did not come in on a regular basis, police investigators found that "[o]n rainy nights when there are few customers, waitresses don't even have train fare for the ride home." Such conditions left the women open to sexual advances by customers. "That's why I'd go with them," admitted one former waitress, who had drifted into an Asakusa delinquent gang, to a writer for the women's magazine *Women's Salon (Fujin saron)* in 1931.[107]

Moreover, café owners pressured their staffs to offer "erotic service" as a means to attract and keep free-spending customers, who were increasingly rare as the economy declined in the late 1920s. Osaka's cafés were particularly notorious for these methods, but Tokyo establishments by no means enjoyed an impeccable reputation. In any case, Osaka entrepreneurs rapidly took over sections of the Ginza, thus fueling Tokyo authorities' fears of an increase in unregulated commercial licentiousness. The number of cafés and bars grew at an explosive pace. In 1929, the MPD reported that there were 6,187 cafés and 13,849 waitresses in Tokyo; three years later, there were more than 7,500 cafés and nearly 23,000 waitresses.[108]

As with the fallen office girl, various commentators argued that waitresses were victims of gender and class oppression. No one wrote more persuasively of these matters than Hayashi Fumiko, whose *Diary of a Vagabond* is filled with the voices of women who have suffered at the hands of men in whom they had mistakenly placed their trust. As one character laments: "'Never leave me, okay?' or 'I've fallen for you.' You know, I've had enough of foolish things like love and endearments. These promises don't mean a thing. The man who did this to me is even a member of the Diet. As soon as he got me pregnant, he was out the door. If you bear an illegitimate child, everybody says that you're a modern girl, but it's still shameless." In 1929, an MPD officer also explained that while half of the waitresses and dancers his agents had detained acted from a desire for money, the other half had been corrupted and exploited by delinquent *mobos,* mainly well-to-do types, who took sport in such behavior.[109] Such experiences may also have led waitresses to see casual

Figure 9. Café Ultra, Ueno, 1937. Kuwabara Kineo. The placard on the right reads, "The ease of a coffee shop with the steaminess of a café—a passion factory." The one on the left reads, "Enjoy a cheerful cup of coffee in the uninterrupted company of an Ultra girl!" The sign on the door (center) reads, "Waitresses wanted—urgent, due to popular demand." Courtesy of Kuwabara Kineo.

prostitution as an acceptable activity. As U.S. historian Christine Stansell has observed, prostitution could "be an act of shrewdness, prompted by a woman's comprehension of the power relations in which she found herself. . . . To sell her favors for money was a logical countermove in a sexual system in which men might take what they could get—sometimes through rape—and turn their backs on the consequences. To exact a price from a man, hard cash, must have held some appeal to a woman whose last lover had just skipped off scot-free." But while prostitution was rarely "a deliberate bid for control," it could, in some cases, provide waitresses with the means to enter, again to use Stansell's words, "the urban youth culture to which they aspired." (The same may be said for those low-paid office workers, however few or many they may have been, who chose to commodify their erotic behavior.)[110]

To the Metropolitan Police Department, of course, prostitution and urban youth culture equally merited repression. In mid-1929, at the same time that they rounded up *mobo* and *moga* in the various entertainment districts, the police imposed strict new controls on cafés. One news report quoted MPD Superintendent Maruyama Tsurukichi (nicknamed "The Demon") on the goals of this new approach: "Let's make it clear: we're going to crack down on all of them. The plan is to wipe out dance halls and turn cafés into cafeterias. Waitresses: what in the world are they? They put on white aprons and say things to their customers like, 'Let's run off together on the Odakyū line.'" (Maruyama was referring to a lyric from the popular "Tokyo Marching Song.") Like his counterparts in Osaka, Maruyama succeeded in eliminating the *desen* system and in regulating café décors as part of his effort to turn waitresses into upstanding working women. But café owners found other ways of imposing charges on their employees, and erotic service remained a fixture at many establishments, especially those off the main thoroughfares, prompting further police interventions. Meanwhile, the police implemented a regime of strict surveillance with regard to the activities of café and bar waitresses, who were prohibited, among other things, from leaving work in the company of their customers.[111]

The fact that many of these customers were college and middle-school students most outraged "Demon" Maruyama and the middle-class moral reform groups, such as the Women's Christian Temperance Union (WCTU) and the Salvation Army, with which he had long been allied. As the superintendent fumed, "[Led on by waitresses,] students who live off their parents, don't study at all, and spend their time in cafés give such big tips using money they've never earned. It's disgraceful.

In the first place, they're students!"[112] Following the 1929 crackdowns, Ginza cafés began posting signs refusing entry to students in uniform, but these were voluntary measures. Most students in fact couldn't afford the Ginza cafés, where one had to spend a huge sum to be considered a good customer. But cafés in other districts, particularly Kanda, with its many schools, continued to see students as valuable customers, and some cafés tried to attract them with free drink coupons. And in Shinjuku, where the railway station serving as a hub for commuters from the Western suburbs also functioned as a meeting point for daters, police officers reported their astonishment at seeing "female students, waitresses, and middle-school boys in various combinations."[113]

Dance halls, where young men could pay to spend time in the arms of a taxi dancer and possibly arrange to meet her after hours, proved equally appalling to moral reformers. The first halls opened in 1925, and in Tokyo in the same year, the MPD issued an ordinance prohibiting "underage students" from entering them. Osaka Prefecture outlawed dance halls in 1927, but they continued to thrive in the capital, prompting new crackdowns by the MPD's juvenile delinquency and vice brigades in 1929 that compelled a number of halls to close. Reformers such as the WCTU's Hayashi Utako wholeheartedly endorsed these measures, remarking that dance halls were inappropriate to a society in which young people had not been taught how to relate to members of the opposite sex.[114] But students, as well as other young men, continued to dance and to look for dates. And while dancers had to be increasingly cautious about going out with their clients for fear of losing their jobs and their police-issued dancer's permits, police in the mid-1930s continued to report problems with dancers who took "students, *yotamono*, and wealthy men" as their lovers; one police officer also opined that female students and other young women who played in dance halls would most likely become delinquents, get pregnant, leave home, and wind up as dancers themselves.[115] Some students, picking up where the pre-1923 *peragoro* left off, spent their evenings chasing dancers from the revues in Asakusa; others, in middle schools as well as colleges, continued to venture into the unlicensed brothels of Tamanoi and Kameido. The greatest number, however, simply spent hours in coffee shops *(kissaten)* conversing, listening to music, or looking at the young waitresses who, unlike those in cafés and bars, did not offer erotic service. Echoing their Meiji predecessors, police officers argued that such students were likely to spend their tuition fees in these places and then turn to mugging or extortion to support their habits.[116]

In response, the MPD in 1929 began to summon the parents of "class-cutting students" from the provinces in order to have them take their children out of Tokyo. Police raids also targeted students in movie theaters or eateries during final examination weeks, students shuffling down the streets of Kanda in step with the jazz emanating from café entrances, or students simply walking around snacking on roasted potatoes. In 1934, with the active prodding of the WCTU and other reform groups and the consent of college administrators and education officials, the MPD issued strict prohibitions against students frequenting cafés, bars, coffee shops, and other establishments that employed waitresses.[117] Not every student was a student, though. Many boys who did not attend any schools frequently masqueraded as students in order to play in cafés and meet girls (or, in a few cases, kidnap them); in one instance, the *Tokyo Asahi* reported that a group of schoolgirls in Senjū had pooled their money to buy college uniforms for their boyfriends, neighborhood delinquents, so that they could go out to "play *moga* and *mobo*" in the Ginza, Shinjuku, and Asakusa. As one educator involved in secondary-school extracurricular surveillance programs remarked after a 1935 inspection, "The most difficult problem was determining who was a student and who was not. . . . Today, everyone between the ages of 15 and around 20 wears a student outfit" (as, in fact, did many in their early twenties).[118] The police and their allies strove to distinguish between real and fake students and thus to reinforce status and class hierarchies, but the confusion of visible markers also led, conversely, to the imperative of making everyone conform to the behavioral norms of dependent adolescents.

Police campaigns against student profligacy coincided with government crackdowns on radicalism in Japan's universities and higher schools, particularly after many students were swept up in the mass arrests of suspected communists and communist sympathizers on March 15, 1928. Although contemporary observers treated these two developments separately, both targeted deviant behavior that was often attributed to pernicious "foreign" influences—be they Marxist theory or jazz rhythms—that contravened Japanese national morality and threatened to subvert the emperor-centered national polity. By the early 1930s, left-wing student radicalism had been effectively suppressed and, in the wake of the Manchurian Incident, many young leftists had converted to nationalism.[119] In the eyes of the MPD, however, students at play posed a continuing threat because they had not awakened to their true responsibilities as Japanese subjects.

The outbreak of war with China in July 1937 only exacerbated police anger at students' alleged indifference to Japan's "national emergency." In February 1938, Tokyo officers conducted a massive three-day sweep in which they arrested 7,373 youths (7,032 males and 341 females) in cafés, coffee shops, movie theaters, billiard halls, mah-jongg clubs, department stores, and other amusement centers. Slightly over half of those detained were in fact working or unemployed youths as opposed to enrolled students (some were fake students), but the presence of large numbers of students fueled further police actions, which the media labeled "student roundups."[120] In June, officers focused in particular on the neon-lit streets around Waseda University, where "drinking and eating establishments and mah jongg clubs surround the academy like the walls of a castle." Explained MPD Superintendent Abe Genki: "I'm not saying that it's always bad for students to go to coffee shops, billiard halls, or mah-jongg parlors, but I want them to think more seriously about the current situation. At a time when their brothers are risking their lives for the state in battle at the front, how can [students] use money that their parents have sweated for on the home front to immerse themselves in the indolent atmosphere of coffee shops and bars? The issue is their state of mind."[121]

During the Waseda roundup, however, many of those arrested were guilty of nothing more than having spent their lunch breaks or free time in off-campus dining establishments—a necessity, given the paucity of on-campus lounges or eating facilities.[122] As with prior police sweeps, it often took very little in order for students to be labeled as both a social problem and an object of special protection. One young man, detained while going to see newsreels of the China war during a free moment of the day, fumed to a journalist, "When I asked what was wrong with viewing a healthy picture, the plainclothesman in charge answered that I should not have gone to the movies in my university uniform. I should have gone home first, he said, obtained my parents' permission and then gone with some member of my family—just like a primary-school child." The detective, more like the strict schoolmarm than the people's nursemaid, urged the young man: "Put your hand over your heart and think. . . . If [you don't understand], you must spend the night here and think."[123]

In response, students and administrators from Waseda University and even some Ministry of Education officials denounced the MPD for its unjustified, excessive morals policing. Waseda, furthermore, had cultivated a spirit of independence since its establishment during the Meiji-era

Movement for Freedom and People's Rights; thus, the preservation of university autonomy was at stake. To secure this, university officials promised to strengthen their "spiritual education" programs and student leaders pledged to conduct their own efforts to keep students from engaging in behavior unbecoming their status. The police, however, refused to cease their interventions, instead taking a wait-and-see attitude.[124] Meanwhile, in Waseda, according to one report, "all waitresses between the ages of 16 and 35 were compelled to leave the employ of tearooms and cafés catering to student trade by the end of August [1938]. . . . The very young girls and middle-aged waitresses beyond the pale of this decree were ordered to dress modestly and inconspicuously." Faced with these and other regulations affecting furnishings, illumination, and window curtains, most cafés around the university soon went out of business.[125]

The threat of student roundups affected not only colleges but also secondary schools. In June 1938, for example, Education Minister Araki Sadao—an army officer known for his close ties to the ultranationalist "Imperial Way" faction that had staged a failed coup d'état in February 1936—admonished an assembly of normal-school principals not to wait for other agencies to exercise their policing powers but rather to take the initiative in enforcing discipline and uplifting students' characters. And one month after the Waseda incidents, the Ministry of Education warned middle-school and girls'-high-school students to rectify their behavior lest they become the next targets of police actions. Girls in particular were denounced for their "modern" ways: going to the movies, chatting in coffee shops using incomprehensible mixtures of foreign words, neologisms, and masculine speech, and seeking autographs from actors, all-girl revue actresses, athletes, and foreigners.[126] The outbreak of war and the increasing military role in civil government not only fueled new concerns with the "spiritual mobilization" of students, but also permitted police agents and middle-class reformers to realize their long-standing desire to delimit the spaces of student activity and "purify" student life.

Police campaigns against youth culture had been a constant feature of urban life since the turn of the century, but their scope and intensity clearly grew in response to officials' and reformers' perceptions that interwar modernization had radically destabilized orthodox constructions of class, status, family, gender, and sexuality and that national crises, especially Japan's growing military involvement on the Asian continent, required the reinforcement of behavioral norms linking modernity to self-discipline and sacrifice in the name of nation and empire. By the late 1930s, police interventions had greatly constrained the more flamboyant manifestations of urban youth culture—from street toughs to modern girls, modern boys, and pleasure-seeking students—and had imposed tight controls on the behavior of those young people, particularly café waitresses, whose work required their presence in the morally dubious spaces of popular entertainment. Eventually, police officers were joined on the streets by "children's loving protection commissioners" *(jidō aigo iin)* appointed by the Justice Ministry and "children's educational protection commissioners" *(jidō kyōgo iin)* deputized by the Home Ministry.[127]

Repressive measures could not, of course, address the many factors that had led young people into the worlds of play or delinquency in the first place; on the contrary, the state's increasing reliance on such heavy-handed approaches only underscored the persistent shortcomings of reformers' efforts to construct a comprehensive system of socialization and protection. In this regard, although sensational allegations of middle-class decadence greatly perturbed middle-class reformers who feared for their own legitimacy as standard-bearers of Japanese national progress, the question of how to integrate young members of the working classes into society remained a potentially greater problem. And notwithstanding the notoriety of the café waitress—who attracted the attention of reformers as much because of her alleged effect on middle-class morality as from a concern for her own needs—social policy authorities treated the conditions governing young male workers' lives as the core issue in need of resolution. Indeed, many vocational guidance experts continued to believe that women's careers should be centered on the home, with paid work serving at most as a supplement to a man's income.[128] In a labor market dominated by small, unstable businesses, however, those experts could guarantee most of their young male clients neither decent working conditions nor certain career (or marital) futures. And in a rapidly changing society in which the dominant ideology linked individual male fulfillment to post-elementary schooling and middle-class careers, employment experts sought to dissuade working-class boys from pursuing such ambitions. Nor, in contrast to relatively successful efforts by the army and by civilian ministries to mobilize and indoctrinate rural youths, did the state and its allies provide an effective regime of continuing education and recreation that might compensate for the everyday deprivations experienced by young clerks and apprentices, who continued to form the main pool of delinquents processed by the juvenile courts and other agencies. As the following chapter shows, the onset of war would present urban working youths with new economic challenges and opportunities, but the expansion and prolongation of conflict only exacerbated authorities' long-standing fears regarding the indiscipline and alienation of these youths, and prompted aggressive new measures to ensure their conformity to national goals.

CHAPTER 6

Juvenile Delinquency and the National Defense State

From July 1937 to August 1945, as Japan fought a war to establish first a "New Order in East Asia" and then a "Greater East Asia Co-Prosperity Sphere," the Japanese state conscripted an increasing number of adult workers into the military and mobilized hundreds of thousands of elementary- and middle-school graduates to replace them as "industrial warriors" *(sangyō senshi)* in the nation's munitions factories. By early 1943, authorities estimated that "from fifty to eighty percent of workers in important industries are youths, and in particular virtually all of those working in aircraft manufacture are aged fifteen to twenty."[1] As the prominence of young workers increased, so did elite anxieties. Police agents repeatedly swept through the streets of Tokyo, Osaka, and other cities, rounding up thousands of young workers allegedly engaged in criminal or immoral behavior, while juvenile corrections, social work, labor management, and education experts produced a constant stream of articles, reports, and conferences about the dangers that a mass of inadequately socialized industrial warriors posed to themselves and the nation. As the cabinet's January 1943 Outline of Emergency Measures for the Protective Guidance of Working Youths *(Kinrō seishōnen hodō kinkyū taisaku yōkō)* reveals, this social group occupied a central position, along with spies and thought-criminals, in the regime's schema of internal threats.

The wartime discourse on delinquency constituted a principal channel for elites to articulate their visions of social order and sweeping social change, and fears of delinquency (but not necessarily a real upsurge in such behavior) facilitated the expansion of the network of agencies to protect working youth, provide them with "daily life guidance" *(seikatsu shidō)*, and mobilize workplaces, homes, and communities for this purpose. Wartime protection and guidance increasingly fused the functions of educator, personnel manager, social worker, and probation officer; they involved not only an intensification of surveillance within existing hierarchical relationships but also a reconfiguration and expansion of the space in which youth could be disciplined. As part of a broad project that contemporaries called *rensei* (training), programs for working youth featured a stridently martial mode of intensive physical and spiritual cultivation, often in *dōjō* settings, rooted in the ideology of selfless sacrifice for the divine emperor and the ineffable national polity. But in the interest of productivity, wartime socialization measures also emphasized middle-class notions of rational life-course planning, economy, and hygiene, thereby attracting the support of numerous labor scientists, personnel managers, educational reformers, and social workers.[2] The goal of these efforts, as one juvenile court officer put it, was to "provide young workers with a sense of the national significance of their work, . . . cultivate their desire for self-improvement, [and] prevent them from keeping part of their lives concealed."[3]

These programs were thus the product of both long-term strategies and the new possibilities to which total war had given birth. Middle-class advocates of juvenile protection had since the time of Tomeoka Kōsuke emphasized the importance of cultivating productive workers, training national subjects, and guiding young people and families in their daily lives; and the Home, Justice, and Education ministries had mobilized a growing number of agencies for the surveillance and socialization of urban youth. But total war, by expanding the size of the "precocious" working element and the urban space that bred it, and by imbuing the rhetoric of national struggle with a concreteness and immediacy that it earlier had lacked, gave these strategies greater salience and practical force—as did the fact that they were now applied by a state intent on establishing "a structure of national unanimity in politics, economy, culture, education, and all other realms of national life."[4] In a word, the nation at arms was also a national reformatory. As in previous years, however, the politics of everyday life ensured that even totalizing projects did not yield total results. Still, many of the policing techniques applied during the wartime years would continue to bolster Japan's social order for decades after the demise of the regime that produced them.

MOBILIZATION AND THE PROBLEM
OF URBAN WORKING YOUTH

The state's efforts to mobilize workers and increase productivity began shortly after the outbreak of war with China in 1937. In 1938, following extensive negotiations between the army and the Home Ministry, the government expanded the latter's Social Bureau into a new Welfare Ministry, which assumed primary responsibility for labor administration and the conservation of manpower, and nationalized all employment agencies in order to coordinate their operations according to state requirements. The following year, the government established plans for the expansion of productive forces, to be implemented through annual labor mobilization plans.[5] Although these plans called for mobilizing adult women, such efforts remained constrained by an ideological environment that defined married women's proper role as bearers of children and moral defenders of the home. The state also mobilized Korean laborers in growing numbers, but this supply was not sufficient to meet demand.[6] Under these circumstances, authorities looked to young people, many of them from the countryside, to assume critical roles in urban munitions factories. Labor mobilization plans for 1940, for example, called for primary- and middle-school graduates to provide 50 percent of the required manpower supply, and new regulations restricted the employment of young workers in nonessential (i.e., peacetime) industries, including many of the small commercial shops that had previously relied on youth labor.[7] Within the vocational guidance bureaucracy, earlier rhetoric of respecting the needs of the individual child now yielded to arguments that prioritized the interests of the state.[8]

Demands for labor only grew as the war in China dragged on, and especially after the conflict expanded into an all-out struggle against the United States and its allies in December 1941. In October 1941, the government began conscripting males aged sixteen to thirty-nine and unmarried women aged sixteen to twenty-four for labor service, sending them "white letters" instead of the "red letters" that went to military conscripts. As the military draft cut deeper into the workforce, the government lowered the minimum age for male labor conscription from sixteen in 1941 to twelve in 1944, and employment agencies required elementary schools to supply new graduates according to a rigorous quota system.[9] By 1943, as noted earlier, contemporaries estimated that younger workers comprised the great majority of the workforce in

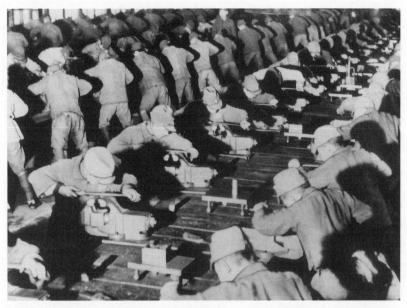

Figure 10. Young "industrial warriors" at work in the youth school of Hitachi's Kameari plant. Tokyo, 1942. Source: The Asahi Shimbun Company.

domestic factories and mines, and nearly all of those working in aircraft plants in particular.[10] This massive demographic shift provoked widespread elite consternation and fueled reports of mounting crime and delinquency.

In the public eye, young factory workers were "overnight nouveaux riches."[11] Demand for labor had boosted wages, and by 1939, many workers in their late teens and early twenties earned over one hundred yen per month, more than many white-collar workers.[12] Authorities feared that these youths were wasting their wages at movie theaters, cafés, or even unlicensed brothels—for example, one Tokyo newspaper in 1939 reported the case of a twenty-year-old who spent eighty-five yen on alcohol and women before being detained for drunken and disorderly conduct.[13] Once in thrall to these vices, arose the common refrain, young workers would turn to crime when their wages ran out. Rising incomes, moreover, appeared to entail rising assertiveness on the part of subordinate classes. A 1939 Justice Ministry internal report noted that in Osaka, teenage workers resisted police officers who tried to detain them for their "spendthrift" ways. "I earned this money," one of the boys said. "What's wrong with my spending it as I please?"[14] According to veteran Tokyo social worker Kusama Yasoo, such attitudes reflected lower-class youths' lack of cultivation, their family deficiencies, and their susceptibility to the influence of bad friends. Similarly, labor scientist Kirihara Shigemi, a prolific writer on the problems of young workers, contrasted their lack of supervision and their free spending habits to conditions in the homes of his respectable readers, "where youths aged fifteen to eighteen receive meticulous oversight and protection."[15]

Representations of extravagance and autonomy could, however, be misleading, particularly once real wages dropped dramatically during the Pacific War years in the face of endemic commodity shortages and inflation. A 1942 study of young workers in sixty-nine machine factories in the Tokyo area reported, for example, that 79 percent of youths in large plants and 66 percent of those in smaller shops earned less than fifty yen per month. After employers deducted compulsory savings and health insurance fees and, in the case of dormitory residents, room and board costs, most youths were left with little money for extravagant expenditures; many also remitted their wage packets to their parents in exchange for small allowances.[16] Authorities feared that deprivation would also lead to delinquency, and cited reports of youths who stole to pay for recreational activities or simply to obtain basic articles of clothing. And to the mass of rural youths conscripted into the urban labor force, mobilization was anything but liberating. As one conscript noted in a 1942 interview, the combination of low wages, poor conditions, and harsh punishments "really makes you feel as though you're in jail."[17] Many observers also lamented that wartime conditions had made young males rough: they formed gangs, made crude weapons, and accosted others in the streets. The thriving black market also offered some youths an opportunity to make extra money, either by selling stolen factory tools or by blackmailing businessmen who violated price controls. Unwholesome housing, stultifying working conditions, and exposure to the vices of older workers also figured prominently in the litany of corrupting influences.[18]

The police approached this problem, as was their custom, by assiduously rounding up young people on the streets. From August 31 to September 4, 1942, Tokyo police rounded up 9,900 "delinquent youths," most of them factory workers, during a massive sweep through the city's popular amusement areas. Over the following month, Tokyo agents detained nearly 29,000 youths for delinquent behavior. In Osaka as well, from July 27 to August 5, 1942, police detained 4,445 young males,

some older than twenty-five, for having committed criminal or delinquent acts; roughly half were identified as juvenile factory workers
(shōnenkō).[19] Given the precedent of the 1938 student roundups (which
had actually netted more working youths than school enrollees), as well
as the prudish intolerance of the police, it seems safe to assume that most
of those detained, especially the younger ones, had done little more than
smoke, go to cafés, eateries, or cinemas, or loiter on the streets (if they
went in groups, they may well have been considered gangs).

Students in middle schools, higher schools, normal schools, and colleges also entered factories in increasing numbers, but because they were
mobilized as school or class units or as "labor service brigades" with
their teachers assigned to supervise them, and no doubt because of their
more elite or upwardly mobile class positions, they did not figure in the
discourse on delinquency among young workers. In 1942, moreover,
Tokyo police reported that student misbehavior had declined over the
course of the war.[20] Female students also undertook factory work (also
in supervised brigades), as did unmarried women, but official sources
offer virtually no discussion of crime or delinquency among women in
factories during the wartime years. Personnel managers did apparently
fear receiving reports of young female workers involved in after-hours
sexual "incidents" with their male coworkers, as Kirihara noted briefly
in a 1941 address to juvenile justice experts. But such worries did not
translate into a moral panic over female delinquency. Indeed, police
crackdowns on modern girls and café waitresses in the 1920s and early
1930s led to a muting of this general discourse by the wartime years
(although café waitresses continued to figure among the handfuls of
women detained on the streets), and, as in the prewar years, only a
small number of girls and young women appeared in official statistics as
juvenile delinquents.[21]

Even with regard to working boys, however, the increase in the
absolute number of reported cases of juvenile crime and delinquency
was partly, if not largely, due to intensified policing; moreover, sparse
statistics from the wartime period do not necessarily support contemporary claims that factory workers constituted a growing percentage
of the pool of delinquent youths.[22] Many authorities acknowledged that
the problem might have been sensationalized, but they were unwilling to
tolerate any activity or attitude that might impede industrial production.
As one Tokyo police official, writing in the general-interest magazine
Central Review (Chūō Kōron), explained after the August–September
1942 sweep: "Of course, in terms of the overall rate, the proportion of

'juvenile delinquents' among the great number of young factory workers is no doubt low. However, given that we have made an enemy of
America, with its massive productive capabilities, this issue is a problem
that concerns the 'front line' in our hundred-year war of productivity."[23] Justice Ministry officials, meanwhile, sought to avoid a collapse
of the home front, which they cited as a major factor in Germany's
defeat in 1918. Protection Bureau chief Moriyama Takeichirō wrote:
"In particular, in the closing period of the war and the days after its end,
Germany was plagued by a dramatic increase in crime, and the nation's
strength suffered unrecoverable losses due to decadence among young
people and children. As Japan engages in total warfare, we must take
heed of these past developments."[24]

   Japanese reformers of all stripes agreed that the current situation
called for more than just tighter police controls. As Suzuki Shun'ichi, a
noted personnel manager and authority on youth labor issues, summed
it up in a 1941 contribution to the journal of the Imperial Education
Association, "The cause of today's so-called delinquency among young
factory workers . . . lies in the poverty of culture and the lack of education in the workplace."[25] If the factory symbolized what Marx called
the socialization of production under industrial capitalism, such experts
now hoped to turn it into a center for what Christopher Lasch called the
socialization of reproduction, with traditional child-rearing roles taken
over or administered by external agencies. Reformers thus seized on law
enforcement officials' fears to promote programs that envisioned sweeping changes in Japanese people's approaches to work, school, home,
and leisure. While some framed their goals in terms of the reactionary
images of Japan's "beautiful customs" and emperor-centered values,
they all shared a decades-old modernist desire to create an efficient society of self-activating subjects freed from the alienation and vices plagu-
ing industrial capitalism. Declared Kirihara Shigemi: "Young workers'
daily life guidance urgently requires that the entire society be turned
into an organization of production."[26]

YOUTH CONTINUATION SCHOOLS
AND FACTORY DORMITORIES

Youth continuation schools *(seinen gakkō)* constituted the core element
in the growing regime of training and surveillance. First established in
1935, these schools fused existing supplemental schools (established
after 1900) and youth training centers (established in 1926), offering

courses in civics and national morality, vocational subjects, and a healthy dose of military drill. They thus responded to both educators' long-standing calls to expand post-elementary educational opportunities for the working masses and the army's ongoing desire to prepare adolescents for conscription. However, unlike earlier facilities that targeted mainly rural youth, the wartime schools developed rapidly in urban areas after 1939, when attendance became compulsory for all males aged twelve to nineteen who were not enrolled in higher elementary or secondary institutions. Public youth schools, often housed in local elementary schools, offered a few hours of classes and drill each day to students from neighboring factories; in contrast, larger enterprises established their own private schools.[27] Not everyone attended a school, however. As one Tokyo education official wrote in 1941, "Given the fact that most young workers who get in trouble are not enrolled in youth schools, . . . making them students is the first step in preventing incidents."[28]

To experts such as Kirihara Shigemi, who became head of the welfare department of the government's Imperial Rule Assistance Association (Taisei Yokusankai), total war required the creation of school curricula that were relevant to the actual operations of factory life, as well as military training that would prepare technologically sophisticated soldiers of a "mechanized national defense army." To implement daily life guidance, Kirihara called for all youths to be housed in dormitories or supervised residences. These should in general be modeled upon warships, which represented efficiency, strength, and beauty; in contrast, "soft, homey" facilities or "café" ambiences only impeded productivity. Insubordinate delinquents, he added, "should be shipped off to remote islands in the Southern region and put to work building military facilities."[29] Kirihara found positive examples in both the Japanese Army and the Hitler Youth, which he saw as the key to Germany's military successes. "Through this organization," he wrote, "the state has taken all of Germany's youth away from their homes, and herein lies the success and strength of the training program."[30] But Kirihara took care to emphasize that the system he envisioned would not destroy the "family system," that pillar of Japan's purportedly unique national polity. Rather, he claimed, taking youths away from their homes taught them to be better family men upon their return. Paradoxically, then, for the family to be strong, it had to be relieved of its role in socializing the young.

One should not assume that Kirihara considered these proposals to be wartime expedients. Since the 1920s, Japanese labor scientists and vocational guidance experts had questioned both families' and schools' competence in preparing children for productive, healthy working lives. Like other intellectuals or government officials concerned with developing a planned economy or new agencies of mass mobilization, Kirihara saw the war as a chance to effect permanent, radical changes to improve national productivity. His increasingly militaristic tone may in part have been calculated to maintain his standing in state circles, but by the late 1930s many Japanese experts did hail the Nazi regime's regimented apprentice training and labor service programs as the most dynamic model for modernizing worker education.[31]

Larger manufacturing plants' private schools and dormitories offer the most striking examples of managerial efforts to encompass and reshape every aspect of young workers' lives. At Nihon Seikō's Tamagawa ball-bearing plant, for example, a 1942 report declared, "Administration of the youth school has replaced labor management." The factory director doubled as school principal, his staff helped administer the school, and school and plant staff oversaw the dormitories, assisted by group leaders appointed from among the residents. Students were encouraged to "discover joy in work itself" and develop "a vision of labor that responds to the demands of the times" as well as to entrust themselves to and obey their superiors absolutely.[32] Nihon Kōgaku's 1943 guidelines prescribed that factory managers live with young workers in dormitories to guide them "from the moment they wake to the moment they go to sleep." Daily routines included bows toward the imperial shrine at Ise and prayers for imperial troops and workers' families, spiritual lectures and instruction in "national manners," and physical exercise. Administrators also encouraged each young worker to develop a plan of his life course and stage-by-stage financial needs (seikatsu sekkei), offered guidance in the proper use of money, and promoted postal savings accounts. On the day after wages were distributed, supervisors investigated each youth's holdings and channeled a part of each wage packet into various savings plans—which went to finance the war effort. Supervisors also urged dormitory residents to keep daily journals and personal account ledgers, which supervisors later inspected.[33] Others used "daily life composition" exercises (seikatsu tsuzurikata), a pedagogic technique pioneered by leftist teachers to awaken their pupils' proletarian consciousness, as a means of gauging youth-school students' attitudes toward their jobs. At Seikōsha in Honjo Ward, managers even instructed dormitory residents in the proper way to take off and arrange their bathroom slippers, and exhorted them "not to spill even one drop of urine" outside the toilet.[34] School and factory staff also endeavored to subject commuting youths to the same types of guidance.

By 1942, more than three thousand private factory schools accommodated 541,700 male and 189,512 female students; two years later, the number of male and female students reached 780,181 and 233,357, respectively.[35] Not all school programs were as thoroughgoing as the aforementioned examples, but most dormitories attached to larger factories did in fact rely on military forms of regulation, with movements and activities guided by bugle calls or commands from supervisors, many of whom were decommissioned soldiers.[36] Yet according to some critics such as personnel manager Suzuki Shun'ichi, strict discipline forced youths to "live like monks"; they then sought release in the workplace, borrowing cigarettes from older workers and engaging in idle conversation. On occasion, the harsh regime provoked violent resistance. In one instance, youth-school students severely beat their dormitory supervisor because he failed to keep his promises to improve living conditions and provide more radios.[37] In order to preempt the development of organized resistance or youth subcultures, Nihon Seikō's Tamagawa plant issued regulations that stated: "Dormitory residents are not recklessly to form or join groups, nor are they to hold assemblies or publish magazines or pamphlets."[38]

Small factories posed a different set of problems—and observers noted that most delinquents were employed in such establishments.[39] According to one report, labor-starved owners of smaller plants readily hired workers dismissed as delinquents by larger factories, choosing to overlook the workers' misbehavior in order to keep them on the job. These employers also proved particularly hostile to the local public youth schools. Some simply felt that they had not hired boys in order to send them to school. Others feared that young workers might learn at school about better conditions in other factories. As a result of such contacts, one factory owner complained, youths' feelings toward their employer wavered, the factory's "family atmosphere" was destroyed, and the youths "went bad."[40] The "family atmosphere" to which he referred may well have been more rhetorical than real, but this employer and many others like him clearly saw the problem of youth labor in a different light from educational authorities. Moreover, "dormitories" run by small factories bore little similarity to reformers' ideals—at times, as one police investigator reported, they were nothing more than refurbished chicken coops.[41] Meanwhile, observers of both small and large plants remarked that most adult workers had been raised under traditional apprenticeship modes, "enduring repeated blows to the head" as they acquired their skills. Having been socialized in this manner, stated one personnel manager in 1943, they were hardly cut out to serve as daily life guidance instructors. More often, critics charged, foremen endeavored to mitigate workplace tensions by pressing young subordinates to go out drinking or to brothels.[42] Preventing juvenile delinquency, in other words, also necessitated reforming adult workers and employers.

Judging from limited evidence, it appears that youths also responded ambivalently toward the schools. Many no doubt saw the opportunity for continuing education, especially vocational training, as a means of social advancement. But observers noted students' complaints that the schools in fact provided little specialized training and no formal vocational credentials, "without which neither factory nor society will take them seriously."[43] In contrast, youths expressed the greatest satisfaction with military drill—primarily because it was their sole opportunity for recreation.[44]

Ultimately, factories did subsume "education" in the work process— not as part of a modernizing reformist agenda such as Kirihara's, but because managers reduced school time and extended work hours to meet increased production demands. A 1944 report by the Kyōchōkai, a leading labor relations and social policy institute, noted bleakly: "Factories, constrained by 'productivity first' ideology, consider education to be a secondary issue." During the final years of the war, the Ministry of Education sought to transform all post-elementary schools into factories, and to minimize the amount of time workers spent off the shop floor.[45] The youth schools' functions, along with those of dormitories, were thus reduced to surveillance, military drill, and spiritual indoctrination or exhortation. As a negative force, schools' delinquency prevention departments (kyōgobu) could be very effective, with teachers encouraging youths to police each other: for example, one boy in an industrializing town in Yamanashi Prefecture reported that "diehard" students (kōha, the same term as for ruffians) patrolled the area near the train station and movie theater, beating students who appeared to be shirking their duties.[46] Meanwhile, the expansion of military conscription to include first nineteen-year-olds (in December 1943) and then eighteen-year-olds (in October 1944) drew large numbers of young people away from the schools.[47]

Youth schools constituted part of a broader transformation in Japan's educational system that also touched younger children. In 1941, the Ministry of Education, "in order to give the rising generation a more thorough basic training as Japanese subjects," revised the elementary-school curriculum into "a small number of principal lessons designed as a whole to exalt national spirit, develop the capacity for scientific pursuits, elevate the physical standard and refine sentiments."[48] In the newly renamed national schools (kokumin gakkō), rituals such as shrine visits, military commemorations, and the reading of imperial rescripts, as well as labor service, occupied a growing share of the school calendar; physical education assumed a more rigorous martial character, and official boys' organizations conducted after-school drills and patriotic exercises. Revisions also stipulated that the two-year, vocation-oriented higher elementary course would become mandatory (although wartime exigencies forced the state to suspend implementation).[49] And, for the first time in the history of Japan's modern school system, the government eliminated the exemption of poor children from the obligation to attend school—not out of any "notions of charity or individualistic ideas of equality," as one admirer of the measure explained, but rather as a "welfare policy for constructing the national defense state."[50] Given wartime conditions, however, the effects of this reform were not immediately felt.

Similarly, the structural impact of the youth continuation schools became most evident after 1945. These institutions closed shortly after Japan's defeat, but with enrollments exceeding three million in 1943, they set the stage for the postwar state's implementation of compulsory secondary education.[51] The growth of links among schools, factories, and dormitories, particularly in larger establishments, marked an important step in reformers' decades-old campaigns to turn adolescent urban wage-laborers into disciplined, dependent youth. And as administrators applied militarized methods to inculcate national subjectivity and improve the quality of younger workers, they also endeavored to make working-class lifestyles conform to middle-class values of diligence, planning, economy, and hygiene.

STORM TROOPS OF THE FACTORY?
THE GREATER INDUSTRIAL YOUTH BRIGADES

This combination of militarized training and middle-class reformism also underpinned the youth activities of the Greater Japan Industrial Patriotic Association (Sanpō), another critical agency for labor socialization. Developed in the late 1930s by the Home and Welfare ministries as a statist alternative to labor-union-based mediation between employers and workers, Sanpō drew inspiration from the Nazi model of "shop communities" administered by the German Labor Front (DAF). Plant-level Sanpō units were to provide the setting for a new harmony between management and labor that transcended class distinctions and enabled the pursuit of productivity in the service of the nation. In fact, Sanpō delegitimized the organized interests of labor while leaving the power of management unchecked. As Sheldon Garon has noted, officials increasingly "hoped to use the industrial patriotic units to rally grass-roots support for . . . new ordinances to regulate wages, hours, employment, and dismissals."[52]

To date, studies of Sanpō have focused largely on its role as a state-imposed replacement for labor unions, and have often treated it as moribund.[53] However, Sanpō also ran education and welfare programs that attracted a large number of progressive social engineers intent on improving the welfare of the workforce, creating a new labor culture, devising productive forms of leisure, and rationalizing household economies in wartime Japan. Prominent women, including Tanno Setsuko, Japan's first female factory inspector, and Akamatsu Tsuneko, formerly head of the women's section of the Japan General Federation of Labor, joined Sanpō's Daily Life Guidance Department. Sanpō also absorbed two other organizations: the Labor Nutrition Association, an external branch of the Welfare Ministry; and the Japan Labor Science Research Institute, whose left-leaning members (including Kirihara Shigemi) had since the 1910s conducted studies on worker fatigue, plant conditions, and other issues relating to industrial efficiency and welfare, and had placed their expertise at the service of their nation in its moment of mounting international crisis.[54] Leftist women such as Miyamoto Yuriko also applauded Sanpō's efforts to keep young workers from "losing to temptation" and seeing "their youths eaten away" by visits to the unlicensed brothels.[55]

In 1940, a Welfare Ministry subcommittee on daily life guidance for youth called for measures "to renovate lethargic, unwholesome everyday lives plagued by materialism and individualism, and to lead the people to conduct wholesome, cheerful leisure activities based on the fundamental principles of the national polity." As specific goals, the report enumerated "embodiment of the imperial spirit, cultivation of respect for labor, complete awareness of the current situation, promotion of a desire to learn, training in group life, elevation of personal tastes, promotion of a healthy lifestyle, and rationalization of economic life."

To achieve these ends, the subcommittee proposed the establishment of a system of Industrial Patriotic Youth Brigades (Sangyō Hōkoku Seinentai), under the aegis of Sanpō.[56] The report reflected the ideas of subcommittee chairman Gonda Yasunosuke, an expert on mass leisure who had worked for both the left-leaning Ōhara Social Problems Research Institute and the Ministry of Education, and who now found inspiration in Nazi organizations such as the German Labor Front (DAF) and Kraft durch Freude (KdF, or Strength Through Joy).[57]

Beginning in March 1941, the Welfare Ministry's Labor Bureau and prefecture Sanpō directors vigorously promoted the establishment of these youth brigades in factories employing more than fifty young workers. Guidelines provided for the establishment of two types of organizations: a boys' section for workers younger than twenty, and a young men's section for those aged twenty to twenty-five. Boys were to live in dormitories and undergo round-the-clock training (in practice, however, many younger workers, especially nonconscript local youths, commuted). Activities for young men, who had completed youth schools and military service, would center on nonresidential Industrial Patriotic Youth Clubs located near factories. The brigades would also have access to *dōjō*-type facilities for outdoor group training retreats. Officials also called for the establishment of brigades for girls in the workforce, but the Welfare Ministry's Labor Bureau, considering young women in factories to be objects of protection rather than training, chose to leave this matter to employers' discretion.[58]

In a 1941 book addressed to young workers, Gonda explained that the Sanpō youth brigades were to be "storm troops of the factory" who would "take up the front line" in the battle to "eliminate the stagnant, decadent workplace atmosphere fostered by older workers through either ignorance or ill will."[59] In practice, however, the majority of factory managers and Sanpō officials bridled at the notion of shop floors dominated by younger workers. Obata Tadayoshi, who became director of the Greater Japan Sanpō Association in 1942, recalled that as a factory manager during the depression-ridden early 1930s, he had experienced the most trouble with single male workers under the age of twenty-five, who were likely to defy management and engage in "disquieting behavior." Upon taking charge of Sanpō, Obata was shocked to discover "an extremely dangerous attitude" among "provocateurs engaging in the same kinds of activities that caused me the greatest difficulty as a factory manager." He immediately moved to eliminate dangerous youth-department programs and shift the focus of youth activities to training.[60] Given that youth brigades were under the leadership of factory youth-school principals who were frequently factory managers, it seems unlikely that many of the new organizations would have challenged traditional structures of authority, as the Hitler Youth had in its early years during the 1930s before it was reined in and bureaucratized. Even prior to Obata's measures, a report from Tokyo noted that the storm troops of Gonda's vision were in fact little more than a "color guard" *(girei butai)* for workplace ceremonies.[61] But managers were determined to eliminate even rhetorical suggestions of the legitimacy of autonomous youth action.

On the other hand, managers, Sanpō officials, and other state agents did mobilize the youth brigades to police members' morals and behavior, often through systems of collective responsibility, while seeking to inspire young workers' wholehearted participation in projects to increase production and enhance national defense capabilities. And throughout the wartime years, officials organized numerous training programs for youth brigade leaders. Mobilization techniques included reading circles, in which, a training manual explained, participants should be encouraged to share their thoughts, refine their understanding of workplace life, develop a desire to learn, and enhance their self-awareness as "industrial youth, imperial youth, and youth of Japan, the leader of Greater East Asia."[62]

Given that most information on Sanpō youth brigades is derived from official sources, one can only hypothesize concerning the effectiveness of this program. One the one hand, a large number of young workers joined the organization: approximately 1.5 million youths in 1943. In Tokyo, according to a 1944 Metropolitan Police Department report, 916 brigades contained roughly 150,000 male and 30,000 female members. On the other hand, to protect their managerial prerogatives from intervention by Sanpō officials, many large factories did not form youth brigades. Where brigades were established, moreover, their administration and activities often overlapped with those of the normal Sanpō units, in effect obscuring the specific youth-centered identity of the program.[63] Meanwhile, Sanpō youth activities had little if any impact on the mass of factories employing fewer than fifty young workers, which were not required to establish such organizations.

Finally, as in the case of youth continuation schools, the demands of increased production severely hampered the implementation of Sanpō educational activities. Workplace pressures, material shortages, family concerns, and general enervation no doubt proved a major stumbling block to the new programs, particularly in the closing years of the war. Military drill and "color guard" activities may have been a welcome diversion from factory tasks, or they may have been yet another tedious imposition. Spiritual training and observance of various daily rituals may have elicited reactions ranging from active self-reflection to unthinking performance, resentment, or resistance. And in the work-place, youthful "storm troopers" were in fact just another form of industrial cannon fodder.

Still, at the most basic level, youth brigades functioned as mutual policing organizations and significantly restricted the ability of young workers to engage in autonomous activities. Moreover, Sanpō ideology rhetorically assigned youths an elevated status that corresponded to their growing prominence in the workforce. These young people, most of whom were of rural background, formed part of a cohort who entered school and came of age after the demise of "Taishō Democracy" of the 1920s, in a period increasingly dominated by a militaristic world-view and ultranationalist discourse. Labor scientists reported that in interviews and questionnaires, the majority of working youth showed that they were earnest about their jobs, concerned to develop as work-ers, and motivated to serve their nation; at the same time, many were disturbed by what they saw as the corruption or inefficiency of adult workers and managers. To some of these young people, identification as Sanpō youth, hollow as it seems today, may have compensated for mate-rial deprivations and authoritarian impositions in various aspects of everyday life.[64] Those trained as unit leaders or deputies, moreover, almost certainly benefited from an enhanced sense of self-worth and local power, although their enthusiasm (like that of "diehard" youth-school students discussed earlier) may well have antagonized their peers. If they survived the war, these young men no doubt carried the youth brigade experience into their adult careers, and may have deployed the wartime organizational techniques and group ideology in their every-day lives as workers or community members. On the other hand, those seen as lacking the requisite discipline and motivation faced increas-ingly harsh forms of training and surveillance.

REEDUCATION AND PROBATION

Authorities built up the "protective guidance network" to deal with alleged miscreants. The wartime years witnessed a rapid expansion of the juvenile court system, with new courts established in major population and industrial centers: Fukuoka, Hiroshima, Sendai, and Sapporo. By January 1942, officials realized their long-standing desire to have the provisions of the Juvenile Law applied throughout the country. (Officials also established a juvenile court in Seoul.) Although the new courts employed small staffs, their establishment led to a major increase (290 percent) in the number of cases to which protective measures were applied.[65]

Protective guidance entailed the increasing penetration of the shop floor by the agencies of juvenile correction and the creation of new facilities to isolate and reeducate delinquents. In 1941, for example, Tokyo Juvenile Court officers oversaw the establishment of a Young Worker Guidance Association *(seishōnenkō hodō kyōkai)* in Kawasaki City, the principal manufacturing district in Kanagawa Prefecture. The association, staffed by former police officers and middle-school educators, conducted surveys of young workers, developed protection programs for youths who switched or left jobs (and for those who committed or appeared likely to commit crimes), and operated consultation centers for employers, youths, and other concerned parties. In response, employers reported more cases of delinquency to the juvenile court. The court soon inaugurated a similar association, in conjunction with local Sanpō officials, in Sago-chō in Tokyo's Jōtō Ward, and planned to establish an association in each factory district in Tokyo. This network expanded even further when the government's 1943 Outline of Emergency Measures for the Protective Guidance of Working Youths and ancillary guidelines ordered the establishment of new surveillance committees at the shop, enterprise, prefectural, regional, and national levels.[66]

Meanwhile, a network of special training centers or *dōjō* employed various techniques, some harsher than others, to turn problem workers into self-activating subjects. The mildest reeducation sessions, administered by factory managers, targeted youths whose absenteeism, insubordination, or indolence threatened to disrupt productivity. An article in the December 1942 issue of the journal *Sanpō* described one such session, conducted for delinquent conscript workers at a factory near Tokyo.

Each morning, participants rose at 5:00 and cleaned the premises. They then performed ritual ablution *(misogi)* and one hour of spiritual practices. After breakfast, which began and ended with the recitation of declarations of gratitude for benevolence received, youths spent their mornings on physical education (gymnastics or parading) and moral instruction. The afternoon hours were devoted to work, with participants performing tasks such as weeding, hauling dirt, and leveling ground in parks in workers' neighborhoods. After dinner came "practices of the child's heart," such as singing and light play or movie viewing, and then another hour of prayer. The day concluded with "reflection," as well as individual interviews and instruction for participants whose activities "lacked sincerity" or who "caused incidents." On the fourth day, the group offered prayers at the shrine of the Meiji Emperor, at Yasukuni Shrine, where Japan's war dead were enshrined, and at Sengakuji Temple in Takanawa, which housed the tombs of the forty-seven loyal *rōnin* celebrated in the *Chūshingura* as exemplars of selfless commitment to the way of the warrior. By the end of the session, according to the reporter, trainees had "completely abandoned the feeling of being a group of delinquent or lazy workers" and had "turned into a group of pupils in the company of a teacher who was their friend." These youths had learned to regret their past behavior and appreciate the blessings bestowed on them by parents and supervisors. They performed prayers "with an earnestness and spiritual unity not seen in regular spiritual instruction courses," and were prepared to return to the industrial battle as new men.[67]

Even if the short-term effects were as this glowing report described, experts questioned the long-term results. At a 1943 meeting with juvenile social workers, Suzuki Shun'ichi, the noted personnel manager, reported that thirty-six delinquents he had recently trained at a special center had resumed their old behavior as soon as they returned to the shop floor. "From the perspective of educational protection, the workplace atmosphere is extremely bad," he observed. "Factory managers understand the problem, but they are unable to devote any resources to addressing it." Participants at a 1943 round-table meeting of personnel managers and juvenile justice agents (including Suzuki) voiced similar concerns.[68] Yet these worries did not prevent employers from continuing to rely on the training programs, especially after the 1943 Outline of Emergency Measures called for their systematic use.

Factories sent more recalcitrant workers to month-long sessions in training halls administered by prefectural governments or Sanpō associations; those workers whose conduct still did not improve, and those who committed criminal offenses or demonstrated such proclivities, received more intensive, boot-camp-style reeducation at the hands of the Justice Ministry, which converted its national training schools and private reform agencies for this purpose. One Justice official offered this

explanation of the training project: "It is fundamentally people with
strong selves who become criminals. . . . If in a short period of time we
can exhaust them mentally and physically—this does not mean that we
beat them—then we will be able to break down their selves and they
will be reborn as Japanese. It is from this belief that we have adopted
short-term drilling programs."[69] The official's rather defensive reference
to corporal punishment suggests that a "spare the rod, spoil the child"
mentality may well have governed the training camps—as it did regular
army training programs. Although the army was not directly involved
in the Justice Ministry's programs, administrators appear to have
encouraged trainees to "volunteer" for military service as a sign of their
nationalist awakening, and a number of them did so.

Youths who completed the drilling sessions were placed in private
juvenile protection associations on or adjacent to factory premises for
periods of four to six months, after which those deemed ready for full
reintegration were discharged and placed under the supervision of probation officers attached to each factory.[70] A few were sent to the
colonies or to areas under Japanese military occupation. Between 1938
and 1942, the juvenile courts had shipped several hundred young people
over to Manchuria, but officials judged the project a failure, apparently
because the youths selected had been "of bad character" and because of
a lack of adequate integration measures on the continent. In 1942, however, the Fukuoka Juvenile Court reported a more profitable approach:
it placed a number of delinquents in a private academy whose director
then sent them to a factory he operated under the auspices of the army
in Northern China. Proper drilling, explained the Fukuoka court director, was the key to the success of any such program.[71] Meanwhile, to
expedite court operations and minimize disruptions in production, the
Justice Ministry ordered juvenile court officers to circulate among factories, conduct background surveys of workers reported as delinquent,
and adjudicate cases on the spot; the courts also began appointing plant
staff members as probation officers. Just as the youth continuation
schools and Sanpō youth brigades sought to fuse the disciplinary mechanisms of factory, classroom, and dormitory, these training programs
effaced the line between labor management and juvenile corrections.

Like other agencies, the Justice Ministry reported that its training
programs achieved positive results, and the juvenile courts began to pre-
scribe drilling for youths whose offenses were so petty that in earlier
years their files would have remained unopened.[72] An enthusiastic
Moriyama Takeichirō envisioned expanding the intensive drilling system

into a mass-production process targeting roughly forty thousand youths per year. "If we can send these youths off to the nation's important industrial sectors," he stated, "we will have truly manifested the modern significance of juvenile protection operations."[73] Starting as an emergency wartime measure, the camps were to become an integral pedagogic component of an advanced industrial society. The state, however, never realized Moriyama's vision. Personnel and material shortages led to administrative retrenchment within the Justice Ministry, while intensified air raids hampered the implementation of new operations. Nonetheless, drilling and training sessions continued until the closing months of the war, and provided templates not only for postwar juvenile corrections programs but also for the employee training retreats that became a staple of Japanese enterprise culture during the high-growth era from the 1950s to the 1970s.[74]

ENGAGING FAMILIES AND COMMUNITIES

New disciplinary agencies did not limit their focus to working youths but also, like earlier social work and probation programs, targeted their homes and communities. As Narita Ryūichi has observed, the increasing concentration of the population in industrial areas during wartime entailed a greater systematization of urban space and standardization of lifestyles, and permitted a variety of organizations, such as women's and neighborhood groups, to play an important role in the allocation of resources and in the promotion of norms of public health.[75] Fears of delinquency also impelled this process.

Sanpō's daily life guidance programs constituted a prime example of authorities' efforts to mobilize and discipline families and communities. At the national level, for example, Sanpō worked to generate public support through annual "young industrial warrior protection weeks." Plans for 1943 included newspaper and radio campaigns, as well as bringing members of the Greater Japan Women's Association into factory dormitories to serve as "dorm mothers for a day."[76] Individual factories also sent parents of dormitory residents monthly reports that discussed their children's work attitudes, income, and expenditures; and factories dispatched youth-school instructors to investigate conditions in the homes of commuting workers.[77] In the Osaka region, according to one survey, a number of companies opened counseling centers in workers' neighborhoods and one plant even established its own system of local welfare commissioners. According to this survey, employers reported "marked spiritual effects," including "enhanced trust and closeness between factories and families," "improvement in workers' thought," and "prevention of delinquency," as well as a decline in absenteeism and worker separation rates. Noda Shin'ichi of the Osaka Regional Labor Council declared: "One will be able to speak of the correct form of labor management when it has extended from the factory to the family, and succeeds in integrating the two." "It is clear," he added, "that factories must extend their grasp over the home."[78]

As in previous efforts, grasping the home meant training mothers as agents of socialization and surveillance. Education officials, recognizing that the mobilization of women for wartime tasks threatened to leave children neglected or improperly trained, promoted "home education" programs through which mothers' associations and similar groups, which had existed in various elementary schools prior to the war but grew rapidly following its outbreak, would "uplift family life" and "promot[e] thrift and savings" based on "results of studies in [the] modern sciences of education and domestic economy." This position accorded with that of the Welfare Ministry, which implemented numerous policies to protect mothers and children as part of its drive to improve human resources.[79] Even the Education Ministry's manifesto of the "traditional" ideology of the patriarchal family and family-state, the 1944 draft of *Fundamental Principles of the Household (Ie no hongi)*, embraced this more feminized configuration of the domestic sphere: "The mother does not simply perform the duties of a subordinate to the patriarch and father. She also raises her child to succeed his father as head of the household and as a subject of the lord, ready to perform great tasks in the service of the nation. She dedicates every bit of her life to her child. . . . Here lies the great desire of Japanese motherhood, which by far surpasses instinctive motherly love."[80] Ironically, the state's effort to protect Japan's "beautiful customs" against the influence of Western liberalism and individualism thus hinged on the continued diffusion of child-rearing practices and home economics originating in Anglo-American models of middle-class life.

As the Ministry of Education had foreseen, however, wartime demands prevented mothers from becoming the stalwart agents that government officials required. In 1942, for example, Tokyo probation officer Uetani Chie, herself a woman, reported that mothers of young factory workers gave the boys money to eat dinner at food shops before coming home. For women to resort to such measures, lamented Uetani, "makes family life meaningless and eliminates mothers' authority and compassion," while leaving young boys open to unwholesome influences.[81] The fact remained, however, that distributing rations and other home-front activities (not to mention labor service) severely taxed housewives' time and energy, while food shortages in the home often made eating out a necessity. (Uetani complained that families, not eateries, should be receiving the scarce provisions.) The state was incapable of resolving the fundamental material problems of home-front life, but officials and reformers persisted in their efforts to guide women's daily lives.[82]

Where mothers could not fulfill this mission, community councils and neighborhood associations, Sanpō, schoolteachers, welfare commissioners and child-protection agents, and, of course, the police, provided surveillance. Private associations linked to the juvenile courts also established consultation centers *(shōnen hogo sōdansho)* whose staff conducted mental evaluations, home visits, and "parent reeducation," and could arrange for problem children to be placed in more appropriate settings. In Tokyo, to coordinate these overlapping operations, welfare agents opened two juvenile guidance centers *(shōnen shidōsho)* in the working-class districts of Ōji and Fukagawa, which were designated as models for a new system of "educational protection precincts" *(kyōgo chiku).*[83]

Yet while reformers strove to cast "a net for the prevention of delinquency," many working-class families sought to wriggle free. Counseling center personnel lamented, for example, that they "get many cases from families of good standing, whereas the lower classes stay away." This was not surprising, given that the youth protection project continued to be driven in good measure by middle-class reformers' desire, in a manner paralleling the colonial project, to "civilize" or "assimilate" the lower classes. (In this vein, one can note Kirihara Shigemi's 1940 characterization of working-class families as susceptible to collapse because of their "weak capacity for ensuring the cohesion of individual personalities.")[84] In contrast, employers enthusiastically relied on the counseling centers to discipline conscript workers, particularly once authorities stepped up their short-term drilling programs.[85]

Working parents did, however, avail themselves of those facilities that met their immediate needs, such as new public after-school centers for their younger children. Authorities in several cities inaugurated such programs in response to Welfare Ministry findings that the number of elementary-school pupils displaying problematic tendencies—mainly "laziness," "stubbornness," and "lying," rather than larceny or other criminal activity—had increased dramatically from 1937 to 1942. Parents need not have accepted officials' definition of the problem, however, to appreciate the services of a supplemental caregiver. (Indeed, the statistical increase itself, as a leading Welfare Ministry official admitted, may have been due to different surveying methods in 1937 and 1942.)[86] Wartime concerns over delinquency thus gave birth—albeit on a limited scale—to social services that have since become a standard resource for many working parents throughout Japan.

Community socialization programs reflect the modern Japanese state's unrelenting determination—like that of the Tokugawa rulers—to weave society into an organically linked system of well-regulated local units. These programs struggled in the face of material shortages, conscription, air raids and evacuation, and other disruptions of urban life during 1944 and 1945, but they left important precedents for postwar counseling centers, home education programs, and campaigns to create a delinquency-free, "bright society." Moreover, the protective precinct model evolved into a nationwide system of district councils for youth countermeasures *(seishōnen taisaku chiku kyōgikai)*—councils that boast remarkably high degrees of popular participation.[87]

Sociologist Sonya O. Rose suggests, "Moral discourse especially intensifies . . . when perceptions of difference and diversity are particularly problematic. . . . War, especially total war, transforms the everyday in unparalleled ways, as women and men take up new opportunities with unforeseen consequences. Thus, war's liberating potential threatens the very unity that the nation is supposed to represent."[88] While Rose develops this argument in relation to episodes in which young European and American women's active pursuit of sexual relations was labeled "subversive," her observations apply equally to discourses on juvenile delinquency in Japan and elsewhere.

Indeed, during the total-war years from the 1930s to 1945, elites in virtually all of the principal belligerent countries feared that social dislocations had unleashed waves of delinquency. Such outbreaks were often diagnosed as manifestations of "alien" influences. Nazi authorities, for example, contended with gangs of working-class "Edelweiss Pirates" who asserted their autonomy not only by maintaining a distinctive subculture but also by attacking members of the Hitler Youth, an organization they resented for its overbearing presence and elite-dominated structure. In some cases, Pirate gangs went so far as to participate in more coordinated resistance activities. Meanwhile, groups of upper-middle-class German "swing youth" held dance parties, listened to jazz, and spoke English to demonstrate their rejection of the National Socialist order. Nazi authorities responded by sending delinquents to labor camps and eventually to special juvenile concentration camps where inmates were compelled to demonstrate their fitness as members of the "national community" or face even harsher consequences as "community aliens"; for according to the Nazi discipline of criminal biology, delinquency could be defined as a symptom of racial degeneracy. Many of those committed were subsequently sterilized and sent to psychiatric hospitals or other concentration camps. Authorities also publicly hanged groups of Pirates who abetted the resistance.[89] In the United States as well, the 1943 zoot-suit riots, violent clashes between white servicemen (and sometimes policemen) and gangs of young Mexican-American and African-American zoot-suiters in Los Angeles, Detroit, New York, and other cities, highlighted both the wartime tensions and abiding racial cleavages of American society. According to Stuart Cosgrove, "The zoot-suit was a moral and social scandal in the eyes of the authorities, not simply because it was associated with petty crime and violence, but because [by requiring so much cloth] it openly snubbed the laws of rationing." To mainstream society, its wearers appeared to be flouting the demands of service to and sacrifice for the nation; and a number of politicians claimed, without providing evidence, that Axis agents had instigated the riots.[90]

The Japanese regime did not confront such cases of deliberate nonconformism or political resistance among young people; and as some contemporaries suggested, the scale of delinquency among working youth may actually have been relatively small.[91] But because the presence of even one delinquent was thought to corrupt the entire workplace, the mere threat of misbehavior called forth heavy-handed efforts to secure conformity and cooperation. To this end, authorities constructed a socialization system in which "traditional" Japanese practices such as Shintō-influenced *misogi* ablution and prayer, Zen meditation, and expressions of gratitude for imperial and parental benevolence blended with "modern" techniques of mass mobilization, surveillance, personnel management, physical cultivation, supervised diary writing, and life-course planning. School, factory, barracks, and *dōjō* overlapped in a network of training centers characterized by their concern with every aspect and moment of young workers' lives. Employers and state agents also used daily life guidance programs to expand their influence within communities and homes, mobilizing the people for not only military but also economic warfare.

These programs paralleled the regime's "imperialization" *(kōminka)*
and "harmonization" *(kyōwa)* programs to turn colonial Koreans and
Taiwanese into active "Japanese" subjects, as well as the "fusion"
(yūwa) programs to socialize and police the *burakumin* minority within
Japan.[92] Like those policies, measures for working youth represented
not simply a response to wartime mobilization but also the culmination
of a long-term process through which subaltern groups were to be
assimilated to the nation-state and the industrial capitalist economy.
For "becoming Japanese" involved the acceptance not simply of nativist
and martial ideologies but also of middle-class values and habits. These
norms would retain their power even after the more egregiously militaristic elements of national identity were stripped away in the years
after 1945.

Like other aspects of Japan's wartime imperial program, juvenile protection and socialization activities were by no means foolproof, nor
were they all necessarily implemented as planned. Conflicts of interest
among various groups, and resistance from employers wary of ceding
authority to external agencies, often slowed the reformist agenda. As
educational reformer Kido Mantarō declared, "One can lecture workers on service in the workplace and industrial patriotism, but if employers are still greedily pursuing profit, training efforts will be fruitless."[93]
Moreover, many working-class families vigorously defended their children (and the money they brought home) from reformers' intrusions.
And given the burdens that war imposed on people's everyday lives,
daily life guidance and home education could not prevent widespread
absenteeism and dissatisfaction among the labor force, including the
young.

Nonetheless, one should not slight the significance of wartime socialization and protection measures. The immediate result of these projects
was the spread of a dense net of surveillance agencies over Japanese
working youth and their families. Training and policing programs may
not have turned young people or their mothers into the exact models
that state authorities envisioned, but mobilization into various campaigns no doubt served to sustain people's commitment to official goals.
As Louise Young has suggested with respect to the Japanese state's
Manchurian emigration policies, the "over-organized character of the
movement, the duplication and overlapping of effort, the endless make-
work tasks, all served to get as many people as possible thinking, talking,
working for, and believing in the . . . project, thus building a consensus
behind the empire."[94] Officials, moreover, did not abandon their efforts

even as air raids flattened entire cities and drove the surviving population into the countryside. National mobilization was for them a long-term process that neither began nor ended with the military conflict; indeed, it was the most crucial element in the organization of a modern polity.

But the most long-lasting legacy of wartime mobilization was surely the standardization of lifeways across the archipelago through the accelerated movement of young Japanese into cities and factories.[95] This trend created both a crisis and an opportunity for the wartime regime, which proceeded to implement measures for the socialization of young urban workers about which earlier generations of reformers had only dreamed—measures that in turn contributed, as we shall see in the following pages, to the subsequent elaboration of postwar Japan's "miraculous" pedagogic regime.

Epilogue

The Century of Juvenile Protection

By the time of Japan's defeat in 1945, government officials, professionals, social reformers, religious groups, and local notables had constructed a regime of socialization premised on the notion that every aspect of a young person's life should be rendered visible and subject to intensive guidance. Notwithstanding occasional caveats about the sanctity of the "Japanese family system," state agents and their allies endeavored to diffuse new norms of domestic life and render homes more permeable to external authority. They sought to reshape the content and style of schooling to enhance morality, improve discipline, and facilitate young people's transition to the world of productive work. They worked to restrict youths' engagement with the realms of popular culture and leisure. And they maintained specialized institutions to train those who could not be contained in family or community settings. The reactions of young people, families, and employers to reformers' initiatives ranged from willing cooperation to resentment or outright hostility. When new pedagogic or welfare technologies proved insufficient, however, a zealous police force stood ready to intervene.

Juvenile protection programs and the rhetoric used to describe them underwent a number of important shifts over the period covered in this study, but the juvenile protection project as a whole revealed a high degree of ideological consistency. From late-Meiji Protestants such as Tomeoka Kōsuke to wartime Justice Ministry officials such as Moriyama

Takeichirō, champions of juvenile protection argued that the proper training of youth was the key to creating a healthy society that could face the challenges of modernity, and thus the key to fortifying Japan's position as an industrial, imperial power in a fiercely competitive international order. While some experts, particularly during the age of Taishō Democracy, spoke of the importance of children's rights or individual fulfillment, preventing delinquency was above all a matter of cultivating and allocating human resources across class and gender categories, and thus of promoting national efficiency.

Many of Japan's social, economic, and political structures have changed since 1945, as have the overarching international paradigms shaping them. Defeat led to the dismantling of Japan's overseas empire, the demilitarization and democratization of the political system, the constitutionally enshrined rejection of war as a means of settling international conflicts, and the country's eventual reemergence as a peace-time economic power prospering within a security framework defined by hegemonic U.S. power. These transformations, however, have by no means diminished authorities' belief that their nation must continue to struggle for survival in a harsh world, nor have they mitigated concerns for youth as a source of national strength or weakness. Just as many of Japan's prewar political and economic elites played leading roles in the postwar system, disciplinary projects from Japan's imperial era continue to provide templates for anti-delinquency activities today.[1]

Indeed, postwar government officials moved quickly to reconstruct and expand the juvenile protection network. In 1949, the prime minister's office established the Council for Youth Problem Countermeasures (Seishōnen Mondai Taisaku Kyōgikai, which after 1966 was known as the Youth Problems Deliberative Council, Seishōnen Mondai Shingikai) to coordinate delinquency prevention efforts at the national level. Parallel agencies appeared at the prefectural, municipal, and ward levels, and in turn spawned numerous committees within communities. Since 1951, the Bright Society Campaign, one of several such "people's movements" (kokumin undō), has brought together a broad range of government agencies, welfare organizations, and community groups in an effort to prevent crime and delinquency.[2] In their study of juvenile delinquency in Tokyo's Arakawa Ward during the 1960s, Hiroshi Wagatsuma and George De Vos reported a high degree of volunteer participation in such activities—which they viewed as evidence that "the community is alert and readily aroused to action." What the authors did not perceive, however, is the extent to which such "alertness" is the product of persistent mobilization and coordination by state agencies, including a highly interventionist police force.[3] And as a plethora of postwar home education programs demonstrates, authorities continue to emphasize the importance of having parents, but especially mothers, play active roles in preventing delinquency and policing community life.[4]

Of course, U.S. Occupation officials implemented a number of changes to policies toward young people at risk. The 1947 Child Welfare Law *(Jidō fukushi hō)* replaced the earlier Educational Protection Law (formerly the Reformatory Law) and the 1933 Child Abuse Prevention Law with a comprehensive set of measures that devoted more attention to issues of human rights. The 1948 Juvenile Law raised the upper age of the juvenile category from eighteen to twenty, placed juvenile offenders under the jurisdiction of a new system of family courts, greatly reduced the authority of procurators, established new specialized reformatories, and abolished the old private protective associations.[5] Yet with regard to both of these new laws, the continued reliance not only on professional caseworkers but also on an extensive network of volunteer social workers and probation officers suggests that one of Japan's key mechanisms for mobilizing society to protect the young has not fundamentally changed since the early twentieth century. Writing of the family court system, one scholar has recently argued that "reliance on unsalaried volunteer probation officers (VPOs) is a preeminent example of community based corrections in Japan and remarkable for international criminal justice."[6]

Postwar educational reforms also facilitated the extension of prewar and wartime models of policing. Whereas middle-school students constituted a relatively privileged minority prior to 1945, since 1947 the state has required that all children attend the three-year middle school course. In many public middle schools, teachers continue to patrol amusement centers and other hot spots, and "daily life guidance" has often verged on an obsessive compulsion, like that of both Meiji-era student oversight departments and wartime factory youth schools, to expunge even the slightest hint of deviation from carefully prescribed routines and dress codes. As Rebecca Erwin Fukuzawa has shown, middle-school teachers meticulously investigate students' eating, sleeping, and spending habits, and use this information to assess the quality of their charges' home life—in particular, mothers' attitudes toward domestic responsibility. Fukuzawa's account, from the 1980s, of one group of teachers' zealous, highly methodical investigation of candy eating—to them, the sign of a severe break-down in student discipline—also supports the view that at least some postwar instructors have inherited the role of "criminologist" from their prewar predecessors.[7]

Japan's rapid economic growth and general prosperity have also led to a marked decrease in the number of adolescents entering the work-force after completing compulsory schooling. By 1954, more than half of those graduating middle school continued to high school; this figure reached 80 percent in 1970 and has exceeded 95 percent since the 1980s.[8] Hence, the majority of Japan's adolescents have been subjected to longer periods of pedagogic surveillance and spend more time in school uniforms, which identify the "protected" population and greatly facilitate the policing process.[9] This rapid expansion of the cat-egory of student should not obscure the socioeconomic and cultural divisions within that cohort, which were already becoming apparent during the 1920s and 1930s. Studies by Thomas Rohlen, Ikuya Sato, and others in the affluent 1970s and 1980s demonstrate that many stu-dents do not fit the norms of scholastic behavior promoted by educators, middle-class reformers, and the police, and that schools themselves differ according to their position in the structures of social mobility. Policing efforts, moreover, have been most marked in those schools with students from less advantaged backgrounds—the sorts of institu-tions that follow in the steps of the wartime public youth schools.[10] Young people on the margins, meanwhile, run the risk of placement in detention centers and training schools which continue to combine dis-courses of clinical case analysis and daily life guidance with strict modes of discipline—like "a world run by high school physical educa-tion teachers," in the words of one boy.[11] Many youths, however, have been kept from marginalization by both a strong economy and school-to-work transition programs which, drawing on prewar and wartime precedents, rely on close contacts among employment agencies, employ-ers, and schools.[12]

Yet while Japan's disciplined, relatively well-integrated workforce and low rates of delinquency and overall crime have earned the envy of other industrialized societies, Japanese authorities continue to find much cause for worry. Since the 1970s, for example, juveniles have comprised at least 40 percent, and sometimes more than 50 percent, of those arrested for penal code offenses.[13] The majority of these cases have involved shoplifting or other types of petty larceny, and recidi-vism rates have remained extremely low; but as in the prewar era, the media and the police have cultivated public anxiety by disseminating a steady stream of sensational images of youthful indiscipline and deviant youth subcultures. Whereas accounts of juvenile misbehavior in the late 1940s and early 1950s centered on impoverished young people whose lives had been shattered by the war, commentators during the "economic miracle" years, echoing their interwar predecessors, shifted their focus to the phenomenon of "hedonistic" delinquency among students from "average," economically comfortable homes.[14] In the 1970s and 1980s, public fears of youthful alienation amid great affluence turned into a moral panic over hot-rodding and rough play by motorcycle gangs *(bōsōzoku)*, some of which drew on the traditions of *kōha* ruffian style (in its non-homoerotic mode).[15] Since the mid-1980s, reports on "problem behavior" such as bullying and school violence have also served to focus attention on the stress and strain endemic to the nation's highly competitive educational system.

To many Japanese observers, the 1990s appear to have brought a virtual breakdown in social authority over youth. A century after the emergence of the *jogakusei* problem, casual prostitution or "compensated dating" *(enjo kōsai)* among high-school and even middle-school girls has constituted a prominent object of public concern (and curiosity), to which the government responded in 1999 by enacting a new Law for Punishing Acts Related to Child Prostitution and Child Pornography, and for Protecting Children.[16] Although this particular phenomenon may not be as extensive as media reports suggest, the spread of cell phones and the Internet, ready access to a variety of part-time service jobs, the increasing popularity of styles such as hair dying or bleaching among youths of both sexes, and the massive daily flows of young people into globalized urban play-spaces such as Tokyo's Shibuya do indeed appear to be straining, if not overwhelming, the ability of many schools to ensure students' adherence to institutional regulations and norms of Japanese adolescence. While authorities repeat their time-honored calls for expanded pedagogic cooperation among schools, families, communities, and protective agencies, the police have redoubled their interventions: in 2003, for example, officers across Japan provided "guidance" to 1.1 million minors for smoking, roaming the streets at night, or other activities seen as precursors of criminal behavior.[17]

A second panic has erupted since 1997, spurred by reports of teen crimes including knifings, beatings of homeless people or older salarymen, and a handful of gruesome murders such as the 1997 decapitation of a boy in Kōbe. The media's avid coverage of these cases has fostered images of a younger generation inured to violence and callous in its brutality; indeed, such coverage facilitated the revision of the Juvenile Law in 2001 to lower the age of criminal responsibility from sixteen to fourteen. Although violent crimes by young people actually occurred with greater frequency in the 1960s and 1980s (and the absolute numbers remain very low), such images no doubt reflect the anxieties of a society that, following the collapse of the economic bubble in 1993, has spent the better part of the last decade in the throes of recession.[18] Recent studies, however, have begun to suggest that the economic downturn has triggered a breakdown in high-school-to-work transition mechanisms and the creation of a large pool of idle youths beyond the reach of traditional socialization agencies.[19] Whether authorities act to develop new surveillance and socialization mechanisms in response to these changes remains to be seen.

Each outpouring of concern over juvenile delinquency and crime has prompted what one reporter has called "a new round of soul-searching about Japan's education system and the way children are raised."[20] And in each case, critics have pointed to the usual suspects in their search for an explanation. These include urbanization and atomization; the breakdown of the family and of effective parenting techniques; an excessive focus on exams and credentialism in education; mounting materialism and commercialism; and the glut of harmful forms of popular culture and opportunities for illicit sexual activity. To this mix, many progressive critics have added attacks on what they see as the fundamentally undemocratic nature of Japanese society and the persistence of prewar militarist, authoritarian attitudes in the educational system—as evinced, for example, in one middle-school principal's remark in the 1980s that schools and businesses should use Imperial Army tactical manuals for organizational guidance. Conservative or neonationalist critics, on the other hand, have attacked the lack of moral education in Japanese schools, an excessively permissive social climate, and the rampancy of poorly digested concepts of democracy, individual freedom, and human rights—thereby suggesting that Japan's defeat and subsequent occupation by the United States set in motion processes that undermined the moral certitudes and social discipline of the (idealized) pre-1945 national community.[21]

As these developments reveal, discourses on juvenile delinquency continue to figure prominently in efforts to organize class, status, gender, national, and racial identities in Japan. And if today's "Japanese are losing their ethical moorings," as one prominent psychiatrist has noted, they have been losing them for a long time—indeed, for as long as authorities have been trying to anchor them.[22] More than any quantitative measure of juvenile misbehavior, it is the overwrought anxiety concerning delinquency and the persistent efforts to mobilize society to prevent it that have characterized the century-long project to create ideal subjects in modern Japan.

Notes

INTRODUCTION

1. *Tōkyō Asahi shinbun*, August 3, 1927, evening edition, p. 1; ibid., August 13, 1927, evening edition, p. 7 (hereafter abbreviated as *TAS*). *Hōritsu shinbun*, August 5, 1927, p. 19.

2. On the Tokugawa state and status, see for example Herman Ooms, *Tokugawa Village Practice: Class, Status, Power, Law* (Berkeley: University of California Press, 1996), 323 for "production and delivery of tribute"; see also David L. Howell, *Geographies of Identity in Nineteenth-Century Japan* (Berkeley: University of California Press, 2005), and the sources cited in chapter 1, notes 4 and 5.

3. For a collection of early modern child-rearing guides, see Yamazumi Masami and Nakae Kazue, eds., *Kosodate no sho*, 3 vols. (Tokyo: Heibonsha, 1976); see also Kojima Hideo, "Japanese Concepts of Child Development from the Mid-Seventeenth to the Mid-Nineteenth Century," *International Journal of Behavioral Development* 9, no. 3 (1986): 315–29; Hiroko Hara and Mieko Minagawa, "From Productive Dependents to Precious Guests: Historical Changes in Japanese Children," in *Japanese Childrearing: Two Generations of Scholarship*, ed. David W. Shwalb and Barbara J. Shwalb (New York and London: Guilford Press, 1996), 9–30.

4. See for example Takashi Fujitani, *Splendid Monarchy: Power and Pageantry in Modern Japan* (Berkeley: University of California Press, 1996), esp. 19–21; Sheldon Garon, *Molding Japanese Minds: The State in Everyday Life* (Princeton, NJ: Princeton University Press, 1997); Sabine Frühstück, *Colonizing Sex: Sexology and Social Control in Modern Japan* (Berkeley: University of California Press, 2003); Susan L. Burns, "Constructing the National Body: Public Health and the Nation in Nineteenth-Century Japan," in *Nation Work: Asian Elites and National Identities*, ed. Timothy Brook and Andre Schmid (Ann Arbor: University of Michigan Press, 2000), 17–49; and Narita Ryūichi,

"Women and Views of Women within the Changing Hygiene Conditions of Late Nineteenth and Early Twentieth-Century Japan," *U.S.-Japan Women's Journal, English Supplement* 8 (1995): 64–86. For earlier approaches, see for example Kenneth B. Pyle, "The Technology of Japanese Nationalism: The Local Improvement Movement, 1900–1918," *Journal of Asian Studies* 33, no. 1 (November 1973): 51–65, and Ariizumi Sadao, "Meiji kokka to minshū tōgō," in *Iwanami kōza Nihon rekishi*, ed. Asao Naohiro et al., vol. 17 (Tokyo: Iwanami Shoten, 1976), 222–62.

5. For perspectives on the social construction of delinquency and other forms of deviance, see Howard S. Becker, *Outsiders: Studies in the Sociology of Deviance* (New York: The Free Press, 1973), esp. 1–18; Michel Foucault, *Discipline and Punish: The Birth of the Prison*, trans. Alan Sheridan (New York: Vintage Books, 1979); Jacques Donzelot, *The Policing of Families*, trans. Robert Hurley (New York: Pantheon, 1979); John R. Gillis, *Youth and History: Tradition and Change in European Age Relations, 1770–Present* (New York and London: Academic Press, 1974), esp. 133–83; and Anthony M. Platt, *The Child Savers: The Invention of Delinquency* (Chicago and London: University of Chicago Press, 1977). For histories of juvenile corrections in Japan that do not address the social construction of the problem, see for example Shigematsu Kazuyoshi, *Shōnen chōkai kyōikushi* (Tokyo: Daiichi Hōki Shuppan, 1976); Kyōsei Kyōkai, ed., *Shōnen kyōsei no kindaiteki tenkai* (Tokyo: Kyōsei Kyōkai, 1984); and Moriya Katsuhiko, *Shōnen no hikō to kyōiku* (Tokyo: Keisō Shobō, 1977). For works that do begin to address this issue, see Katō Hiroshi, *Fukushiteki ningenkan no shakaishi: yūsei shiso to hikō, seishinbyō o tōshite* (Kyoto: Kōyō Shobō, 1996), and Kano Masanao, "Furyō shōnen bunka toshite no eiga," in *Musei eiga no kansei*, vol. 2 of *Kōza Nihon eiga*, ed. Imamura Shōhei et al. (Tokyo: Iwanami Shoten, 1986), 320–34.

6. For the widely used phrase *treasures of the nation*, see for example Matsumoto Kōjirō, "Katei no sekinin," *Jidō kenkyū* 8, no. 6 (June 1905): 10. For the terminology of childhood and youth as developed by early-twentieth-century experts, see Takashima Heizaburō, *Jidō shinri kōwa* (Tokyo: Kōbundō Shoten, 1909), 24–29. On the gendering of the *shōjo*, see for example Jennifer Robertson, *Takarazuka: Sexual Politics and Popular Culture in Modern Japan* (Berkeley: University of California Press, 1998), 63–66.

7. For "radicalism of the streets," see Yamamoto Akira, "Taishū seikatsu no henka to taishū bunka," *Iwanami kōza Nihon rekishi*, vol. 19 (Tokyo: Iwanami Shoten, 1976), esp. 305. On interwar discourses of modernity, see Harry Harootunian, *Overcome by Modernity: History, Culture, and Community in Interwar Japan* (Princeton, NJ: Princeton University Press, 2000), and Miriam Silverberg, "Constructing the Japanese Ethnography of Modernity," *Journal of Asian Studies* 51, no. 1 (February 1992): 30–54.

8. For a discussion of the new middle class and social policy formation, see Desley Deacon, *Managing Gender: The State, the New Middle Class, and Women Workers, 1830–1930* (Melbourne: Oxford University Press, 1989). I treat these issues in detail in David R. Ambaras, "Social Knowledge, Cultural Capital, and the New Middle Class in Japan, 1895–1912," *Journal of Japanese Studies* 24, no. 1 (Winter 1998): 1–33.

9. On the concept of "moral entrepreneurs," see Becker, *Outsiders,* 147–63; as applied to the juvenile reform movement in the United States, see Platt, *The Child Savers.* On professionals and social knowledge, see Robert Dingwall, introduction to *The Sociology of the Professions: Doctors, Lawyers, and Others,* ed. Robert Dingwall and Philip Lewis (New York: St. Martin's Press, 1983); Dietrich Rueschemeyer, "Professional Autonomy and the Social Control of Expertise," in ibid.; Dietrich Rueschemeyer and Theda Skocpol, eds., *States, Social Knowledge, and the Origins of Modern Social Policies* (Princeton, NJ: Princeton University Press, 1996); and Foucault, *Discipline and Punish.*

10. On concerns to prevent social dislocations, see for example Kenneth B. Pyle, "The Advantages of Followership: German Economics and Japanese Bureaucrats, 1890–1925," *Journal of Japanese Studies* 1, no. 1 (Autumn 1974): 127–64; Sheldon Garon, *The State and Labor in Modern Japan* (Berkeley: University of California Press, 1987); and Jeffrey E. Hanes, *The City as Subject: Seki Hajime and the Reinvention of Modern Osaka* (Berkeley: University of California Press, 2002).

11. On the transmission and adaptation of European chronicles of colonial and urban "darkness," see Maeda Ai, "Gokusha no yūtopia," in *Toshi kūkan no naka no bungaku,* vol. 5 of *Maeda Ai chosakushū* (Tokyo: Chikuma Shobō, 1989), 123–30. For these discourses in England, see Deborah Epstein Nord, "The Social Investigator as Anthropologist: Victorian Travellers among the Urban Poor," in *Visions of the Modern City: Essays in History, Art, and Literature,* ed. William Sharpe and Leonard Wallock (Baltimore and London: Johns Hopkins Univeristy Press, 1987), 122–34; and Susan Thorne, "'The Conversion of Englishmen and the Conversion of the World Inseparable': Missionary Imperialism and the Language of Class in Early Industrial Britain," in *Tensions of Empire: Colonial Cultures in a Bourgeois World,* ed. Frederick Cooper and Ann Laura Stoler (Berkeley: University of California Press, 1997), 238–62. For France, see Eugen Weber, *Peasants into Frenchmen: The Modernization of Rural France, 1870–1914* (Stanford, CA: Stanford University Press, 1976), 485–96.

12. On gender and erotic exchanges in the interwar years, see for example Miriam Silverberg, "The Modern Girl as Militant," in *Recreating Japanese Women, 1600–1945,* ed. Gail Lee Bernstein (Berkeley: University of California Press, 1991), 239–66; Miriam Silverberg, "The Café Waitress Serving Modern Japan," in *Mirror of Modernity: Invented Traditions of Modern Japan,* ed. Stephen Vlastos (Berkeley: University of California Press, 1998), 208–25; and Minami Hiroshi, ed., *Nihon modanizumu no kenkyū: shisō, seikatsu, bunka* (Tokyo: Bureen Shuppan, 1982).

13. Matsumoto Kōjirō, *Katei ni okeru jidō kyōiku* (Tokyo: Kokkōsha, 1906), 2. On new forms of domesticity and child-rearing strategies in modern Japan, see for example Sharon H. Nolte and Sally Ann Hastings, "The Meiji State's Policy toward Women, 1890–1910," in *Recreating Japanese Women, 1600–1945,* ed. Gail Lee Bernstein, 151–74; Fukaya Masashi, *Ryōsai kenbo shugi no kyōiku* (Nagoya: Reimei Shobō, 1998); Jordan Sand, "At Home in the Meiji Period: Inventing Japanese Domesticity," in Vlastos, ed., *Mirror of Modernity,* 191–207; Sawayama Mikako, "Kosodate ni okeru otoko to onna,"

in *Nihon josei seikatsushi,* vol. 4, ed. Joseishi Sōgō Kenkyūkai (Tokyo: Tōkyō Daigaku Shuppankai, 1990), 125–62; Sawayama Mikako, "Kyōiku kazoku no seiritsu," in *Kyōiku: tanjō to shūen,* vol. 1 of *Sōsho umu, sodateru, oshieru: tokumei no kyōiku shi,* ed. Henshū Iinkai (Tokyo: Fujiwara Shoten, 1990), 108–31; and Kathleen S. Uno, *Passages to Modernity: Motherhood, Childhood, and Social Reform in Early Twentieth Century Japan* (Honolulu: University of Hawai'i Press, 1999).

14. On the historical traditions of youth, see for example Gillis, *Youth and History;* and David Matza, "The Subterranean Traditions of Youth," *Annals of the American Academy of Political and Social Science* 228 (1961): 102–18.

15. This formulation draws on Satadru Sen, "A Separate Punishment: Juvenile Offenders in Colonial India," *Journal of Asian Studies* 63, no. 1 (February 2004), 82. On juvenile penitentiaries for youths convicted of more serious offenses, which are beyond the scope of this study, see Shigematsu, *Shōnen chōkai kyōikushi;* and Kyōsei Kyōkai, ed., *Shōnen kyōsei no kindaiteki tenkai.*

16. This approach draws on, for example, Linda Gordon, *Heroes of Their Own Lives: The Politics and History of Family Violence, Boston, 1880–1960* (New York: Viking, 1988); Mary E. Odem, *Delinquent Daughters: Protecting and Policing Adolescent Female Sexuality in the United States, 1885–1920* (Chapel Hill: University of North Carolina Press, 1995); see also Eric C. Schneider, *In the Web of Class: Delinquents and Reformers in Boston, 1810s–1930s* (New York: New York University Press, 1992); and Tamara K. Hareven, "The History of the Family and the Complexity of Social Change," *American Historical Review* 96, no. 1 (February 1991), esp. 121–23.

17. On literary representations of urban space and life, see Maeda, *Toshi kūkan no naka no bungaku.* See also Judith R. Walkowitz, *City of Dreadful Delight: Narratives of Sexual Danger in Late-Victorian London* (Chicago: University of Chicago Press, 1992); and Deborah Epstein Nord, *Walking the Victorian Streets: Women, Representation, and the City* (Ithaca, NY: Cornell University Press, 1995).

18. Yasushi Yamanouchi, "Total War and System Integration: A Methodological Introduction," in *Total War and "Modernization,"* ed. Yasushi Yamanouchi, J. Victor Koschmann, and Ryūichi Narita (Ithaca, NY: East Asia Program, Cornell University, 1998), 3–39.

19. For one example, see "Toshi no hattatsu to furyō shōnen," reprinted in Sakaguchi Shizuo, *Furyō shōnen no kenkyū* (Tokyo: Nakamura Yasuke, distributed by Nihon Keisatsu Shinbunsha, 1917), 54–68.

20. On rural youth as a "problem" in the Tokugawa and Meiji eras, see for example Ujiie Mikito, *Edo no shōnen* (Tokyo: Heibonsha, 1994); Michiko Tanaka, "Village Youth Organizations (Wakamono Nakama) in Late Tokugawa Politics and Society" (Ph.D. diss., Princeton University, 1982); and Miyachi Masato, *Nichi-Ro sengo seijishi no kenkyū* (Tokyo: Tōkyō Daigaku Shuppankai, 1982), 46–69. On youth groups, reservist organizations, and youth training centers, see ibid; Richard J. Smethurst, *A Social Basis for Prewar Japanese Militarism: The Army and the Rural Community* (Berkeley: University of California Press, 1974); Leonard A. Humphreys, *The Way of the Heavenly Sword: The Japanese*

Army in the 1920s (Stanford, CA: Stanford University Press, 1995), esp. 91–93. For studies that emphasize the ambivalent mentalities of rural youths in these associations, see Kano Masanao, "Sengo keiei to nōson kyōiku: Nichi-Ro sensōgo no seinendan undō ni tsuite," *Shisō* 521 (November 1967): 42–59; and Kano Masanao, *Taishō demokurashii no teiryū: "dozoku" teki seishin e no kaiki* (Tokyo: Nihon Hōsō Shuppan Kyōkai, 1973), 29–32, 95–134.

21. Population figures are drawn from Tōyō Keizai Shinpōsha, ed., *Meiji Taishō kokusei sōran* (Tokyo: Tōyō Keizai Shinpōsha, 1975), 637; and Tōyō Keizai Shinpōsha, ed., *Kanketsu Shōwa kokusei sōran* (Tokyo: Tōyō Keizai Shinpōsha, 1991), 1:33–35. For histories of Tokyo, see Tōkyō hyakunenshi Henshū Iinkai, ed., *Tōkyō hyakunenshi*, 7 vols. (Tokyo: Tōkyō-to, 1979–80); Ishizuka Hiromichi and Narita Ryūichi, *Tōkyō-to no hyakunen* (Tokyo: Yamakawa Shuppansha, 1986); Edward Seidensticker, *Low City, High City: Tokyo from Edo to the Earthquake* (New York: Alfred A. Knopf, 1983); and Edward Seidensticker, *Tokyo Rising: The City since the Great Earthquake* (New York: Knopf, distributed by Random House, 1990).

22. Christine Stansell, *City of Women: Sex and Class in New York, 1789–1860* (Urbana: University of Illinois Press, 1987), xiv. On the symbolic centrality of Tokyo, see Henry D. Smith, "Tokyo as an Idea: An Exploration of Japanese Urban Thought until 1945," *Journal of Japanese Studies* 4, no. 1 (Winter 1978): 45–80; Narita Ryūichi, "Teito Tōkyō," in *Iwanami Kōza Nihon tsūshi*, ed. Asao Naohiro et al., vol. 16 (Tokyo: Iwanami Shoten, 1993), 175–214; and Yoshimi Shun'ya, "(Sōsetsu) Teito Tōkyō to modanitii no bunka seiji," in *Kakudai suru modanitii: 1920–30 nendai 2*, vol. 6 of *Iwanami kōza kindai Nihon no bunkashi*, ed. Komori Yōichi et al. (Tokyo: Iwanami Shoten, 2002), 1–62. For a succinct overview of Japan's modern urban development, see Narita Ryūichi, "Kindai toshi to minshū," in *Toshi to minshū*, ed. Narita Ryūichi, vol. 9 of *Kindai Nihon no kiseki* (Tokyo: Yoshikawa Kōbunkan, 1993), 1–56.

CHAPTER 1

1. Shihōshō, ed., *Tokugawa kinrei kō goshū*, vol. 5 (Tokyo: Yoshikawa Kōbunkan, 1932), 440–55.

2. See for example Tanaka, "Village Youth Organizations"; Nakayama Tarō, *Nihon wakamono shi* (Tokyo: Parutosusha, 1983); and Tani Teruyuki, *Wakamono nakama no rekishi* (Tokyo: Nihon Seinenkan, 1984). For a discussion of the category of "youths" in terms of the discourse of male-male sexuality, see Gregory M. Pflugfelder, *Cartographies of Desire: Male-Male Sexuality in Japanese Discourse, 1600–1950* (Berkeley: University of California Press, 1999), esp. 29–44.

3. Rough ages can be inferred from broader contextual information. See for example Gary P. Leupp, *Servants, Shophands, and Laborers in the Cities of Tokugawa Japan* (Princeton, NJ: Princeton University Press, 1992), 57–61, and Minami Kazuo, *Bakumatsu Edo shakai no kenkyū* (Tokyo: Yoshikawa Kōbunkan, 1978), 211.

4. Howell, *Geographies of Identity;* see also David L. Howell, "Territoriality and Collective Identity in Tokugawa Japan," *Daedalus* 127, no. 3 (Summer 1998): esp. 106–7. In English, see Ooms, *Tokugawa Village Practice,* and John W. Hall, "Rule by Status in Tokugawa Japan," *Journal of Japanese Studies* 1, no. 1 (Autumn 1974): 39–49. For overviews in Japanese, see Asao Naohiro, ed., *Mibun to kakushiki,* vol. 7 of *Nihon no kinsei,* ed. Tsuji Tatsuya and Asao Naohiro (Tokyo: Chūō Kōronsha, 1992). See also Mizumoto Kunihiko, "Mura kyōdōtai to mura shihai"; Yoshida Nobuyuki, "Chōnin to chō"; and Yokota Fuyuhiko, "Shokunin to shokunin shūdan," all in *Kōza Nihon rekishi,* vol. 5, ed. Nihonshi Kenkyūkai and Rekishigaku Kenkyūkai (Tokyo: Tōkyō Daigaku Shuppankai, 1985), 117–226.

5. Mary Elizabeth Berry, "Public Life in Authoritarian Japan," *Daedalus* 127, no. 3 (Summer 1998), 141. See also Herman Ooms, *Tokugawa Ideology: Early Constructs, 1570–1680* (Princeton, NJ: Princeton University Press, 1985). On sumptuary regulations, see for example Donald H. Shively, "Sumptuary Regulation and Status in Early Tokugawa Japan," *Harvard Journal of Asiatic Studies* 25 (1964–65): 123–64.

6. Eiko Ikegami, *The Taming of the Samurai: Honorific Individualism and the Making of Modern Japan* (Cambridge, MA, and London: Harvard University Press, 1995), 204–6; Ono Susumu, Satake Akihiro, and Maeda Kingorō, eds., *Iwanami Kogo jiten* (Tokyo: Iwanami Shoten, 1974), s.v. "Kabukimono," 321.

7. Kitajima Masamoto, "Kabukimono: sono kōdō to ronri," in *Kinseishi no gunzō* (Tokyo: Yoshikawa Kōbunkan, 1977), 113–31; see also Ikegami, *The Taming of the Samurai,* ch. 10. On male-male sexuality, especially the political threat of *shudō* ties, see Pflugfelder, *Cartographies of Desire,* 128–32. See also Ujiie, *Edo no shōnen,* 141–60, on the lineages of eroticized "fraternal allegiances."

8. Information on this case is taken from Kitajima, "Kabukimono," 119–21; Ikegami, *The Taming of the Samurai,* 208–9; and "Otorii Ichibyōe gumi no koto," *Keichō kenmon shū,* reprinted in *Nihon shomin seikatsu shiryō shūsei,* vol. 8, ed. Miyamoto Tsuneichi and Haraguchi Torao (Tokyo: San'ichi Shobō 1969), 561–63.

9. "Otorii Ichibyōe gumi no koto," 561.

10. Kitajima, "Kabukimono," 134–38. On the formation of the urban lower class and the hiring of warrior servants, see Yoshida Nobuyuki, "Nihon kinsei toshi kasō shakai no sonzai kōzō," *Rekishigaku kenkyū* 534 (October 1984): 2–8. On the changing nature of service, lengths of employment contracts, and the role of employment agencies, see also Leupp, *Servants, Shophands, and Laborers,* 15–28, 69–72.

11. Yoshida, "Nihon kinsei toshi kasō shakai," 6.

12. Kitajima, "Kabukimono," 138–39. On servants, bosses, and gambling in samurai residences, see also Yoshida, "Nihon kinsei toshi kasō shakai," 5; and Leupp, *Servants, Shophands, and Laborers,* 117.

13. Bitō Masahide, *Genroku jidai,* vol. 19 of *Nihon no rekishi* (Tokyo: Chūō Kōronsha, 1987), 88–96, 102; Kitajima, "Kabukimono," 135–40; Kodama Kōta, *Genroku jidai,* vol. 16 of *Nihon no rekishi* (Tokyo: Chūō Kōronsha, 1966), 80–82.

14. Nishiyama Matsunosuke et al., eds., *Edogaku jiten* (Tokyo: Kōbundō, 1984), s.v. "Otokodate," 298–300; Bitō, *Genroku jidai*, 96–98; Kitajima, "Kabukimono," 140–44; Kodama, *Genroku jidai*, 80–93; Gary P. Leupp, "The Five Men of Naniwa: Gang Violence and Popular Culture in Genroku Osaka," in *Osaka: The Merchants' Capital of Early Modern Japan*, ed. James L. McClain and Wakita Osamu (Ithaca, NY: Cornell University Press, 1999), 128. For one account of the life and murder of Banzuiin Chōbei, see A. B. Mitford, *Tales of Old Japan* (Rutland, VT, and Tokyo: Charles E. Tuttle Company, 1966), 90–124.

15. Kitajima, "Kabukimono," 141–42, 149; Kodama, *Genroku jidai*, 84–86; Bitō, *Genroku jidai*, 106; Nishiyama Matsunosuke, "Edokko," in *Edo chōnin no kenkyū*, vol. 2, ed. Nishiyama Matsunosuke (Tokyo: Yoshikawa Kōbunkan, 1973), 53–54.

16. Katō Takashi, "Governing Edo," in *Edo and Paris: Urban Life and the State in the Early Modern Era*, ed. James L. McClain, John M. Merriman, and Ugawa Kaoru (Ithaca, NY: Cornell University Press, 1994), 50–51.

17. These measures are discussed in Bitō, *Genroku jidai*, 86–89; and Kitajima, "Kabukimono," 141, 144–50. On *kabuki*, see Donald H. Shively, "*Bakufu* vs. *Kabuki*," *Harvard Journal of Asiatic Studies* 18, nos. 3–4 (December 1955), 326–54; and Pflugfelder, *Cartographies of Desire*, 112–16.

18. Hishikawa Moronobu, *Konokorokusa*, quoted in Bitō, *Genroku jidai*, 106–7; for a similar contrast, written over a century later, see Buyō Inshi, *Seji kenmonroku* (1816), in *Kinsei shakai keizai sōsho*, vol. 1, ed. Honjo Eijirō et al. (Tokyo: Kaizōsha, 1926), 211–12.

19. Nishiyama Matsunosuke, *Edo Culture: Daily Life and Diversions in Early Japan, 1600–1868*, trans. Gerald Groemer (Honolulu: University of Hawai'i Press, 1997), 212–16; Nishiyama, "Edokko," 54–59.

20. Pflugfelder, *Cartographies of Desire;* the quoted passages are on 98–99, 131–32.

21. Ujiie, *Edo no shōnen*, esp. 141–46; Pflugfelder, *Cartographies of Desire*, 133; see ibid., 131–32, for examples from other domains.

22. Katsu Kokichi, *Musui's Story: The Autobiography of a Tokugawa Samurai*, trans. Teruko Craig (Tuscon: The University of Arizona Press, 1988), 60.

23. Ibid., 59–69; see also 23–46 for an account of an earlier episode of running away.

24. See ibid., 41, for a reference to this possibility.

25. Morisue Yoshiaki et al., eds., *Seikatsushi 2*, vol. 16 of *Taikei Nihonshi sōsho*, ed. Andō Yoshio et al. (Tokyo: Yamakawa Shuppansha, 1966), 336–48; see also Teruko Craig, "Introduction," in Katsu, *Musui's Story*, xi–xiv; and Marius B. Jansen, *The Making of Modern Japan* (Cambridge, MA: The Belknap Press of Harvard University Press, 2000), 101–11.

26. Buyō Inshi, *Seji kenmonroku*, 19. On nineteenth-century samurai and townsmen sharing a common language rooted in the city's popular culture, see Henry D. Smith II, "The Edo-Tokyo Transition: In Search of Common Ground," in *Japan in Transition: From Tokugawa to Meiji*, ed. Marius B. Jansen and Gilbert Rozman (Princeton, NJ: Princeton University Press, 1986), 361.

27. Katsu, *Musui's Story*, 71–108; the quoted passage is on 106.

28. Anne Walthall, "Edo Riots," in McClain, Merriman, and Ugawa, eds., *Edo and Paris*, 413–15; the quoted passage is on 414; Takeuchi Makoto, "Festivals and Fights: The Law and the People of Edo," in ibid., 386–91; Morisue et al., eds., *Seikatsushi 2*, 356–57.

29. Kokushi daijiten Henshū Iinkai, ed., *Kokushi daijiten*, vol. 3 (Tokyo: Yoshikawa Kōbunkan, 1983), s.v. "Kansei no kaikaku," 860–62; the quoted passage is on 861. See also Herman Ooms, *Charismatic Bureaucrat: A Political Biography of Matsudaira Sadanobu, 1758–1829* (Chicago: University of Chicago Press, 1975), 77–104.

30. Ujiie, *Edo no shōnen*, 130–38. On the symbolic manipulation and questionable veracity of these rumors, see ibid., and Walthall, "Edo Riots," 415–18.

31. Ōkurashō, ed., *Nihon zaisei keizai shiryō*, vol. 7 (Tokyo: Zaisei Keizai Gakkai, 1925), 772. The first paragraph is translated in Takeuchi, "Festivals and Fights," 402.

32. Tani, *Wakamono nakama no rekishi*, 107–8.

33. Takeuchi, "Festivals and Fights," 402; a similar injunction followed in 1798. Late-nineteenth-century sources on Tokyo customs, which carried over from Edo practices, indicate that boys joined the neighborhood *wakaishu* at the age of seventeen or eighteen. See Hirade Kojirō, *Tōkyō fūzokushi*, vol. 1, in *Meiji bunka shiryō sōsho*, vol. 12, ed. Ōtō Tokihiko (Tokyo: Kazama Shobō, 1960), 27. For a literary account, see Higuchi Ichiyō, "Takekurabe" (1895–96), in *Higuchi Ichiyō*, ed. Tsubouchi Yūzō, vol. 17 of *Meiji no bungaku* (Tokyo: Chikuma Shobō, 2000), 122.

34. Takeuchi, "Festivals and Fights," 384–86.

35. Ibid., 397–98, 402–3; the quoted passages are on 397, 402–3. See also Ujiie, *Edo no shōnen*, esp. 118–19, on rising perceptions of children and young people as a threat.

36. Katō, "Governing Edo," 57; see also 53–58 on neighborhood administration.

37. Takeuchi, "Festivals and Fights," 385–86, 399–405. See also Nishiyama et al., eds., *Edogaku jiten*, s.v. "Kenka," 582–83; and Yoshida Nobuyuki, "Yatagorō Genshichi no shō: oyabun, tōrimono no isō," in *"Kamiyui Shinza" no rekishi sekai*, ed. Yoshida Nobuyuki, vol. 19 of *Asahi hyakka Nihon no rekishi bessatsu: rekishi o yominaosu* (Tokyo: Asahi Shinbunsha, 1994), 48–56.

38. For a discussion of notions of territoriality in the world of the Edo common people, see Yoshida, "Yatagorō Genshichi no shō," 54–56.

39. On firefighter wakamono, see for example the 1839/7/7 entry in Fujiokaya [Sudō] Yoshizō, *Fujiokaya nikki*, in *Kinsei shomin seikatsu shiryō*, ed. Suzuki Tōzō and Koike Shōtarō (Tokyo: San'ichi Shobō, 1987–95), 2:107. On firefighters, see William Kelly, "Incendiary Actions: Fires and Firefighting in the Shogun's Capital and the People's City," in McClain, Merriman, and Ugawa, eds., *Edo and Paris*, 310–31; and Ikegami Akihiko, "Edo hikeshi seido no seiritsu to tenkai," in Nishiyama, ed., *Edo chōnin no kenkyū*, 5:91–170. On the fish markets, see Yoshida Nobuyuki, *Seijuku suru Edo*, vol. 17 of *Nihon no rekishi* (Tokyo: Kōdansha, 2002), 286–326.

40. *Fujiokaya nikki*, entry for 1851/7/17, discussed in Yoshida, *Seijuku suru Edo*, 341. On the connections among firefighters, artisan bosses, *wakamono*,

and *yose,* see Nishiyama et al., eds., *Edogaku jiten,* s.v. "Yose," 527–28, and "Kōdan," 528–29.

41. Yoshida, "Yatagorō Genshichi no shō," 54–55.

42. See for example Terakado Seiken, *Edo hanjō ki* (1834), in *Shin Nihon koten bungaku taikei,* vol. 100 (Tokyo: Iwanami Shoten, 1996), 150–56. On bosses' dual roles, see for example Tsukada Takashi, *Mibunsei shakai to shimin shakai: kinsei Nihon no shakai to hō* (Tokyo: Kashiwa Shobō, 1992), 42–51.

43. For the text of an 1811 prohibition, see Shihōshō, ed., *Tokugawa kinrei kō goshū,* 5:550; for tattoos coming alive, see Terakado, *Edo hanjō ki,* 153. See also Tamaru Eri, "Otokodate no bunka," in Yoshida, ed., *"Kamiyui Shinza" no rekishi sekai,* 44–45.

44. See for example the critique of rural youth extravagance by Confucian scholar Yamada Sansen in 1834, quoted in Ujiie, *Edo no shōnen,* 193. On rural youth as a social problem, see ibid., 192–253; Tanaka, "Village Youth Organizations"; and Tani, *Wakamono nakama no rekishi.*

45. Edicts reprinted in Shigematsu, *Shōnen chōkai kyōikushi,* 67.

46. Takayanagi Kaneyoshi, *Edo jidai hinin no seikatsu,* vol. 21 of *Seikatsushi sōsho* (Tokyo: Yūzankaku, 1971), 28; see also Shigematsu, *Shōnen chōkai kyōikushi,* 74–77.

47. Santō Kyōden [Kitao Masanobu], *Edo umare uwaki no kabayaki* (1787), in *Kibyōshi sharebon shū,* ed. Mizuno Minoru, vol 58 of *Nihon koten bungaku taikei* (Tokyo: Iwanami Shoten, 1958), 148–49; see also the discussion in Noguchi Takehiko, *Edo wakamono kō* (Tokyo: Sanseidō, 1986), 137–40. For moralizers' criticisms, see for example Buyō Inshi, *Seji kenmonroku,* 172.

48. Ishikawa Ken, *Wagakuni ni okeru jidōkan no hattatsu* (Chiba: Seishisha, 1976), 115.

49. Ibid., 116. On earlier state efforts to promote moral education in private schools for Edo commoners *(terakoya),* see Karasawa Tomitarō, *Zōho Nihon kyōiku shōshi: kindai izen* (Tokyo: Seibundō Shinkōsha, 1978), 163. On the shogunate's educational ideology, see Ronald P. Dore, *Education in Tokugawa Japan* (Berkeley: University of California Press, 1965), esp. 232.

50. On tenants' sons, see Buyō Inshi, *Seji kenmonroku,* 201–3. On pickpockets, see especially Osatake Takeki, *Bakuto to suri no kenkyū* (Tokyo: Shinsensha, 1969); on state use of pickpocket leaders as police agents *(meakashi* or *tesaki),* see Kyūji Shimonkai, ed., *Kyūji shimon roku: Edo bakufu yakunin no shōgen* (Tokyo: Iwanami Shoten, 1986), 1:286. The 1796 edict on education suggests that local officials encouraged families to disown their problem children. Ishikawa, *Wagakuni ni okeru jidōkan no hattatsu,* 115.

51. Leupp, *Servants, Shophands, and Laborers,* 73; see ibid., 57–61, for data on the age structure and general youth of the servant population.

52. On socialization in merchant houses, see for example Hayashi Reiko, *Edodana hankachō* (Tokyo: Yoshikawa Kōbunkan, 1982); Hayashi Reiko, "Edodana no seikatsu," in Nishiyama, ed., *Edo chōnin no kenkyū,* 2:94–138; Hayashi Reiko, "Noren no uchigawa de," in *Shōnin no katsudō,* ed. Hayashi Reiko, vol. 5 of *Nihon no kinsei* (Tokyo: Chūō Kōronsha, 1992), 169–95; Nishizaka Yasushi, "Kinsei toshi to ōdana," in *Toshi no jidai,* ed. Yoshida Nobuyuki, vol. 9 of *Nihon no kinsei* (Tokyo: Chūō Kōronsha, 1992), 197–217;

and Morisue et al., eds., *Seikatsushi* 2, 248–59, which also discusses artisans' apprentices. On servant/apprentice types and functions in general, see Leupp, *Servants, Shophands, and Laborers*, 41–64.

53. Hayashi, *Edodana hankachō*, 115–79; Hayashi, "Edodana no seikatsu," 125–35; and Hayashi, "Noren no uchigawa de," 172–74. On kitchen hands *(daidokorokata)*, see Nishizaka, "Kinsei toshi to ōdana," 199–203.

54. Hayashi, *Edodana hankachō*, 142–46; see also ibid., 115–18. For examples from other merchant houses, particularly that of the Mizuguchiya merchant house in Nagoya, see Shigematsu, *Shōnen chōkai kyōikushi*, 49–53.

55. Buyō Inshi, *Seji kenmonroku*, 201.

56. Hayashi, "Edodana no seikatsu," 129.

57. See the cases in Shihōshō, ed., *Tokugawa kinrei kō goshū*, vol. 3 (Tokyo: Yoshikawa Kōbunkan, 1931), 436–41. On banishment, see Ishii Ryōsuke, *Edo no keibatsu* (Tokyo: Chūō Kōronsha, 1992), 78–81.

58. See for example Tsukada Takashi, *Kinsei Nihon mibunsei no kenkyū* (Kōbe: Hyōgo Buraku Mondai Kenkyūjo, 1987), esp. 205–337; and Takayanagi, *Edo jidai hinin no seikatsu*.

59. Tsukada, *Kinsei Nihon mibunsei no kenkyū*, 216.

60. Shihōshō, ed., *Tokugawa kinrei kō goshū*, 5:444; Takayanagi, *Edo jidai hinin no seikatsu*, 19–20; see also Higuchi Hideo, *Edo no hankachō* (Tokyo: Jinbutsu Ōraisha, 1963), 78–79. For evidence of a growing trend toward lenience toward children, see Shigematsu, *Shōnen chōkai kyōikushi*, 35–36, 62.

61. Tsukada, *Kinsei Nihon mibunsei no kenkyū*, 311, 320–22; Takayanagi, *Edo jidai hinin no seikatsu*, 34.

62. Minami Kazuo, *Edo no shakai kōzō* (Tokyo: Hanawa Shobō, 1969), 81–82; Daniel V. Botsman, *Punishment and Power in the Making of Modern Japan* (Princeton, NJ: Princeton University Press, 2004), ch. 4.

63. On the growth of the unregistered population, see Takayanagi, *Edo jidai hinin no seikatsu*, 35. On Sadanobu's poor relief policies, see Yoshida Nobuyuki, *Kinsei kyodai toshi no shakai kōzō* (Tokyo: Tōkyō Daigaku Shuppankai, 1991), 3–38.

64. For English-language studies of the Edo stockade, see Botsman, *Punishment and Power*, ch. 4; and Leupp, *Servants, Shophands, and Laborers*, 165–75. For studies in Japanese, see for example Ninsoku Yoseba Kenshōkai, ed., *Ninsoku yoseba shi: wagakuni jiyūkei, hoan shobun no genryū* (Tokyo: Sōbunsha, 1974); Hiramatsu Yoshirō, *Edo no tsumi to batsu* (Tokyo: Heibonsha, 1988); Minami, *Edo no shakai kōzō*, 90–144; and Tsukada, *Mibunsei shakai to shimin shakai*, 67–98. On Shingaku, see Janine Anderson Sawada, *Confucian Values and Popular Zen: Sekimon Shingaku in Eighteenth-Century Japan* (Honolulu: University of Hawai'i Press, 1993); and Robert N. Bellah, *Tokugawa Religion: The Values of Pre-Industrial Japan* (Glencoe, IL: Free Press, 1957).

65. Shigematsu, *Shōnen chōkai kyōikushi*, 39–40; Minami, *Edo no shakai kōzō*, 117. For the Nakai brothers' ideas, see Nakai Riken, "Jukkei bōgi" (ca. 1785), in *Nihon keizai taiten*, vol. 23, ed. Takimoto Seiichi (Tokyo: Keimeisha, 1929), 707–16; Nakai Chikuzan, *Sōbō kigen* (1789), in ibid., 535–36; and Botsman, *Punishment and Power*.

66. Minami, *Edo no shakai kōzō*, 121–22.

67. Shigematsu, *Shōnen chōkai kyōikushi*, 68. This law thus substituted banishment for the death penalty.

68. Ibid., 45.

69. For analyses of the stockade and the status system, see Tsukada, *Mibunsei shakai to shimin shakai*, 67–98, esp. 94–96; and Botsman, *Punishment and Power*. For a view of the stockade as part of the disciplining of a new proletariat, see Leupp, *Servants, Shophands, and Laborers*, 165–75. For 1840s reports of recidivism, see Minami, *Edo no shakai kōzō*, 132. For 1869 inmate data, see Shigematsu, *Shōnen chōkai kyōikushi*, 1023–24. For stockade-like institutions and related practices in the first decade of the Meiji era, see ibid., 105–11, and Sumiya Mikio, *Nihon chinrōdō shiron* (Tokyo: Tōkyō Daigaku Shuppankai, 1974), 79–80.

70. On the crisis of the early nineteenth century, see for example H.D. Harootunian, "Late Tokugawa Culture and Thought," in *The Nineteenth Century*, ed. Marius B. Jansen, vol. 5 of *The Cambridge History of Japan* (Cambridge: Cambridge University Press, 1989), 168–258; and David L. Howell, "Hard Times in the Kantō: Economic Change and Village Life in Late Tokugawa Japan," *Modern Asian Studies* 23, no. 2 (1989): 349–71. On productivist ideologies, see also Morimoto Jun'ichirō, *Tokugawa jidai no yūminron* (Tokyo: Miraisha, 1985).

71. On Tokugawa diplomacy, see for example Ronald P. Toby, *State and Diplomacy in Early Modern Japan: Asia in the Development of the Tokugawa Bakufu* (Princeton, NJ: Princeton University Press, 1984); Arano Yasunori, *Kinsei Nihon to higashi Ajia* (Tokyo: Tōkyō Daigaku Shuppankai, 1988); and Howell, *Geographies of Identity*. For overviews of the nineteenth-century crisis in foreign relations and the political process leading to the Meiji Restoration, see W.G. Beasley, "The Foreign Threat and the Opening of the Ports," and Marius B. Jansen, "The Meiji Restoration," both in Jansen, ed., *The Nineteenth Century*.

72. For overviews of the Meiji Restoration, see for example Yasumaru Yoshio, "1850–70 nendai no Nihon: Ishin henkaku," in *Iwanami kōza Nihon tsūshi*, vol. 16, ed. Asao Naohiro et al. (Tokyo: Iwanami Shoten, 1993), 1–64, and the various essays in ibid.; and the essays in Jansen, ed., *The Nineteenth Century*.

CHAPTER 2

1. "Tōkyō no hinmin" part 2, *Jiji shinpō*, October 18, 1896, in *Meiji Tōkyō kasō seikatsushi*, ed. Nakagawa Kiyoshi (Tokyo: Iwanami Shoten, 1994), 103–7; the quoted passage is on 107. This reportage appeared in six parts, on October 11, 18, and 25, and November 1, 22, and 29, 1896, and is reprinted in full in ibid., 90–153; all references are to this reprinted version. Naruse Kametarō is a fictitious name assigned by poorhouse manager Adachi Kenchū, who recorded the interview (see below). Kametarō's age is reported as eleven, but this was most likely according to the traditional mode of reckoning; he was thus ten, or possibly nine, years old. On Tokyo as a showcase of modernity, see Smith, "Tokyo as an Idea."

2. Hirade Kojirō, *Tōkyō fūzokushi*, vol. 1, in *Meiji bunka shiryō sōsho*, vol. 12, ed. Ōtō Tokihiko (Tokyo: Kazama Shobō, 1960), 52–53. For "interesting materials," see Hensō Kisha, "Asakusa kōen no hitoyo: ichigatsu kokonoka yoru no sukettchi," part 1, *Shin kōron* 26, no. 2 (February 1911): 90.

3. Matsubara Iwagorō, *Shakai hyappōmen* (1897), in *Meiji bunka shiryō sōsho*, vol. 12, ed. Ōtō Tokihiko, 284. For metaphors of delinquency as disease, "miasma," or "bacillus," see for example Tomeoka Kōsuke, *Kanka jigyō no hattatsu* (Tokyo: Keiseisha Shoten, 1897), 145; and Tomeoka Kōsuke, *Katei Gakkō* (Tokyo: Keiseisha Shoten, 1901), 78–79, reprinted in *Nihon jidō mondai bunken senshū*, vol. 1, ed. Jidō Mondaishi Kenkyūkai (Tokyo: Nihon Tosho Sentā, 1983).

4. See for example Carol Gluck, *Japan's Modern Myths: Ideology in the Late Meiji Period* (Princeton, NJ: Princeton University Press, 1985).

5. Shijō Gakushirō, quoted in Yamamoto Tokushō, "Furō shōnen ni tsukite," part 1, *Jidō kenkyū* 8, no. 10 (October 1905): 16. On the time-space of modern Japan, see Fujitani, *Splendid Monarchy;* and Tessa Morris-Suzuki, *Re-Inventing Japan: Time, Space, Nation* (Armonk, NY, and London: M.E. Sharpe, 1998), esp. 9–34. See also Benedict Anderson, *Imagined Communities: Reflections on the Origins and Spread of Nationalism* (London and New York: Verso, 1991).

6. For a recent discussion of colonizing power within Japan, see Sabine Frühstück, *Colonizing Sex: Sexology and Social Control in Modern Japan* (Berkeley: University of California Press, 2003).

7. For the distinction between strategies and tactics, see Michel de Certeau, *The Practice of Everyday Life*, trans. Steven Rendall (Berkeley: University of California Press, 1984), esp. 29–42.

8. For an overview of economic developments in this period, see for example Takafusa Nakamura, *Economic Growth in Prewar Japan*, trans. Robert A. Feldman (New Haven, CT: Yale University Press, 1983); and Ishii Kanji, *Nihon keizaishi*, 2d ed. (Tokyo: Tokyo Daigaku Shuppankai, 1991).

9. Population figures are drawn from Naikaku Tōkeikyoku, ed., *Dai 14 kai Nihon teikoku tōkei nenkan* (Tokyo: Tōkeikyoku, 1895), 63; Naikaku Tōkeikyoku, ed., *Dai 36 kai Nihon teikoku tōkei nenkan* (Tokyo: Tōkeikyoku, 1918), 28; Tōyō Keizai Shinpōsha, ed., *Meiji Taishō kokusei sōran* (Tokyo: Tōyō Keizai Shinpōsha, 1975), 642–45; and Gluck, *Japan's Modern Myths,* 33. On the composition of the lower class, see Yoshida Kyūichi, *Nihon hinkonshi: seikatsushateki shiten ni yori mazushisa no keifu to sono jittai* (Tokyo: Kawashima Shoten, 1984), 224–36. For contemporary depictions of lower-class life, see for example Matsubara Iwagorō, *Saiankoku no Tōkyō* (1893) (Tokyo: Iwanami Shoten, 1992); Matsubara, *Shakai hyappōmen;* Yokoyama Gennosuke, *Nihon no kasō shakai* (1899) (Tokyo: Iwanami Shoten, 1949); Yokoyama Gennosuke, *Kasō shakai tanpōshū*, ed. Tachibana Yūichi (Tokyo: Shakai Shisōsha, 1990); and the various reports collected in Nakagawa, ed., *Meiji Tōkyō kasō seikatsushi.*

10. Yokoyama, *Nihon no kasō shakai,* 295. For an overview of the growing significance of social problems after 1895, see Matsunaga Shōzō, "Shakai mondai no hassei," in *Iwanami kōza Nihon rekishi,* ed. Asao Naohiro et al., vol. 16 (Tokyo: Iwanami Shoten, 1976), 241–80.

11. *Shakai zasshi* 1, no. 1 (April 1897): 1–2, quoted in Kawai Takao, "Kaidai," in *Meijiki shakaigaku kankei shiryō*, ed. Kawai Takao, vol. 1 (Tokyo: Ryūkei Shosha, 1991), 15–16. For information about turn-of-the-century study groups and their members, see Kawai, "Kaidai," 1–13; and Akamatsu Katsumaro, *Nihon shakai undō shi* (Tokyo: Iwanami Shoten, 1970), esp. 62–75.

12. For Tomeoka's ideas on philanthropists, see Tomeoka Kōsuke, *Jizen mondai* (Tokyo: Keiseisha Shoten, 1898), esp. 17–20. For attacks on Christianity, see Gluck, *Japan's Modern Myths*, esp. 132–34. I discuss the new middle class and the role of Protestantism in greater detail in Ambaras, "Social Knowledge," 1–33.

13. Pyle, "The Advantages of Followership," 127–64; the quoted passage is on 150. See also Garon, *The State and Labor in Modern Japan*, 25–29.

14. On the Hinmin Kenkyūkai, see Ikeda Yoshimasa, *Nihon shakai fukushishi* (Kyoto: Hōritsu Bunkasha, 1986), 374–77; and Ichibangase Yasuko, "Kaidai," in *Senzenki shakai jigyō shiryō shūsei*, vol. 1, ed. Shakai Fukushi Chōsa Kenkyūkai (Tokyo: Nihon Tosho Sentā, 1985), 10.

15. Gluck, *Japan's Modern Myths*, esp. 174–77; Miyachi, *Nichi-Ro sengo seijishi no kenkyū*; Andrew Gordon, *Labor and Imperial Democracy in Prewar Japan* (Berkeley: University of California Press, 1991), 11–79; Okamoto Shunpei, "The Emperor and the Crowd: The Historical Significance of the Hibiya Riot," in *Conflict in Modern Japanese History: The Neglected Tradition*, ed. Tetsuo Najita and J. Victor Koschmann (Princeton, NJ: Princeton University Press, 1982), 258–75. On the Ashio Mine riot, see Nimura Kazuo, *The Ashio Riot of 1907: A Social History of Mining in Japan*, trans. Terry Boardman and Andrew Gordon, ed. Andrew Gordon (Durham, NC: Duke University Press).

16. Pyle, "The Technology of Japanese Nationalism," 51–65; Gluck, *Japan's Modern Myths*, ch. 6; Miyachi, *Nichi-Ro sengo seijishi no kenkyū*.

17. See for example Naimushō Chihōkyoku, ed., *Kanka kyūsai jigyō kōenshū*, 2 vols. (Tokyo: Naimushō Chihōkyoku, 1909), reprinted in *Senzenki shakai jigyō shiryō shūsei*, vols. 18–20, ed. Shakai Fukushi Chōsa Kenkyūkai (Tokyo: Nihon Tosho Sentā, 1985). All subsequent references to this work refer to this reprint edition. On charity associations, see Ikeda, *Nihon shakai fukushishi*, 375–78.

18. Ogawa Shigejirō, "Kyōiku to hanzai to no kankei," part 2, *Shakai zasshi* 1, no. 10 (February 1898): 12–13. All references to this journal are to the reprint in Kawai, ed., *Meijiki shakaigaku kankei shiryō*, vols. 1–2.

19. Adachi Kenchū, *Koji akka no jōkyō* (manuscript, 1895), reprinted in *Nihon jidō mondai bunken senshū*, vol. 2, ed. Jidō Mondaishi Kenkyūkai (Tokyo: Nihon Tosho Sentā, 1983), esp. 35–36. Other versions of this text, some with slightly different contents, appeared as Adachi Kenchū, *Kyūji akka no jōkyo tsuketari shūyōhō* (Tokyo: Tōkyō-shi Yōikuin, 1898); and Adachi Kenchū, "Koji akka no jōkyō," *Shakai zasshi* 1, no. 12 (April 1898): 31–38.

20. Adachi, *Koji akka no jōkyō*, 11–14; see also "Sakkon no hinminkutsu: Shiba Shin'ami chō no tansa," *Hōchi shinbun*, November 25, 1897, in Nakagawa, ed., *Meiji Tōkyō kasō seikatsushi*, 169–70; and Hirade, *Tōkyō fūzokushi*, 1:36–39. On children put out as street performers in Boston, see Gordon, *Heroes of Their Own Lives*, 39–42.

21. "Tōkyō no hinmin" part 4, *Jiji shinpō,* November 1, 1896, in Nakagawa, ed., *Meiji Tōkyō kasō seikatsushi,* 122–28; "Furōji akka no jitsurei: dai ni rei," *Tōkyō Yōikuin geppō* 60 (February 25, 1906), reprinted in *Adachi Kenchū kankei shiryō: jiyū minken undō kara shoki shakai fukushi jigyō,* ed. Naitō Jirō (Tokyo: Sairyūsha, 1982), 293–94 (hereafter abbreviated as *AKKS*). On the fish market in the Meiji era, see Seidensticker, *Low City, High City,* 83.

22. The formulation "prayer and play" is taken from Nam-lin Hur, *Prayer and Play in Late Tokugawa Japan: Asakusa Sensōji and Edo Society* (Cambridge, MA, and London: Harvard University Asia Center, 2000).

23. Matsubara, *Shakai hyappōmen,* 284. For another report on Asakusa as a "den of evil" *(makutsu),* see Futaba-sei (pseudonym), "Asakusa Kōen," parts 1–3, *Chūō kōron,* no. 191 (February 1905): 89–94; no. 192 (March 1905): 87–93; and no. 194 (May 1905): 95–102. For Asakusa in the Meiji and Taishō eras, see Tōkyō-shi Asakusa Kuyakusho, *Asakusa-ku shi,* 2 vols. (Tokyo: Bunkaidō Shoten, 1914); Yoshimi Shun'ya, *Toshi no doramaturugii: Tōkyō, sakariba no shakaishi* (Tokyo: Kōbundo, 1987), 194–218; and Seidensticker, *Low City, High City.*

24. Hensō Kisha, "Asakusa kōen no hitoyo," part 1, p. 90.

25. "Tōkyō no hinmin," parts 2–4, in Nakagawa, ed., *Meiji Tōkyō kasō seikatsushi,* 107–28; Adachi, *Kyūji akka no jōkyō,* 30–32; Adachi, *Koji akka no jōkyō,* 69–78.

26. "Furōji akka no jitsurei: dai ichi rei," *Tōkyō Yōikuin geppō* 60 (February 25, 1906), in *AKKS,* 291–93.

27. Ibid., and "Furōji akka no jitsurei: dai ni rei," 293–94.

28. Adachi, *Kyūji akka no jōkyō,* 28.

29. "Furōji akka no jitsurei: dai jūyon rei," *Tōkyō Yōikuin geppō* 70 (December 25, 1906), in *AKKS,* 314–15. For similar declarations, see *AKKS,* 306, 310–11.

30. "Furōji akka no jitsurei: dai jūichi rei," *Tōkyō Yōikuin geppō* 68 (October 25, 1906), in *AKKS,* 309–10.

31. Matsubara, *Shakai hyappōmen,* 289.

32. "Furōji akka no jitsurei: dai jū rei," *Tōkyō Yōikuin geppō* 67 (September 25, 1906), in *AKKS,* 306.

33. Adachi Kenchū, "Kitsukai suri matawa settō ni kansuru no jikkyō," *Kokka Gakkai zasshi* 12, no. 138 (1898): 805–6; "Shōnen to hanzai," *Hōritsu shinbun* 247 (December 5, 1904): 1. On this spate of arson cases as a stimulus to new legislation to deal with juvenile delinquency, see Namae Takayuki, "Wagakuni jidō hogo jigyō no hatten katei to sono dōkō," part 2, *Shakai jigyō* 30, nos. 6–7 (June–July, 1947): 15. On slum youth scavenging at fire scenes, see Tengai Bōbō Sei (Yokoyama Gennosuke), "Shakai kansatsu," *Mainichi shinbun,* May 11, 1895, reprinted in Tachibana, ed., *Kasō shakai tanpōshū,* 46–47.

34. Sakuma Chōkei, *Ginmi no kuden,* reprinted in *Edo jidai hanzai keibatsu jireishū,* ed. Hara Taneaki and Osatake Takeki (Tokyo: Kashiwa Shobō, 1982), 265–66.

35. On continuities between *hinin* and ragpickers, see Ōgushi Natsumi, *Kindai hisabetsu burakushi kenkyū* (Tokyo: Akashi Shoten, 1980), 27. For an

example of contemporary perceptions of ragpickers as nonhuman, see Yokoyama, *Nihon no kasō shakai*, 38.

36. For the 1896 estimate of 300 street beggars and 150 juvenile ragpickers, see "Tōkyō no hinmin," parts 1 and 5, in Nakagawa, ed., *Meiji Tōkyō kasō seikatsushi*, 99, 134. For the 1917 police estimate of two thousand lower-class vagrants and thieves, excluding ragpickers, see Sakaguchi, *Furyō shōnen no kenkyū*, 147. Neither of these estimates included female street performers.

37. Adachi, "Koji akka no jōkyō," 38; Yokoyama, *Nihon no kasō shakai*, esp. 295; see also Matsubara, *Shakai hyappōmen*.

38. Adachi, "Koji akka no jōkyō," 36–37; Tomeoka Kōsuke, "Shakai seisaku toshite no kanka jigyō," in *Katei Gakkō dai ni hen*, ed. Tomeoka Kōsuke (Tokyo: Keiseisha Shoten, 1902), 31–32, reprinted in *Nihon jidō mondai bunken senshū*, vol. 1, ed. Jidō Mondaishi Kenkyūkai (Tokyo: Nihon Tosho Sentā, 1983). See also Matsubara, *Shakai hyappōmen*, 284; and Yokoyama, *Nihon no kasō shakai*, 50.

39. Quoted from *Shinsen Tōkyō meisho zue, Shitaya-ku no bu*, in *Meiji Tōkyō meisho zue*, ed. Asakura Haruhiko and Tsuchida Michifumi (Tokyo: Tōkyōdō Shuppan, 1992), 2:57. On flophouses, bedding, and other conditions, see Tengai Bōbō Sei (Yokoyama Gennosuke), "Tokai no hanmen" (1896), in Tachibana, ed., *Kasō shakai tanpōshū*, 81–90; Yokoyama, *Nihon no kasō shakai*, 48, 54–59; and Taiga Kyoshi (Sakurada Bungo), *Hintenchi kikankutsu tankenki* (1890), in Nakagawa, ed., *Meiji Tōkyō kasō seikatsushi*, 72–73. For an 1891 association of slums and cholera, see Kure Bunsō, "Tōkyō fuka hinmin no jōkyō," *Sutachisuchikku zasshi*, January 20, 1891, in Nakagawa, ed., *Meiji Tōkyō kasō seikatsushi*, 82. See also Ishizuka Hiromichi, *Nihon kindai toshi ron: Tōkyō, 1868–1923* (Tokyo: Tōkyō Daigaku Shuppankai, 1991), esp. 84–106; and Narita, "Teito Tōkyō," 186–87.

40. For example, Yokoyama, *Nihon no kasō shakai*, 49–52, 39, 326; English translation of "enviously ogling" (326) from Eiji Yutani, "*Nihon no kasō shakai* of Yokoyama Gennosuke" (Ph.D. diss., University of California, Berkeley, 1985), 544. See also Yatsuhama Tokusaburō, *Kasō shakai kenkyū* (Tokyo: Bungadō, 1920), 143–155.

41. On children in Shitaya's Mannenchō, see *Shinsen Tōkyō meisho zue, Shitaya-ku no bu*, 2:57. For the Samegahashi painting, see "Samegahashi no yūbe," *Fūzoku gahō* 277 (October 1903). On children hunting mice for bounty at the encouragement of Tokyo hygiene authorities, see *TAS*, January 12, 1900, and February 17, 1900, both reprinted in *Tōkyō hyakusai*, vol. 3 of *Asahi shinbun hyakunen no kiji ni miru*, ed. Asahi Shinbunsha (Tokyo: Asahi Shinbunsha, 1979), 54. On slum parents praising scavenging children, see Ishida Magotarō, "Hinmin jidō no kazokuteki kankei," *Jidō kenkyū* 6, no. 5 (May 1903): 30–31. On lower-class children's scavenging activities and their family economies in the early Meiji period, see Nakagawa Kiyoshi, "Senzen Tōkyō no toshi kasō," in *Toshi to gijutsu*, ed. Hayashi Takeshi and Koyano Seigo (Tokyo: United Nations University Press, 1995), 96. On scavenging and petty theft as part of working-class family economies in late-nineteenth- and early-twentieth-century England, see Stephen Humphries, *Hooligans or Rebels? An Oral History of Working-Class Childhood and Youth, 1889–1939* (Oxford: Blackwell, 1995), 150–73.

42. Yamamoto, "Furō shōnen ni tsukite," part 1, 17–18.

43. Nihon Gakudōkai, ed., *Akudō kenkyū* (Tokyo: Nanbokusha, 1916), 56–60. See also Yatsuhama Tokusaburō, "Shishō no kenkyū," *Kyūsai kenkyū* 2, no. 12 (December 25, 1914): 60–80.

44. Garon, *Molding Japanese Minds*, ch. 3. For a literary view from the commoners' side, see Higuchi, "Takekurabe," 98–148; in English: Higuchi Ichiyō, "Growing Up," trans. Edward Seidensticker, in *Modern Japanese Literature: From 1868 to the Present Day*, ed. Donald Keene (New York: Grove Press, 1956), 70–110.

45. Matsunaga, "Shakai mondai no hassei," 251–55; Tanaka Katsufumi, "Gimu kyōiku no rinen to hōsei," in *Kōza Nihon kyōikushi*, vol. 3, ed. Kōza Nihon kyōikushi Henshū Iinkai (Tokyo: Daiichi Hōki Shuppankai, 1984), 41–70; Katōda Keiko, "Wagakuni ni okeru hinji kyōiku: Tōkyō-shi tokushu jinjō shōgakkō no seiritsu to tenkai," *Shakai fukushi* 23 (1982): 88–89 (Tokyo: Nihon Joshi Daigaku Shakai Fukushi Gakka).

46. Yamada Kikusaburō, "Hinji no rōdō, chingin oyobi tori no machi," *Tōkyō-shi Kyōikukai zasshi* 89 (December 1912): 18.

47. On elementary-school-age children as a percentage of the industrial labor force, see Matsunaga, "Shakai mondai no hassei," 247. Ministry of Education directive *(kunrei)* no. 10, 1900, quoted in Tanaka, "Gimu kyōiku no rinen to hōsei," 64. On rural girls, family economies, and textile labor, see E. Patricia Tsurumi, *Factory Girls: Women in the Thread Mills of Meiji Japan* (Princeton, NJ: Princeton University Press, 1990).

48. "Fuka hinmin no shinkyō," part 6, *Chōya shinbun*, April 1, 1886, in Nakagawa, ed., *Meiji Tōkyō kasō seikatsushi*, 24; Yokoyama, *Nihon no kasō shakai*, 84. For conditions in the weaving establishments, see ibid., 93–127; and Tsurumi, *Factory Girls*, 174–80.

49. For the nostalgic view, see Tomeoka Kōsuke, "Kanka kyōiku ron," *Keisatsu Kyōkai zasshi* 66 (December 15, 1905), in *Tomeoka Kōsuke chosakushū*, 5 vols., ed. Dōshisha Daigaku Jinbun Kagaku Kenkyūjo (Kyoto: Dōmeisha, 1978–81), 2:184. For masters' unscrupulous behavior, see Yamamoto Tokushō, "Furō shōnen ni tsukite," part 3, *Jidō kenkyū* 8, no. 12 (December 1905): 16–18. For a different analysis, see Yokoyama, *Nihon no kasō shakai*, 84.

50. For the critique of the Osaka system, see Yatsuhama Tokusaburō, "Osaka no detchi seido" ("Keian no kenkyū," part 3), *Kyūsai kenkyū* 2, no. 1 (January 25, 1914): 52–53. For a summation of Ogawa's arguments on this theme, see Ogawa Shigejirō, "Shōnen rōdōsha no hogo," *Kyūsai kenkyū* 1, no. 1 (August 20, 1913): 6–7.

51. Ogawa, "Shōnen rōdōsha no hogo"; Nojiri Seiichi, "Kanka kyūsai jigyō to futsū kyōiku," in Naimushō Chihōkyoku, ed., *Kanka kyūsai jigyō kōenshū*, 2:314. On the Factory Law, see Garon, *The State and Labor in Modern Japan*, 26–29.

52. Nakagawa, "Senzen Tōkyō no toshi kasō," esp. 75–96. According to Ishizuka Hiromichi, one in two Tokyo residents in 1907 was an immigrant. Ishizuka, *Nihon kindai toshi ron*, 13–14.

53. Tengai Bōbō Sei (Yokoyama Gennosuke), "Kasō shakai no shin genshō: kyōdō nagaya," in Nakagawa, ed., *Meiji Tōkyō kasō seikatsushi,* 198–99.

54. Uno, *Passages to Modernity,* esp. 43, 59. For a fictional account of children's play based on the author's observations of life in a neighborhood on the fringes of the Yoshiwara licensed quarter, see Higuchi, "Takekurabe." For studies of the United States and England, see for example David Nasaw, *Children of the City: At Work and Play* (New York: Oxford University Press, 1985), and Humphries, *Hooligans or Rebels?*

55. Shigematsu, *Shōnen chōkai kyōikushi,* 114–16.

56. Information on the *chōjikan* is drawn from ibid., 116–37, 161–62; "thoughts of rebelliousness or murder" quoted from p. 118. For a discussion of Ohara Shigechika and the emergence of the prison in modern Japan, see Botsman, *Punishment and Power.*

57. Moriya, *Shōnen no hikō to kyōiku,* 19; Botsman, *Punishment and Power.*

58. Berry's report is reprinted in Shigematsu, *Shōnen chōkai kyōikushi,* 301–5; sections of Onoda's report, which was published in 1889 as *Taisei kangoku mondoroku,* are reprinted in ibid., 306–19.

59. Ibid., 139–41, 147.

60. Moriya, *Shōnen no hikō to kyōiku,* 24–25; Shigematsu, *Shōnen chōkai kyōikushi,* 151–52, 171–72.

61. Moriya, *Shōnen no hikō to kyōiku,* 34. On parents' reluctance, see for example the Chiba Kankain petition to the Diet, December 1893, in Kyōsei Kyōkai, ed., *Shōnen kyōsei no kindaiteki tenkai,* 201; on criticisms of the *chōjijō,* see ibid., 94–99. On disabled children committed to the *chōjijō,* see Shigematsu, *Shōnen chōkai kyōikushi,* 174–75. On prefectural assemblies, see ibid., 152.

62. Kozaki Hiromichi, "Chōkyōin o mōkezaru bekarazaru no gi," *Rikugō zasshi* 3 (December 11, 1880), reprinted in *Meiji bunka zenshū,* vol. 18, ed. Yoshino Sakuzō (Tokyo: Nihon Hyōronsha, 1928), 406–8. For early Meiji discussions and studies of Western reformatories, see for example "Eikoku ganjiin no setsu," trans. Yasuda Jirōkichi, *Shinjuku nisshi* 2 (1869/4), reprinted in ibid., 35–36; Kido Takayoshi, *The Diary of Kido Takayoshi,* vol. 2, trans. Sidney Devere Brown and Akiko Hirota (Tokyo: The University of Tokyo Press, 1985), 141; and Shigematsu, *Shōnen chōkai kyōikushi,* esp. 121, 272–99. On Protestantism in early Meiji Japan, see Irwin Scheiner, *Christian Converts and Social Protest in Meiji Japan* (Berkeley: University of California Press, 1970). On Protestant reform movements in the United States, see for example Paul Boyer, *Urban Masses and Moral Order in America, 1820–1920* (Cambridge, MA: Harvard University Press, 1978).

63. Shigematsu, *Shōnen chōkai kyōikushi,* 323–24, 328–40; Kyōsei Kyōkai, ed., *Shōnen kyōsei,* 197–201. On Buddhist involvement in social work as a response to Christian activism, see Yoshida Kyūichi, *Nihon kindai Bukkyō shakaishi kenkyū* (Tokyo: Kawashima Shoten, 1991); and James Edward Ketelaar, *Of Heretics and Martyrs in Meiji Japan: Buddhism and Its Persecution* (Princeton, NJ: Princeton University Press, 1990), esp. 133–35.

64. On the Tōkyō Kankain, see "Tōkyō Kankain sōgyōki" (1896), in *Meiji bunka shiryō sōsho*, vol. 6, ed. Kaji Ryūichi (Tokyo: Kazama Shobō, 1961), 215–32; and Kyōsei Kyōkai, ed., *Shōnen kyōsei*, 100–111.

65. Adachi republished his 1895 proposal in Adachi Kenchū, "Gaisen'in o okosu no gi," *Yōikuin geppō* 54 (August 25, 1905), in *AKKS*, 271–74. On the establishment of the Tokyo City Poorhouse reformatory division, see Shibusawa Seien Kinen Zaidan Ryūmonsha, ed., *Shibusawa Eiichi denki shiryō*, vol. 24 (Tokyo: Shibusawa Eiichi denki shiryō Kankōkai, 1959), 343–78; and Tōkyō-shi Yōikuin, ed., *Yōikuin rokujūnenshi* (Tokyo: Tōkyō-shi Yōikuin, 1933).

66. Report on the conference by Samuel J. Barrows, quoted in Negley Teeters, *Deliberations of the International Penal and Penitentiary Congresses: Questions and Answers, 1872–1935* (Philadelphia: Temple University Bookstore, 1949), 97, n. 14. For Ogawa's report on the conference, see Ogawa Shigejirō, *Gokujidan* (Tokyo: Tōkyō Shoin, 1901), 325–95.

67. Ogawa Shigejirō, "Miyoshi Taizō Shi sōritsu no kanka gakkō ni tsuite shokan o shirusu," *Kangoku zasshi* 8, nos. 3–4 (April 1900), reprinted in *Ogawa Shigejirō shū*, ed. Doi Yōichi and Endō Kōichi (Tokyo: Ōtori Shoin, 1980), 82. For Ogawa's 1903 doctoral dissertation on the treatment of juvenile offenders, see Ogawa Shigejirō, *Miseinen hanzaisha no shogū*, reprinted in *Ogawa Shigejirō chosaku senshū*, vol. 1, ed. Ogawa Hakase Ibun Kankōkai (Tokyo: Nihon Hyōronsha, 1942). For Home Ministry explorations of the possibility of establishing public reformatories since the 1880s, see Kyōsei Kyōkai, ed., *Shōnen kyōsei*, 99–100.

68. "Shūgiin Kanka hōan daiichi dokkai: Shūgiin giji sokkiroku dai 30 gō 616–618 kō" (February 19, 1900), reprinted in *Taishō shōnen hō*, vol. 1, ed. Morita Akira, vol. 18 of *Nihon rippō shiryō zenshū* (Tokyo: Shinzansha, 1993), 81–82.

69. Ogawa comments in "Kizokuin Kanka hōan tokubetsu iinkai giji sokkiroku daiichi gō" (February 22, 1900), reprinted in ibid., 117–18; see also 106, 114.

70. See for example Suzuki Kaichirō, ed., *Tōkyō Shōnen Shinpanjo jūnenshi* (Tokyo: Nihon Shōnen Hogo Kyōkai Tōkyō Shibu, 1935), 12–13.

71. "Kizokuin Kanka hōan tokubetsu iinkai giji sokkiroku daiichi gō" (February 22, 1900), reprinted in Morita, ed., *Taishō shōnen hō*, 1:105; and "Furyō shōnen ni kansuru chōsa," in "Shūgiin Kanka hō chū kaisei hōritsu an iinkai giroku (dai 5 rui dai 29 gō)," session 4 (March 13, 1908), in ibid., 165–66.

72. Shigematsu, *Shōnen chōkai kyōikushi*, 485–596; Moriya, *Shōnen no hikō to kyōiku*, 28–29.

73. For the Diet proceedings concerning the revision of the Reformatory Law, see Morita, ed., *Taishō shōnen hō*, 1:122–222; the revised articles are enumerated on 122. On Justice Ministry responses, see Suzuki, ed., *Tōkyō Shōnen Shinpanjo jūnenshi*, 14–17.

74. "Shūgiin Kanka hō chū kaisei hōritsu an iinkai giroku (dai 5 rui dai 29 gō)," sessions 2–4 (February 26 and March 13, 1908); "Shūgiin daiichi dokkai ni tsuzuki, dai ni dokkai" (Shūgiin giji sokkiroku dai 15 gō 300–301 kō), all reprinted in Morita, ed., *Taishō shōnen hō*, 1:124–74, esp. 131–33, 154–55,

171–72; Tokonami statements quoted from 132, 155. For a similar statement by a prominent reformer, see Tomeoka Kōsuke, "Kanka jigyō jisshi hōhō" (1912), in *Tomeoka Kōsuke Kun koki kinenshū*, ed. Makino Toraji (Tokyo: Tomeoka Kōsuke Kun Koki Kinen Jimusho, 1933), 492–93, reprinted as vol. 21 of *Denki sōsho* (Tokyo: Ōzorasha, 1987).

75. Kyōsei Kyōkai, ed., *Shōnen kyōsei*, 257.

76. *Hōritsu shinbun*, May 5, 1917, p. 14. The Home Ministry's 1901 Regulations for the Implementation of the Reformatory Law (Kanka hō shikō kisoku) included provisions for the types of education to be provided for girls. Reprinted in Tomeoka, *Katei Gakkō*, 194–96.

77. For the 1908 police survey, see Ōbinata Sumio, *Keisatsu no shakaishi* (Tokyo: Iwanami Shoten, 1993), 34–35. For similar survey results from 1914, see Yatsuhama, "Shishō no kenkyū," 67. For one statement that female juvenile delinquency included unlicensed sex work, see Nihon Gakudōkai, ed., *Akudō kenkyū*, 124. On the 1916 anti-prostitution campaign, see Maruyama Tsurukichi, *Gojūnen tokorodokoro* (Tokyo: Dai Nihon Yūben Kōdansha, 1934), 196–213.

78. Biographical information on Tomeoka is taken from the following sources: Tomeoka Kōsuke, "Katei Gakkō sōsetsu ni itaru made," in *Tomeoka Kōsuke Kun koki kinenshū*, ed. Makino Toraji, 29–39; Endō Kōichi, "'Shokutaku' toshite no Tomeoka Kōsuke," *Meiji Gakuin ronsō*, vols. 352–53: series *Shakaigaku, shakai fukushigaku kenkyū*, nos. 65–66 (March 1984), esp. 289–92; and Fujii Tsunefumi, *Fukushi kokka o tsukutta otoko: Tomeoka Kōsuke no shōgai, 1864–1934* (Tokyo: Hōsei Shuppan, 1992). Tomeoka's textbook is Tomeoka Kōsuke, *Kanka jigyō no hattatsu* (Tokyo: Keiseisha Shoten, 1897). For early books on the Family School, see Tomeoka, *Katei Gakkō* and Tomeoka, ed., *Katei Gakkō dai ni hen*. On the Police and Prisons School, see Baron Kanétaké Ōura, "The Police of Japan," in *Fifty Years of New Japan*, ed. Marcus B. Huish, comp. Shigénobu Ōkuma (London: Smith, Elder, and Co., 1909), 1:294; and Baron Suyematsu [Kenchō], "Police," in *Japan by the Japanese*, ed. Alfred Stead (New York: Dodd, Mead and Co., 1904), 506–9.

79. For Tomeoka's shift from a more heredetarian to a more environmentalist approach, see Tomeoka, "Kanka jigyō to sono kanrihō," 139–40. The characterization of Morrison's work is quoted from Platt, *The Child Savers*, 39. Morrison's classic text is William Douglas Morrison, *Juvenile Offenders* (London: T. Fisher Unwin, 1896). On criminological debates in Europe and the United States, see for example Platt, *The Child Savers*, 15–45; David Garland, *Punishment and Welfare: A History of Penal Strategies* (Hampshire, England: Gower, 1985), 73–111; and David G. Horn, *Social Bodies: Science, Reproduction, and Italian Modernity* (Princeton, NJ: Princeton University Press, 1994), 28–34.

80. For Tomeoka's rural agenda and "health, spirit, and vitality," see Tomeoka Kōsuke, "Tokai to inaka," *Jindō* 51 (July 5, 1909): 2; and Tomeoka, "Kanka jigyō jisshi hōhō," 456–57. For a discussion of anti-urbanism in late-Meiji ideology, with reference to Tomeoka, see Gluck, *Japan's Modern Myths*, 190–91.

81. Tomeoka, ed., *Katei Gakkō dai ni hen*, 162–71. Tomeoka also recognized that more difficult types of delinquents, like pickpockets and thieves,

might require barracks-style discipline, at least in the initial stages of reform. Ibid., 45–47. On ideas of the home, see for example Muta Kazue, "Images of the Family in Meiji Periodicals: The Paradox Underlying the Emergence of the 'Home'," *U.S.-Japan Women's Journal, English Supplement* 7 (1994): 53–71; Nishikawa Yūko, "The Changing Form of Dwellings and the Establishment of the Katei (Home) in Modern Japan," *U.S.-Japan Women's Journal, English Supplement* 8 (1995): 3–36; Sand, "At Home in the Meiji Period"; and Ambaras, "Social Knowledge."

82. Tomeoka, "Kanka jigyō jisshi hōhō," 471–75; "Kankainchō kyōgikai," entry for December 1, 1910, in *Tomeoka Kōsuke nikki,* ed. Tomeoka Kōsuke nikki Henshū Iinkai (Tokyo: Kyōsei Kyōkai, 1979), 3:551–54. For "civil morality," see Gluck, *Japan's Modern Myths,* chap. 5.

83. Tomeoka, "Kanka jigyō jisshi hōhō," 463–64; Sakai Yoshisaburō, "Kanka kyōiku ni okeru tanjihi no keiken," in Tomeoka, ed., *Katei Gakkō dai ni hen,* 77–82. For reports of mental and physical weakness, see Tomeoka Kōsuke, "Shintai no hanzai kōi ni oyobosu eikyō," in ibid., 89–95; and Tōkyō-shi Yōikuin, *Meiji 33 nendo Tōkyō-shi Yōikuin dai 29 kai hōkoku* (Tokyo: Tōkyō-shi Yōikuin, 1900), 45.

84. Koshio Takatsune, "Furyō shōnen no shurui," part 2, Jindō 17 (September 15, 1906): 7.

85. Arima Shirōsuke, "Shōnen hanzaisha no kun'iku," in Naimushō Chihōkyoku, ed., *Kanka kyūsai jigyō kōenshū,* 2:899.

86. Yatsuhama, *Kasō shakai kenkyū,* 291–93; the quoted passage is on 293. On the benefits of vocational education, see Kawatsu Shichirō, "Kanka jigyō to kōgyō kyōiku," in Naimushō Chihōkyoku, ed., *Kanka kyūsai jigyō kōenshū,* 1:436–37. For reservations about a full-blown vocational-school approach to reforming younger children, see Ogawa Shigejirō, "Kanka jigyō no honshitsu oyobi soshiki," *Kyūsai kenkyū* 2, nos. 10–12, and vol. 3, no. 1 (October 1914–January 1915), reprinted in *Ogawa Shigejirō chosaku senshū,* vol. 1, ed. Ogawa Hakase Ibun Kankōkai, 272–73.

87. Tomeoka, "Kanka jigyō jisshi hōhō," 469.

88. Tomeoka Kōsuke, "Kawagoe Yōnenkan o miru," *Kangoku Kyōkai zasshi* 17, no. 7 (July 20, 1904), reprinted in *Tomeoka Kōsuke chosakushū,* 2:83. For similar arguments, see Tejima Seiichi, "Kyūsai to shokugyō," *Jizen* 3, no. 2 (July 30, 1911): 22–37.

89. Ogawa, "Kanka jigyō no honshitsu oyobi soshiki," esp. 267–72; see also Ueda Kyūkichi, *Hogo kyōiku* (Tokyo and Osaka: Hōbunkan, 1911), 58–65.

90. Arima, "Shōnen hanzaisha no kun'iku," 913.

91. On administrative and budget problems, see Namae Takayuki, "Genkō Kanka hō ni tsuite," part 1, *Kyūsai kenkyū* 3, no. 2 (February 25, 1915): 80–82. On reformatories' staffing and implementation problems, see for example Ogawa, "Kanka jigyō no honshitsu oyobi soshiki," 252–53; and Ichi Kisha, "Inokashira Gakkō," *Jizen* 1, no. 2 (October 30, 1910): 87, 95–96.

92. Shibusawa Seien Kinen Zaidan Ryūmonsha, ed., *Shibusawa Eiichi denki shiryō,* 24:397, 402. Ichi Kisha, "Inokashira Gakkō," 89, puts the number of

Tokyo City Poorhouse reformatory admissions up to the year 1905 at 125, less than the 160 reported by Yamamoto.

93. Family School escape rates in "Kōshiritsu kankain no genjō," report included in Diet proceedings reprinted in Morita, ed., *Taishō shōnen hō*, 1:166–67; this also includes escape rates for the Tokyo Kankain, another private reformatory. For one study of the Family School, see Doi Yōichi, "Katei Gakkōshi kenkyū nōto: Sugamo Katei Gakkō o chūshin ni," *Shakai jigyōshi kenkyū* 2 (October 1974): 51–84.

94. *Tomeoka Kōsuke nikki*, 2:190, 192.

95. Ibid., 168–70. See also Kobayashi Hitomi, "Katei Gakkō to Koshio Juku ni kansuru kōsatsu: kanka kyōiku ni okeru 'katei' to 'gakkō'," *Kyōiku-gaku kenkyū* 58, no. 2 (June 1991): 23–24.

96. *Tomeoka Kōsuke nikki*, 2:192–95.

97. Information on the Shūsai Gakuen is from Hashimoto Shizuka, "Shūsai Gakuen no genkyō," in *Dai go kai kanka kyūsai kōenshū*, ed. Naimushō Chihōkyoku (Tokyo: Naimushō Chihōkyoku, 1913), 682–85; and Aida Yoshio, "Tōkyō-fu ni furitsu kankain no saichi o nozomu," *Shakai fukuri* 16, no. 8 (August 1932): 60–61.

98. Kobayashi, "Katei Gakkō to Koshio Juku," 24–26.

99. For reformatory directors' remarks, see "Zenkoku kankainchō kaigi," in *Tomeoka Kōsuke nikki*, 3:644–48; Namae's comments are in Namae Takayuki, "Genkō kankahō ni tsuite," part 2, *Kyūsai kenkyū* 3, no. 3 (March 25, 1915): 90.

100. For example, Ōhama Takashi, "Kyōto furyō shōnen kyūchisaku," part 1, *Hōritsu shinbun*, September 20, 1912, pp. 5–6.

101. "Incomprehensible" quoted in Shigematsu, *Shōnen chōkai kyōikushi*, 427. For Tomeoka's remarks, see Tomeoka, "Kawagoe yōnenkan o miru," 77. On the *yōnenkan* under Ogawa's influence, see Shigematsu, *Shōnen chōkai kyōikushi*, 391–463, 497–504; Moriya, *Shōnen no hikō to kyōiku*, 48–53; Hayasaki Haruka, "Shōnen hanzaisha no kun'iku," in Naimushō Chihōkyoku, ed., *Kanka kyūsai jigyō kōenshū*, 1:114–54; and Ueda, *Hogo kyōiku*.

102. Shigematsu, *Shōnen chōkai kyōikushi*, 513. The *chōjijō* had been formally abolished at the time of the revision of the Penal Code in 1907; however, they continued to operate as *yōnenkan* on a provisional basis.

103. Ogawa Shigejirō, "Kankain no tōsō jiko," *Kyūsai kenkyū* 2, no. 1 (January 25, 1914): 74–76.

104. Miyake Kōichi, "Furyō shōnen ni tsuite," *Keisatsu Kyōkai zasshi* 209 (1914): 6–8.

105. Miyake Kōichi and Ikeda Ryūtoku, "Furyō shōnen chōsa hōkoku," *Jidō kenkyū* 12, no. 9 (March 1909): 313–18.

106. On the Musashino Gakuin, see Kyōsei Kyōkai, ed., *Shōnen kyōsei*, 258–67. For reports and proposals by Musashino officers and psychiatrists associated with the Home Ministry, see Naimushō Shakaikyoku, ed., *Kanka kyōiku shiryō (Musashino Gakuin kenkyū hōkoku)* (Tokyo: Naimushō Shakaikyoku, 1921); Naimushō Shakaikyoku, ed., *Kankain shūyō jidō kanbetsu chōsa hōkoku* (Tokyo: Naimushō Shakaikyoku, 1925); and Naimushō

Shakaikyoku, ed., *Kankain shūyō jidō kanbetsu chōsa hōkoku fuhyō* (Tokyo: Naimushō Shakaikyoku, 1923), all reprinted in *Senzen Nihon shakai jigyō chōsa shiryō shūsei*, vol. 5, ed. Shakai Fukushi Chōsa Kenkyūkai (Tokyo: Keisō Shobō, 1990), 69–136.

107. Mimura Haruyo, "Furyō shōjo no kyōiku," in *Dai go kai kanka kyūsai kōenshū*, ed. Naimushō Chihōkyoku (Tokyo: Naimushō Chihōkyoku, 1913), 662–68. See also Miyoshi Akira, *Arima Shirōsuke* (Tokyo: Yoshikawa Kōbunkan, 1967), 173–82. The *Greater Learning for Women* is translated and reprinted in Basil Hall Chamberlain, *Things Japanese; Being Notes on Various Subjects Connected with Japan for the Use of Travellers and Others* (London: J. Murray, 1905); the quoted passages are on 502 and 507.

108. Quoted in Uno Riemon, "Kōjo daraku no keiro," *Kyūsai kenkyū* 3, no. 1 (January 25, 1915): 73.

109. Tomeoka, "Kanka jigyō to sono kanrihō," 225–27; see also Ueda, *Hogo kyōiku,* 149–52. On gendered treatments of sexual delinquency in the United States, see for example Steven Schlossman and Stephanie Wallach, "The Crime of Precocious Sexuality: Female Juvenile Delinquency in the Progressive Era," *Harvard Educational Review* 48, no. 1 (February 1978): 69.

110. For one example of police placing a girl in a geisha house, see Nihon Gakudōkai, ed., *Akudō kenkyū*, 114–15. On regulations governing young girls' entry into such establishments, see Ōbinata, *Keisatsu no shakaishi,* 42–43. On the use of the Women's Christian Temperance Union and Salvation Army shelters, see *Hōritsu shinbun,* May 28, 1917, p. 13; see also Maruyama, *Gojūnen tokorodokoro,* 205.

111. Directive from Local Affairs Bureau Chief Yamagata Isaburō to prefectural governors, May 15, 1901, in Tomeoka, ed., *Katei Gakkō dai ni hen,* 197–98.

112. Ishikawa Koreyasu, "Tōkyō-fuka no kyōiku," *Shakai zasshi* 1, no. 12 (April 1898): 52.

113. Ibid., 51–54; Katōda, "Wagakuni ni okeru hinji kyōiku," 88–89; Tanaka, "Gimu kyōiku no rinen to hōsei," 333–54; Matsunaga, "Shakai mondai no hassei," 251–55. On education levels among Osaka's factory workers, see Yokoyama, *Nihon no kasō shakai,* 179–82.

114. Betchaku Atsuko, "Tōkyō-shi Mannen Jinjō Shōgakkō ni okeru Sakamoto Ryūnosuke no gakkō keiei to kyōikukan," *Tōkyō Daigaku Kyōiku Gakubu kiyō* 30 (1990): 32. On private schools for the poor in Tokyo, see Ishii Shōji, *Kindai no jidō rōdō to yakan shōgakkō* (Tokyo: Akashi Shoten, 1992), chap. 3.

115. Betchaku Atsuko, "Tōkyō-shi 'tokushu shōgakkō' no setsuritsu katei no kentō: chiiki to no kattō ni shiten o atete," *Nihon no kyōiku shigaku* 38 (1995): 160–63; and Katōda, "Wagakuni ni okeru hinji kyōiku," 86–98.

116. Katoda, "Wagakuni ni okeru hinji kyōiku," 88, 90–93. For photographs of bathing and medical examinations at Samegahashi Special Elementary School in Yotsuya Ward, see *Tōkyō-shi Kyōikukai zasshi* 29 (February 10, 1907): n.p.; for a photograph of children at the same school having their hair cut and dressed, see Tōkyō Shiyakusho Shishi Hensan Kakari, ed., *Tōkyō annai* (Tokyo: Shōkadō, 1907), 2:201. On the Mikasa Elementary School programs,

see Imai Etsuzō, "Tokushu kyōiku to shakai jigyō," *Toshi kyōiku* 205 (October 1921): 20–22.

117. Satō Tadashi, "Tokushu shōgakkō zakkan," *Tōkyō-shi Kyōikukai zasshi* 31 (April 10, 1907): 38; see also Ume No Ya, "Tokushu shōgakkō ni tsuite," *Tōkyō-shi Kyōikukai zasshi* 61 (October 10, 1910): 42.

118. Sakamoto Ryūnosuke, "Hinminkutsu jidō no seiheki to sono kyōiku," *Shin kōron* 27, no. 1 (January 1912): 212–13.

119. Fujioka Shin'ichirō, "Saimin shitei no kyōiku to tokubetsu sagyō," *Tōkyō-shi Kyōikukai zasshi* 86 (November 10, 1911): 14–22, esp. 15; Satō Tadashi, "Kinrō gakkyū," *Toshi kyōiku* 185 (February, 1920): 19–23. See also Katoda, "Wagakuni ni okeru hinji kyōiku," 94–95; Betchaku, "Tōkyō-shi Mannen Jinjō Shōgakkō," 37–38.

120. On assemblies for graduates, see "Onkyūkai," *Tōkyō-shi Kyōikukai zasshi* 53 (February 10, 1909): 10–11. On night schooling, see Ishii, *Kindai no jidō rōdō to yakan shōgakkō*, 93–118.

121. The quote is from Satō Tadashi, "Tokushu shōgakkō zakkan," 40. For surveys, see for example Tōkyō-shi Reigan Jinjō Shōgakkō, "Katei chōsa," *Toshi kyōiku* 83 (August 1911): 6–8; and Katōda, "Wagakuni ni okeru hinji kyōiku," 93–94, 98–100. On the Mikasa Elementary School food distribution program, see Imai, "Tokushu kyōiku to shakai jigyō," 22–23.

122. Tagawa Daikichirō, "Tokushu shōgakkō no ichi," *Toshi kyōiku* 82 (July 1911): 19. On the support committee's activities, see for example "Tamahime nagaya rakusei shiki," *Toshi kyōiku* 92 (May 1912): 62; "Yōji hoiku jigyō no shinsetsu," *Jizen* 4, no. 4 (May 30, 1913): 99–100; and Katōda, "Wagakuni ni okeru hinji kyōiku," 95–96.

123. Katōda, "Wagakuni ni okeru hinji kyōiku," 90–91.

124. Nihon Gakudōkai, ed., *Akudō kenkyū*, 18–20; Ishii, *Kindai no jidō rōdo to yakan shōgakkō*, 91–92. On similar tensions in a private charity school in Shitaya Ward (one that was supplanted by the Mannen special elementary school), see Ishida, "Hinmin jidō no kazokuteki kankei," 29–30.

125. Ueda, *Hogo kyōiku*, 149–52.

126. Yamamoto Tsunehiko, *Kindai Nihon toshi kyōkashi kenkyū* (Tokyo: Reimei Shobō, 1972), 85–87 (for the contents of the lecture program), 101–2 (for the *Miyako shinbun* article, dated May 9, 1910).

127. Tanaka Tarō, "Nakute wa naranu hito to nare," *Toshi kyōiku* 94 (July 1912): 8–10. See also Yamamoto, *Kindai Nihon toshi kyōkashi kenkyū*, 178–97.

128. Tagawa Daikichirō, "Shōjiki mono no hanashi," *Tōkyō-shi Kyōikukai zasshi* 78 (April 1911): 60; and Yamamoto, *Kindai Nihon toshi kyōkashi kenkyū*, 197.

129. Betchaku, "Tōkyō-shi 'tokushu shōgakkō' no setsuritsu katei," 167, 169–70.

130. *TAS*, June 12, 1921, in *Shinbun shūsei Taishō hennenshi*, vol. for 1921, part 2, ed. Meiji Taishō Shōwa Shinbun Kenkyūkai (Tokyo: Meiji Taishō Shōwa Shinbun Kenkyūkai, 1969–88), 409. For information on graduates' employment, see for example "Saimin shitei no shūgyō betsu," *Jizen* 3, no. 4 (April 1912): 101–2; and Katōda, "Wagakuni ni okeru hinji kyōiku," 101–2.

131. On the elimination of the special schools, see Katōda, "Wagakuni ni okeru hinji kyōiku," 100; and Ikeda, *Nihon shakai fukushishi,* 571–72. On shifting slum demographics and the comparison to the Ainu, see Koyata Yajūrō, "Tokushu shōgakkō jidō no zōgen wa nani ni yoru ka," *Toshi kyōiku* 202 (July 1921): 12–16; the quoted passage is on 15.

132. Maeda Ai, "Gokusha no yūtopia," in *Toshi kūkan no naka no bungaku,* vol. 5 of *Maeda Ai chosakushū* (Tokyo: Chikuma Shobō, 1989), 123–30; see also Narita, "Teito Tōkyō," 198–202. Matsubara, *Saiankoku no Tōkyō,* is the clearest example of this modeling. For discussions of the overlapping discursive formations of class and race in Europe, see Nord, "The Social Investigator as Anthropologist"; Thorne, "The Conversion of Englishmen"; and Weber, *Peasants into Frenchmen.*

133. Tomeoka, "Kanka jigyō jisshi hōhō," 470–71. For an account of one of Tomeoka's own nocturnal safari-like forays into Asakusa, from which he returned with a street urchin in tow as a "memento," see *Tomeoka Kōsuke nikki,* 3:321–22, entry for April 24, 1911.

134. Kashima Kōji, *Taishō no Shitayakko* (Tokyo: Seiabō, 1976), excerpted at www.aurora.dti.ne.jp/~ssaton/bungaku/kasima.html (accessed December 1, 2002).

135. See for example Yokoyama, *Nihon no kasō shakai,* 51–52.

136. Sakamoto Ryūnosuke, "Saiminkutsu no joshi," *Fujin shinpō* 207 (September 28, 1914): 16–17. Kathleen Uno has also written of a "yawning cultural gap" between middle-class day-care workers and working-class families in early-twentieth-century urban Japan. See Uno, *Passages to Modernity,* 64; see also 63–72.

137. Toshitani Nobuyoshi, "Oya to kyōshi no chōkaiken," in *Chiiki jūmin to kyōikuhō no sōzō,* vol. 4 of *Nihon Kyōikuhō Gakkai nenpō* (Tokyo: Yūhikaku, 1975), 198.

138. Yamamoto Tokushō, "Furō shōnen ni tsukite," part 3, *Jidō kenkyū* 8, no. 12 (December 1905): 12–13.

CHAPTER 3

1. Ishikawa Tengai, *Tōkyōgaku* (1909), in *Meiji bunka shiryō sōsho,* vol. 12, ed. Ōtō Tokihiko (Tokyo: Kazama Shobō, 1960), 486. For the concept of moral panics, see Stanley Cohen, *Folk Devils and Moral Panics: The Creation of the Mods and Rockers,* 3d ed. (London and New York: Routledge, 2002).

2. On the establishment of the student section, see Bō Tōkyokusha, "Furyō gakusei no ni dai keitō," *Shin kōron* 27, no. 10 (October 1912): 223. On the 1912 roundup, see Keishichō shi Hensan Iinkai, ed., *Keishichō shi Meiji hen* (Tokyo: Keishichō shi Hensan Iinkai, 1958), 525–26.

3. On the transformations of late-Meiji Japanese society and reactions to those developments, see Gluck, *Japan's Modern Myths.* See also Oka Yoshitake, "General Conflict after the Russo-Japanese War," in Najita and Koschmann, eds., *Conflict in Modern Japanese History: The Neglected Tradition,* 197–225.

4. Yamamoto Seikichi, *Gendai no furyō seinen tsuketari furyō joshi* (Tokyo: Shunyōdō, 1914), 204–5.

5. On "adolescent races" and colonial policy, see G. Stanley Hall, *Adolescence: Its Psychology and Its Relations to Physiology, Anthropology, Sociology, Sex, Crime, Religion, and Education*, 2 vols. (New York: D. Appleton and Company, 1905), 2:648–748, esp. 648 (for a succinct statement of the identification of "primitive men and women" or "savages" with childhood and adolescence).

6. For descriptions of students' clothing, see Karasawa Tomitarō, *Gakusei no rekishi: gakusei seikatsu no shakaishiteki kōsatsu*, vol. 3 of *Karasawa Tomitarō chosakushū* (Tokyo: Gyōsei, 1991); Honda Masuko, *Jogakusei no keifu: saishoku sareru Meiji* (Tokyo: Seidosha, 1990). For fictionalized descriptions of delinquent students' sartorial styles in the early 1910s, see Hamamoto Hiroshi, "Yozakura no koro," and "Jūnikai shita no shōnentachi," in Hamamoto Hiroshi, *Furyō shōnen* (Tokyo: Edo Shoin, 1947).

7. For secondary-school, specialized-school, and girls'-higher-school enrollments, see Government of Japan, Research and Statistics Division, Minister's Secretariat, Ministry of Education, Science, and Culture, *Japan's Modern Educational System: A History of the First Hundred Years* (Tokyo: Printing Bureau, Ministry of Finance, 1980), 456. The category of secondary school also included normal schools, which in 1912 enrolled nearly 28,000 students who received free tuition and stipends in exchange for commitments to become public school teachers. Other categories of students included those in the handful of elite public higher schools and imperial universities, those in higher normal schools, and a few hundred young women in women's normal and higher normal schools. For figures, see ibid. On declining ages of middle-school students after 1895, see Earl H. Kinmonth, *The Self-Made Man in Meiji Japanese Thought: From Samurai to Salaryman* (Berkeley: University of California Press, 1981), 216. On secondary-school students as percentage of their age cohort, see Amano Ikuo, *Gakureki no shakaishi: kyōiku to Nihon no kindai* (Tokyo: Shinchōsha, 1996), 123. On specialized schools, see ibid., 90–96, 207–24; and Byron K. Marshall, *Learning to Be Modern: Japanese Political Discourse on Education* (Boulder, CO: Westview Press, 1994), 68–69.

8. On the costs of schooling, see Amano, *Gakureki no shakaishi*, 123; and the findings of Fukaya Masashi, cited in Saitō Toshihiko, *Kyōsō to kanri no gakkōshi: Meiji kōki chūgakkō kyōiku no tenkai* (Tokyo: Tōkyō Daigaku Shuppankai, 1995), 53. For a discussion of the various "strata" of youth, see Tajima Hajime, "Kyōdōtai no kaitai to 'seinen' no shutsugen," in *Kyōiku: tanjō to shūen*, vol. 1 of *Sōsho umu, sodateru, oshieru: tokumei no kyōikushi*, ed. Henshū Iinkai (Tokyo: Fujiwara Shoten, 1990), esp. 37–45. On the "dual structure" of youth education that separated elites from the working-class (and primarily rural) majority, see Miyasaka Kōsaku, *Kindai Nihon no seinenki kyōiku*, vol. 3 of *Miyasaka Kōsaku chosakushū* (Tokyo: Akashi Shoten, 1995); and Marshall, *Learning to Be Modern*, esp. 62–72. On youth groups and military reservist associations that socialized and mobilized nonstudent youths for community and national purposes, see Smethurst, *A Social Basis for Prewar Japanese Militarism*; and Kano, "Sengo keiei to nōson kyōiku."

9. On students carrying weapons, see for example Ubukata Toshirō, *Meiji Taishō kenbunshi* (Tokyo: Chūō Kōronsha, 1978). For "virtually a fashion," see

"Jihyō," *Shakai* 2, no. 11 (March 1900): 64. All references to this journal are to the reprint in *Meijiki shakaigaku kankei shiryō*, vols. 3–8, ed. Kawai Takao (Tokyo: Ryūkei Shosha, 1991).

10. Information on gangs, unless otherwise noted, is from Sakaguchi, *Furyō shōnen no kenkyū*, 105–18. Sakaguchi's personal recollection is in ibid., 5. On exaggerated membership figures, see Pflugfelder, *Cartographies of Desire*, 220.

11. Tomeoka Kōsuke, "Gakusei fūki mondai," *Shakai* 2, no. 15 (June 1900): 65–66. For a chart of gang names, see Sakaguchi, *Furyō shōnen no kenkyū*, 109–12. On local-origin groups, see for example Narita, "Kindai toshi to minshū," 20–21; and Kimura Naoe, *"Seinen" no tanjō: Meiji Nihon ni okeru seijiteki jissen no tenkan* (Tokyo: Shinyōsha, 1998), 157–60.

12. For a description of one such group, see Ōsugi Sakae, *The Autobiography of Ōsugi Sakae*, trans. Byron K. Marshall (Berkeley: University of California Press, 1992), 63–64; see also ibid., 43–90, for his description of delinquent student life in a middle school in Niigata Prefecture and in a military cadet school in Nagoya.

13. The terms *kōha* and *nanpa* are used by Mori Ogai in his autobiographical novel of 1870s school life, *Uita sekusuarisu* (1909), in *Ōgai zenshū*, vol. 5, ed. Kinoshita Mokutarō et al. (Tokyo: Iwanami Shoten, 1971–75), 83–179. The rivalry between these student types figures prominently in Tsubouchi Shōyō's novel *Tōsei shosei katagi* (1885–86), in *Tsubouchi Shōyō shū*, vol. 16 of *Meiji bungaku zenshū*, ed. Okitsu Kaname et al. (Tokyo: Chikuma Shobō, 1969), 59–163. For secondary discussions, see Donald Roden, *Schooldays in Imperial Japan: The Culture of a Student Elite* (Berkeley: University of California Press, 1980), 26–28; Pflugfelder, *Cartographies of Desire*, 212–25; and Furukawa Makoto, "The Changing Nature of Sexuality: The Three Codes Framing Homosexuality in Modern Japan," *U.S.-Japan Women's Journal, English Supplement* 7 (1994), 101.

14. The statement from Seigi Kurabu can be found in Sakaguchi, *Furyō shōnen no kenkyū*, 117–18. The characters *keikan*, the new term for sodomy, were censored in the original. On the construction of sodomy as a criminal act, see Pflugfelder, *Cartographies of Desire*, and Furukawa, "The Changing Nature of Sexuality." For one example of student groups fighting over a "beautiful boy," see *Tokyo nichinichi shinbun*, October 29, 1899, in *Shinbun shūsei Meiji hennenshi*, ed. Nakayama Masayasu et al., 15 vols. (Tokyo: Zaisei Keizai Gakkai, 1934–36), 10:458.

15. Ujiie, *Edo no shōnen*, 150–51; Pflugfelder, *Cartographies of Desire*, 132–33, 212–13. On domain schools and Tokugawa education more generally, see Dore, *Education in Tokugawa Japan*.

16. Pflugfelder, *Cartographies of Desire*, 216.

17. Quoted in Gillis, *Youth and History*, 113.

18. Shibusawa Seika, *Asakusakko* (Tokyo: Mainichi Shuppansha, 1966), 26. On the "Satsuma habit," see Pflugfelder, *Cartographies of Desire*, esp. 210.

19. Furukawa, "The Changing Nature of Sexuality," 101–5, 112–14; see also Pflugfelder, *Cartographies of Desire*, 221–22. The quoted passage is from "Gakusei no dai daraku: Sōryū Gidan no koto," *Yorozu chōhō*, March 7, 1900, p. 3.

20. Pflugfelder, *Cartographies of Desire*, 193–234.

21. On the Justice Club, see Sakaguchi, *Furyō shōnen no kenkyū*, 109.

22. Bō Tōkyokusha, "Furyō gakusei no ni dai keitō," 224. The author is most likely MPD Inspector Yamamoto Seikichi.

23. Roden, *Schooldays in Imperial Japan*, 24–25.

24. Chamberlain, *Things Japanese*, 133–34.

25. Kimura, *"Seinen" no tanjō*, esp. 64–98, 320 n. 22; Soeda Tomomichi, *Enka no Meiji Taishō shi* (Tokyo: Iwanami Shoten, 1970); and Kurata Yoshihiro, *Meiji Taishō no minshū goraku* (Tokyo: Iwanami Shoten, 1980), 98–115. See also Kinmonth, *The Self-Made Man*, 81–116, for a broader discussion of the significance of politics in students' aspirations; and Maeda Ai, *Kindai dokusha no seiritsu* (Tokyo: Iwanami Shoten, 1993), esp. 157–60, 182–84, on the relationship between early-Meiji students' reading practices and their enthusiasm for politics and nationalism. For a discussion of some of the most important political novels that inspired young people at this time, see G. B. Sansom, *The Western World and Japan* (Tokyo: Charles E. Tuttle Company, 1984), 400–417.

26. Jason G. Karlin, "The Gender of Nationalism: Competing Masculinities in Meiji Japan," *Journal of Japanese Studies* 28, no. 1 (Winter 2002): 58–68.

27. Kimura, *"Seinen" no tanjō*, 42–131; see ibid., 55–56, for a succinct statement of this thesis. On the introduction of the term *seinen* by Japanese promoters of the Young Men's Christian Association (established 1880), see Tajima, "Kyōdōtai no kaitai to 'seinen' no shutsugen," 38.

28. Tokutomi Sohō, *Shin Nihon no seinen*, and *Shōrai no Nihon*, both in *Tokutomi Sohō shū*, vol. 4 of *Gendai Nihon bungaku zenshū* (Tokyo: Kaizōsha, 1930), 3–53 and 54–128; Kimura, *"Seinen" no tanjō*, esp. 17–50, 249–300. *Shin Nihon no seinen* first appeared in 1885 as *Dai jūkyū seiki Nihon no seinen oyobi sono kyōiku*. For analyses of Tokutomi's thought and influence, see John D. Pierson, *Tokutomi Sohō: A Journalist for Modern Japan* (Princeton, NJ: Princeton University Press, 1980); Kenneth B. Pyle, *The New Generation in Meiji Japan: Problems of Cultural Identity, 1885–1895* (Stanford, CA: Stanford University Press, 1969); and Sumiya Mikio, "Meiji nashonarizumu no kiseki," in *Tokutomi Sohō, Yamaji Aizan*, ed. Sumiya Mikio, vol. 40 of *Nihon no meicho* (Tokyo: Chūō Kōronsha, 1971), esp. 9–37. For Tokutomi's modification of Spencer's schema, see Kinmonth, *The Self-Made Man*, 100; and Peter Duus, "Whig History, Japanese Style: The Min'yusha Historians and the Meiji Restoration," *Journal of Asian Studies* 33, no. 3 (May 1974): 421–22.

29. Quoted in Kinmonth, *The Self-Made Man*, 129–30.

30. Kimura, *"Seinen" no tanjō*, 282–98; the quoted passage is on 292. On *Shōnen'en*, see also Kinmonth, *The Self-Made Man*, 121–31.

31. The quotes are from Kurata, *Meiji Taishō no minshū goraku*, 105, 108.

32. Kimura, *"Seinen" no tanjō*, 108–13; the quoted passages are on 112–13. On directives targeting students and politics, see Gluck, *Japan's Modern Myths*, 22, 107, 117; Maeda, *Kindai dokusha no seiritsu*, 158.

33. Soeda, *Enka no Meiji Taishō shi*, esp. 100–101. For a fictionalized depiction of a criminal *enka* singer, based on the author's encounters with the delinquent underworld, see Hamamoto, "Jūnikai shita no shōnentachi," 179–227.

34. Murakami Aisen, "Furyō seinendan ni kyakubun to naru no ki," *Shin kōron* 26, no. 12 (December 1911): 95.

35. On delinquents and school athletic events, see Rankai Rōshi (pseudonym), "Furyō seinendan no uchimaku," part 2, *Shin kōron* 26, no. 6 (June 1911): 384. Gang names are from Sakaguchi, *Furyō shōnen no kenkyū,* 109–12; for another police officer's comments on *kōha*/ruffian delinquents' self-image as *sōshi* and street knights, see Yamamoto, *Gendai no furyō seinen,* 46.

36. On *sōshi undōkai,* see Kimura, *"Seinen" no tanjō,* 64–78. For denunciations of similar competitions between groups of children and youths in Ibaraki Prefecture in the 1880s, see Ujiie, *Edo no shōnen.*

37. On the rise of school field days, see Yoshimi Shunya et al., *Undōkai to Nihon kindai* (Tokyo: Seikyūsha, 1999).

38. On *bankara* style, see Karlin, "The Gender of Nationalism," 68–76.

39. Sakaguchi, *Furyō shōnen no kenkyū,* 128–29; Murakami, "Furyō seinendan ni kyakubun to naru no ki."

40. For the persistence of these styles and stories, see Tōkyō-shi Asakusa Kuyakusho, *Asakusa-ku shi,* 2:603–15; and Yamamoto, *Kindai Nihon toshi kyōkashi kenkyū,* 362–70. For a twentieth-century memoir of the gambling underworld, see Saga Junichi, *Confessions of a Yakuza,* trans. John Bester (Tokyo, New York, and London: Kodansha International, 1991).

41. Hamamoto, "Jūnikai shita no shōnentachi," 181–82.

42. On social criticisms and discussions of youth problems in this period, see Oka, "General Conflict after the Russo-Japanese War;" and Gluck, *Japan's Modern Myths,* esp. 157–78.

43. Bō Tōkyokusha, "Furyō gakusei no ni dai keitō," 223.

44. For an actual record of *nanpa*-style profligacy ca. 1891, see Maeda Ai, "Shosei no kozukai chō," in *Genkei no Meiji,* vol. 4 of *Maeda Ai chosakushū* (Tokyo: Chikuma Shobō, 1989), 73–76.

45. See for example "Gakusei ni kansuru fūki mondai," *Jidō kenkyū* 2, no. 8 (April 1900): 1–2; Tomeoka, "Gakusei fūki mondai," 66; Yamagata Tōkon (Nunokawa Magoichi), "Kyōshi gakusei fūki taihai no seishitsu," *Shakai zasshi* 1, no. 14 (July 1898): 4–10; Yamagata Tōkon (Nunokawa Magoichi), "Gakusei kenkyūkai o mōkeyo," *Shakai* 2, no. 16 (July 1900): 75–76; *Tomeoka Kōsuke nikki,* 3:322, entry for April 24, 1911; and Kinmonth, *The Self-Made Man,* 219. On archery galleries, see Shibusawa, *Asakusakko,* 14–16. A *Yorozu chōhō* commentary in 1900 on the Righteous Blue Dragon Gang claimed that the group included a "department" for accosting women alongside its departments for *nanshoku,* eating and drinking without paying, and firing pistols. "Gakusei no dai daraku: Sōryū Gidan no koto," *Yorozu chōhō,* March 7, 1900, p. 3.

46. "Rappa bushi," in *Meiji nenkan hayari uta,* appendix to *Riyōshū shūi,* ed. Takano Tatsuyuki and Ōtake Shiyō (Tokyo: Rikugōkan, 1915).

47. Kaminaga Ryōgetsu, "Matsu no koe" (1907), in ibid.

48. On naturalism, see Jay Rubin, *Injurious to Public Morals: Writers and the Meiji State* (Seattle: University of Washington Press, 1984), 55–142. On boarding houses, see Tomeoka, "Gakusei fūki mondai," 65; Hibino Hiroshi, *Seinen shijo daraku no riyū tsuketari sono kyōkyūhō* (Tokyo: Kinkōdō, 1907), 99–110; Ishikawa, *Tōkyōgaku,* 491–93; and Karasawa, *Gakusei no rekishi,*

107–12. For a report of prostitutes masquerading as schoolgirls in order to ply their trade in student lodgings in Kanda and Hongō, see *Tōkyō nichinichi shinbun,* June 25, 1902, reprinted in Nakayama et al., eds., *Shinbun shūsei Meiji hennenshi,* 10:431.

49. *Yorozu chōhō,* July 20, 1906, reprinted in Hara Masao, *Shikijō to seinen* (Tokyo, Eisei Shinpōsha, 1906), 179–82. See also "Gakusei ryūhei no ichi ni," *Chūō kōron* 21, no. 8 (August 1906), discussed in Wada Atsuhiko, "Sei no sōchi to dokusho no sōchi: *Chūō kōron,* itsudatsu no kyōfu," *Bungei to hihyō* 70 (October 1994), available online at http://fan.shinshu-u.ac.jp/~wada/report/tyuuouf.html (accessed January 29, 2003).

50. See for example "Haikara bushi" (1907), a popular song that catalogues the fashions of girls at prominent Tokyo schools, in Takano and Ōtake. eds., *Meiji nenkan hayari uta.* See also Tayama Katai's 1907 short story "Shōjo byō" (about a Tokyo white-collar worker's obsession with *jogakusei* he sees on the train each day, and the fatal accident that this fetish provokes), in *Tayama Katai shū,* ed. Yoshida Seiichi, vol. 67 of *Meiji bungaku zenshū* (Tokyo: Chikuma Shobō, 1968), 64–71. On this text and its urban social context, see Alisa Freedman, "Commuting Gazes: Schoolgirls, Salarymen, and Electric Trains in Tokyo," *Journal of Transport History* 23, no. 1 (March 2002), 23–36.

51. Soeda, *Enka no Meiji Taishō shi,* 81.

52. Kaminaga, "Matsu no koe." For a later fictionalized account of a *jogakusei*'s degradation, at the hands of an army officer, see Ozaki Shirō, "Meiji daraku jogakusei," in Ozaki Shirō, *Meiji daraku jogakusei* (Tokyo: Shinchōsha, 1955), 5–52.

53. Hara, *Shikijō to seinen,* 107–8.

54. For "playing at husband and wife," see *Gifu nichinichi shinbun,* May 30, 1908, p. 3. I wish to thank Stewart Lone for introducing me to this article, as well as to other *Gifu nichinichi* articles cited in this chapter. Oguri Fūyō's novel *Seishun* is discussed in Honda, *Jogakusei no keifu;* the reference to the abortion is on 165. For the *enka* song "Omoi kusa," see Soeda, *Enka no Meiji Taishō shi,* 147–48.

55. S.M. Sei, "Furyō seinendan Kozakura gumi no katsudō buri o miyo," *Shin kōron* 30, no. 8 (August 1915): 68–72. For other discussions of *nanpa* techniques, see for example Yamamoto, *Gendai no furyō seinen,* 49 ff.; and Sakaguchi, *Furyō shōnen no kenkyū,* 131–37.

56. S.M. Sei, "Furyō seinendan Kozakura gumi," 70–72.

57. Ibid., 70.

58. Yamamoto, *Gendai no furyō seinen,* 49.

59. S.M. Sei, "Furyō seinendan Kozakura Gumi," 68–69.

60. A.A. Gerow, "Swarming Ants and Elusive Villains: Zigomar and the Problem of Cinema in 1910s Japan," *CineMagaziNet! On-Line Research Journal of Cinema* 1 (August 1996), available at www.cmn.hs.h.kyoto-u.ac.jp/NO1/SUBJECT1/ZIGOMAR.HTM (accessed January 3, 2004); see also Yamamoto, *Kindai Nihon toshi kyōkashi kenkyū,* 144–45.

61. Hen Genshi (pseudonym), "Yamanote o ōkō suru kōtō furyō shōjodan no shinsō," *Shin kōron* 31, no. 1 (January 1916): 85–89.

62. Hamamoto, "Yozakura no koro," 26. On the city as theater, urban flaneurs' subjectivity, and their narratives of the dark zones of Victorian London,

see Nord, *Walking the Victorian Streets,* and Walkowitz, *City of Dreadful Delight.*

63. Yamamoto, *Gendai no furyō seinen,* 182–85.

64. Walkowitz, *City of Dreadful Delight,* 249 n. 16.

65. For press and police reports of fallen *jogakusei,* as well as of working girls masquerading as *jogakusei,* who supported themselves by sleeping with Chinese exchange students, see *Gifu nichinichi shinbun,* June 14, 1907, p. 5; and Yamamoto, *Gendai no furyō seinen,* 159–60.

66. Middle school student figures are from Kuwabara Sanji, *Tōkyō-fu kōritsu chūgakkō kyōikushi* (Tokyo: Takayama Honten, 1981), 80. Roundup figures are from Keishichō shi Hensan Iinkai, ed., *Keishichō shi Meiji hen,* 525–26. The list of six hundred students is mentioned in Bō Tōkyokusha, "Furyō gakusei no ni dai keitō," 223–24.

67. Police precinct reports are discussed in "Tōkyō no rimen (4): jogakusei no daraku," part 2, *Gifu nichinichi shinbun,* May 30, 1908, p. 3; Yamamoto's observations can be found in Yamamoto, *Gendai no furyō seinen,* 158.

68. Furukawa, "The Changing Nature of Sexuality," 112–13.

69. Tomeoka Kōsuke, "Kanka jigyō to sono kanrihō," in Naimushō Chihōkyoku, ed., *Kanka kyūsai jigyō kōenshū,* 2:132–36.

70. Hara Taneaki, "Katei kyōiku to hanzai to no kankei," *Shakai zasshi* 1, no. 8 (December 1897): 7–10; Katsuura Tomoo, "Chūryū ijō no katei ni fukanzen no gakusei no deru riyū" *Shin kōron* 24, no. 6 (June 1909): 17; "queens" is quoted from this source. See also Tomeoka, "Kanka jigyō to sono kanrihō," 132–36; Yamamoto, *Gendai no furyō seinen,* esp. 220–21. For other criticisms of upper-class households and upper-class licentiousness, see for example Sakai Toshihiko, "Gūkan," *Katei zasshi* 1, no. 3 (June 1903), in *Sakai Toshihiko zenshū,* ed. Yamakawa Hitoshi et al. (Tokyo: Chūō Kōronsha, 1933), 2:313–15; and "Jōryū shakai no zokuron," *Fujin shinpō* 42 (October 25, 1900): 1.

71. Hara, *Shikijō to seinen,* 146–48.

72. Kojima Hideo, "Japanese Concepts of Child Development from the Mid-Seventeenth to the Mid-Nineteenth Century," *International Journal of Behavioral Development* 9, no. 3 (September 1986): 315–29, cited in Anne Walthall, "The Life Cycle of Farm Women in Tokugawa Japan," in Bernstein, ed., *Recreating Japanese Women, 1600–1945,* 45.

73. Ototake Iwazō, *Furyōji kyōikuhō* (Tokyo: Meguro Shoten, 1910), 40–82. For an early example of this genre, see Ōmura Jintarō, *Jidō kyōheiron* (Tokyo: Seika Shoin, 1900), reprinted in *Nihon jidō mondai bunken senshū,* vol. 15, ed. Jidō Mondaishi Kenkyūkai (Tokyo: Nihon Tosho Sentā, 1984).

74. Takashima Heizaburō, "Jidō kenkyū," in Naimushō Chihōkyoku, ed., *Kanka kyūsai jigyō kōenshū,* 2:485, 616, and 631; Ototake, *Furyōji kyōikuhō,* 67–70.

75. See for example Takashima Heizaburō, "Jidō to shakai," *Jidō kenkyū* 3, no. 7 (January 1901): 9–15.

76. Ototake, *Furyōji kyōikuhō,* 34–35.

77. Takashima Heizaburō, "Shakai ni okeru katei no chii o ronzu," *Jidō kenkyū* 5, no. 8 (October 1902): 18; Matsumoto Kōjirō, "Katei ni okeru jidō kenkyū," *Jidō kenkyū* 6, no. 10 (October 1903): 17–24.

78. Takashima Heizaburō, *Jidō shinri kōwa* (Tokyo: Kōbundō Shoten, 1909), 5. On calls to women to attend lectures and study, see for example Matsumoto, "Katei ni okeru jidō kenkyū," 18–19. See also Takeda Shinjirō, "Kanka kyōiku ni tsuite," parts 1–2, *Jidō kenkyū* 18, no. 11 (June 1915): 396–99, and no. 12 (July 1915): 429–36. On *ryōsai kenbo* ideology, see for example Nolte and Hastings, "The Meiji State's Policy toward Women, 1890–1910," 151–74; and Fukaya, *Ryōsai kenbo shugi no kyōiku.* On the class inflections of good wife, wise mother, see Uno, *Passages to Modernity.*

79. Sawayama, "Kyōiku kazoku no seiritsu," 108–31.

80. Matsumoto Kōjirō, "Katei no sekinin (Jidō Kenkyūkai ni oite)," *Jidō kenkyū* 8, no. 6 (June 1905): 9–10.

81. Takashima, *Jidō shinri kōwa,* 146–48.

82. Takashima often explicitly framed his analyses in terms of adolescents' situation in the secondary and tertiary school systems. See for example Takashima Heizaburō, "Seinenki oyobi sono kyōiku," parts 1–2, *Jidō kenkyū* 5, no. 4 (June 1902): 5–10, and no. 5 (July 1902): 11–21. On this transformation of class-based norms into "'natural' attributes of adolescence," see Gillis, *Youth and History,* chs. 3–4; the quoted passage is on p. 114.

83. This summary is based on Takashima, "Seinenki oyobi sono kyōiku"; Takashima, "Jidō kenkyū," 641–697; and Takashima, *Jidō shinri kōwa,* 467–548. For Hall's original text, see Hall, *Adolescence.*

84. "Barbarians with knowledge" quoted in Hayashi Masayo, "Kindai Nihon no 'seishōnen' kan ni kansuru ichi kōsatsu: 'gakkō seito' no kitsuen mondai no seisei, tenkai katei o chūshin ni," *Kyōiku shakaigaku kenkyū* 56 (1995): 68. For Hall's view of adolescence as a critical stage between savagery and higher stages of racial development, see Hall, *Adolescence,* 1:44–50.

85. Yamamoto, *Gendai no furyō seinen,* 3–4, 203–5, 225; passage cited on 204–5. For earlier denunciations of the inappropriateness of Westernized educational content and the promulgation and interpretations of the Imperial Rescript on Education, see Gluck, *Japan's Modern Myths,* 102–56; Marshall, *Learning to Be Modern,* 52–62; and Mark E. Lincicome, *Principle, Praxis, and the Politics of Educational Reform in Meiji Japan* (Honolulu: University of Hawai'i Press, 1995).

86. This discussion is based upon the following sources: Yamamoto, *Gendai no furyō seinen,* esp. 3–4, 22–23, 225–39; Yamamoto Nobutaka, "Kinji seinen gakuseikai no genshō ni tsukite," part 4, *Jidō kenkyū* 9, no. 12 (December 1906): 8–16; Sakaguchi, *Furyō shōnen no kenkyū,* 49–50; and Tomeoka Kōsuke, "Kanka kyōiku ron," *Keisatsu Kyōkai zasshi* 66 (December 15, 1905), in *Tomeoka Kōsuke chosakushū,* 2:183–84.

87. Sasakura Shinji, *Chūgaku kyōiku ni kansuru kenkyū* (1899), quoted in Miyasaka, *Kindai Nihon no seinenki kyōiku,* 50. See also Roden, *Schooldays in Imperial Japan;* Kinmonth, *The Self-Made Man;* and Marshall, *Learning to Be Modern.*

88. Saitō, *Kyōsō to kanri,* 112–13. See also Kinmonth, *The Self-Made Man,* esp. ch. 5, and Gluck, *Japan's Modern Myths,* 204–12. For discussion of the emergence of academic credentialism in children's magazines, see Narita Ryūichi, "'Shōnen sekai' to dokusho suru shōnentachi: 1900 nen

zengo, toshi kūkan no naka no kyōdōsei to sai," *Shisō* 845 (November 1994), esp. 207–8.

89. Yamamoto Nobutaka, "Kinji seinen gakuseikai no genshō ni tsukite," part 3, *Jidō kenkyū* 9, no. 11 (November 1906): 19–26.

90. Quoted in Government of Japan, *Japan's Modern Educational System*, 119.

91. For doubts concerning teachers, see for example Hara, *Shikijō to seinen*, 11–12.

92. Yamamoto, *Gendai no furyō seinen*, 143–44.

93. On sex education debates, see for example Kuriki Yōshō, "Seiteki kyōiku ron: furyō shōnen furyō shōjo no zōka to no kankei," *Shin kōron* 28, no. 11 (December 1913): 1–6; Hara, *Shikijō to seinen;* Wada, "Sei no sōchi to dokusho no sōchi"; and Frühstück, *Colonizing Sex,* 55–82.

94. Saitō, *Kyōsō to kanri,* 216–17; see also Monbushō Futsū Gakumukyoku, *Zenkoku chūgakkō ni kansuru shochōsa* (Tokyo: Monbushō, April 1907 and June 1909 editions).

95. Saitō, *Kyōsō to kanri,* 173–96, 203–37. For a study of school regulations covering a longer time period, see Takano Keiichi, *Seito kihan no kenkyū: seito kisoku no hō shakaigakuteki mikata, kangaekata* (Tokyo: Gyōsei, 1987). On the development of similarly strict regulations in the First Higher School during the late 1880s and 1890s, see Roden, *Schooldays in Imperial Japan,* 59. For the growing influence of Herbartianism in Japanese educational circles, see Lincicome, *Principle, Praxis, and the Politics of Educational Reform,* 95–102, 197–203. On increasing regimentation and cloistering of adolescent youth in European schools during the nineteenth century, see Gillis, *Youth and History,* esp. 105–9. Whether or not specific European school disciplinary methods influenced Japanese educators is not clear.

96. "Tōkyō Furitsu Daiichi Chūgakkō saisoku" (1909), reprinted in *Tōkyō kyōikushi shiryō taikei,* vol. 8, ed. Tōkyō Toritsu Kyōiku Kenkyūjo (Tokyo: Tōkyō Toritsu Kyōiku Kenkyūjo, 1973), 286; Saitō, *Kyōsō to kanri,* 259–82.

97. "Tōkyō Furitsu Daiyon Chūgakkō seito chūi jikō" (1902), reprinted in *Tōkyō kyōikushi shiryō taikei,* 8:278.

98. Gluck, *Japan's Modern Myths,* 169–72.

99. The following information is taken from Monbushō Futsū Gakumukyoku, "Gakkō seito kōgai torishimari ni kansuru chōsa," *Teikoku kyōiku* 321 (April 10, 1909): 72–83. See also Saitō, *Kyōsō to kanri,* 196–203.

100. "Gakkō seito kōgai torishimari ni kansuru chōsa," 81–82.

101. Saitō, *Kyōsō to kanri,* 237–47. On student monitors and peer sanctions in some domain schools during the Tokugawa period, see Dore, *Education in Tokugawa Japan,* 101–6; in higher schools during the prewar years, see Roden, *Schooldays in Imperial Japan,* 147–50.

102. Yamamoto, *Gendai no furyō seinen,* 244–45. For discussions of expulsion rates and sample statistical charts, see Satō Norio, "Chūtō kyōikukai ni okeru furyō seito no kanka," in Naimushō Chihōkyoku, ed., *Kanka kyūsai jigyō kōenshū,* 1:605–6; and Monbushō Futsū Gakumukyoku, *Zenkoku chūgakkō ni kansuru shochōsa,* April 1907 and June 1909 editions.

103. Fukui Hikojirō, "Katei oyobi kyōiku," *Jindō* 3 (July 15, 1905): 12.

104. Hashizume Kōichirō, *Chūgakusei to katei no kyōyō* (Tokyo: Jitsugyō no Nihonsha, 1912), 194; and see 189–219 for advice on how to transfer into vocational schools and how to deal with schools' disciplinary measures. See also Yamamoto, "Kinji seinen gakuseikai no genshō ni tsukite," part 4, 19; and Saitō, *Kyōsō to kanri*, 63–64.

105. Bō Tōkyokusha, "Furyō gakusei no ni dai keitō," 223–25; *Gifu nichinichi shinbun*, May 26, 1908, p. 5.

106. On parents and public reformatories, see Sakaguchi, *Furyō shōnen no kenkyū*, 209–11; and Itō Shikyō, "Museki matawa tafuken no furyō shōnen," *Jizen* 2, no. 1 (July 30, 1910): 75. See also Kyōsei Kyōkai, ed., *Shōnen kyōsei*, 201, for an 1893 account of parents' views of the juvenile carceral facilities *(chōjijō)* that preceded the reformatories.

107. Takeda Shinjirō's remarks can be found in *Daiikkai kankainchō kyōgikai sokkiroku*, ed. Kankainchō Kyōgikai (1910), reprinted in *Nihon jidō mondai bunken senshū*, vol. 24, ed. Jidō Mondaishi Kenkyūkai (Tokyo: Nihon Tosho Sentā, 1984), 160–61. See also Takeda, "Kanka kyōiku ni tsuite," part 1, 399; and *Tomeoka Kōsuke nikki*, 3:256–57.

108. Nojiri Seiichi, "Kanka kyūsai jigyō to futsū kyōiku," in Naimushō Chihōkyoku, ed., *Kanka kyūsai jigyō kōenshū*, 2:299–300; Arimatsu Hideyoshi, "Keisatsu gyōsei to kanka jigyō," in ibid., 2:819–20.

109. Kyōsei Kyōkai, ed., *Shōnen kyōsei*, 143.

110. Ibid., 145; see also "Tōkyō Kankain," *Jizen* 1, no. 1 (July 30, 1909): 107.

111. Okanishi Shigesaburō, ed., *Tōkyō Kankain keiri ippan* (Tokyo: Tōkyō Kankain Hazawa Bunko, 1903), statistical appendix (no page number).

112. Nishimura's logbooks, as copied into Tomeoka Kōsuke's diary, are reproduced in *Tomeoka Kōsuke nikki*, 2:85–155.

113. Ibid., 2:91, 96, 106–7, 116, 119, 129–30; the quoted passage is on 107.

114. Ibid., 2:98–99, 101–2; the quoted passage is on 98.

115. Ibid., 2:122–23; Nishimura refers to having been rebuked by Tomeoka on 2:148.

116. Kyōsei Kyōkai, ed., *Shōnen kyōsei*, 139–40. For a 1912 report that Takase was (again?) making plans to open a girls' reformatory, see *Hōritsu shinbun*, February 15, 1912, p. 12.

117. See for example Mimura Haruyo, "Joshi kankasei no shogū," *Jizen* 2, no. 1 (July 1910): 80; and Kawahara Masu, "Daraku josei no kyōsei," *Jizen* 2, no. 1 (July 1910): 87–91. On the Salvation Army Women's Home, see the 1911 entry in *Tomeoka Kōsuke nikki*, 3:357.

118. Hibino, *Seinen shijo daraku no riyū*, 55. On the evolution of the school system and debates over education, see Marshall, *Learning to Be Modern*, 51–89; and Lincicome, *Principles, Praxis, and the Politics of Educational Reform*, which is attentive to issues of pedagogic theory.

CHAPTER 4

1. Miyagi Tamayo, "Shōnen to hanzai: aru tamashii no hatten," *Fujin no tomo* 23, no. 3 (March 1929): 40–49; descriptions of home environment can be found on 45, 47.

2. On the rise of this regulated space, see Donzelot, *The Policing of Families,* esp. 88–89; Gilles Deleuze, "Foreword: The Rise of the Social," in ibid., ix–xvii; and Horn, *Social Bodies.*

3. For standard accounts of this period, see Eguchi Keiichi, *Futatsu no taisen,* vol. 14 of *Taikei Nihon no rekishi* (Tokyo: Shōgakkan, 1993); Asao Naohiro et al., eds., *Iwanami kōza Nihon tsūshi,* vol. 18 (Tokyo: Iwanami Shoten, 1994); and Imai Seiichi, *Taishō demokurashii,* vol. 23 of *Nihon no rekishi* (Tokyo: Chūō Kōronsha, 1988). For political analyses in English, see Gordon, *Labor and Imperial Democracy;* Michael Lewis, *Rioters and Citizens: Mass Protest in Imperial Japan* (Berkeley: University of California Press, 1990); and Sheldon Garon, "State and Society in Interwar Japan," in *Historical Perspectives on Contemporary East Asia,* ed. Merle Goldman and Andrew Gordon (Cambridge, MA: Harvard University Press, 2000), 155–82. For the "economic muddle," see Hugh T. Patrick, "The Economic Muddle of the 1920s," in *Dilemmas of Growth in Prewar Japan,* ed. James W. Morley (Princeton, NJ: Princeton University Press, 1971), 211–66.

4. Kusama Yasoo, "Dai Tōkyō no chimata ni shutsubotsu suru furyō shōnen," *Shakai to kyūsai* 4, no. 11 (February 1921): 7. On social, economic, and cultural developments, see Minami Hiroshi and Shakai Shinri Kenkyūjo, *Taishō bunka: 1905–1927* (Tokyo: Keisō Shobō, 1987); Minami Hiroshi, *Shōwa bunka: 1925–1945* (Tokyo: Keisō Shobō, 1987); Minami Hiroshi, ed., *Nihon modanizumu no kenkyū: shisō, seikatsu, bunka* (Tokyo: Bureen Shuppan, 1982); Yamamoto, "Taishū seikatsu no henka to taishū bunka," 302–36; Harootunian, *Overcome by Modernity;* and Silverberg, "Constructing the Japanese Ethnography of Modernity," 30–54. On fears of delinquency after the Great Kantō Earthquake, see Mawatari Toshio and Sandaya Hiraku, *Fukkō to jidō mondai* (Tokyo: Teito fukkō sōsho Kankōkai, 1924), esp. 53–56.

5. For the phrase "go-fast imperialism," see Louise Young, *Japan's Total Empire: Manchuria and the Culture of Wartime Imperialism* (Berkeley: University of California Press, 1998), 115–80.

6. For juvenile Penal Code infractions, 1914–19, see Yamaoka Mannosuke, "Shōnen hogo seido ni tsuite," *Hōritsu shinbun,* January 28, 1921, pp. 3–4. On MPD arrests in 1924 and 1928, see Gotō Yomokichi, "Furyō shōnen shōjo ni tsuite" part 1, *Kyōiku jiron,* no. 1455 (November 15, 1925): 20; "Tōkyō fuka ni okeru furyō shōnen shirabe," *Shakai jigyō ihō,* November 1929: 7–10, appendix to *Shakai jigyō* 13, no. 8 (November 1929). For 30,000 names on Tokyo police blacklists, see *TAS,* May 8, 1928, morning edition, p. 7. For the 1934 juvenile crime rate in Tokyo, see Suzuki Kaichirō, "Tōkyō-shi ni okeru shōnen hanzai ritsu: shōnen hanzai no tokushitsu ni kansuru kenkyū," *Shōnen hogo* 1, no. 7 (July 1936): 2–6.

7. For overall population figures, see Tōyō Keizai Shinpōsha, ed., *Kanketsu Shōwa kokusei sōran,* 1:33–35. On immigration and age cohorts from 1920 to 1930, see Ōkado Masakatsu, "Nōson kara toshi e: seishōnen no idō to 'kugaku,' 'dokugaku,'" in Narita, ed., *Toshi to minshū,* 174–75.

8. On the Heibonsha Encyclopedia, see Kano, "Furyō shōnen bunka toshite no eiga," 324. For examples of book-length studies, see Nakamura Kokyō et al., ed., *Shōnen furyōka no keiro to sono kyōiku* (Tokyo: Nihon Seishin Igakkai,

1921); Gōzu Shigeki, *Furyō shōnen ni naru made* (Tokyo: Ganshōdō, 1922); Suzuki Kaichirō, *Furyō shōnen no kenkyū* (Tokyo: Daitōkaku, 1923); Furuya Shintarō, *Aa shōnen* (Osaka: Kyōgaku Sōchōsha, 1930); and Iijima Mitsuyasu, *Kanka kyōiku: furyō shōnen no kenkyū* (Tokyo: Shōkado Shoten, 1931).

9. Mawatari and Sandaya, *Fukkō to jidō mondai*, 63. On children's rights, see also for example Nishiyama Tetsuji, *Kyōiku mondai: kodomo no kenri* (1918), reprinted in *Gendai Nihon jidō mondai bunken senshū*, vol. 6, ed. Jidō Mondaishi Kenkyūkai (Tokyo: Nihon Tosho Sentā, 1988).

10. On social solidarity theories, see Yoshida Kyūichi, *Gendai shakai jigyōshi kenkyū* (Tokyo: Kawashima Shoten, 1990), 93–103; Ishida Takeshi, "Kindai Nihon ni okeru 'shakai fukushi' kanren kannen no hensen," in *Kindai Nihon no seiji bunka to gengo shōchō*, ed. Ishida Takeshi (Tokyo: Tōkyō Daigaku Shuppankai, 1983), 175–232; and Garon, *Molding Japanese Minds*, 51. On child-protection policies, see Katoda Keiko, "Taishō ki ni okeru 'jidō mondai' to 'jidō hogo'," in *Shakai fukushi no Nihonteki tokushitsu*, ed. Yoshida Kyūichi (Tokyo: Kawashima Shoten, 1986), 328–59; Ikeda, *Nihon shakai fukushishi*, 560–81; Tago Ichimin, *Shakai jigyō* (1922), in *Tago Ichimin, Yamasaki Iwao shū*, ed. Satō Susumu, vol. 5 of *Shakai fukushi koten sōsho* (Tokyo: Koto Shoin, 1982), 11–16, 44–73. On day-care centers in this period, see Uno, *Passages to Modernity*, 89–138.

11. Motoji Shinkuma, "Shōnen hanzai no yobō to shakaiteki kyōryoku," *Hōgaku Kyōkai zasshi* 39, no. 3 (March 1921): 1–38; the quoted passage is on p. 8.

12. On the establishment of the Home Ministry Social Bureau, see Garon, *The State and Labor*, 94–95. On Tokyo agencies, see Tōkyō-to Shakai Fukushi Kyōgikai sanjūnenshi Kankō Iinkai, ed., *Tōkyō-to Shakai Fukushi Kyōgikai sanjūnenshi* (Tokyo: Tōkyō-to Shakai Fukushi Kyōgikai, 1983), 13; "Shakaika shinsetsu," *Tōkyō-fu Jizen Kyōkai hō* 9 (April 1920): 94; and Sally Ann Hastings, *Neighborhood and Nation in Tokyo, 1905–1937* (Pittsburgh, PA: University of Pittsburgh Press, 1995), 38–43.

13. On social work training courses, see Kyōsei Kyōkai, ed., *Shōnen kyōsei*, 267–70; and Yoshida, *Gendai shakai jigyōshi kenkyū*, 56–57, 77–78. On women's social work opportunities, see also Margit Nagy, "Middle-Class Working Women during the Interwar Years," in Bernstein, ed., *Recreating Japanese Women, 1600–1945*, 208.

14. See for example Tōkyō-shi Shakaikyoku, *Tōkyō-shi Yōshōnen Hogosho ni okeru hogo jidō jōkyō* (Tokyo: Tōkyō-shi Shakaikyoku, 1924); and Nakai Shin'ichirō, "Tōkyō-shi no yōshōnen hogo jigyō," *Tōkyō-shi kōhō* 1506 (April 12, 1928): 667–69.

15. Tōkyō-fu Shakaika, "Jidō hogoin setchi shuisho," *Tōkyō-fu Jizen Kyōkai hō* 10 (June 1920): 63–67; *Nihon shakai jigyō nenkan*, 1921 edition, ed. Ōhara Shakai Mondai Kenkyūjo (Osaka: Ōhara Shakai Mondai Kenkyūjo Shuppanbu, 1921), 69–71; Tōkyō-fu Gakumubu Shakaika, *Honfu ni okeru jidō hogo jigyō no gaikyō*, *Shakai chōsa shiryō*, no. 10 (Tokyo: Tōkyō-fu Gakumubu Shakaika, 1930). Figures for the years after 1929 are not available.

16. Garon, *Molding Japanese Minds*, 52–56; the quoted passage is on 53. See also Ōmori Makoto, "Toshi shakai jigyō seiritsuki ni okeru chūkansō to

minponshugi: Ōsaka-fu hōmen iin seido no seiritsu o megutte," *Hisutoria* 97 (December 1982): 58–77; Ikeda, *Nihon shakai fukushishi,* 510–17; and Hastings, *Neighborhood and Nation,* 86–88. On a slightly earlier Tokyo Prefecture Charity Association experiment with "relief commissioners" *(kyūsai iin)* composed of individuals with specialized welfare knowledge, see Ikeda, *Nihon shakai fukushishi,* 513–15; and *Tōkyō-to Shakai Fukushi Kyōgikai sanjūnenshi,* 16–18.

17. On the "popularization of the police" and the establishment of police personal counseling centers, see Ōbinata, *Keisatsu no shakaishi,* 122–67. See also Elise B. Tipton, *The Japanese Police State: The Tokkō in Interwar Japan* (Honolulu: University of Hawai'i Press, 1990), 80–85, and 35–39 (for the ideology of the police as "nursemaids"). On the subsequent establishment of an MPD Social Section, see "Keishichō ni 'shakai ka': hinkonsha kyūsai no tame," *Shakai fukuri* 14, no. 3 (March 1930): 102–3. On the establishment of the modern Japanese police, see also D. Eleanor Westney, *Imitation and Innovation: The Transfer of Western Organizational Patterns to Meiji Japan* (Cambridge, MA: Harvard University Press, 1987).

18. On the establishment of the committee and research institute, see *Hōritsu shinbun,* June 30, 1918, p. 11; and *Tōkyō-fu Gakumubu Shakaika, Honfu ni okeru jidō hogo jigyō no gaikyō,* 6. For institute reports, see Tōkyō-fu (Daiyō) Jidō Kenkyūjo, *Ippan jidō, furyōji, seishin hakujakuji ni kansuru tōkeiteki chōsa* (Tokyo: Takinokawa Gakuen, 1933); and Fujimoto Katsumi, "Yōhogo shōnen no kanbetsu ni tsuite," *Shakai fukuri* 18, no. 7 (July 1934): 56. For an overview of the development of counseling centers, see Yasuda Seimei Shakai Jigyōdan, ed., *Nihon no jidō sōdan: Meiji, Taishō kara Shōwa e,* 2 vols. (Tokyo: Kawashima Shoten, 1969–70).

19. See for example Kondō Kenzō, "Hinji kyōiku to sono kaiko," parts 1–4, *Kyōiku jiron,* no. 1464 (February 15, 1926): 37–41; no. 1465 (February 25, 1926): 38–41; no. 1466 (March 5, 1926): 38–40; and no. 1467 (March 15, 1926): 39–41. See also Katōda, "Wagakuni ni okeru hinji kyōiku," 93–94. On mothers' associations, see for example Kondō Kenzō, "Furyōji kyōiku shōdan (2)," *Kyōiku jiron,* no. 1573 (February 25, 1929): 31. On mothers' meetings in day-care centers, see Uno, *Passages to Modernity,* 104–6, 125–26.

20. Azuma Masako, "Shōnen no furyōka to kōgai kyōgo jigyō," *Shakai jigyō* 18, no. 3 (June 1936): 109–15.

21. Nikai Gen'ichi, "Tōkyō-fu Chūtō Gakkō Hodō Kyōkai no setsuritsu ni tsuite," *Teikoku kyōiku* 684 (November 1, 1935): 12–19; the quoted passage is on 15. See also Okada Minoru, "Kōgai hodōjō no shomondai," *Teikoku kyōiku* 685 (November 15, 1935): 7–11.

22. Suzuki, *Furyō shōnen no kenkyū,* 14–16, Suzuki Kaichirō, "Shōnen shinpanjo no tenbō," in *Tōkyō Shōnen Shinpanjo jūnenshi,* ed. Suzuki Kaichirō (Tokyo: Nihon Shōnen Hogo Kyōkai Tōkyō Shibu, 1935), 277–79; Moriya, *Shōnen no hikō to kyōiku,* 73–74. On Hara Taneaki's reform work, see for example *Hōritsu shinbun,* September 20, 1914, pp. 5–7. For Justice officials' and jurists' discussions of juvenile courts in the West, see Shigematsu, *Shōnen chōkai kyōikushi,* esp. 580–96; Kyōsei Kyōkai, ed., *Shōnen kyōsei;* and the documents collected in Morita, ed., *Taishō Shōnen hō,* 2 vols. On juvenile

courts in the United States, see for example Platt, *The Child Savers;* Steven L. Schlossman, *Love and the American Delinquent: The Theory and Practice of "Progressive" Juvenile Justice, 1825–1920* (Chicago and London: University of Chicago Press, 1977); Schneider, *In the Web of Class;* and Odem, *Delinquent Daughters.*

23. For the deliberations and drafts leading to the final passage of the Juvenile Law, see especially Morita Akira, "Taishō jūichinen shōnen hō no rippō katei: hikaku hōshiteki gaikan," in Morita, ed., *Taishō Shōnen hō,* 1:3–68, and the documents collected in ibid., vols. 1–2.

24. See for example Ogawa Shigejirō, "Hi shōnen hō ron," in *Ogawa Shigejirō chosaku senshū,* ed. Ogawa Hakase Ibun Kankōkai, 1:427–62; and "Jidō hogo no kenchi yori shōnen hōan o ronzu," *Jindō* 188 (February 15, 1921): 2–4. The latter article was no doubt written by Tomeoka Kōsuke.

25. For the Home Ministry's bill, see "Jidō hogo iin hōan" (Home Ministry, December 23, 1919), in Morita, ed., *Taishō shōnen hō,* 1:498–99. On conflicts between the Home Ministry and the Justice Ministry, see Garon, *The State and Labor,* 131–36; and Tipton, *The Japanese Police State,* 106–19, which also refers to compromises and shared views of the need to suppress communism and anarchism.

26. Yamaoka Mannosuke, "Shōnen hogo seido ni tsuite," *Hōritsu shinbun,* January 28, 1921, pp. 3–4; the quote on "spirit of social solidarity" is from p. 4; Yamaoka Mannosuke, "Shōnen hōan no konpon seishin," *Shakai to kyūsai* 4, no. 7 (October 1920): 4–5; and Yamaoka Mannosuke, "Shakai seisaku to shōnenhan no hogo," *Tōkyō nichinichi shinbun,* January 21, 1921, in *Shinbun shūsei Taishō hennenshi,* vol. for 1921, part 1, pp. 214–15.

27. Namae Takayuki, "Shōnen hō ni tsuite no shokan," *Teikoku kyōiku* 453 (April 1, 1920): 98–99.

28. Morita, "Taishō jūichinen shōnen hō no rippō katei," 42–68, and the documents in Morita, ed., *Taishō Shōnen hō,* vols. 1–2; Moriya, *Shōnen no hikō to kyōiku,* 84–85. For the text of the law and ancillary regulations, see also Suzuki, ed., *Tōkyō shōnen shinpanjo jūnenshi,* 61–99.

29. On the decline in criminal prosecutions, which appear to have involved largely recidivists, see Moriya, *Shōnen no hikō to kyōiku,* 94–95; Ishida Kōkichi, "Shōnen hō jisshigo Tōkyō ku saibansho ni okeru hanzai shōnen ni tsuite no chōsa," *Hōsōkai zasshi* 4, no. 9 (September 1926): 61–72; and Ishida Kōkichi, "Shōnen hanzai ni tsuite no chōsa," *Hōsōkai zasshi* 5, no. 7 (July 1927): 112–28. For statistics on the continuing use of penal measures in areas beyond the juvenile courts' jurisdiction, see "Kenkyo ni kakaru furyō shōnen shobun shirabe," *Shakai jigyō ihō,* September 1930: 22–24, appendix to *Shakai jigyō* 14, no. 6 (September 1930). Fifteen-year information on juvenile court cases is calculated from Shihō Hogo Kyōkai, ed., *Shihō hogo jigyō nenkan,* vol. 1 (Tokyo: Shihō Hogo Kyōkai, 1940), 10–16. All subsequent references to this title are to vol. 1. Types of crime are based on ten-year statistics, 1923–1932, in Tōkyō Shōnen Shinpanjo, *Shōnen hogo tōkei: ji Taishō jūni nen shi Shōwa shichi nen* (Tokyo: Tōkyō Shōnen Shinpanjo, 1933), 3–11; see also *Shihō hogo jigyō nenkan,* 246–47, for 1937 figures. For types of youths, see *Shōnen hogo tōkei,* 36–40; the graph titled "Shōnen no shokugyō (Osaka Shōnen Shinpanjo

no bu)," in Nihon Shōnen Hogo Kyōkai, *Hogo tōkei zushū* (Osaka: Nihon Shōnen Hogo Kyōkai Ōsaka Shibu, 1932), no page number; for Tokyo, see "Shōwa kunenchū shirabe shokugyōbetsu hikaku zu," *Tokufū* 6, no. 6 (July 1935), no page number.

30. For "all of the court's personnel are Christians," see J.O., "Shōnen shinpanjo o miru: ai to hōritsu to," *Jindō* 237 (July 15, 1925): 9. Biographical data on Miyagi (Ueda) Tamayo is taken from Haga Noboru et al., ed., *Nihon josei jinmei jiten* (Tokyo: Nihon Tosho Sentā, 1993), 1009. Personnel information is from Suzuki, ed., *Tōkyō shōnen shinpanjo jūnenshi*, 107–23. For Tokunaga's work, see for example Ōtani-ha Honganji Shakaika, ed., *Shōnen hogo ippan* (Kyoto: Ōtani-ha Shūmusho Shakaika, 1932). For examples of Shinbori's work, see Shinbori Tetsugaku, "Gure no hanashi," parts 1–3, *Jidō kenkyū* 32, no. 8 (November 1928): 198–202; no. 9 (December 1928): 221–26; and no. 10 (January 1929): 241–45. For writings by the Christian director of the Osaka Juvenile Court, see for example Furuya, *Aa shōnen*; and Furuya Shintarō, *Jūjiro ni tatsu shōnen* (Osaka: Kyōgaku Sōchōsha, 1930).

31. Personnel information is from Suzuki, ed., *Tōkyō shōnen shinpanjo jūnenshi*, 107–23; and Shihō Hogo Kyōkai, ed., *Shihō hogo jigyō nenkan*, 161 and 311.

32. On public outreach programs, see Suzuki, ed., *Tōkyō shōnen shinpanjo jūnenshi*, 249–75; and Shihō Hogo Kyōkai, ed., *Shihō hogo jigyō nenkan*, 101–3. On the Juvenile Protection Women's Association, see *Nihon shakai jigyō nenkan*, 1926 edition, ed. Ōhara Shakai Mondai Kenkyūjo (Osaka: Ōhara Shakai Mondai Kenkyūjo, 1926), 159; and *Ōsaka Asahi shinbun*, March 2, 1925, in *Shinbun shūsei Taishō hennenshi*, vol. for 1925, part 1, p. 781. For "socialization of protection," see Moriyama Takeichirō, "Shōnen hogo no shakaika e," *Shōnen hogo* 1, no. 1 (January 1936): 5–11.

33. For one recollection of this rocky start and eventual cooperation in Osaka, see Furuya Shintarō, "Ōsaka shōnen shinpanjo kaikoroku," *Shakai jigyō kenkyū* 23, no. 10 (October 1935): 202–3. For ongoing criticism of the Justice Ministry's approach, see Kikuchi Shuntei, "Yōhogo jidō jimu uchiawasekai," *Tōkyō-fu Shakai Jigyō Kyōkai hō* 13, no. 8 (August 1929): 87–89. For one juvenile court officer's view of the differences between the Juvenile Law and the Reformatory Law, or between social and criminal policies, see Ōtani-ha Honganji Shakaika, ed., *Shōnen hogo ippan*, 21. For one slum school teacher's criticism of colleagues who relied on strip searches and police-like methods, see Kondō Kenzō, "Watakushi wa kakushite furyōji o kyōsei shita," *Jidō kenkyū* 29, no. 6 (March, 1926): 194.

34. For Gotō's case, presented as a first-person testimonial by the youth in question, see Gotō Fumio, "Aru hogo shōnen no minouebanashi," parts 1–2, *Tōkyō-fu Shakai Jigyō Kyōkai hō* 13, no. 3 (March 1929): 37–47, and no. 4 (April 1929): 41–61. On durations of casework, see for example Tōkyō-fu Gakumubu Shakaika, *Shōwa ninen honfu toriatsukai furyō jidō jōkyō, Shakai chōsa shiryō*, no. 8 (Tokyo: Tōkyō-fu Gakumubu Shakaika, 1929) 46–47. On durations of probation, see for example Shihō Daijin Kanbō Hogoka, *Shihō hogo tōkei shū* (Tokyo: Shihō Daijin Kanbō Hogoka, 1936), 5. On runaways from apprenticeships, see Tōkyō-fu Shakaika, "Honfu ni okeru jidō hogo jōkyō

to sono keika: dai-ichi bu, furyō, furō jidō no bu," *Tōkyō-fu Shakai Jigyō Kyōkai hō* 27 (March 1926): 9–11.

35. Nakagawa Kiyoshi, "Senzen Nihon no hinkon no seikaku: sono jittai to ninshiki," in Yoshida, ed., *Shakai fukushi no Nihonteki tokushitsu*, esp. 284–96; see also Nakagawa, "Senzen Tōkyō no toshi kasō," 61–117.

36. Tōkyō-fu Shakaika, "Honfu ni okeru jidō hogo jōkyō to sono keika," 21–28; Tōkyō Shōnen Shinpanjo, *Shōnen hogo tōkei*, 34–35.

37. Gotō, "Aru hogo shōnen no minouebanashi," part 2; the quote is on p. 41.

38. For the phrase "reorganizing the home," see Tōkyō-fu Shakaika, "Honfu ni okeru jidō hogo jōkyō to sono keika," esp. 28.

39. This case is reported in Tōkyō-fu Shakaika, "Honfu ni okeru jidō hogo jōkyō to sono keika," 146–49. On the 1904 Supreme Court decision, see Toshitani, "Oya to kyōshi no chōkaiken," 199–200.

40. See for example "Kanojo no kokuhaku: aru hogo dantai ni te," part 2, *Tokufū* 6, no. 10 (November 1935): 29–30. For family, generational, and gender tensions related to working girls' use of money and time for leisure and pleasure in the United States, see Odem, *Delinquent Daughters*, 157–84; Gordon, *Heroes of Their Own Lives*, 187–93; and Kathy Peiss, *Cheap Amusements: Working Women and Leisure in Turn-of-the-Century New York* (Philadelphia, PA: Temple University Press, 1987).

41. Tōkyō-fu Shakaika, "Honfu ni okeru jidō hogo jōkyō to sono keika," 74–80. On stepparents and family conflicts in the United States, see Gordon, *Heroes of Their Own Lives*, 200–202.

42. This case is reported in Tōkyō-fu Gakumubu Shakaika, *Shōwa ninen honfu toriatsukai furyō jidō jōkyō*, 68–79.

43. "Kanojo no kokuhaku," part 2, pp. 29–30.

44. See for example Tōkyō-fu Gakumubu Shakaika, *Honfu ni okeru jidō hogo jigyō no gaikyō*, 60–66.

45. Tōkyō-fu Shakaika, "Tōkyō-fu jidō hogoin no kankei seru jidō jōkyō," *Tōkyō-fu Shakai Jigyō Kyōkai kaihō* 15 (September 1921): 90–91.

46. Miyagi, "Shōnen to hanzai," 40.

47. Fukudō (pseudonym), "Nihon de yuitsu no joshi kanka jigyō," *Hōritsu shinbun*, November 5, 1925, pp. 16–18.

48. "Furyō shōnen mondai ni kansuru zadankai," *Shakai jigyō* 11, no. 6 (September 1927): 75.

49. On probation officers' fears of entering delinquents' homes, see "Shōnen hō o kataru zadankai," *Shōnen hogo* 1, no. 4 (April 1936): 29–30. On commissioned probation officers' arrogance and misbehavior, see Furuya, "Ōsaka shōnen shinpanjo kaikoroku," 201. On steps to professionalize the commissioned probation officer system, see Shihō Hogo Kyōkai, ed., *Shihō hogo jigyō nenkan*, 113–27.

50. Honjo Mutsuo, "Shiroi kabe," in *Honjo Mutsuo, Suzuki Kiyoshi shū*, vol. 31 of *Nihon puroretaria bungaku shū* (Tokyo: Shin Nihon Shuppansha, 1987), 122, 124–26.

51. Ibid., 121. For the phrase "an education like everyone else gets" *(hitonami no kyōiku)*, uttered by a women requesting that her son be admitted to the

Reigan Elementary School, see Kondō Kenzō, "Saimin no seikatsu to dōtoku," *Teikoku kyōiku* 483 (October 1, 1922): 22. On the types of services parents requested, see Kondō Kenzō, "Hinji kyōiku to sono kaiko (4)," *Kyōiku jiron,* no. 1467 (March 15, 1926): 40.

52. See for example Kondō, "Saimin no seikatsu to dōtoku"; and Kondō Kenzō, "Saimin josei no kankyō oyobi shinri," *Teikoku kyōiku* 487 (February 1, 1923): 28–64. Kondō later criticized himself for having passed cruel judgments based on superficial perceptions. See Kondō Kenzō, "Donzoko seikatsu no hiai (2)," *Kyōiku jiron,* no. 1573 (February 25, 1929): 33.

53. For other examples of concocted stories, see Tōkyō-fu Gakumubu Shakaika, *Shōwa ninen honfu toriatsukai furyō jidō jōkyō,* 49–68; and Fujii Koto, "Uso o tsuku onna," *Tokufū* 6, no. 4 (May 17, 1935): 25–34.

54. Honjo, "Shiroi kabe," 115–20.

55. For educational levels of children and parents in cases examined by the Tokyo Prefecture Child Research Institute, see Fujimoto, "Yōhogo shōnen no kanbetsu ni tsuite," 51. The Tokyo Social Bureau study, conducted by Matsui Senju, is cited in Ishihara Yoshiharu, "Furyō shōnen mondai," *Shakai fukuri* 16, no. 8 (August 1932): 42; this article represents the paternalistic view. For a critical view of mental test findings, see for example Teruoka Gitō and Kirihara Shigemi, *Rōdō kagaku ron* (Tokyo: Chikura Shobō, 1933), 171–76. For a discussion of ethnic, class, and educational factors in intelligence tests of delinquents at Boston's highly regarded Judge Baker Clinic, see Schneider, *In the Web of Class,* 184.

56. For a novelistic description of medical examinations, see Honjo, "Shiroi kabe," 125–28. On symbolic violence in education, see for example Pierre Bourdieu and Jean-Claude Passeron, *Reproduction in Education, Society, and Culture,* trans. Richard Nice (London: SAGE Publications, 1977); and Stanley William Rothstein, *Schools and Society: New Perspectives in American Education* (Englewood Cliffs, NJ: Merrill, 1996). For a discussion of class and cultural divides between teachers and students in Chicago, see Howard Becker, "Social Class Variations in the Teacher-Pupil Relationship," (1952), reprinted in *Howard Becker on Education,* ed. Robert O. Burgess (Buckingham: Open University Press, 1995), 31–43.

57. Ōkado, "Nōson kara toshi e," esp. 177–78.

58. Nikai, "Tōkyō-fu Chūtō Gakkō Hodō Kyōkai no setsuritsu ni tsuite," 12; Tokyo figures are from ibid., 19, and Okada, "Kōgai hodōjō no shomondai," 7.

59. Morikawa Yoshiaki, "Gakusei hanzai no keitai to gen'in," *Shōnen hogo* 1, no. 2 (February 1936): 29, 32–36. See also Ishihara Yoshiharu, "Fuka shōnen shokugyō shōkai jigyō to sore ni tomonau shomondai," *Shakai fukuri* 17, no. 4 (April 1933): 74–75; and Watanabe Ikkō, "Chūgakkō ni okeru furyō keikō no sōki hakken," *Jidō hogo* 7, no. 7 (July 1937): 11–12.

60. Koyata Gengorō, "Gakusei kansatsu yodan," *Shōnen hogo* 1, no. 1 (January 1936): 105–6.

61. Watanabe, "Chūgakkō ni okeru furyō keikō no sōki hakken," 9–18. On methods at girls' schools, see Nakanishi Keijirō, "Jogakkō ni okeru furyō keikō no sōki hakken to sono yobōhō," *Jidō hogo* 7, no. 8 (August 1937): 17–32.

For federation leaders' rejection of the "school-police attitude," see Nikai, "Tōkyō-fu Chūtō Gakkō Hodō Kyōkai no setsuritsu ni tsuite," 14.

62. Ōsaka Asahi shinbun, March 2, 1925, in Shinbun shūsei Taishō hennen-shi, vol. for 1925, part 1.

63. Suzuki Kaichirō, Ko no tame ni naku (Tokyo: Shōkadō, 1934), 62–63, 69–70, 229–31.

64. Ibid., 147–48.

65. TAS, May 6, 1928, morning edition, p. 5.

66. Tōkyō-fu Shakaika, "Honfu ni okeru jidō hogo jōkyō to sono keika," 159–68.

67. Suzuki, Ko no tame ni naku, 204–20.

68. For the case of the widow and her son, see Sawaki Shōun, "Shōnen o kansatsu suru kokoro," Shakai jigyō kenkyū 25, no. 8 (August 1937): 80–86. On bribes and elementary-school teachers, see the comments by Fujioka Shin'ichirō in "Furyō shōnen mondai ni kansuru zadankai," 76.

69. Tōkyō-fu Shakaika, "Honfu ni okeru jidō hogo jōkyō to sono keika," 48–59. For types of treatments used in all cases of juvenile delinquents handled by the Social Section from 1920 to 1929, but not the results, see Tōkyō-fu Gakumubu Shakaika, Honfu ni okeru jidō hogo jigyō no gaikyō, 10–13.

70. Statistics from Shihō Hogo Kyōkai, ed., Shihō hogo jigyō nenkan, 19–21. For a criticism of some probation officers' "mechanical" methods and reports, see Suzuki Kaichirō, "Shōnen hogo no tame ni," Shōnen hogo 1, no. 1 (January 1936): 15–16. For a report on one case handled by a district welfare commissioner, mainly through the Tokyo City Children's Shelter, see "Hikari aru seikatsu e: hogosho no aru shōnen," in Tōkyō-shi Shakaikyoku, Tōkyō-shi hōmen iin toriatsukai jitsureishū (Tokyo, 1929), 118–28; reprinted in Tōkyō-shi Shakaikyoku chōsa hōkokushū, vol. 1 of Nihon kindai toshi shakai chōsa shiryō shūsei, ed. Kingendai Shiryō Kankōkai (Tokyo: SBB Shuppankai, 1995), 134–44. For an account of one schoolteacher's personalized approach, see Kondō, "Watakushi wa kakushite furyōji o kyōsei shita," 194–99.

71. Yoshio Sugimoto, An Introduction to Japanese Society (Cambridge: Cambridge University Press, 1997), 249–51.

72. Ōtani-ha Honganji Shakaika, ed., Shōnen hogo ippan, 48. On the family system ideology, see for example Kano Masanao, Senzen "ie" no shisō (Tokyo: Sōbunsha, 1983).

73. Suzuki's observations are in Suzuki, ed., Tōkyō shōnen shinpanjo jūnen-shi, 142. Narita's views are in Narita Katsurō, "Seishin eisei shisō to shōnen hogo," part 5, Shōnen hogo 2, no. 6 (June 1937): 84–87.

74. Suzuki, Ko no tame ni naku, 224. See also Suzuki, Furyō Shōnen no kenkyū, 1–9, for an earlier expression of the idea that the harmonious, loving katei (rather than the kazoku) was the foundation of the nation/state. On the relationship between the ie (patriarchal household) and the katei, see Sand, "At Home in the Meiji Period," 191–207; and Muta, "Images of the Family in Meiji Periodicals," 53–71. On the ubiquity of surveillance/power, see for example Foucault, Discipline and Punish.

75. Takeda Shinjirō, "Kankain seito ni taisuru taigū kaizen to bunrui shūyō ni tsuite," Jindō 293 (March 15, 1930): 9. See also Yamamoto Keiji, "Kanka hō

happu mansanjusshūnen o mukauru ni saishite," *Shakai fukuri* 14, no. 3 (March 1930): 62–64. For statistics on reformatories, see for example Naimushō Shakaikyoku Shakaibu, *Kanka jigyō ni kansuru tōkei* (Tokyo: Naimushō, 1926 and 1927 editions).

76. The play was first published as Fujimori Seikichi, "Nani ga kanojo o sō saseta ka," *Kaizō* 9, no. 2 (February 1927): literary supplement, 1–81.

77. For the text of the 1933 Juvenile Educational Protection Law and ancillary regulations, see Kōseishō Shakaikyoku Jidōka, ed., *Jidō hogo kankei hōki* (Tokyo: Kōseishō Shakaikyoku Jidōka, 1938), 1–40, reprinted in *Senzenki shakai jigyō shiryō shūsei*, vol. 15, ed. Shakai Fukushi Chōsa Kenkyūkai (Tokyo: Nihon Tosho Sentā, 1985). For escape rates, see for example Naimushō Shakaikyoku Shakaibu, *Kanka jigyō ni kansuru tōkei* (1926 and 1927 editions). For subsequent criticisms, see for example Aoki Seishirō, "Shōnen kyōgo no shōrai o kataru," *Jidō hogo* 11, no. 1 (January 1941): 13–14.

78. Shihō Hogo Kyōkai, ed., *Shihō hogo jigyō nenkan*, 166.

79. Ibid., 30–31, 65, 165–87. Little information exists regarding the treatment of Korean delinquents.

80. Miyagi Chōgorō, "Jisshi kaiko," in Suzuki, ed., *Tōkyō shōnen shinpanjo jūnenshi*, 323–27.

81. "Kōtō no sukui no sono: Fukugyō Chisankai o miru," parts 1–2, *Shōnen hogo* 3, no. 1 (January 1938): 62–66, and no. 2 (February 1938): 88–91.

82. Ōtani-ha Honganji Shakaika, ed., *Shōnen hogo ippan*, 54–55, 60.

83. *TAS*, June 20, 1930, morning edition, p. 11. See also Moriya, *Shōnen no hikō to kyōiku*, 103–4.

84. *TAS*, June 11, 1931, morning edition, p. 7; and *TAS*, June 12, 1931, evening edition, p. 2.

85. *Hōritsu shinbun*, July 15, 1927, pp. 4–5.

86. "Nagashima Jikan kunji" (1936), in Shihō Hogo Kyōkai, ed., *Shihō hogo jigyō nenkan*, 125–26.

87. On the Legal Protection Operations Law, which governed juvenile corrections agencies and programs for the rehabilitation of ex-convicts and leftwing thought criminals, see Moriya, *Shōnen no hikō to kyōiku*, 116–18. On training courses for juvenile protection workers, see Kyōsei Kyōkai, ed., *Shōnen kyōsei*, 486–90. The Japan Juvenile Protection Association had organized occasional seminars throughout the 1930s.

88. Calculated from data in Shihō Hogo Kyōkai, ed., *Shihō hogo jigyō nenkan*, 19–21.

89. For the 1942 discussion of escapes, see Hashimoto Katsutarō, *Shōnen no seikaku to kankyō* (Tokyo: Dōbunkan, 1942), 176–79. On sexual practices in protective associations, see for example Maeda Takeo, "Itaku hogo ni kansuru shiken," *Tokufū* 12 (March 15, 1935): 18; and Nihon Shōnen Shidōkai Yōshōnen Kyōka Kenkyūbu, ed., *Shōnen furyōka to sono taisaku (shōhon), dai isshū* (Tokyo: Nihon Shōnen Shidōkai, 1937), 51. On tattooing, see Shinbori Tetsugaku, "Gaitō shōnen no hanashi," part 2, *Shakai fukuri* 16, no. 5 (May 1932): 67. For the concept of "underlives," tied to that of total institutions, see Erving Goffman, *Asylums: Essays on the Social Situation of Mental Patients and Other Inmates* (Chicago: Aldine Publishing Co., 1962), 304–5.

90. See for example Suzuki, "Shōnen hogo no tame ni," 15–16; and "Shōnen kyōgo ni kansuru zadankai: Shōnen kyōgo hō jisshi o kinenshite," *Jidō hogo* 4, no. 10 (October 1934): 38–39. On the operations of the Judge Baker Foundation, see Schneider, *In the Web of Class,* 170–88; and Peter C. Holloran, *Boston's Wayward Children: Social Services for Homeless Children, 1830–1930* (Rutherford, NJ: Fairleigh Dickinson University Press, 1989), esp. 230–37.

91. *TAS*, August 2, 1931, evening edition, p. 2; "Furyōsei jidō mondai ni kansuru shūdankai," part 1, *Jidō kenkyū* 35, no. 11 (February 1932): 247–50.

92. Narita Katsurō, "Seishin eisei shisō to shōnen hogo," part 4, *Shōnen hogo* 2, no. 4 (April 1937): 24–25.

93. Nihon Shōnen Shidōkai Yōshōnen Kyōka Kenkyūbu, ed., *Shōnen furyōka to sono taisaku,* 54–55; Hashimoto Katsutarō, *Nihon seishin eisei undō no ichi kōsatsu* (Tokyo: Nihon Shōnen Shidōkai, 1934), 18–23; Ōta Shūsui, "*Shōnen furyōka to sono taisaku* o yomu," *Jidō hogo* 8, no. 4 (April 1938): 63–64. See also comments by youth workers in "Danshuhō seitei ni taisuru sanpi," *Shakai jigyō kenkyū* 24, no. 10 (October 1936): 46–52.

94. Sumiko Otsubo, "Problematizing State Power: Eugenic Legislation in Wartime Japan" (paper presented at the annual meeting of the Association for Asian Studies, San Diego, California, March 9, 2000), esp. 36; Sumiko Otsubo, "Feminist Maternal Eugenics in Wartime Japan," *U.S.-Japan Women's Journal, English Supplement* 17 (1999): 39–76. Narita Katsurō and his colleagues did play key roles in promoting mental hygiene programs in the postwar juvenile corrections system. Elmer H. Johnson, *Japanese Corrections: Managing Convicted Offenders in an Orderly Society* (Carbondale: Southern Illinois University Press, 1996), 159.

95. Henry D. Smith, II, "The Nonliberal Roots of Taishō Democracy," in *Japan Examined: Perspectives on Modern Japanese History,* ed. Harry Wray and Hilary Conroy (Honolulu: University of Hawai'i Press, 1983), 191–98; Garon, "State and Society in Interwar Japan."

96. Garon, *Molding Japanese Minds,* 49–57.

97. See for example Gordon, *Heroes of Their Own Lives,* 76; and Schneider, *In the Web of Class,* 151–53.

98. Suzuki, *Ko no tame ni naku,* 223. For a theoretical discussion of enforcement agencies' strategies to justify their continued existence, see Becker, *Outsiders,* 157.

CHAPTER 5

1. *Ōsaka Mainichi shinbun,* September 22, 1929, in *Shinbun shūsei Shōwa hennenshi,* ed. Meiji Taishō Shōwa Shinbun Kenkyūkai (Tokyo: Meiji Taishō Shōwa Shinbun Kenkyūkai, 1955–), 1929, part 3, p. 925 (hereafter abbreviated as *SSSHS*).

2. For one instance of radicalization, see Kaneko Fumiko, *The Prison Memoirs of a Japanese Woman,* trans. Jean Inglis (Armonk, NY: M. E. Sharpe, 1991), 168–248; see also the transcript of Kaneko's interrogation in *Reflections on the Way to the Gallows: Rebel Women in Prewar Japan,* translated and edited with an introduction by Mikiso Hane (New York: Pantheon, 1990), 119–24.

3. The phrase "cheap, plentiful" appears in Ishizumi Harunosuke, *Ginza kaibōzu daiippen hensenshi* (Tokyo: Marunouchi Shuppan, 1934), reprinted in *Sakariba, uramachi,* vol. 2 of *Kindai shomin seikatsushi,* ed. Minami Hiroshi et al. (Tokyo: San'ichi Shobō, 1984), 287. On Asakusa amusements, see for example Ishizumi Harunosuke, *Asakusa keizaigaku* (Tokyo: Bunjinsha, 1933), reprinted in ibid., 245–85; and Zakō Jun, *Asakusa Rokku wa itsumo modan data: opera, rebyū, sutorippu* (Tokyo: Asahi Shinbunsha, 1984), 68–69. For a study of Tokyo's *sakariba* (thriving places), see Yoshimi, *Toshi no doramaturugii;* Seidensticker, *Low City, High City;* and Seidensticker, *Tokyo Rising.*

4. "Furyō shōnen mondai ni kansuru zadankai," *Shakai jigyō* 11, no. 6 (September 15, 1927): 77, 79; see also Iijima Mitsuyasu, "Teito ni okeru furyō shōnen no jissai to sono bōshisaku," part 2, *Jidō kenkyū* 31, no. 10 (January 1928): 242.

5. Marshall, *Learning to Be Modern,* 93.

6. Government of Japan, *Japan's Modern Educational System,* 456; for middle-school application figures and their relationship to enrollments, both nationwide and in Tokyo, see Kuwabara, *Tōkyō-fu kōritsu chūgakkō kyōikushi,* 81, 112–14, 159–60, 261.

7. Namae Takayuki, "Shokugyō jidō ni taisuru jidai no yōkyū," *Shakai jigyō* 10, no. 9 (December 1926): 6–14; the quoted passage is on 8.

8. For "people's middle schools," see Noguchi Entarō, *Kōtō shōgakkō no kenkyū* (Tokyo: Teikoku Kyōiku Kai, 1926), quoted in Ōkado Masakatsu, "Gakkō kyōiku to shakai idō: tokainetsu to seishōnen," in *Nihon no kindai to shihonshugi: kokusaika to chiiki,* ed. Nakamura Masanori (Tokyo: Tōkyō Daigaku Shuppankai, 1992), 172. For political parties' education platforms, see Marshall, *Learning to Be Modern,* 93. For *zaibatsu*-controlled firms' hiring policies, see Sumiya Mikio, *Nihonteki yōsei seido no keisei,* vol. 2 of *Nihon shokugyō kunren hattenshi,* ed. Sumiya Mikio and Koga Hiroshi (Tokyo: Nihon Rōdō Kyōkai, 1977), esp. 183.

9. Ōkado, "Gakkō kyōiku to shakai idō," 172–75; Government of Japan, *Japan's Modern Educational System;* and Marshall, *Learning to Be Modern,* 93–94.

10. Yamada Sakuzō, "Shokugyō shidō no hitsuyō o ronjite sono hōan ni oyobu," *Toshi kyōiku* 168 (September 1918): 4–10; the quoted passage is on 5. On the new managerial and technocratic ideologies, see for example William Tsutsui, *Manufacturing Ideology: Scientific Management in Twentieth Century Japan* (Princeton, NJ: Princeton University Press, 1998); and Chalmers Johnson, *MITI and the Japanese Miracle: The Growth of Industrial Policy, 1925–1975* (Tokyo: Charles E. Tuttle Co., 1982).

11. For the progressive education argument, see Tōkyō Shisei Chōsakai, *Toshi kyōiku no kenkyū* (Tokyo: Tōkyō Shisei Chōsakai, 1926), esp. 284–93, 315, 598–99; and Toyohara Matao, "Shōnen shōjo to shokugyō shidō," part 2, *Tōkyō-fu Shakai Jigyō Kyōkai hō* 28 (June 1926): 52–54. For a basic exposition of Dewey's ideas, see John Dewey, *The School and Society: Being Three Lectures by John Dewey Supplemented by a Statement of the University Elementary School* (Chicago: University of Chicago Press, 1907). For the "social service" argument, see Tanino Iwao, "Gakkō kyōiku to shokugyō shidō,"

Shakai jigyō 13, no. 1 (April 1929): 20. For a compendium of lectures on vocational guidance, see Monbushō Futsū Gakumukyoku, ed., *Shokugyō shidō*, 2 vols. (Tokyo: Shakai Kyōiku Kyōkai, 1924).

12. Lincicome, *Principle, Praxis, and the Politics of Educational Reform*, 244; "Jidō seito no kosei sonchō oyobi shokugyō shidō ni kansuru ken," November 25, 1927, in *Jidō kankei hōki shū*, ed. Tōkyō-fu Gakumubu Shakaika, *Shakai jigyō shiryō*, no. 23 (Tokyo: Tōkyō-fu Gakumubu Shakaika, 1935), 95–96, reprinted in *Senzenki shakai jigyō shiryō shūsei*, vol. 15, ed. Shakai Fukushi Chōsa Kenkyūkai (Tokyo: Nihon Tosho Sentā, 1985).

13. Moriya Shigeo, "Shokugyō shidō," *Tōkyō-fu Shakai Jigyō Kyōkai hō* 31 (March 1927): 15–16. For a study of the vocational guidance movement in Weimar Germany, see Elizabeth Harvey, *Youth and the Welfare State in Weimar Germany* (Oxford: Clarendon Press, 1993). On vocationalism and vocational guidance programs in Chicago, see David John Hogan, *Class and Reform: School and Society in Chicago, 1880–1930* (Philadelphia: University of Pennsylvania Press, 1985), 138–93.

14. Toyohara Matao, "Shōnen shōjo to shokugyō shidō," part 1, *Tōkyō-fu Shakai Jigyō Kyōkai hō* 27 (March 1926): 184–87; the phrase "common, traditional" is on 186–87. For "vocational cripples," see Moriya, "Shokugyō shidō," 14. For an earlier exposition, see Yamada, "Shokugyō shidō no hitsuyō."

15. Yasuda Seimei Shakai Jigyōdan, ed., *Nihon no jidō sōdan*, 1:102–7, 125–28; this source also contains information on the establishment of counseling centers in Osaka and elsewhere. On Tokyo, see also Maki Ken'ichi, "Tōkyō ni okeru shōnen shokugyō shidō no jissai to shiryō ni tsuite," *Shakai jigyō* 13, no. 1 (April 1929): 50–51.

16. "Shōnen shokugyō shōkai ni kansuru ken imei tsūchō," July 8, 1925; "Shōnen shokugyō shōkai ni kansuru ken tsūchō," July 25, 1925; "Shōnen shokugyō shōkai ni kansuru ken," October 19, 1925; and "Shōnen shokugyō shōkai ni kansuru ken," February 10, 1926, in Tōkyō-fu Gakumubu Shakaika, ed., *Jidō kankei hōki shū*, 96–100.

17. 1932 figures (for the year from June 1, 1931 to May 30, 1932) are from Chūō Shokugyō Shōkai Jimukyoku, ed., *Shokugyō shōkai nenpō*, 1932 ed. (Tokyo: Chūō Shokugyō Shōkai Jimukyoku, 1934), 68–73; see also Akasaka Renzō, "Shōgakkō sotsugyōsei no shūshoku mondai," *Shakai fukuri* 17, no. 2 (February 1933): 9–10. For a discussion of trends in the 1930s, see Saguchi Kazurō, "Nihon no naibu rōdō shijō: 1960 nendaimatsu no henyō o chūshin toshite," in *Keizai riron e no rekishiteki paasupekutibu*, ed. Yoshikawa Hiroshi and Okazaki Tetsuji (Tokyo: Tōkyō Daigaku Shuppankai, 1990), 224. For lists of employment agencies, see for example *Shokugyō shōkai nenpō*, 1931 and 1932 editions.

18. Ishihara Yoshiharu, "Tōkyō fuka ni okeru shōnen shokugyō shōkai jigyō," *Tōkyō-fu Shakai Jigyō Kyōkai hō* 15, no. 10 (October 1931): 63; Ishihara Yoshiharu, "Fuka shōnen shokugyō shōkai jigyō to sore ni tomonau shomondai," *Shakai fukuri* 17, no. 4 (April 1933): 71–73. See also Ōkado, "Gakkō kyōiku to shakai idō," and Ōkado, "Nōson kara toshi e," 174–95.

19. For the 1932 survey figures, see Tōkyō-fu Gakumubu Shakaika, *Rōdō jidō chōsa, dai ni bu, Shakai chōsa shiryō* no. 20 (Tokyo: Tōkyō-fu Gakumubu

Shakaika, 1933), 6, reprinted in *Shōnen rōmusha,* vol. 6 of *Rōdōsha seikatsu chōsa shiryō shūsei: kindai Nihon no rōdōsha zō, 1920–1930 nendai,* ed. Nakagawa Kiyoshi (Tokyo: Seishisha, 1995). For Kawasaki's observations about office girls and examinations, see Kawasaki Natsu, *Shokugyō fujin o kokorozasu hito no tame ni* (Tokyo: Genjinsha, 1932), 196, reprinted in *Kindai fujin mondai meicho senshū zoku hen,* vol. 10, ed. Nakajima Kuni et al. (Tokyo: Nihon Tosho Sentā, 1982). For a discussion of lower-class women's aspirations for social mobility in the 1920s, see Margit Maria Nagy, "'How Shall We Live?': Social Change, the Family Institution, and Feminism in Prewar Japan" (Ph.D. diss., University of Washington, 1981), esp. 138–54.

20. For an analysis of *Shōnen kurabu*'s content and editorial strategies, including the column by "Kyūbei," see Iwahashi Ikurō, *Shōnen kurabu to dokushatachi* (Tokyo: Zōnsha, 1988). On programs for youth department employees, see Noma Seiji, *Watakushi no hansei, Shūyō zatsuwa* (Tokyo: Noma Kyōiku Kenkyūjo, 1999), 417–21, 444–46. Several of the most successful works that appeared in the magazine, including Satō's *Aa gyokuhai ni hana ukete,* have been republished in *Shōnen kurabu meisakusen,* vols. 1–3, ed. Katō Ken'ichi (Tokyo: Kōdansha, 1966). For an analysis of these novels, see Kuwabara Saburō, *Shōnen kurabu no koro: Shōwa zenki no jidō bungaku* (Tokyo: Keiō Tsūshin, 1987). This discourse, of course, represented an expansion of trends already evident in the first decades of the century. See Kinmonth, *The Self-Made Man;* Gluck, *Japan's Modern Myths,* 204–11; and Narita, "'Shōnen sekai' to dokusho suru shōnentachi."

21. Ishihara, "Fuka shōnen shokugyō shōkai jigyō to sore ni tomonau shomondai," 71–73. For girls'-school graduates applying to the Tokyo Municipal Women's and Children's Employment Agency, see *TAS,* February 13, 1933, morning edition, p. 9. On the labor market for female domestic servants, see Okuda Akiko, "Jochū no rekishi," in *Semegiau onna to otoko: kindai,* ed. Okuda Akiko, vol. 5 of *Onna to otoko no jikū,* ed. Tsurumi Kazuko et al. (Tokyo: Fujiwara Shoten, 1995), 376–401.

22. For "extremely clear understanding," see *TAS,* February 13, 1933, morning edition, p. 9. For "reveres the ruling class," see Akasaka, "Shōgakkō sotsugyōsei no shūshoku mondai," 11. For figures nationwide by job category, see for example *Shokugyō shōkai nenpō,* 1931 ed., 86–87; and 1932 ed., 70.

23. Ishihara, "Fuka shōnen shokugyō shōkai jigyō to sore ni tomonau shomondai," 74–75.

24. On night students and office boys as delinquents, see *Yomiuri shinbun,* May 31, 1925, in *Shinbun shūsei Taishō hennenshi,* vol. for 1925, p. 631; *TAS,* June 7, 1929, evening edition, p. 2; *Hōritsu shinbun,* August 5, 1927, p. 19; and "Furyō shōnen mondai ni kansuru zadankai," 77, 81.

25. Ishihara, "Tokyo fuka ni okeru shōnen shokugyō shōkai jigyō," 59; *TAS,* February 21, 1931, morning edition, p. 7; *TAS,* July 30, 1931, morning edition, p. 3. On (middle-class) women's work as a danger to home and family, see also Ishihara Yoshiharu, "Furyō shōnen mondai," *Shakai fukuri* 16, no. 8 (August 1932): 43; Yamada Waka, "Shōnen Hogo Kyōkai no setsuritsu ni tsuite," *Aikoku fujin* 516 (April 1, 1925): 9–10; and Nagy, "Middle-Class Working Women," 199–216.

26. For discussions of "struggling students" and delinquency, see for example "Furyō shōnen mondai ni kansuru zadankai" 78; *TAS*, January 24, 1927, morning edition, p. 7; *TAS*, April 11, 1933, morning edition, p. 5; and Suzuki, *Ko no tame ni naku*, 156–57, 296–97. See also Kaneko, *The Prison Memoirs of a Japanese Woman*, 175–214, for an account of her hardships as a struggling student.

27. *TAS*, February 8, 1930, morning edition, p. 7.

28. See for example *TAS*, December 28, 1927, morning edition, p. 11; *TAS*, February 8, 1930, morning edition, p. 7; Shiina Ryūtoku, "Ankoku no chimata ni naku," *Keimu gahō* 305 (Seoul: Chōsen Keisatsu Kyōkai, September 1938): 99–103; and Shinbori Tetsugaku, *Meian no Asakusa to furyō shōnen* (Tokyo: Hokutō Shobō, 1936), 57–58. For a discussion of discourses on and campaigns against white slavery in Toronto in the early twentieth century, see Carolyn Strange, *Toronto's Girl Problem: The Perils and Pleasures of the City, 1880–1930* (Toronto, Buffalo, and London: University of Toronto Press, 1995), 96–102.

29. Stephen Vlastos, "Agrarianism without Tradition: The Radical Critique of Prewar Japanese Modernity," in *Mirror of Modernity: Invented Traditions of Modern Japan*, ed. Stephen Vlastos, 79–94; the quoted passage is on 89. See also Thomas R.H. Havens, *Farm and Nation in Modern Japan: Agrarian Nationalism, 1870–1940* (Princeton, NJ: Princeton University Press, 1974); and Kerry Smith, *A Time of Crisis: Japan, the Great Depression, and Rural Revitalization* (Cambridge, MA: Harvard University Press, 2003).

30. *TAS*, June 27, 1931, morning edition, p. 10. For Tokugawa-era commentators' laments about young women's desire to find positions as housemaids in Edo, see Leupp, *Servants, Shophands, and Laborers*, 67.

31. On vocational guidance, local economies, and alumni success stories, see Ōkado, "Gakkō kyōiku to shakai idō," 178; on continuing supply-demand imbalances at employment agencies, see for example Tomita Yukio, "Shōnen shokugyō shōkai jigyō no nanten," *Shakai jigyō kenkyū* 24, no. 3 (March 1936): 35.

32. Ishihara Yoshiharu, "Shokugyō shōnen shōjo no hanzai oyobi jisatsu no shuin oyobi dōki ni tsuite," *Shakai fukuri* 16, no. 10 (October 1932): 97–108; see also Kitamura Reiji, "Bakuro saru beki shōnen rōdō no genjō," *Shakai fukuri* 15, no. 3 (March 1931): 14–19; Iso Ryōtarō, "Totei shōnenkō mondai," parts 1–5, *Jidō hogo* 12, no. 10 (October 1933): 19–24; no. 11 (November 1933): 24–31; no. 12 (December 1933): 30–35; vol. 13, no. 1 (January 1934): 34–39; and no. 2 (February 1934): 39–45.

33. Tokunaga Sunao, "Tanin no naka" (1939), in *Tokunaga Sunao shū* 2, vol. 25 of *Nihon puroretaria bungakushū* (Tokyo: Shin Nihon Shuppansha, 1987), 252–53. While set in a provincial town, Tokunaga's story applies as well to conditions in the larger cities.

34. *Yomiuri shinbun*, January 18, 1929, in *SSSHS* 1929, part 1, p. 212.

35. *TAS*, February 8, 1930, morning edition, p. 7; Ishihara, "Shokugyō shōnen shōjo no hanzai oyobi jisatsu no shuin oyobi dōki ni tsuite."

36. Isomura Eiichi, "Shōnen shokugyō mondai no shakaiteki igi," *Shakai jigyō* 13, no. 1 (April 1929): 3.

37. Survey information is discussed in Ishihara Yoshiharu, "Nenshō rōdō seikatsusha mondai," parts 1–2, *Shakai fukuri* 21, no. 7 (July 1937): 21–30, and no. 8 (August 1937): 86–100.

38. Tokunaga Sunao, "Hikōki kozō," in *Tokunaga Sunao shū* 2, 205. On younger sons of poor families as a significant pool of internal migrants, see James B. White, "Internal Migration in Prewar Japan," *Journal of Japanese Studies* 4, no. 1 (1978): 85.

39. *TAS*, February 21, 1931, morning edition, p. 7. For "aptitude tests are meaningless," see Iso, "Totei shōnenkō mondai," part 3, 31. Labor exchanges also reported that employers were targeting graduates of the compulsory elementary course over those leaving the higher elementary program. *TAS*, February 3, 1930, morning edition, p. 7.

40. On maids and rape, see Okuda, "Jochū no rekishi."

41. Ishihara, "Shokugyō shōnen shōjo no hanzai oyobi jisatsu no shuin oyobi dōki ni tsuite," 97–108; the quoted passage is on 107.

42. Chūō Shakai Jigyō Kyōkai Shakai Jigyō Kenkyūjo, *Furyō jidō to shokugyō to no kankei* (Tokyo: Chūō Shakai Jigyō Kyōkai Shakai Jigyō Kenkyūjo, 1936), 26.

43. Kokushi daijiten Henshū Iinkai, ed., *Kokushi daijiten*, vol. 7 (Tokyo: Yoshikawa Kōbunkan, 1986), s.v. "Shōten hō," 566. For a transcript of Miyoshi's radio broadcast, see Miyoshi Toyotarō, "Shōten'in ni tsuite," *Shakai fukuri* 20, no. 5 (May 1936), 81–88.

44. For "nihilism" and "thoughts of only sex," see Iso, "Totei shōnenkō mondai," part 5, 39–45. On Osaka merchants' calls for government action against cafés, see Murashima Yoriyuki, *Kanraku no ōkyū kafuee* (Tokyo: Bunka Seikatsu Kenkyūkai, 1929), reprinted in *Kyōraku, sei*, vol. 10 of *Kindai shomin seikatsushi*, ed. Minami Hiroshi et al. (Tokyo: San'ichi Shobō, 1990), esp. 359–60.

45. On continuing education facilities in Tokyo in the 1920s, see Tōkyō Shisei Chōsakai, *Toshi kyōiku no kenkyū*. On youth groups, youth training centers, and disparities between rural and urban enrollments, see Smethurst, *A Social Basis for Prewar Japanese Militarism;* Humphreys, *The Way of the Heavenly Sword*, esp. 91–93; and Takano Yoshihiro, *Seinen gakkōshi* (Tokyo: San'ichi Shobō, 1992), which also discusses urban-rural disparities in the older vocational supplementary schools.

46. On youth groups in Tokyo, see Hastings, *Neighborhood and Nation*, 104–15. On the national system, see Smethurst, *A Social Basis for Prewar Japanese Militarism*. For proposals concerning youth groups or organized leisure activities for working youths, see for example Kondō Kenzō, "Furyōji kyōiku shōdan," part 2, *Kyōiku jiron*, no. 1573 (February 25, 1929): 28–29; and Miyoshi, "Shōten'in ni tsuite," 81–88. For one Tokyo City experiment with a Commercial and Industrial Young Men's Cultivation Association, see Tōkyō Shiyakusho, *Shōnen rōmusha ni kansuru chōsa* (Tokyo: Tōkyō Shiyakusho, 1929), 1–4, reprinted in Nakagawa, ed., *Shōnen rōmusha*. On earlier lectures and recreational assemblies for young factory workers and apprentices in Tokyo, see Yamamoto, *Kindai Nihon toshi kyōkashi kenkyū*, 83–84. On opportunities and obstacles facing female workers in larger textile factories, see

Barbara Molony, "Activism among Women in the Taishō Cotton Textile Industry," in Bernstein, ed., *Recreating Japanese Women, 1600–1945*, 226–27.

47. Higuchi, "Growing Up," 70–110; the quoted passage is on 90. For the original, see Higuchi, "Takekurabe" (1895–96), 98–148; the quoted passage is on 122. Whereas Higuchi writes of youths aged "seventeen or eighteen," Seidensticker has adjusted the text to reflect the modern mode of calculating ages. On continuities in neighborhood youth group activity from Edo to Tokyo, see also Hirade, *Tōkyō fūzokushi*, vol. 1. For Sakaguchi's discussion of the decline of student ruffians and the rise of working-class gangs, see Sakaguchi, *Furyō shōnen no kenkyū*, 119; see also Komino Naozō, "Machi no shōnen fūzokushi (3): furyō shōnen no jingi," *Shōnen hogo* 3, no. 3 (March 1938): 56. On the more general continuity of commoner culture across the 1868 divide, see Ogi Shinzō, *Tōkei shomin seikatsushi kenkyū* (Tokyo: Nippon Hōsō Shuppan Kyōkai, 1979); and Smith, "The Edo-Tokyo Transition," 363–65. On working-class gambling in Tokyo's Fukagawa district in the 1920s, see Saga, *Confessions of a Yakuza*.

48. For examples of gang behavior, see *TAS*, June 13, 1927, morning edition, p. 7; *TAS*, November 1, 1927, morning edition, p. 7; *TAS*, November 24, 1928, morning edition, p. 11; and *Tōkyō nichinichi shinbun*, February 25, 1932, in *Shinbun shūsei Shōwa hennenshi*, vol. for 1932, ed. Taishō Shōwa Shinbun Kenkyūkai (Tokyo: Taishō Shōwa Shinbun Kenkyūkai, 1969), 121; the latter refers to the Kantō Blue Dragons (Kantō Seiryūdan).

49. "Furyō shōnen mondai ni kansuru zadankai," 78; Iijima Mitsuyasu, "Teito ni okeru furyō shōnen no jissai to sono bōshisaku," part 1, *Jidō kenkyū* 31, no. 9 (December 1927): 214–15; Sekine Ryūji, "'Yotamon' o kataru," part 1, *Shakai fukuri* 18, no. 7 (July 1934), 41–44; Komino, "Machi no shōnen fūzokushi (3): furyō shōnen no jingi," 54–58. For "Eddie Polo-ing," see Satō Hachirō, *Asakusa* (Tokyo: Seikōkan Shoten, 1932), 141. On the persistence of turf fights and violent subcultures of construction workers, see for example *TAS*, June 21, 1927, morning edition, p. 7; and *TAS*, May 24, 1932, morning edition, p. 7. For theoretical discussions of subculture and style, see Stuart Hall and Tony Jefferson, eds., *Resistance through Rituals: Youth Subcultures in Postwar Britain* (London: Hutchinson, 1976); and Dick Hebdige, *Subculture: The Meaning of Style* (London: Routledge, 1995).

50. *TAS*, June 7, 1928, morning edition, p. 7. For a report of one Japanese youth who drifted over to Manchuria and became a delinquent while working in a café, see *Manshū nichinichi shinbun*, November 4, 1935, p. 2.

51. Eve Rosenhaft, "Organising the 'Lumpenproletariat'," in *The German Working Class, 1888–1933: The Politics of Everyday Life*, ed. Richard J. Evans (London: Croom Helm, 1982), 208.

52. On Apache membership as a youthful rite of passage, see Michelle Perrot, "Dans Paris de la Belle Epoque, les 'Apaches', Premières Bandes de Jeunes," in Michelle Perrot, *Les Ombres de l'Histoire: Crime et Châtiment au XIXe Siècle* (Paris: Flammarion, 2001), 354. For a discussion of graduation from Japanese motorcycle gangs in the 1970s and 1980s, see Ikuya Satō, *Kamikaze Biker: Parody and Anomy in Affluent Japan* (Chicago: University of Chicago Press, 1991).

53. Tōkyō-fu Shakaika, "Honfu ni okeru jidō hogo jōkyō to sono keika," 162.

54. Suzuki, *Furyō shōnen no kenkyū*, 103–18, also 86–87. For the 1925 MPD action, see Keishichō shi Hensan Iinkai, ed., *Keishichō shi Taishō hen* (Tokyo: Keishichō shi Hensan Iinkai, 1960), 679–81.

55. Ishizumi Harunosuke, *Asakusa urabanashi* (Tokyo: Bungei Shijōsha, 1927), 184; Suzuki, *Furyō shōnen no kenkyū*, 110–11. For a report about similar behavior by a gang based in Shitaya, see *TAS*, November 28, 1929, evening edition, p. 2.

56. Perrot, "Dans Paris de la Belle Epoque," 358.

57. Iijima Mitsuyasu, "Teito ni okeru furyō shōnen no jissai to sono bōshisaku," parts 2–3, *Jidō kenkyū* 31, no. 10 (January 1928): 24–43, and no. 11 (February 1928): 277; *TAS*, June 27, 1927, morning edition, p. 7; and *TAS*, June 28, 1927, morning edition, p. 7.

58. For the *yotamono* interview and students affecting street-tough styles, see Sekine Ryūji, "'Yotamon' o kataru," part 2, *Shakai fukuri* 18, no. 8 (August 1934): 22; and Komino, "Machi no shōnen fūzokushi (3): furyō shōnen no jingi," 54–56, 58. For students as no match for "pure" delinquents, see "Furyō gakusei no jissai o kataru zadankai," *Tokufū* 6, no. 9 (October 17, 1935): 35. For police warnings, see for example "Furyō gakusei no taisaku o kiku," ibid., 60. On student toughs, see also Suzuki, *Furyō shōnen no kenkyū*, and Suzuki, *Ko no tame ni naku*. For reports of knife fights between *yota* groups from different secondary schools, often low-grade private middle schools or vocational schools, see for example *TAS*, February 2, 1933, morning edition, p. 7; and *TAS*, January 9, 1934, morning edition, p. 11.

59. Joan Neuberger, *Hooliganism: Crime, Culture, and Power in St. Petersburg, 1900–1914* (Berkeley: University of California Press, 1993), 32.

60. The Takushoku students episode is reported in *TAS*, October 15, 1934, evening edition, p. 2. On early links between *bankara* and continental adventurers *(tairiku rōnin)*, see Karlin, "The Gender of Nationalism," 70–71. On Manchuria in the 1920s as a lawless territory that attracted many Japanese, see for example Saga, *Confessions of a Yakuza*, 122–23. For one report of Japanese *yotamono* gangs in colonial Seoul, see *Keijō nippō*, November 5, 1937, p. 5.

61. On delinquents becoming political thugs, see the comments by MPD Inspector Iijima in "Furyō shōnen mondai ni kansuru zadankai," 80. On labor organizing in Tokyo, see Gordon, *Labor and Imperial Democracy;* see also Garon, *The State and Labor;* Stephen S. Large, *Organized Workers and Socialist Politics in Interwar Japan* (Cambridge and New York: Cambridge University Press, 1981); and Stephen E. Marsland, *The Birth of the Japanese Labor Movement: Takano Fusatarō and the Rōdō Kumiai Kiseikai* (Honolulu: University of Hawai'i Press, 1989). On German Communist Party (KPD) overtures to working-class "cliques," see Rosenhaft, "Organising the 'Lumpenproletariat'."

62. For police crackdowns on hawkers and criminal gangs, see for example *TAS*, July 30, 1931, evening edition, p. 2; and *TAS*, August 27, 1932, evening edition, p. 2, which reports on young toughs leading a gang with both a "youth" and an "adult" section.

63. Ishizumi Harunosuke, *Kojiki urabanashi* (Tokyo: Bunjinsha Shuppanbu, 1929), reprinted in *Rumin,* ed. Hayashi Hideo, vol. 4 of *Kindai minshū no kiroku* (Tokyo: Shinjinbutsu Ōraisha, 1971), 379.

64. Sekine, "'Yotamon' o kataru," part 2, pp. 22–23.

65. *TAS,* August 24, 1929, evening edition, p. 2.

66. Sekine, "'Yotamon' o kataru," part 2, pp. 23–24.

67. Quoted in Kawabata Yasunari, *Asakusa kurenaidan,* in Kawabata Yasunari, *Asakusa kurenaidan, Asakusa matsuri* (Tokyo: Kōdansha, 1996), 179.

68. For accounts of street-fighting girls with pride in their turf, see Ishizumi, *Kojiki urabanashi,* 379; Satō, *Asakusa,* 168–88; and Tamagawa Shinmei, *Boku wa Asakusa no furyō shōnen: jitsuroku Satō Hachirō den* (Tokyo: Sakuhinsha, 1991), 81–85, 114–20.

69. Suzuki, *Furyō shōnen no kenkyū,* 83; Kawabata Yasunari also picked up on this story in *Asakusa kurenaidan,* 25.

70. The quoted passage is from Tsukimigusa (pseudonym), "Sawa Morino," *Asakusa* 2 (October 1919): 18. On opera actresses, eroticism, and *peragoro,* see also Kusama Yasoo, "Dai Tōkyō no chimata ni shutsubotsu suru furyō shōnen," *Shakai to kyūsai* 4, no. 11 (February 1921): 10–11; Ishizumi Harunosuke, *Asakusa onna urabanashi* (Tokyo: Bunjinsha Shuppanbu, 1930), 61–83, 215–18; Tamagawa, *Boku wa Asakusa no furyō shōnen,* 101–4; and Seidensticker, *Low City, High City,* 73. For a broader discussion of the Asakusa opera, see Zakō, *Asakusa Rokku wa itsumo modan datta,* 35–81. The *peragoro* may have been the successors of turn-of-the-century groups known as *dōsuru ren,* who were enthusiasts of traditional storytelling performances by young women called *musume gidayu.* See Kurata, *Meiji Taishō no minshū goraku,* 162–63.

71. For Hamamoto's stories, see Hamamoto Hiroshi, *Asakusa no hi* and *Zoku Asakusa no hi* (1937), in *Taishū bungaku taikei,* vol. 23, ed. Ōfutsu Jirō, Kawaguchi Matsutarō, and Kimura Takeshi (Tokyo: Kōdansha, 1973), 287–382; and Hamamoto Hiroshi, "Tamako," in Hamamoto, *Furyō shōnen,* 103–44. For views of actresses' wages and materialism, see Kusama, "Dai Tōkyō no chimata," and Ishizumi, *Asakusa onna urabanashi.* For another literary treatment of the opera demimonde, see Tanizaki Jun'ichirō, *Kōjin* (1920), in *Tanizaki Jun'ichirō zenshū,* vol. 7 (Tokyo: Chūō Kōronsha, 1967), 27–212.

72. *Hōritsu shinbun,* June 8, 1919, p. 12; Ishizumi, *Asakusa onna urabanashi,* 74–75, 216. On the Tokugawa *bakufu*'s efforts to police the theater, see especially Shively, "*Bakufu* vs. *Kabuki,*" 231–62. For Meiji-Taishō police regulations of theaters, see Ishizuka, *Nihon kindai toshi ron,* 149–62; and Ōbinata, *Keisatsu no shakaishi,* 30–43. On actresses and the theater, see Ayako Kano, *Acting Like a Woman in Modern Japan: Theater, Gender, and Nationalism* (New York: Palgrave, 2001).

73. Ishizumi, *Asakusa urabanashi,* 185–200; the quoted passage is on 186; Ishizumi, *Kojiki urabanashi,* 380–84; Kusama Yasoo, "Nikumenai furyō shōjo no hanashi," *Fujin kōron* 16, no. 6 (June 1931), reprinted in Kusama Yasoo, *Kindai Nihon no donzoko shakai,* ed. Isomura Eiichi (Tokyo: Akashi Shoten, 1992), 395–403. For newspaper reports, see for example *TAS,* August 11, 1929, evening edition, p. 2; and *TAS,* September 28, 1934, evening edition, p. 2.

74. Kawabata, *Asakusa kurenaidan;* the phrase "modern geisha" *(modan hidarizuma)* appears on 114. Maeda's analysis is in Maeda Ai, "Gekijo toshite no Asakusa," in Maeda, *Toshi kūkan no naka no bungaku;* the quoted passage is on p. 299. For experts' alarms about working-class delinquents preying on women in the shelters set up after the earthquake, see Mawatari and Sandaya, *Fukkō to jidō mondai,* esp. 53–56.

75. Kawabata, *Asakusa kurenaidan,* 110–11.

76. Satō Hachirō, "Furyō shōjo no ryūkō," *Kaizō* 13, no. 5 (May 1931): 125–27. For "ideology of hedonism," see *TAS,* August 7, 1929, morning edition, p. 7.

77. The quotation in the section title is from *TAS,* June 7, 1929, evening edition, p. 2. The article described the nature of young people's delinquent play in various parts of Tokyo; "up-tempo love" referred to the style of male-female interaction in the Ginza, the heart of the "modern" *(modan)* cityscape.

78. Satō Takeshi, "Modanizumu to Amerikaka: 1920 nendai o chūshin toshite," in Minami, ed., *Nihon modanizumu no kenkyū,* 29; see also Silverberg, "The Modern Girl as Militant," 239–66; and Barbara Sato, *The New Japanese Woman: Modernity, Media, and Women in Interwar Japan* (Durham, NC: Duke University Press, 2003), esp. 45–77.

79. Tanizaki Jun'ichirō, *Chijin no ai* (1924–25), in *Tanizaki Jun'ichirō zenshū,* vol. 10 (Tokyo: Chūō Kōronsha, 1967), 1–302. In English: Junichirō Tanizaki, *Naomi,* trans. Anthony Chambers (New York: Alfred A. Knopf, 1985).

80. Sato, *The New Japanese Woman,* 48.

81. Tōkyō-shi Shakaikyoku, ed., *Fujin jiritsu no michi* (Tokyo: Tōkyō-shi Shakaikyoku, 1925), reprinted in *Kindai fujin mondai meicho senshū zokuhen,* vol. 7, ed. Nakajima Kuni (Tokyo: Nihon Tosho Sentā, 1982); Kawasaki Natsu, *Shokugyō fujin o kokorozasu hito no tame ni* (Tokyo: Genjinsha, 1932), reprinted in Nakajima, ed., *Kindai fujin mondai meicho senshū zokuhen,* vol. 10; Maeda Hajime, *Shokugyō fujin monogatari* (Tokyo: Tōyō Keizai Shuppanbu, 1929), reprinted in *Kindai josei bunken shiryō sōsho,* vol. 32, ed. Nakajima Kuni (Tokyo: Ōzorasha, 1993); Tōkyō Joshi Shūshoku Shidōkai, ed., *Tōkyō joshi shūshoku annai* (Tokyo: Tōkyō Joshi Shūshoku Shidōkai, 1936), reprinted in *Kindai josei bunken shiryō sōsho,* vol. 39, ed. Nakajima Kuni (Tokyo: Ōzorasha, 1994); see also Tazaki Noriyoshi, "Josei rōdō no shoruikei," in *Nihon josei seikatsushi,* vol. 4, ed. Joseishi Sōgō Kenkyūkai, 164–90; Nagy, "Middle-Class Working Women"; Silverberg, "The Modern Girl as Militant," 257–58; and Sato, *The New Japanese Woman,* esp. 114–30.

82. 1924 Tokyo numbers are drawn from Silverberg, "The Modern Girl as Militant," 256; 1932 figures are from Kawasaki, *Shokugyō fujin o kokorozasu hito no tame ni,* 30–32. The firms included in this survey all employed or were capable of employing at least thirty workers or were capitalized at 500,000 yen or higher.

83. Nagy, "Middle-Class Working Women," 211; Sato, *The New Japanese Woman,* esp. 118–27. On women in public in Victorian London, see Walkowitz, *City of Dreadful Delight.* On eroticized narratives of "type-writer girls" in England and the United States in the early twentieth century, see Christopher

Keep, "The Cultural Work of the Type-Writer Girl," *Victorian Studies* 40, no. 3 (Spring 1997): 401–26.

84. *TAS*, December 10, 1924, in *Shinbun shūsei Taishō hennenshi*, vol. for 1924, p. 903.

85. *Tōkyō nichinichi shinbun*, April 20, 1927, and April 21, 1927, both in *Shōwa nyūsu jiten*, ed. Shōwa Nyūsu Jiten Hensan Iinkai (Tokyo: Mainichi Komyunikeshonzu, 1990), 1:699.

86. Asahara Rokurō, "Marunouchi no tenjō," in *Yoshiyuki Eisuke to sono jidai: modan toshi no hikari to kage*, ed. Yoshiyuki Kazuko and Saitō Shinji (Tokyo: Tōkyō Shiki Shuppan, 1988), 141–51.

87. *Hogaraka ni ayume*, directed by Ozu Yasujirō; story by Shimizu Hiroshi; script by Ikeda Tadao, 1930, rereleased by Shochiku Hōmu Bideo, videocassette.

88. For women's inherent "seduceability" and men's inherent "delinquency," see Ichikawa Genzō, *Seishun jidai: sono tokushoku to sono kyōiku* (Tokyo: Meiji Tosho Kaisha, 1930).

89. Gotō's comments can be found in *Tōkyō nichinichi shinbun*, May 4, 1927, in *SSSHS*, 1927, part 2, p. 367. Salary information is drawn from Obama Toshinari, "Shoninkyū shirabe," *Chūō kōron* 45, no. 7 (July 1930): 296–301.

90. *Hogaraka ni ayume*, directed by Ozu Yasujirō.

91. *Naniwa eregii*, directed by Mizoguchi Kenji; written by Fujiwara Tadashi, Mizoguchi Kenji, et al., produced by Daiichi Eigasha, distributed by Shōchiku Kinema, 1936, redistributed by Shōchiku Films, Ltd., videocassette.

92. *Tōkyō nichinichi shinbun*, May 4, 1927, in *SSSHS*, 1927, part 2, p. 367; *TAS*, May 4, 1927, evening edition, p. 2; *TAS*, May 7, 1927, evening edition, p. 2; *TAS*, May 10, 1927, morning edition, p. 7; *Tōkyō nichinichi shinbun*, July 6, 1927, in *SSSHS*, 1927, part 3, p. 64. See also Iijima Mitsuyasu, "Teito ni okeru furyō shōnen no jissai to sono bōshisaku," part 4, *Jidō kenkyū* 31, no. 12 (March 1928): 312–13; and Sato, *The New Japanese Woman*, 62–63. For the female victim becoming a criminal, see *TAS*, September 13, 1927, morning edition, p. 7.

93. Asahara, "Marunouchi no tenjō"; the quoted passage is on p. 143; Tanizaki, *Chijin no ai*.

94. *TAS*, August 3, 1927, evening edition, p. 1.

95. Sato, *The New Japanese Woman*, 130–48.

96. For women's complaints, see Maeda, *Shokugyō fujin monogatari*, 112–20; and Tazaki, "Josei rōdō no shoruikei," 194–95. On working women as "sexual accoutrements," see Sato, *The New Japanese Woman*, 119–25; the phrase is on 119.

97. See for example Ogawa Takeshi, *Ryūsenkei abekku* (Tokyo: Marunouchi Shuppan, 1935), in *Kyōraku, sei*, ed. Minami Hiroshi et al., 381–439; and Minami Hiroshi's explanatory comments in ibid., 448.

98. Narita Ryūichi, "Sei no chōryō: 1920 nendai no sekushuaritii," in *Jendā no Nihonshi*, vol. 1, *Shūkyō to minzoku, shintai to seiai*, ed. Wakita Haruko and S.B. Hanley (Tokyo: Tōkyō Daigaku Shuppankai, 1994), esp. 541–60. On middle-school students reading sexology magazines, see *Yomiuri shinbun*, May 29, 1923, in *Shinbun shūsei Taishō hennenshi*, vol. for 1923, pp. 268–69;

for an example of a student's sex-related inquiry to a woman's magazine and the discussion by a panel (most of whom were male authorities), see "Chūgakusei no seikatsu ni aru iroiro no mondai," *Fujin no tomo* 27, no. 7 (July, 1933): 52–55. On women's groups' appeals to the Home Ministry, see *TAS*, July 19, 1928, evening edition, p. 2.

99. *TAS*, May 27, 1927, evening edition, p. 2; *TAS*, June 22, 1927, evening edition, p. 2; *TAS*, June 24, 1927, evening edition, p. 2; *TAS*, July 13, 1927, morning edition, p. 11. On family planning and abortion in prewar Japan, see Frühstück, *Colonizing Sex*, esp. 116–51; and Tiana Norgren, *Abortion before Birth Control: The Politics of Reproduction in Postwar Japan* (Princeton, NJ: Princeton University Press, 2001), 22–35.

100. For the 1929 roundups, see *TAS*, August 7, 1929, morning edition, p. 7. For the 1932 detentions, see *TAS*, September 20, 1932, morning edition, p. 11; and *TAS*, September 23, 1932, morning edition, p. 11.

101. For studies of the café and waitresses in English, see Silverberg, "The Café Waitress Serving Modern Japan," 208–25; and Elise K. Tipton, "The Café: Contested Space of Modernity in Interwar Japan," in *Being Modern in Japan: Culture and Society from the 1910s to the 1930s,* ed. Elise K. Tipton and John Clark (Honolulu: University of Hawai'i Press, 2000), 119–36.

102. Kusama Yasoo, *Jokyū to baishōfu* (Tokyo: Bonjinsha, 1930), 62–65, 96–99, 114–15, 118–20, 142–44, reprinted in *Kindai fujin mondai meicho senshū zokuhen,* vol. 9, ed. Nakajima Kuni (Tokyo: Nihon Tosho Sentā, 1982). For a fictional account of an office worker turned unlicensed prostitute turned café waitress, see Nagai Kafū, "During the Rains" (1931), in *During the Rains and Flowers in the Shade: Two Novellas by Nagai Kafū,* trans. Lane Dunlop (Stanford, CA: Stanford University Press, 1994), 3–133.

103. Kusama, *Jokyū to baishōfu,* 106–7; see also Matsuzaki Tenmin, *Ginza* (Tokyo: Ginbura Gaidosha, 1927), 83.

104. Murashima, *Kanraku no ōkyū kafuee,* 320–21; Hayashi Fumiko, *Diary of a Vagabond,* trans. Joan E. Ericson, in Joan E. Ericson, *Be a Woman: Hayashi Fumiko and Modern Japanese Women's Literature* (Honolulu: University of Hawai'i Press, 1997), 166; see also 169–70, 202. See also Silverberg, "The Café Waitress," 221.

105. See for example *Tōkyō nichinichi shinbun,* July 9, 1927, in *SSSHS* 1927, part 3, p. 106.

106. Murashima, *Kanraku no ōkyū kafuee,* 324–33; Tipton, "The Café," 127–32.

107. For "rainy nights," see *TAS*, May 17, 1928, morning edition, p. 7. For "That's why I'd go with them," see Tsuji Saburō, "Furyō shōjo Michiko no hanashi," *Fujin saron* 3, no. 3 (March 1931): 228–29.

108. 1929 figures are from Kusama, *Jokyū to baishōfu,* 63; 1932 figures are from Tanaka Tetsuo, *Keishichō monogatari: hiwa hyakunen* (Tokyo: Kasumigaseki Shuppankai N. T. Jigyōbu, 1974), 199–200. On erotic service, see, in addition to the above, Ishizumi, *Ginza kaibōzu daiippen hensenshi,* 324–25; Tipton, "The Café," 127–32; Silverberg, "The Café Waitress," 211–21; and Seidensticker, *Tokyo Rising,* 53–62. For an example of waitresses opposing erotic service, see *TAS*, May 6, 1932, evening edition, p. 2.

109. Hayashi, *Diary of a Vagabond*, 174; *Yomiuri shinbun*, May 15, 1929, p. 7, in *SSSHS* 1929, part 2, p. 430.

110. Stansell, *City of Women*, 189, 185.

111. Maruyama is quoted in *TAS*, September 15, 1929, morning edition, p. 11; see also *Yomiuri shinbun*, August 1, 1929, p. 7, in *SSSHS*, 1929, part 3, pp. 320–21. For WCTU appreciation of Maruyama's measures, see the statement by Moriya Azuma in *TAS*, August 7, 1929, morning edition, p. 7. On the crackdowns, see also Garon, *Molding Japanese Minds*, 106–10; Minami, *Shōwa bunka;* Ōbinata Sumio, *Tennōsei keisatsu to minshū* (Tokyo: Nihon Hyōron-sha, 1987), 203–5; and Tipton, "The Café," 127–32.

112. *TAS*, September 15, 1929, morning edition, p. 11. For Maruyama's cooperation with Christian reform groups during the 1916 MPD campaign against unlicensed prostitution, see Maruyama, *Gojūnen tokorodokoro,* 196–213. For Maruyama's ongoing interaction with reform groups, many of them Protestant, see *Shakai jigyōka daihyōsha kondankai* (Tokyo: Keishichō, 1929).

113. On students not being welcome in Ginza cafés, see Seidensticker, *Tokyo Rising,* 62, referring to Takeda Rintarō's 1934 novel *Ginza Hattchō*. On coupons from cafés near schools, see Hatano Keiji, "Furyō gakusei no nikki oyobi shuki," *Jidō kenkyū* 30, no. 6 (September 1926): 189. For police reactions to daters at Shinjuku Station, see *TAS*, June 7, 1929, evening edition, p. 2.

114. Murashima, *Kanraku no ōkyū kafuee,* 356–59; *TAS*, May 26, 1929, evening edition, p. 2; *TAS*, September 8, 1929, evening edition, p. 2; *TAS*, September 20, 1929, morning edition, p. 11. Hayashi Utako's remarks can be found in *Ōsaka Mainichi shinbun*, August 18, 1927, in *SSSHS*, 1927, part 3. See also Garon, *Molding Japanese Minds*, 106–10; E. Taylor Atkins, *Blue Nippon: Authenticating Jazz in Modern Japan* (Durham, NC: Duke University Press, 2001), 93–95, 113–21; and Minami, *Shōwa bunka*, 164–66.

115. On students in dance halls, see for example *TAS*, May 12, 1931, morning edition, p. 7; for an earlier account of dancers "sinking their teeth" into a wealthy student, see *TAS*, February 20, 1931, morning edition, p. 7. Police comments on young women can be found in "Furyō gakusei no jissai o kataru zadankai," *Tokufū* 6, no. 9 (October 1935): 40–41. For one dancer's views, see Ogawa, *Ryūsenkei abekku,* 426.

116. On students and revues, see for example *TAS*, July 18, 1930, evening edition, p. 2. On unlicensed brothels, see for example *Miyako shinbun*, March 4, 1930, p. 13; and *TAS*, March 5, 1930, evening edition, p. 2.

117. For expelling students from the capital, see *TAS*, September 20, 1929, morning edition, p. 11. For roundups during final exam week, see *Tōkyō jiji shinpō*, February 9, 1930, and *Chugai shōgyō shinbun*, February 14, 1930, both in *Shinbun shūsei Shōwa hennenshi*, vol. for 1930, ed. Shinbun Shūsei Shōwa hennenshi Kankōkai (Tokyo: Shinbun Shūsei Shōwa hennenshi Kankōkai, n.d.), 92, 104. For students moving to jazz music or eating roasted potatoes, see *TAS*, September 20, 1932, morning edition, p. 11. For the 1934 regulations, see Keishichō shi Hensan Iinkai, ed., *Keishichō shi, Shōwa zenpen* (Tokyo: Keishichō shi Hensan Iinkai, 1962), 825–29; and Garon, *Molding Japanese Minds,* 106–10.

118. For girls buying uniforms for their delinquent boyfriends, see *TAS,* June 26, 1933, morning edition, p. 11. Educator's remarks can be found in "Furyō gakusei mondai zadankai," *Tokufū* 6, no. 10 (November 17, 1935): 42–43. For the case of a delinquent impersonating a student in order to entrap a young woman and sell her into prostitution, see Shiina, "Ankoku no chimata ni naku." See also Kawabata, *Asakusa kurenaidan,* 55–56.

119. On student radicalism and its suppression, see Henry DeWitt Smith, II, *Japan's First Student Radicals* (Cambridge, MA: Harvard University Press, 1972); Richard H. Mitchell, *Thought Control in Prewar Japan* (Ithaca, NY: Cornell University Press, 1976); and Marshall, *Learning to Be Modern,* 101–10, 129–33. On Japanese jazz, see Atkins, *Blue Nippon.*

120. *TAS,* February 16, 1938, morning edition, p. 11; *TAS,* February 25, 1938, evening edition, p. 2, both in *SSSHS,* 1938, part 1, pp. 428, 542; Keishichō shi Hensan Iinkai, ed., *Keishichō shi, Shōwa zenpen,* 829–31.

121. The description of Waseda is quoted from *Yomiuri shinbun,* June 13, 1938, evening edition, p. 2, in *SSSHS,* 1938, part 2, pp. 793–94; Superintendent Abe is quoted in *TAS,* June 18, 1938, morning edition, p. 11, in ibid., p. 843.

122. *Yomiuri shinbun,* June 13, 1938, evening edition, p. 2, in *SSSHS,* 1938, part 2, pp. 793–94. On the paucity of on-campus facilities, see *TAS,* June 19, 1938, evening edition, p. 2, in ibid., pp. 852–53; see also the comments by Motono Hisako in "Shijo no katei kyōiku to furyōka bōshi o kataru," *Shōnen hogo* 3, no. 4 (April 1938): 40; and Yasuji Ito, "Student Life," *Contemporary Japan* 8, no. 8 (October 1939): 1006–19.

123. Ito, "Student Life," 1013.

124. *Yomiuri shinbun,* June 13, 1938, evening edition, p. 2; *TAS,* June 16, 1938, morning edition, p. 11; *TAS,* June 18, 1938, evening edition, p. 2; *TAS,* June 19, 1938, evening edition, p. 2; *Tōkyō nichinichi shinbun,* June 21, 1938, p. 7, all in *SSSHS,* 1938, part 2, pp. 793–94, 822, 843–44, 852–53, 873. For a subsequent incident in which a group of drunken Waseda students mauled a policeman in a Tsukiji coffee shop, see *TAS,* June 24, 1938, morning edition, p. 11, in ibid., p. 912. On Waseda University's spirit of independence and its reputation as a "Campus of Freedom," see Smith, *Japan's First Student Radicals,* 14–15. For a study of conflicts over the autonomy of Japan's imperial universities, see Byron K. Marshall, *Academic Freedom and the Japanese Imperial University, 1868–1939* (Berkeley: University of California Press, 1992).

125. Ito, "Student Life," 1014–15.

126. *TAS,* June 8, 1938, morning edition, p. 11, in *SSSHS,* 1938, part 2, pp. 740–41; *Tōkyō nichinichi shinbun,* August 20, 1938, p. 4, in *SSSHS,* 1938, part 3, pp. 525–26. For earlier articles on *jogakusei* misbehavior, see for example *TAS,* February 24, 1936, and *Yomiuri shinbun,* March 12, 1936, both in *Shinbun shūsei Shōwa hennenshi,* vol. for 1936, ed. Taishō Shōwa Shinbun Kenkyūkai (Tokyo: Taishō Shōwa Shinbun Kenkyūkai, 1969), 135, 182. On young women as fans of all-female revues, see Robertson, *Takarazuka.* On Araki as Education Minister, see Marshall, *Academic Freedom,* 168–75. As "Bad Company" ("Warui nakama," 1953), Yasuoka Shōtarō's story of middle-school student ennui on the eve of the Pacific War, suggests, some students continued to engage in proscribed behavior. Yasuoka Shōtarō, "Bad Company," trans. Kären Wigen

Lewis, in *The Shōwa Anthology: Modern Japanese Short Stories, volume 1, 1929–1969*, ed. Van C. Gessel and Tomone Matsumoto (Tokyo, New York, and San Francisco: Kodansha International, 1985), 76–99.

127. On the children's loving protection commissioners, see Shihō Hogo Kyōkai, ed., *Shihō hogo jigyō nenkan*, 192–98; Moriya, *Shōnen no hikō to kyōiku*, 106–7, 113–16. For the text of the Educational Protection Law (the revised Reformatory Law) and ancillary regulations relating to educational protection commissioners, see Kōseishō Shakaikyoku Jidōka, ed., *Jidō hogo kankei hōki*, 1–40. On the growth of the system into the wartime years, see Shigematsu, *Shōnen chōkai kyōikushi*, 727.

128. Ōkado, "Gakkō kyōiku to shakai idō," 187 n. 67.

CHAPTER 6

1. Moriyama Takeichirō, "Kinrō seishōnen hodō kinkyū taisaku no jisshi," *Shōnen hogo* 8, no. 3 (March 1943): 6.

2. Terasaki Masao and Senjika Kyōiku Kenkyūkai, eds., *Sōryokusen taisei to kyōiku: kōkokumin "rensei" no rinen to jissen* (Tokyo: Tōkyō Daigaku Shuppankai, 1987), 2–10; David R. Ambaras, "Treasures of the Nation: Juvenile Delinquency, Socialization, and Mobilization in Modern Japan, 1895–1945" (Ph.D. diss., Princeton University, 1999), ch. 5.

3. "Seishōnenkō no furyōka bōshi: Kawasaki Shōnenkō Hodō Kyōkai setsuritsu saru," *Naigai rōdō shūhō* 454 (April 30, 1941): 34.

4. Ministry of Education, *The Way of Subjects* (*Shinmin no michi*, 1941), excerpted and translated in *Japan: A Documentary History*, ed. David J. Lu (Armonk, NY: M.E. Sharpe, 1997), 438.

5. Itō Akihiro, "Senjiki Nihon ni okeru 'jinteki shigen' seisaku: senji dōin to kōtō kyōiku o meguru seiji katei," *Hiroshima Daigaku Daigaku Kyōiku Kenkyū Sentā Daigaku ronshū* 18 (March 1989): 132–35; Garon, *The State and Labor*, 215.

6. On the mobilization of women, see for example Miyake Yoshiko, "Doubling Expectations: Motherhood and Women's Factory Work under State Management in Japan in the 1930s and 1940s," in Bernstein, ed., *Recreating Japanese Women*, 267–95; and Thomas R.H. Havens, *Valley of Darkness: The Japanese People and World War II* (Lanham, MD: University Press of America, 1986), 106–13. On Korean labor, see for example Michael Weiner, *Race and Migration in Imperial Japan* (London: Routledge, 1994).

7. Jerome B. Cohen, *Japan's Economy in War and Reconstruction* (Minneapolis: University of Minnesota Press, 1949), 311; Hōsei Daigaku Ōhara Shakai Mondai Kenkyūjo, ed., *Taiheiyō Sensōka no rōdōsha jōtai*, special edition of *Nihon rōdō nenkan* (Tokyo: Tōyō Keizai Shinpōsha, 1964), sections 1.1.2 and 2.6.1; available online at: http://oohara.mt.tama.hosei.ac.jp/rn/senji1/index.html (accessed September 15, 2003).

8. Ishihara Yoshiharu, "Shinsotsugyō jidō no shūshoku hogo ni tsuite," *Shakai fukuri* 23, no. 3 (March 1939): 12–23.

9. On labor conscription ages, see *Taiheiyō Sensōka no rōdōsha jōtai*, sections 1.1.2, 1.2.2, and 1.3.2; and Cohen, *Japan's Economy*, 276–78, 304–27.

On employment agencies and schools, see "Kokumin gakkō shokugyō shidō jisshi yōkō to shokugyō sōdan yōryō," *Naigai rōdō shūhō* 530 (November 13, 1942): 15–17.

10. Moriyama, "Kinrō seishōnen hodō kinkyū taisaku no jisshi," 6; see also "Seishōnenkō furyōka bōshi ni kansuru kakushō renraku kondankai," *Jidō hogo* 13, nos. 8–9 (August–September 1943), 15.

11. Yoshimura Yukio, "Shōnenkō to sakariba," *Chūō kōron* 57, no. 10 (October 1942): 148.

12. See for example Hatano Keiji, "Nichiyō no asa: shōnen hogoshi nikki," *Jidō kenkyū* 40, no. 1 (November 1939): 7; Kusama Yasoo, "Shōnenkō wa furyōka suru? inshin sangyō no ura ni hisomu furyōka keikō," *Shōnen hogo* 4, no. 9 (April 1939): 17; *Taiheiyō Sensōka no rōdōsha jōtai*, section 2.5.1; and Haruko Taya Cook and Theodore Cook, *Japan at War: An Oral History* (New York: The New Press, 1992), 48–49.

13. Kusama, "Shōnenkō wa furyōka suru?" 17.

14. *Kaidō gijiroku: shōnen shinpanshochō hogo kansatsushochō kyōsei-inchō, Shōwa 14 nen 6 gatsu 1–3 nichi*, ed. Shihō Daijin Kanbō Hogoka, no. 21 of *Shihō hogo shiryō* (Tokyo: Shihō Daijin Kanbō Hogoka, 1939), 176.

15. Kusama, "Shōnenkō wa furyōka suru?" 15; Kirihara Shigemi, *Rōdō to seinen* (Tokyo: Kagakushugi Kōgyōsha, 1940), 211.

16. Kokumin Kōsei Kenkyūkai, "Shōnenkō seikatsu chōsa hōkoku," part 1, *Kōsei mondai* 26, no. 6 (June 1942): 36–39.

17. Quoted in Havens, *Valley of Darkness*, 95–96; see also Naimushō Keihokyoku, ed., *Shakai undō no jōkyō*, vol. for 1942, reprint ed. (Tokyo: San'ichi Shobō, 1972), 437–43; Andrew Gordon, *The Evolution of Labor Relations in Japan: Heavy Industry, 1853–1955* (Cambridge, MA: Council on East Asian Studies, Harvard University, distributed by Harvard University Press, 1988), 275–76, 318. See also "'Shōnen kyōgo to seisanryoku zōkyō' o kataru zadankai," *Jidō hogo* 13, no. 2 (February 1943): 11; and Aikawa Junzō, "Shōnenkō furyōka no gen'in: jitsurei ni motozuite," part 1, *Shōnen hogo* 6, no. 10 (October 1941): 68–70.

18. Ōnishi Terukazu, "Shōnenkō ni arawareta hanzai jōtai," *Shōnen hogo* 5, no. 11 (November 1940): 6–10; Aikawa, "Shōnenkō furyōka no gen'in," part 1, 69–71, and part 2, *Shōnen hogo* 6, no. 11 (November 1941): 75–78; Yoshimura, "Shōnenkō to sakariba"; and Fujii Hideo, *Kinrō seishōnen no furyōka to sono taisaku* (Kyoto: Ritsumeikan Shuppanbu, 1943). On black market crime, see for example "Ōsaka-fu no seishōnenkō no hanzai, furyō kōi no chōsa," *Naigai rōdō shūhō* 472 (September 19, 1941): 20–25; and "Toka ni okeru seishōnen hanzai no genjō o kataru zadankai," *Shōnen hogo* 6, no. 5 (May 1941): 27.

19. On the August–September sweep, see Yoshimura, "Shōnenkō to sakariba," 146–48. For the subsequent roundups of 29,000, see "'Shōnen kyōgo to seisanryoku zōkyō' o kataru zadankai," 9–10. For earlier sweeps, see "Toka ni okeru seishōnen hanzai no genjō." For the Osaka roundups, see Fujii, *Kinrō seishōnen*, 53–54.

20. On student mobilization, see *Taiheiyō Sensōka no rōdōsha jōtai*, sections 1.3.2 and 2.6.1; Cohen, *Japan's Economy*, 304–27; and Itsumi Katsuaki,

"Fuashizumu kyōiku no hōkai: kinrō dōin o chūshin toshite," in *Kōza Nihon kyōikushi*, vol. 4, ed. Kōza Nihon kyōikushi Henshū Iinkai (Tokyo: Daiichi Hōki Shuppan, 1984), 176–210. Police remarks on the decline of student delinquency are from "Sensō to furyō," *Jidō hogo* 12, no. 9 (September 1942): 24–25.

21. Kirihara Shigemi, "Sangyō shōnenkō no shomondai," part 2, *Shōnen hogo* 6, no. 12 (December 1941): 71. Some of the protection and training programs discussed in this chapter did involve young female workers, but these workers remained a secondary, or even incidental, object of concern. On women's mobilization, see Miyake, "Doubling Expectations," and Havens, *Valley of Darkness*. For the contrasting cases of moral panic over women's sexuality in wartime England and the United States, see Sonya O. Rose, "Cultural Analysis and Moral Discourses: Episodes, Continuities, and Transformations," in *Beyond the Cultural Turn: New Directions in the Study of Society and Culture*, ed. Victoria E. Bonnell and Lynn Hunt (Berkeley: University of California Press, 1999), 217–38; and Karen Anderson, *Wartime Women: Sex Roles, Family Relations, and the Status of Women during World War II* (Westport, CT: Greenwood Press, 1981), 103–11.

22. I base this statement on an analysis of juvenile court data from 1936 to 1942; little data is available for the years 1943–45. Chūō Shakai Jigyō Kyōkai, ed., *Nihon shakai jigyō nenkan*, 1943 ed. (Tokyo: Chūō Shakai Jigyō Kyōkai, 1943), 249. For police reports of rising rates of juvenile delinquency nationwide, see ibid., 174. For Tokyo, see "Toka ni okeru seishōnen hanzai no genjō"; for Osaka, see Fujii, *Kinrō seishōnen*, 49–50. These sources do not consider the possibility that rising rates were due to intensified reporting and policing.

23. Yoshimura, "Shōnenkō to sakariba," 148.

24. Moriyama Takeichirō, "Shōnen hogo no senjiteki shimei," *Shōnen hogo* 8, no. 1 (January 1943): 6–7. For an earlier example, see Department of Justice, "Protection and Discipline of Juvenile Delinquents," *Tokyo Gazette* 23 (May 1939): 26.

25. Suzuki Shun'ichi, "Kyōiku mondai toshite no shōnenkō no furyōka," *Teikoku kyōiku* 754 (August 1941): 34–35.

26. Kirihara, *Rōdō to seinen*, 126. For the socialization of reproduction, see Christopher Lasch, *Haven in a Heartless World: The Family Besieged* (New York: W. W. Norton and Company, 1995), xix–xxiv, 3–21. On the concept of reactionary modernism, see Jeffrey Herf, *Reactionary Modernism: Technology, Culture, and Politics in Weimar and the Third Reich* (Cambridge: Cambridge University Press, 1986). On "total-war systems" as a transition from class societies to "system societies," see Yamanouchi, "Total War and System Integration," in Yamanouchi, Koschmann, and Narita, eds., *Total War and "Modernization*," 1–39, esp. 1–5.

27. Takano, *Seinen gakkōshi*; Smethurst, *A Social Basis for Prewar Japanese Militarism*, esp. 41–43. On the expansion of nationalist rituals and military drill in middle schools over the course of the 1930s, with an interesting emphasis on demographic factors, see Yoneda Toshihiko, "Gakkō no gishiki to girei: rekishi no naka de ukibori ni naru mono," in *Gakkō bunka to iu jiba*, vol. 6 of *Kōza gakkō*, ed. Horio Teruhisa et al. (Tokyo: Kashiwa Shobō, 1996), 151–80.

28. "Tōkyō-fu no seinen gakkō seito kōgai seikatsu shidō hōshin," *Naigai rōdō shūhō* 470 (September 5, 1941): 16.

29. Kirihara Shigemi, *Senji rōmu kanri* (Tokyo: Tōyō Shokan, 1942), 113–27; the quoted passages are on 115 and 124–27.

30. Ibid., 97.

31. For Kirihara's views, see for example ibid.; Kirihara, *Rōdō to seinen;* and Kirihara Shigemi, *Shokugyō shidō to rōmu hodō* (Tokyo: Chikura shobō, 1938). On intellectuals and visions of social reorganization, see also William Miles Fletcher III, *The Search for a New Order: Intellectuals and Fascism in Prewar Japan* (Chapel Hill: University of North Carolina Press, 1982); Johnson, *MITI and the Japanese Miracle;* and Satō Hiromi, *Sōryokusen taisei to kyōiku kagaku: senzen Kyōiku Kagaku Kenkyūkai ni okeru "kyōiku kaikaku ron" no kenkyū* (Tokyo: Ōtsuki Shoten, 1997). For praise of the Nazi labor socialization model, see for example Ishihara Yoshiharu, "Shinsotsugyō jidō no shūshoku hogo ni tsuite," *Shakai fukuri* 23, no. 3 (March 1939): 12–23. On Nazi programs, see John Gillingham, "The 'Deproletarianization' of German Society: Vocational Training in the Third Reich," *Journal of Social History* 19, no. 33 (1986): 423–32.

32. "Rōgaku ichinyo o jissen suru Nissei Tamagawa Seinen Gakkō," *Naigai rōdō shūhō* 529 (November 6, 1942): 11–21; the quoted passages are on 11 and 17.

33. "Nihon Kōgaku Ōi kōjō no shōnenkō hodō taisaku o miru," *Naigai rōdō shūhō* 556 (May 21, 1943), 16–19. On wartime savings campaigns, see Sheldon Garon, "Luxury Is the Enemy: Mobilizing Savings and Popularizing Thrift in Wartime Japan," *Journal of Japanese Studies* 26, no. 1 (Winter 2000): 41–78.

34. For "not one drop of urine," see Terasaki et al., eds., *Sōryokusen taisei to kyōiku,* 248. On the use of *seikatsu tsuzurikata* techniques, see Tsurusaki Kahachi, "Shokuba senshi no tsuzurikata kyōshitsu," *Shokugyō shidō* 13, no. 2 (1940): 47–49.

35. Government of Japan, *Japan's Modern Educational System,* 202; Terasaki et al., eds., *Sōryokusen taisei to kyōiku,* 235; and Takano, *Seinen gakkōshi.*

36. Terasaki et al., eds., *Sōryokusen taisei to kyōiku,* 247.

37. "Kinrō seishōnen furyōka bōshi kenkyū zadankai," part 1, *Shōnen hogo* 8, no. 4 (April 1943): 52–57, and part 2, ibid., no. 5 (May 1943): 42–43.

38. "Rōgaku ichinyo o jissen suru Nissei Tamagawa Seinen Gakkō," 21.

39. See for example, "Ōsaka-fu no seishōnenkō no hanzai, furyō kōi no chōsa," 23.

40. Kokumin Kōsei Kenkyūkai, "Shōnenkō seikatsu chōsa hōkoku," part 2, *Kōsei mondai* 26, no. 7 (July 1942): 35–45. For an earlier discussion of the problem of low attendance in Tokyo, see Ishihara Yoshiharu, "Nenshō rōdō seikatsusha mondai," part 2, *Shakai fukuri* 21, no. 8 (August 1937): 98–99.

41. Yoshimura, "Shōnenkō to sakariba," 148.

42. For "blows to the head," see "Kinrō seishōnen furyōka bōshi kenkyū zadankai," part 1, p. 57. For foremen taking subordinates out to play, see Suzuki, "Kyōiku mondai," 36.

43. Kokumin Kōsei Kenkyūkai, "Shōnenkō seikatsu chōsa hōkoku," part 2, p. 36; see also Kirihara, *Senji rōmu kanri*, 115–21; Sumiya, *Nihonteki yōsei seido no keisei*, 273; and Terasaki et al., eds., *Sōryokusen taisei to kyōiku*, 237.

44. Hōsei Daigaku Ōhara Shakai Mondai Kenkyūjo, ed., *Taiheiyō Sensōka no rōdō undō*, special ed. of *Nihon rōdō nenkan* (Tokyo: Tōyō Keizai Shinpō-sha, 1965), 207–8. See also Kokumin Kōsei Kenkyūkai, "Shōnenkō seikatsu chōsa hōkoku," part 2.

45. Kyōchōkai, *Senji rōdō jijō* (Tokyo: Kyōchōkai, 1944), 117; Sumiya, *Nihonteki yōsei seido no keisei*, 273. On the transformation of schooling into factory work, see "Kōjō seinen gakkō oyobi kōkō ni kansuru senji hijō sochi," *Naigai rōdō shūhō* 580 (November 12, 1943): 10–14.

46. Hachihongi Kiyoshi, *Sensō makki no seinen gakkō* (Tokyo: Nihon Tosho Sentā, 1996), 128.

47. Takano, *Seinen gakkōshi*, 203.

48. Department of Education, "The National School System: A Reform of Primary Education," *Tokyo Gazette* 3, no. 9 (March 1940): 327–31. For an earlier government discussion of elementary schooling and national spiritual mobilization, see Naikaku, Naimushō, and Monbushō, *Kokumin seishin sōdōin to shōgakkō kyōiku, Kokumin seishin sōdōin shiryō dai 9 shū* (Tokyo: Naikaku, Naimushō, Monbushō, 1938).

49. On national school curricula, see Government of Japan, *Japan's Modern Educational System;* Terasaki et al., eds., *Sōryokusen taisei to kyōiku*, esp. 101–10; and Havens, *Valley of Darkness*, 26–29. On efforts to create a more modern science curriculum in wartime elementary school reforms, see Ōuchi Hirokazu, "Inpei sareta kioku: kokumin gakkō no 'kindai'," *Gendai shisō* 23, no. 1 (January 1995): 244–47.

50. Shigematsu Takayasu, "Jidō hogo seisaku to kokumin gakkō," *Shakai jigyō* 25, no. 5 (May 1941): 20–21.

51. Government of Japan, *Japan's Modern Educational System;* Takano, *Seinen gakkōshi;* and Ōuchi Hirokazu, "Prewar, Wartime, and Postwar in Education: The Thought and Behavior of Abe Shigetaka," in Yamanouchi, Koschmann, and Narita, eds., *Total War and "Modernization,"* 181–208.

52. Garon, *The State and Labor*, 217.

53. Ernest J. Notar, "Labor Unions and the Sangyō Hōkoku Movement, 1930–1945: A Japanese Model for Industrial Relations" (Ph.D. diss., University of California, Berkeley, 1979); Garon, *The State and Labor;* Gordon, *The Evolution of Labor Relations in Japan*. For a different view, see Saguchi Kazurō, "The Historical Significance of the Industrial Patriotic Association: Labor Relations in the Total-War State," in Yamanouchi, Koschmann, and Narita, eds., *Total War and "Modernization,"* 261–87.

54. *Asahi shinbun*, March 13, 1941; *Taiheiyō Sensōka no rōdō undō*, section 2.3.1; Miura Toyohiko, *Teruoka Gitō: rōdō kagaku o tsukutta otoko* (Tokyo: Riburopōto, 1991), 217–27; Teruoka Gitō, "Nihon Rōdō Kagaku Kenkyūjo no shokunō narabi ni shidō seishin ni tsuite," *Rōdō kagaku kenkyū* 14, no. 3 (1937): 1–4.

55. Miyamoto Yuriko, "Josei shūhyō," *TAS*, June 20, 1940, in *Miyamoto Yuriko zenshū*, vol. 14 (Tokyo: Shin Nihon Shuppansha, 1979), 189.

56. "Seishōnen rōmusha no seikatsu shidō hōsaku," *Naigai shakai mondai chōsa shiryō* 424 (June 5, 1940): 31–32. See also Gonda Yasunosuke, *Sangyō seinen tokuhon* (Tokyo: Kōjimachi Sakai Shoten, 1941), 105–25.

57. Gonda, *Sangyō seinen tokuhon*, 82–84, 143–47. On Gonda, see Silverberg, "Constructing the Japanese Ethnography of Modernity," 30–54; and Harootunian, *Overcome by Modernity*, ch. 3. On the DAF and the KdF, see David Schoenbaum, *Hitler's Social Revolution: Class and Status in Nazi Germany, 1933–1939* (New York: W. W. Norton and Co., 1980); Detlev J. K. Peukert, *Inside Nazi Germany: Conformity, Opposition, and Racism in Everyday Life,* trans. Richard Deveson (New Haven, CT: Yale University Press, 1987); and Ronald Smelser, *Robert Ley: Hitler's Labor Front Leader* (Oxford and New York: Berg Publishers, 1988).

58. Gonda, *Sangyō seinen tokuhon*, 135, 180–96.

59. Ibid., 140–43.

60. Obata Tadayoshi, "Seinen ni kitai suru mono," *Sanpō* 2, no. 7 (July 1943): 4–5.

61. "Tōkyō Sangyō Hōkokukai no seinentai jōkai un'ei hōshin," *Naigai rōdō shūhō* 497 (March 20, 1942): 15–16. On the transformation of the Hitler Youth, see for example Peukert, *Inside Nazi Germany*, 151–52.

62. "Sanpō Chūō Honbu no seinentai rindokukai kaisai shishin," part 1, *Naigai rōdō shūhō* 514 (July 17, 1942): 32. On training sessions, see also "Tōkyō Sangyō Hōkokukai no seinentai jōkai un'ei hōshin," 17; and Terasaki et al., eds., *Sōryokusen taisei to kyōiku*, 267–71. On reading programs, see also Katō Chiyozō, "Kinrō seishōnen no dokusho shidō ni tsuite," *Sanpō* 2, no. 12 (December 1943): 26–31.

63. 1943 figures are from "Sangyō hōkoku seinentai no shidō rinen: 'Sangyō hōkoku seinentai shidō shishin' ni kanren shite," *Sanpō* 2, no. 7 (July 1943): 25; 1944 figures are from Keishichō, *Kinrō gyōsei gaikyō,* reprinted in *Nihon rōdō undō shiryō,* vol. 9, ed. Rōdō Undō Shiryō Iinkai (Tokyo: Tōkyō Daigaku Shuppankai, 1965), 396. On the organizational limits and ambiguities of the Sanpō Youth Brigades, see Kirihara, *Senji rōmu kanri,* 95; and "Tōkyō Sangyō Hōkokukai no seinentai jōkai un'ei hōshin," 15–16.

64. Kirihara, *Rōdō to seinen,* 87–107; Teruoka Gitō, "Kinrō seishōnen no dōkō ni tsuite," in *Shōnen hogo ronshū,* ed. Shihō Hogo Kenkyūjo (Tokyo: Shihō Hogo Kenkyūjo, 1943), 645–70. See also the postwar interviews in "Senji yori shūsen e itsuwarazaru shinkyō o kataru: wakaki sangyō senshi to no ichimon ittō," *Shokugyō shidō* 19, no. 2 (1946): 12–14. On hardships and psychological motivations of young women conscripted into munitions factories, see Miyake, "Doubling Expectations," 291.

65. On the expansion of the juvenile court system, see Shigematsu, *Shōnen chōkai kyōikushi,* 835–36. Nationwide juvenile court data is drawn from *Nihon shakai jigyō nenkan,* 1943, ed. Chūō Shakai Jigyō Kyōkai, 246–49.

66. For guidance associations affiliated with the juvenile courts, see "Seishōnenkō no furyōka bōshi: Kawasaki Shōnenkō Hodō Kyōkai setsuritsu saru," *Naigai rōdō shūhō* 454 (April 30, 1941): 32–34; and Fujiwara Suesaku, "Shōnen hogo jigyō to shakaiteki kyōryoku," *Shōnen hogo* 7, no. 1 (January 1942):

32–33. For the 1943 measures, see "Kinrō seishōnen no hodō o tettei," *Shōnen hogo* 8, no. 3 (March 1943): 70–76.

67. "Chōyō kōin rensei kiroku: tanki tokubetsu rensei o owarite," *Sanpō* 1, no. 12 (December 1942), reprinted in Terasaki et al., eds., *Sōryokusen taisei to kyōiku*, 430–36.

68. Suzuki's comments are in "'Shōnen kyōgo to seisanryoku zōkyō' o kataru zadankai," 12. For comments at the round-table meeting, see "Kinrō seishōnen furyōka bōshi kenkyū zadankai," part 1, pp. 54, 59, 61–62.

69. "Kinrō seishōnen furyōka bōshi kenkyū zadankai," part 2, *Shōnen hogo* 8, no. 5 (May 1943): 47. For an outline of the Justice Ministry's training programs, see *Nihon shakai jigyō nenkan,* 1943, ed. Chūō Shakai Jigyō Kyōkai, 252–58.

70. "Moriyama Hogo Kyokuchō shiji jikō," *Shōnen hogo* 8, no. 9 (September 1943): 10–11.

71. *Kaidō gijiroku: shōnen shinpanshochō hogo kansatsushochō kyōsei-inchō, Shōwa 16 nen 5 gatsu 19–21 nichi,* ed. Shihōshō Hogokyoku, no. 27 of *Shihō hogo shiryō* (Tokyo: Shihōshō Hogokyoku, 1942), 94, 100, 105. See also Headquarters, Army Service Forces, *Civil Affairs Handbook Japan, Section 16: Public Welfare* (Washington, DC: Headquarters, Army Service Forces, 1944), 92.

72. For positive reports, see "Kinrō seishōnen furyōka bōshi kenkyū zadankai," part 2, p. 47; on court policies, see "Moriyama Hogo Kyokuchō shiji jikō," 7.

73. "Moriyama Hogo Kyokuchō shiji jikō," 7–10. For the Nagoya Juvenile Court's establishment in 1943 of a special facility for students, who were admitted in small groups and only for a few days so as not to disrupt their preparation for exams, see Kinoshita Yoshibe, "Tanki rensei to gakusei seito no baai," *Shōnen hogo* 8, no. 3 (March 1943): 10–17.

74. See for example Thomas P. Rohlen, "'Spiritual Education' in a Japanese Bank," *American Anthropologist,* New Series 75, no. 5 (1973): 1542–62.

75. Narita, "Kindai toshi to minshū," 41–55; see also Gregory J. Kasza, *The Conscription Society: Administered Mass Organizations* (New Haven, CT: Yale University Press, 1995).

76. "Zenkoku shōnen sangyō senshi hodō shūkan yōkō," *Sanpō* 2, no. 5 (May 1943): 81–82.

77. See for example "Seishōnenkō no seikatsu shidō jōkyō no chōsa ni tsuite," *Naigai rōdō shūhō* 474 (October 3, 1941): 23–26; "Nihon Kōgaku Ōi kōjō," 17; and Noda Shinichi, "Kōjō katei kan no renraku hōhō ni tsuite," *Sanpō* 2, no. 2 (February 1943): 57–69.

78. Noda, "Kōjō katei kan no renraku," 57–69; the quoted passages are on 57 and 67.

79. Department of Education, "Emphasizing Home Education," *Tokyo Gazette* 3, no. 7 (January 1940): 261–66; the quoted passages are on 265–66. See also "Katei kyōiku shidōsha kōshūkai," *Kyōiku* 8, no. 11 (November 1940): 12–14; and Terasaki et al., eds., *Sōryokusen taisei to kyōiku,* 283–84. For a brief discussion of mothers' associations in day-care centers during the 1920s, see Uno, *Passages to Modernity.* On Welfare Ministry family policies, see Toshitani

Nobuyoshi, "Senji taisei to kazoku: kokka sōdōin taisei ni okeru kazoku seisaku to kazoku hō," in *Kindai Nihon no kazoku seisaku to hō*, vol. 6 of *Kazoku: seisaku to hō*, ed. Fukushima Masao (Tokyo: Tōkyō Daigaku Shuppankai, 1984), 255–362; and Miyake, "Doubling Expectations."

80. Monbushō Kyōgakukyoku, "Ie no hongi (sōkō)," ca. 1944, reprinted in Terasaki et al., eds., *Sōryokusen taisei to kyōiku*, 440.

81. Uetani Chie, "Tojō de hirotta seishōnen no kaiwa kara," *Jidō hogo* 12, no. 2 (February 1942): 10–12.

82. Garon, "Luxury Is the Enemy"; Narita Ryūichi, "Women in the Motherland: Oku Mumeo through Wartime and Postwar," in Yamanouchi, Koschmann, and Narita, eds., *Total War and "Modernization,"* esp. 148–52.

83. On counseling centers affiliated with the juvenile courts, see Tōkyō-fu Gakumubu Shakai Kyōikuka, *Shōnen hogo no mondai ni tsuite*, no. 7 of *Kōgai seikatsu shidō sōsho* (Tokyo: Tōkyō-fu Gakumubu Shakaika, 1940), 82–99; and "Moriyama Hogo Kyokuchō shiji jikō," 6. On the educational protection precincts, see "Fukagawa Ōji ryō shōnen shidōsho kaisetsu saru," *Kōsei jigyō* 27, no. 9 (October 1943): 57–58.

84. Counseling center complaints can be found in *Kaidō gijiroku: shōnen shinpanshochō hogo kansatsushochō kyōseiinchō, Shōwa 15 nen 5 gatsu 15–18 nichi,* ed. Shihō Daijin Kanbō Hogoka, no. 22 of *Shihō hogo shiryō* (Tokyo: Shihō Daijin Kanbō Hogoka, 1940), 56–57; see also "'Shōnen kyōgo to seisanryoku zōkyō' o kataru zadankai," 17. For "a net for the prevention of delinquency," see Mori Kenzō, "Saikin ni okeru yōkyōgo shōnen no dōko to sono taisaku," *Kōsei mondai* 27, no. 11 (November 1943), 7. Kirihara's observation is in Kirihara, *Rōdō to seinen,* 15.

85. "Moriyama Hogo Kyokuchō shiji jikō," 6.

86. Survey results are reported in Kōseishō Seikatsukyoku, *Zenkoku yōkyōgo jidō chōsa hōkokusho* (1943), in *Senzen Nihon shakai jigyō chōsa shiryō shūsei,* vol. 5, ed. Shakai Fukushi Chōsa Kenkyūkai (Tokyo: Keisō Shobō, 1990), 429–44. For Welfare Ministry official Mori Kenzō's comments on the survey, see "Seishōnen furyōka bōshi ni kansuru kakushō renraku kondankai," *Jidō hogo* 13, nos. 8–9 (August–September 1943): 5–6. On anti-delinquency measures in elementary schools, see "Seishōnen no furyōka bōshi ni kansuru kanmin no taisaku," *Naigai rōdō shūhō* 464 (July 18, 1941): 15. On after-school centers in Tokyo, Nagoya, and elsewhere, see "'Shōnen kyōgo to seisanryoku zōkyō' o kataru zadankai," 12–13, 15–16; and Shigematsu, *Shōnen chōkai kyōikushi,* 843–45.

87. On postwar activities, see for example Sōmuchō Seishōnen Taisaku Honbu, ed., *Seishōnen hakusho, 1996* (Heisei 8) edition, *Seishōnen mondai no genjō to taisaku* (Tokyo: Ōkurashō Insatsukyoku, 1997), 3–39; and Hiroshi Wagatsuma and George A. De Vos, *Heritage of Endurance: Family Patterns and Delinquency Formation in Urban Japan* (Berkeley: University of California Press, 1984), 28–34, 38–43, 443–44.

88. Rose, "Cultural Analysis and Moral Discourses," 231–32.

89. Peukert, *Inside Nazi Germany,* 152–74; Michael Burleigh and Wolfgang Wippermann, *The Racial State: Germany 1933–1945* (Cambridge: Cambridge University Press, 1991), 219–27, 237–41.

90. Stuart Cosgrove, "The Zoot-Suit and Style Warfare," *History Workshop Journal* 18 (1984): 81. For general discussions of responses to juvenile delinquency in the United States, see Anderson, *Wartime Women;* for sources on Great Britain, see Harold L., Smith, ed., *Britain in the Second World War: A Social History* (Manchester: Manchester University Press, 1996).

91. Cohen notes that authorities did monitor "dangerous thoughts" among students who were mobilized into factories late in the war and resented their wage levels and working conditions. See Cohen, *Japan's Economy,* 324.

92. On *kōminka,* see Wan-Yao Chou, "The Kōminka Movement in Taiwan and Korea: Comparisons and Interpretations," in *The Japanese Wartime Empire, 1931–1945,* ed. Peter Duus, Ramon H. Myers, and Mark R. Peattie (Princeton, NJ: Princeton University Press, 1996), 40–68; and Leo T.S. Ching, *Becoming "Japanese": Colonial Taiwan and the Politics of Identity Formation* (Berkeley: University of California Press, 2001). On *kyōwa* policies, see Young-Soo Chung and Elise K. Tipton, "Problems of Assimilation: The Koreans," in *Society and the State in Interwar Japan,* ed. Elise K. Tipton (London and New York: Routledge, 1997), 169–92. See also Chang Hyuk-Chu, "Iwamoto shiganhei," in Chang, *Iwamoto shiganhei* (Keijō [Seoul]: Kōa Bunka Shuppan, 1944), 12–58, for the use of juvenile delinquency as a discursive prop to further *kōminka* policies in Korea. For the example of the Ford Motor Company's programs to assimilate immigrant workers to an American lifestyle and work ethic, see Stephen Meyer III, *The Five Dollar Day: Labor Management and Social Control in the Ford Motor Company, 1908–1921* (Albany: State University of New York Press, 1981).

93. Kido Mantarō, "Shōnenkō no furyōka," *Kyōiku* 10, no. 10 (1942): 352.

94. Louise Young, "Imagined Empire: The Cultural Construction of Manchukuo," in Duus, Myers, and Peattie, eds., *The Japanese Wartime Empire,* 90. For a related view of the German case, see Peukert, *Inside Nazi Germany,* 72–74.

95. See for example Narita, "Kindai toshi to minshū"; and Irene B. Taeuber, *The Population of Japan* (Princeton, NJ: Princeton University Press, 1958), 337–43. For the postwar period, see William W. Kelly, "Finding a Place in Metropolitan Japan: Ideologies, Institutions, and Everyday Life," in *Postwar Japan as History,* ed. Andrew Gordon (Berkeley: University of California Press, 1993), 189–216.

EPILOGUE

1. On transwar and postwar history, see for example John Dower, "The Useful War," in *Showa: The Japan of Hirohito,* ed. Carol Gluck and Steven Graubard (New York: W.W. Norton, 1992), 49–70; John Dower, *Embracing Defeat: Japan in the Wake of World War II* (New York: W.W. Norton, 1999); Gordon, ed., *Postwar Japan as History;* Garon, *Molding Japanese Minds;* Yamanouchi, Koschmann, and Narita, eds., *Total War and "Modernization";* and Noguchi Yukio, *1940 nen taisei: saraba "senji keizai"* (Tokyo: Tōyō Keizai Shinpōsha, 1995).

2. These developments are outlined in Sōmuchō Seishōnen Taisaku Honbu, ed., *Seishōnen hakusho*, 1996 (Heisei 8) edition, 3–39.

3. Wagatsuma and De Vos, *Heritage of Endurance*, 443; see also 38–43. On police activities, see David H. Bayley, *Forces of Order: Police Behavior in Japan and the United States* (Berkeley: University of California Press, 1978).

4. See for example Okamoto Hōji, Fukutome Tsuyoshi, and Yahagi Misao, eds., *Gakkō, katei, chiiki to hikō bōshi: seishōnen kenzen ikusei no jissen kara* (Tokyo: Gyōsei, 1983), esp. 120–215.

5. Minoru Shikita and Shinichi Tsuchiya, *Crime and Criminal Policy in Japan: Analysis and Evaluation of the Shōwa Era, 1926–1988* (New York and Berlin: Springer-Verlag, 1992), 256–57. For a study of the development and application of the postwar Juvenile Law, see Moriya, *Shōnen no hikō to kyōiku;* Kyōsei Kyōkai, ed., *Shōnen kyōsei;* and Shigematsu, *Shōnen chōkai kyōikushi.*

6. Johnson, *Japanese Corrections*, 207; see 206–214 for a discussion of the volunteer probation officer system.

7. Rebecca Erwin Fukuzawa, "The Path to Adulthood according to Japanese Middle Schools," *Journal of Japanese Studies* 20, no. 1 (Winter 1994): 61–86, esp. 69–83. See also Gerald LeTendre, "Guiding Them On: Teaching, Hierarchy, and Social Organization in Japanese Middle Schools," *Journal of Japanese Studies* 20, no. 1 (Winter 1994): 37–59; Gerald K. LeTendre, "Disruption and Reconnection: Counseling Young Adolescents in Japanese Schools," in *The Challenge of Eastern Asian Education: Implications for America*, ed. William K. Cummings and Philip G. Altbach (Albany: State University of New York Press, 1997), 101–14; Hayashi Masayuki, *(Zōho) Kanri sareru kodomotachi* (Tokyo: Takushoku Shobō, 1990); and Serizawa Shunsuke, "Genkai toshite no kenryoku," in *Kaitai sareru kodomotachi: shōnen hanzai no seijigaku*, ed. Serizawa Shunsuke (Tokyo: Seikyūsha, 1994), 281–97. In a provocative essay, Serizawa has suggested that educators' obsessive concern with the minutiae of students' appearance is due not only to fears of delinquency but more importantly to the nature of schools as "religious spaces" *(shūkyō kūkan)* in which specific rituals must be performed according to precise rules. Serizawa Shunsuke, "Hikō ga shōmetsu shita," in *Sedai no kōgengaku*, ed. Sanseidō Henshūbu (Tokyo: Sanseidō, 1993), 149–57.

8. Naikaku-fu, ed., *Seishōnen hakusho*, 2001 (Heisei 13) edition, *21 seiki o mukaete no seishōnen kenzen ikusei no arata na torikumi* (Tokyo: Naikaku-fu, 2001), 118. Since the 1970s, at least one-third of Japan's high school graduates have gone on to college. Ibid., 122 (graph).

9. On school uniforms, see Ichiro Tanioka and Daniel Glaser, "School Uniforms, Routine Activities, and the Social Control of Delinquency in Japan," *Youth & Society* 23, no. 1 (September 1991): 50–75.

10. Thomas P. Rohlen, *Japan's High Schools* (Berkeley: University of California Press, 1983); Satō, *Kamikaze Biker;* Robert S. Yoder, "Youth Deviant Behavior, Conflict, and Later Consequences: Comparison of Working and Middle Class Communities in Japan," in *Juvenile Delinquency in Japan: Reconsidering the "Crisis,"* ed. Gesine Foljanty-Jost (Leiden, The Netherlands: Brill, 2003), 129–42. On educational, cultural, recreational, and welfare programs for working youth, which draw in part on prewar and wartime antecedents, see

for example Rōdōshō Rōseikyoku, ed., *Kinrō seishōnen no genjō*, 1988 (Shōwa 63) edition (Tokyo: Ōkurashō Insatsu Kyoku, 1989); and Sōmuchō Seishōnen Taisaku Honbu, ed., *Seishōnen hakusho*, 1996 ed.

11. Karl Taro Greenfeld, *Speed Tribes: Days and Nights with Japan's Next Generation* (New York: Harper Collins, 1994), 47–83; the quoted passage is on 77. See also Anne Metzler, "The Juvenile Training Schools of Japan—Teaching Young Serious Offenders How to Live and 'How to Be'," in Foljanty-Jost, ed., *Juvenile Delinquency in Japan*, 221–52. On the transwar survival of strict training practices in corporations' "spiritual education" institutes, see Rohlen, "'Spiritual Education' in a Japanese Bank," 1542–62.

12. On vocational guidance and the job referral system in vocational high schools, see Kaori Okano, *School to Work Transition in Japan: An Ethnographic Study* (Clevedon, UK: Multilingual Matters Ltd., 1993). For studies that question the efficiency of this system, see Yuki Honda, "The Formation and Transformation of the Japanese System of Transition from School to Work," *Social Science Japan Journal* 7, no. 1 (April 2004): 103–15; and Mary C. Brinton, "Trouble in Paradise: The Youth Labor Market and School-Work Institutions in Japan's Economy," in *The New Economic Sociology of Capitalism*, ed. Richard Swedberg and Victor Nee (Princeton, NJ: Princeton University Press, forthcoming). I wish to thank Dr. Brinton for providing me with a draft of her chapter.

13. Hōmushō Hōmu Sōgō Kenkyujō, ed., *Hanzai hakusho*, 2001 (Heisei 13) edition, *Zōka suru hanzai to hanzaisha* (Tokyo: Zaimushō Insatsukyoku, 2001), section 3.1.1, graph III-2; available online at: http://hakusyo1.moj.go.jp/ (accessed October 21, 2003).

14. Hōmushō Hōmu Sōgō Kenkyujō, ed., *Hanzai hakusho*, 1975 (Shōwa 50) edition, *Saikin no hanzai to hanzaisha no shogū—jidai no shinten to hanzai no henka* (Tokyo: Ōkurashō Insatsukyoku, 1975), section 3.1.2; available online at: http://hakusyo1.moj.go.jp/ (accessed October 20, 2003).

15. See for example Satō, *Kamikaze Biker*, which does not trace the *kōha* style to its Meiji or prewar origins. For fond depictions of contemporary *kōha* subcultures in Japanese schools, see the *Be-Bop High School* series of *manga* (comics) and films.

16. On *enjo kōsai*, see for example Kuronuma Katsushi, *Enjo kōsai: joshi chūkōsei no kiken na hōkago* (Tokyo: Bungei Shunju, 1996). For the text of the child prostitution law, see www.moj.go.jp/KEIJI/ho1.html; in English, www.moj.go.jp/ENGLISH/CRAB/law01.html (accessed June 15, 2004).

17. For police activities, see Keisatsuchō Seikatsu Anzenkyoku Shōnenka, *Shōnen hikō tō no gaiyō: Heisei 14 nen 1–12 gatsu* (2003), 3; available online at: www.npa.go.jp/safetylife/syonen2/heisei14gaiyou.pdf (accessed June 15, 2004).

18. See for example Sonni Efron, "Japan Shaken by Rise in Juvenile Crime," *Los Angeles Times*, October 12, 1997, pp. A1, A15; David Esnault, "Au Japon une jeunesse ultraviolente," *Le Monde Diplomatique*, August 1999, p. 26; Howard W. French, "Japan's Troubling Trend: Rising Teen-Age Crime," *New York Times*, October 12, 1999, p. A6; "Nipping Juvenile Delinquency in the Bud," *Mainichi Daily News/Mainichi Interactive*, January 30, 2002, p. 2,

http://mdn.mainichi.co.jp/news/archive/200201/30/20020130p2a00m00a010000c. html (accessed October 20, 2003); and Yumi Wijers-Hasegawa, "Debate Rages over Juvenile Crime Age Limit," *Japan Times,* July 13, 2003. For examples of sensational coverage of the 1997 Kobe murder, see *Shūkan shinchō* 42, nos. 27–29 (July 1997).

19. Brinton, "Trouble in Paradise"; Honda, "The Formation and Transformation."

20. "Japanese Youth Crime on the Rise," Associated Press report, *The New York Times on the Web,* December 22, 1998, www.nytimes.com/aponline/i/AP-Japan-Youth-Crime.html (accessed March 1, 1999).

21. For a typical approach to analyzing causes of and orchestrating practical responses to delinquency in the 1980s, see Okamoto et al., eds., *Gakkō, katei, chiiki to hikō bōshi.* For the progressive and conservative/neonationalist critiques, see Annette Erbe, "Youth in Crisis: Public Perceptions and Discourse on Deviance and Juvenile Problem Behavior in Japan," in Foljanty-Jost, ed., *Juvenile Delinquency in Japan,* 63–65; Hayashi, *(Zōho) Kanri sareru kodomo-tachi* (see p. 38 for the principal's statement); and Iwao Sumiko, "Problems among Japan's Young," *Japan Echo* 25, no. 3 (June 1998). The government's Youth Problems Deliberative Council has echoed some of these charges, even choosing to title its 2000 report *Overcoming the "Postwar" ("Sengo" o koete).* The report is summarized in Naikaku-fu, ed., *Seishōnen hakusho,* 2001 (Heisei 13) edition, 449–55.

22. Noda Masaaki, quoted in Efron, "Japan Shaken by Rise in Juvenile Crime," A15.

Selected Bibliography

Prewar journal and newspaper titles are followed by the years consulted. Information for individual articles cited from these journals is contained in the backnotes.

Adachi Kenchū. *Adachi Kenchū kankei shiryō: jiyū minken undō kara shoki shakai fukushi jigyō.* Edited by Naitō Jirō. Tokyo: Sairyūsha, 1982.

———. *Koji akka no jōkyō.* MS, 1895. Reprinted in *Nihon jidō mondai bunken senshū,* vol. 2, edited by Jidō Mondaishi Kenkyūkai. Tokyo: Nihon Tosho Sentā, 1983.

———. *Kyūji akka no jōkyo tsuketari shūyōhō.* Tokyo: Tōkyō-shi Yōikuin, 1898.

Amano Ikuo. *Gakureki no shakaishi: kyōiku to Nihon no kindai.* Tokyo: Shinchōsha, 1996.

Ambaras, David R. "Social Knowledge, Cultural Capital, and the New Middle Class in Japan, 1895–1912." *Journal of Japanese Studies* 24, no. 1 (Winter 1998): 1–33.

———. "Treasures of the Nation: Juvenile Delinquency, Socialization, and Mobilization in Modern Japan, 1895–1945." Ph.D. diss., Princeton University, 1999.

Anderson, Benedict. *Imagined Communities: Reflections on the Origins and Spread of Nationalism.* London and New York: Verso, 1991.

Anderson, Karen. *Wartime Women: Sex Roles, Family Relations, and the Status of Women during World War II.* Westport, CT: Greenwood Press, 1981.

Ariizumi Sadao. "Meiji kokka to minshū tōgō." In *Iwanami kōza Nihon rekishi,* vol. 17, edited by Asao Naohiro et al., 222–62. Tokyo: Iwanami Shoten, 1976.

Arima Shirōsuke. "Shōnen hanzaisha no kun'iku." In *Kanka kyūsai jigyō kōenshū,* vol. 2, edited by Naimushō Chihōkyoku, 887–928. 1909.

Reprinted in *Senzenki shakai jigyō shiryō shūsei*, vol. 20, edited by Shakai Fukushi Chōsa Kenkyūkai. Tokyo: Nihon Tosho Sentā, 1985.

Asahara Rokurō. "Marunouchi no tenjō." 1911. Reprinted in *Yoshiyuki Eisuke to sono jidai: modan toshi no hikari to kage,* edited by Yoshiyuki Kazuko and Saitō Shinji, 141–51. Tokyo: Tōkyō Shiki Shuppan, 1988.

Asahi Shinbunsha, ed. *Tōkyō hyakusai.* Vol. 3 of *Asahi shinbun hyakunen no kiji ni miru.* Tokyo: Asahi Shinbunsha, 1979.

Asakura Haruhiko and Tsuchida Michifumi, ed. *Meiji Tōkyō meisho zue.* 2 vols. Tokyo: Tōkyōdō Shuppan, 1992.

Asakusa. 1919–20.

Asao Naohiro, ed. *Mibun to kakushiki.* Vol. 7 of *Nihon no kinsei.* Tokyo: Chūō Kōronsha, 1992.

Atkins, E. Taylor. *Blue Nippon: Authenticating Jazz in Modern Japan.* Durham, NC: Duke University Press, 2001.

Bayley, David H. *Forces of Order: Police Behavior in Japan and the United States.* Berkeley: University of California Press, 1978.

Becker, Howard S. *Outsiders: Studies in the Sociology of Deviance.* New York: The Free Press, 1973.

———. "Social Class Variations in the Teacher-Pupil Relationship." 1952. Reprinted in *Howard Becker on Education,* edited by Robert O. Burgess, 31–43. Buckingham: Open University Press, 1995.

Bernstein, Gail Lee, ed. *Recreating Japanese Women, 1600–1945.* Berkeley: University of California Press, 1991.

Berry, Mary Elizabeth. "Public Life in Authoritarian Japan." *Daedalus* 127, no. 3 (Summer 1998): 133–66.

Betchaku Atsuko. "Tōkyō-shi Mannen Jinjō Shōgakkō ni okeru Sakamoto Ryūnosuke no gakkō keiei to kyōikukan." *Tōkyō Daigaku Kyōiku Gakubu kiyō* 30 (1990): 31–41.

———. "Tōkyō-shi 'tokushu shōgakkō' no setsuritsu katei no kentō: chiiki to no kattō ni shiten o atete." *Nihon no kyōiku shigaku* 38 (1995): 154–73.

Bitō Masahide. *Genroku jidai.* Vol. 19 of *Nihon no rekishi.* Tokyo: Chūō Kōronsha, 1987.

Botsman, Daniel V. *Punishment and Power in the Making of Modern Japan.* Princeton, NJ: Princeton University Press, 2004.

Bourdieu, Pierre, and Jean-Claude Passeron. *Reproduction in Education, Society, and Culture.* Translated by Richard Nice. London: SAGE Publications, 1977.

Boyer, Paul. *Urban Masses and Moral Order in America, 1820–1920.* Cambridge, MA: Harvard University Press, 1978.

Brinton, Mary C. "Trouble in Paradise: The Youth Labor Market and School-Work Institutions in Japan's Economy." In *The New Economic Sociology of Capitalism,* edited by Richard Swedberg and Victor Nee. Princeton, NJ: Princeton University Press, forthcoming.

Burleigh, Michael, and Wolfgang Wippermann. *The Racial State: Germany 1933–1945.* Cambridge: Cambridge University Press, 1991.

Buyō Inshi. *Seji kenmonroku.* 1816. Reprinted in *Kinsei shakai keizai sōsho,* vol. 1, edited by Honjo Eijirō et al. Tokyo: Kaizōsha, 1926.

Certeau, Michel de. *The Practice of Everyday Life*. Translated by Steven Rendall. Berkeley: University of California Press, 1984.

Chamberlain, Basil Hall. *Things Japanese; Being Notes on Various Subjects Connected with Japan for the Use of Travellers and Others*. London: J. Murray, 1905.

Ching, Leo T.S. *Becoming "Japanese": Colonial Taiwan and the Politics of Identity Formation*. Berkeley: University of California Press, 2001.

Chou, Wan-Yao. "The Kōminka Movement in Taiwan and Korea: Comparisons and Interpretations." In *The Japanese Wartime Empire, 1931–1945*, edited by Peter Duus, Ramon H. Myers, and Mark R. Peattie, 40–68. Princeton, NJ: Princeton University Press, 1996.

Chung, Young-Soo, and Elise K. Tipton. "Problems of Assimilation: The Koreans," in *Society and the State in Interwar Japan*, edited by Elise K. Tipton, 169–92. London: Routledge, 1997.

Chūō kōron. 1900–1943.

Chūō Shakai Jigyō Kyōkai, ed. *Nihon shakai jigyō nenkan*. Tokyo: Chūō Shakai Jigyō Kyōkai, 1933–43.

Chūō Shakai Jigyō Kyōkai Shakai Jigyō Kenkyūjo. *Furyō jidō to shokugyō to no kankei*. Tokyo: Chūō Shakai Jigyō Kyōkai Shakai Jigyō Kenkyūjo, 1936.

Chūō Shokugyō Shōkai Jimukyoku. *Shokugyō shōkai nenpō*. 1931–34 editions. Tokyo: Chūō Shokugyō Shōkai Jimukyoku, 1931–34.

Cohen, Jerome B. *Japan's Economy in War and Reconstruction*. Minneapolis: University of Minnesota Press, 1949.

Cohen, Stanley. *Folk Devils and Moral Panics: The Creation of the Mods and Rockers*. 3d edition. London and New York: Routledge, 2002.

Cook, Haruko Taya, and Theodore Cook. *Japan at War: An Oral History*. New York: The New Press, 1992.

Cosgrove, Stuart. "The Zoot-Suit and Style Warfare," *History Workshop Journal* 18 (1984): 77–91.

Craig, Teruko. "Introduction." In *Musui's Story: The Autobiography of a Tokugawa Samurai*, ix–xxi. Translated with an introduction by Teruko Craig. Tuscon: The University of Arizona Press, 1988.

Deacon, Desley. *Managing Gender: The State, the New Middle Class, and Women Workers, 1830–1930*. Melbourne: Oxford University Press, 1989.

Department of Education (Japan). "Emphasizing Home Education." *Tokyo Gazette* 3, no. 7 (January 1940): 261–66.

———. "The National School System: A Reform of Primary Education," *Tokyo Gazette* 3, no. 9 (March 1940): 327–31.

Dingwall, Robert, and Philip Lewis, eds. *The Sociology of the Professions: Doctors, Lawyers, and Others*. New York: St. Martin's Press, 1983.

Doi Yōichi. "Katei Gakkōshi kenkyū nōto: Sugamo Katei Gakkō o chūshin ni." *Shakai jigyōshi kenkyū* 2 (October 1974): 51–84.

Donzelot, Jacques. *The Policing of Families*. Translated by Robert Hurley. New York: Pantheon, 1979.

Dore, Ronald P. *Education in Tokugawa Japan*. Berkeley: University of California Press, 1965.

Dower, John. "The Useful War." In *Showa: The Japan of Hirohito*, edited by Carol Gluck and Steven Graubard, 49–70. New York: W. W. Norton, 1992.

Endō Kōichi. "'Shokutaku' toshite no Tomeoka Kōsuke." *Meiji Gakuin ronsō*, vols. 352–353: series *Shakaigaku, shakai fukushigaku kenkyū*, nos. 65–66 (March 1984): 243–310.

Fletcher, William Miles III. *The Search for a New Order: Intellectuals and Fascism in Prewar Japan*. Chapel Hill: University of North Carolina Press, 1982.

Foljanty-Jost, Gesine, ed. *Juvenile Delinquency in Japan: Reconsidering the "Crisis."* Leiden, The Netherlands: Brill, 2003.

Foucault, Michel. *Discipline and Punish: The Birth of the Prison*. Translated by Alan Sheridan. New York: Vintage Books, 1979.

Freedman, Alisa. "Commuting Gazes: Schoolgirls, Salarymen, and Electric Trains in Tokyo." *Journal of Transport History* 23, no. 1 (March 2002): 23–36.

Frühstück, Sabine. *Colonizing Sex: Sexology and Social Control in Modern Japan*. Berkeley: University of California Press, 2003.

Fujii Hideo. *Kinrō seishōnen no furyōka to sono taisaku*. Kyoto: Ritsumeikan Shuppanbu, 1943.

Fujii Tsunefumi. *Fukushi kokka o tsukutta otoko: Tomeoka Kōsuke no shōgai, 1864–1934*. Tokyo: Hōsei Shuppan, 1992.

Fujimori Seikichi. "Nani ga kanojo o sō saseta ka." *Kaizō* 9, no. 2, literary section (February 1927): 1–81.

Fujin no tomo. 1927–33.

Fujin saron. 1931–33.

Fujiokaya [Sudō] Yoshizō. *Fujiokaya nikki*. Vols. 1–4 of 15. In *Kinsei shomin seikatsu shiryō*, edited by Suzuki Tōzō and Koike Shōtarō. Tokyo: San'ichi Shobō, 1987–95.

Fujitani, Takashi. *Splendid Monarchy: Power and Pageantry in Modern Japan*. Berkeley: University of California Press, 1996.

Fukaya Masashi. *Ryōsai kenbo shugi no kyōiku*. Nagoya: Reimei Shobō, 1998.

Fukuzawa, Rebecca Erwin. "The Path to Adulthood according to Japanese Middle Schools." *Journal of Japanese Studies* 20, no. 1 (Winter 1994): 61–86.

Furukawa Makoto. "The Changing Nature of Sexuality: The Three Codes Framing Homosexuality in Modern Japan." *U.S.-Japan Women's Journal, English Supplement* 7 (1994): 98–127.

Furuya Shintarō. *Aa shōnen*. Osaka: Kyōgaku Sōchōsha, 1930.

Garland, David. *Punishment and Welfare: A History of Penal Strategies*. Hampshire, England: Gower, 1985.

Garon, Sheldon. "Luxury Is the Enemy: Mobilizing Savings and Popularizing Thrift in Wartime Japan." *Journal of Japanese Studies* 26, no. 1 (Winter 2000): 41–78.

———. *Molding Japanese Minds: The State in Everyday Life*. Princeton, NJ: Princeton University Press, 1997.

———. *The State and Labor in Modern Japan*. Berkeley: University of California Press, 1987.

———. "State and Society in Interwar Japan." In *Historical Perspectives on Contemporary East Asia,* edited by Merle Goldman and Andrew Gordon, 155–82. Cambridge, MA: Harvard University Press, 2000.

Gerow, A. A. "Swarming Ants and Elusive Villains: Zigomar and the Problem of Cinema in 1910s Japan." *CineMagaziNet! On-Line Research Journal of Cinema* 1 (August 1996). www.cmn.hs.h.kyoto-u.ac.jp/NO1/SUBJECT1/ZIGOMAR.HTM (accessed January 3, 2004).

Gillingham, John. "The 'Deproletarianization' of German Society: Vocational Training in the Third Reich." *Journal of Social History* 19, no. 33 (1986): 423–32.

Gillis, John R. *Youth and History: Tradition and Change in European Age Relations, 1770–Present.* New York: Academic Press, 1974.

Gluck, Carol. *Japan's Modern Myths: Ideology in the Late Meiji Period.* Princeton, NJ: Princeton University Press, 1985.

Goffman, Erving. *Asylums: Essays on the Social Situation of Mental Patients and Other Inmates.* Chicago: Aldine Publishing Co., 1962.

Gonda Yasunosuke. *Sangyō seinen tokuhon.* Tokyo: Kōjimachi Sakai Shoten, 1941.

Gordon, Andrew. *The Evolution of Labor Relations in Japan: Heavy Industry, 1853–1955.* Cambridge, MA: Council on East Asian Studies, Harvard University, distributed by Harvard University Press, 1988.

———. *Labor and Imperial Democracy in Prewar Japan.* Berkeley: University of California Press, 1991.

———, ed. *Postwar Japan as History.* Berkeley: University of California Press, 1993.

Gordon, Linda. *Heroes of Their Own Lives: The Politics and History of Family Violence, Boston, 1880–1960.* New York: Viking, 1988.

Government of Japan. Research and Statistics Division, Minister's Secretariat, Ministry of Education, Science, and Culture. *Japan's Modern Educational System: A History of the First Hundred Years.* Tokyo: Printing Bureau, Ministry of Finance, 1980.

Greenfeld, Karl Taro. *Speed Tribes: Days and Nights with Japan's Next Generation.* New York: Harper Collins, 1994.

Hachihongi Kiyoshi. *Sensō makki no seinen gakkō.* Tokyo: Nihon Tosho Sentā, 1996.

Hall, G. Stanley. *Adolescence: Its Psychology and Its Relations to Physiology, Anthropology, Sociology, Sex, Crime, Religion, and Education.* 2 vols. New York: D. Appleton and Company, 1905.

Hall, John W. "Rule by Status in Tokugawa Japan." *Journal of Japanese Studies* 1, no. 1 (Autumn 1974): 39–49.

Hall, Stuart, and Tony Jefferson, eds. *Resistance through Rituals: Youth Subcultures in Post-war Britain.* London: Hutchinson, 1976.

Hamamoto Hiroshi. *Asakusa no hi* and *Zoku Asakusa no hi.* 1937. Reprinted in *Taishū bungaku taikei,* vol. 23, edited by Ōfutsu Jirō, Kawaguchi Matsutarō, and Kimura Takeshi, 287–382. Tokyo: Kōdansha, 1973.

———. *Furyō shōnen.* Tokyo: Edo Shoin, 1947.

Hara, Hiroko, and Mieko Minagawa. "From Productive Dependents to Precious Guests: Historical Changes in Japanese Children." In *Japanese Childrearing: Two Generations of Scholarship,* edited by David W. Shwalb and Barbara J. Shwalb, 9–30. New York and London: Guilford Press, 1996.

Hara Masao. *Shikijō to seinen.* Tokyo, Eisei Shinpōsha, 1906.

Hareven, Tamara K. "The History of the Family and the Complexity of Social Change." *American Historical Review* 96, no. 1 (February 1991): 95–124.

Harootunian, H.D. "Late Tokugawa Culture and Thought." In *The Nineteenth Century,* edited by Marius B. Jansen, 168–258. Vol. 5 of *The Cambridge History of Japan.* Cambridge: Cambridge University Press, 1989.

Harootunian, Harry. *Overcome by Modernity: History, Culture, and Community in Interwar Japan.* Princeton, NJ: Princeton University Press, 2000.

Harvey, Elizabeth. *Youth and the Welfare State in Weimar Germany.* Oxford: Clarendon Press, 1993.

Hashimoto Katsutarō. *Shōnen no seikaku to kankyō.* Tokyo: Dōbunkan, 1942.

Hashizume Kōichirō. *Chūgakusei to katei no kyōyō.* Tokyo: Jitsugyō no Nihonsha, 1912.

Hastings, Sally Ann. *Neighborhood and Nation in Tokyo, 1905–1937.* Pittsburgh, PA: University of Pittsburgh Press, 1995.

Havens, Thomas R.H. *Valley of Darkness: The Japanese People and World War II.* Lanham, MD: University Press of America, 1986.

Hayashi Fumiko. *Diary of a Vagabond.* Translated by Joan E. Ericson. In Joan E. Ericson, *Be a Woman: Hayashi Fumiko and Modern Japanese Women's Literature.* Honolulu: University of Hawai'i Press, 1997.

Hayashi Masayo. "Kindai Nihon no 'seishōnen' kan ni kansuru ichi kōsatsu: 'gakkō seito' no kitsuen mondai no seisei, tenkai katei o chūshin ni." *Kyōiku shakaigaku kenkyū* 56 (1995): 65–80.

Hayashi Masayuki. *(Zōho) Kanri sareru kodomotachi.* Tokyo: Takushoku Shobō, 1990.

Hayashi Reiko. *Edodana hankachō.* Tokyo: Yoshikawa Kōbunkan, 1982.

———. "Edodana no seikatsu." In *Edo chōnin no kenkyū,* vol. 2, edited by Nishiyama Matsunosuke, 94–138. Tokyo: Yoshikawa Kōbunkan, 1973.

———. "Noren no uchigawa de." In *Shōnin no katsudō,* edited by Hayashi Reiko, 169–95. Vol. 5 of *Nihon no kinsei.* Tokyo: Chūō Kōronsha, 1992.

Hebdige, Dick. *Subculture: The Meaning of Style.* London: Routledge, 1995.

Herf, Jeffrey. *Reactionary Modernism: Technology, Culture, and Politics in Weimar and the Third Reich.* Cambridge: Cambridge University Press, 1986.

Hibino Hiroshi. *Seinen shijo daraku no riyū tsuketari sono kyōkyūhō.* Tokyo: Kinkōdō, 1907.

Higuchi Hideo. *Edo no hankachō.* Tokyo: Jinbutsu Ōraisha, 1963.

Higuchi Ichiyō. "Growing Up." 1895–96. Translated by Edward Seidensticker. In *Modern Japanese Literature: From 1868 to the Present Day,* edited by Donald Keene, 70–110. New York: Grove Press, 1956.

———. "Takekurabe." 1895–96. In *Higuchi Ichiyō,* edited by Tsubouchi Yūzō, 98–148. Vol. 17 of *Meiji no bungaku.* Tokyo: Chikuma Shobō, 2000.

Hirade Kojirō. *Tōkyō fūzokushi.* 3 vols. Reprinted in *Meiji bunka shiryō sōsho,* vol. 12, edited by Ōtō Tokihiko. Tokyo: Kazama Shobō, 1960.

Hiramatsu Yoshirō. *Edo no tsumi to batsu.* Tokyo: Heibonsha, 1988.

Hōgaku Kyōkai zasshi. 1918–25.

Hogan, David John. *Class and Reform: School and Society in Chicago, 1880–1930.* Philadelphia: University of Pennsylvania Press, 1985.

Holloran, Peter C. *Boston's Wayward Children: Social Services for Homeless Children, 1830–1930.* Rutherford, NJ: Fairleigh Dickinson University Press, 1989.

Hōmushō Hōmu Sōgō Kenkyujō, ed. *Hanzai hakusho.* 1975 (Shōwa 50) edition, *Saikin no hanzai to hanzaisha no shogū—jidai no shinten to hanzai no henka.* Tokyo: Ōkurashō Insatsukyoku, 1975. http://hakusyo1.moj.go.jp/ (accessed October 20, 2003).

———, ed. *Hanzai hakusho.* 2001 (Heisei 13) edition, *Zōka suru hanzai to hanzaisha.* Tokyo: Zaimushō Insatsukyoku, 2001. http://hakusyo1.moj. go.jp/ (accessed October 21, 2003).

Honda Masuko. *Jogakusei no keifu: saishoku sareru Meiji.* Tokyo: Seidosha, 1990.

Honda, Yuki. "The Formation and Transformation of the Japanese System of Transition from School to Work." *Social Science Japan Journal* 7, no. 1 (April 2004): 103–15.

Honjo Mutsuo. "Shiroi kabe." Reprinted in *Honjo Mutsuo, Suzuki Kiyoshi shū,* 106–31. Vol. 31 of *Nihon puroretaria bungakushū.* Tokyo: Shin Nihon Shuppansha, 1987.

Hōritsu shinbun. 1904–42.

Horn, David G. *Social Bodies: Science, Reproduction, and Italian Modernity.* Princeton, NJ: Princeton University Press, 1994.

Hōsei Daigaku Ōhara Shakai Mondai Kenkyūjo, ed. *Taiheiyō Sensōka no rōdō undō.* Special edition of *Nihon rōdō nenkan.* Tokyo: Tōyō Keizai Shinpōsha, 1965.

———, ed. *Taiheiyō Sensōka no rōdōsha jōtai.* Special edition of *Nihon rōdō nenkan.* Tokyo: Tōyō Keizai Shinpōsha, 1964. http://oohara.mt.tama.hosei. ac.jp/rn/senji1/index.html (accessed September 15, 2003).

Hōsōkai zasshi. 1923–29.

Howell, David L. *Geographies of Identity in Nineteenth-Century Japan.* Berkeley: University of California Press, 2005.

———. "Hard Times in the Kantō: Economic Change and Village Life in Late Tokugawa Japan." *Modern Asian Studies* 23, no. 2 (1989): 349–71.

———. "Territoriality and Collective Identity in Tokugawa Japan." *Daedalus* 127, no. 3 (Summer 1998): 105–32.

Humphreys, Leonard A. *The Way of the Heavenly Sword: The Japanese Army in the 1920s.* Stanford, CA: Stanford University Press, 1995.

Humphries, Stephen. *Hooligans or Rebels? An Oral History of Working-Class Childhood and Youth, 1889–1939.* Oxford: Blackwell, 1995.

Hur, Nam-lin. *Prayer and Play in Late Tokugawa Japan: Asakusa Sensōji and Edo Society.* Cambridge, MA: Harvard University Asia Center, 2000.

Iijima Mitsuyasu. *Kanka kyōiku: furyō shōnen no kenkyū.* Tokyo: Shōkado Shoten, 1931.

Ikeda Yoshimasa. *Nihon shakai fukushishi.* Kyoto: Hōritsu Bunkasha, 1986.

Ikegami, Eiko. *The Taming of the Samurai: Honorific Individualism and the Making of Modern Japan.* Cambridge, MA: Harvard University Press, 1995.

Ishida Takeshi. "Kindai Nihon ni okeru 'shakai fukushi' kanren kannen no hensen." In *Kindai Nihon no seiji bunka to gengo shōchō,* edited by Ishida Takeshi, 175–232. Tokyo: Tōkyō Daigaku Shuppankai, 1983.

Ishii Ryōsuke. *Edo no keibatsu.* Tokyo: Chūō Kōronsha, 1992.

Ishii Shōji. *Kindai no jidō rōdō to yakan shōgakkō.* Tokyo: Akashi Shoten, 1992.

Ishikawa Ken. *Wagakuni ni okeru jidōkan no hattatsu.* Chiba: Seishisha, 1976.

Ishikawa Tengai. *Tōkyōgaku.* 1909. Reprinted in *Meiji bunka shiryō sōsho,* vol. 12, edited by Ōtō Tokihiko. Tokyo: Kazama Shobō, 1960.

Ishizuka Hiromichi. *Nihon kindai toshi ron: Tōkyō, 1868–1923.* Tokyo: Tōkyō Daigaku Shuppankai, 1991.

Ishizuka Hiromichi and Narita Ryūichi. *Tōkyō-to no hyakunen.* Tokyo: Yamakawa Shuppansha, 1986.

Ishizumi Harunosuke. *Asakusa keizaigaku.* 1933. Reprinted in *Sakariba, uramachi,* 245–85. Vol. 2 of *Kindai shomin seikatsushi,* edited by Minami Hiroshi et al. Tokyo: San'ichi Shobō, 1984.

———. *Asakusa onna urabanashi.* Tokyo: Bunjinsha Shuppanbu, 1930.

———. *Asakusa urabanashi.* Tokyo: Bungei Shijōsha, 1927.

———. *Ginza kaibōzu daiippen henshi.* 1934. Reprinted in *Sakariba, uramachi,* 286–332. Vol. 2 of *Kindai shomin seikatsushi,* edited by Minami Hiroshi et al. Tokyo: San'ichi Shobō, 1984.

———. *Kojiki urabanashi.* 1929. Reprinted in *Rumin,* 328–95. Vol. 4 of *Kindai minshū no kiroku,* edited by Hayashi Hideo. Tokyo: Shinjinbutsu Ōraisha, 1971.

Itō Akihiro. "Senjiki Nihon ni okeru 'jinteki shigen' seisaku: senji dōin to kōtō kyōiku o meguru seiji katei." *Hiroshima Daigaku Daigaku Kyōiku Kenkyū Sentā daigaku ronshū* 18 (March 1989): 127–47.

Ito, Yasuji. "Student Life." *Contemporary Japan* 8, no. 8 (October 1939): 1006–19.

Itsumi Katsuaki. "Fuashizumu kyōiku no hōkai: kinrō dōin o chūshin toshite." In *Kōza Nihon kyōikushi,* vol. 4, edited by Kōza Nihon kyōikushi Henshū Iinkai, 176–210. Tokyo: Daiichi Hōki Shuppan, 1984.

Iwahashi Ikurō. *Shōnen kurabu to dokushatachi.* Tokyo: Zōonsha, 1988.

Jansen, Marius B., ed. *The Nineteenth Century.* Vol. 5 of *The Cambridge History of Japan.* Cambridge: Cambridge University Press, 1989.

Jidō hogo. 1931–43.

Jidō kenkyū. 1898–1943.

Jindō. 1905–44. Reprint edition. Tokyo: Fuji Shuppan, 1983.

Jizen. 1909–17.

Johnson, Elmer H. *Japanese Corrections: Managing Convicted Offenders in an Orderly Society.* Carbondale: Southern Illinois University Press, 1996.

Kaneko Fumiko. *The Prison Memoirs of a Japanese Woman.* Translated by Jean Inglis, with an introduction by Mikiso Hane. Armonk, NY: M.E. Sharpe, 1991.

Kanka kyōiku. 1923–31.

Kankainchō Kyōgikai, ed. *Daiikkai kankainchō kyōgikai sokkiroku.* 1910. Reprinted in *Nihon jidō mondai bunken senshū,* vol. 24, edited by Jidō Mondaishi Kenkyūkai. Tokyo: Nihon Tosho Sentā, 1984.

Kano Masanao. "Furyō shōnen bunka toshite no eiga." In *Musei eiga no kansei,* 320–34. Vol. 2 of *Kōza Nihon eiga,* edited by Imamura Shōhei et al. Tokyo: Iwanami Shoten, 1986.

———. "Sengo keiei to nōson kyōiku: Nichi-Ro sensōgo no seinendan undō ni tsuite." *Shisō* 521 (November 1967): 42–59.

———. *Senzen "ie" no shisō.* Tokyo: Sōbunsha, 1983.

Karasawa Tomitarō. *Gakusei no rekishi: gakusei seikatsu no shakaishiteki kōsatsu.* Vol. 3 of *Karasawa Tomitarō chosakushū.* Tokyo: Gyōsei, 1991.

Karlin, Jason G. "The Gender of Nationalism: Competing Masculinities in Meiji Japan." *Journal of Japanese Studies* 28, no. 1 (Winter 2002): 41–77.

Kashima Kōji. *Taishō no Shitayakko.* Tokyo: Seiabō, 1976. Excerpted at: www.aurora.dti.ne.jp/~ssaton/bungaku/kasima.html (accessed December 1, 2002).

Kasza, Gregory J. *The Conscription Society: Administered Mass Organizations.* New Haven, CT: Yale University Press, 1995.

Katō Hiroshi. *Fukushiteki ningenkan no shakaishi: yūsei shiso to hikō, seishinbyō o tōshite.* Kyoto: Kōyō Shobō, 1996.

Katoda Keiko. "Taishō ki ni okeru 'jidō mondai' to 'jidō hogo'." In *Shakai fukushi no Nihonteki tokushitsu,* edited by Yoshida Kyūichi, 328–59. Tokyo: Kawashima Shoten, 1986.

———. "Wagakuni ni okeru hinji kyōiku: Tōkyō-shi tokushu jinjō shōgakkō no seiritsu to tenkai." *Shakai fukushi* 23 (1982): 85–103.

Katsu Kokichi. *Musui's Story: The Autobiography of a Tokugawa Samurai.* Translated with an introduction by Teruko Craig. Tuscon: The University of Arizona Press, 1988.

Kawabata Yasunari. *Asakusa kurenaidan.* In Kawabata Yasunari, *Asakusa kurenaidan, Asakusa matsuri.* Tokyo: Kōdansha, 1996.

Kawai Takao, ed. *Meijiki shakaigaku kankei shiryō.* 10 vols. Tokyo: Ryūkei Shosha, 1991.

Kawasaki Natsu. *Shokugyō fujin o kokorozasu hito no tame ni.* 1932. Reprinted in *Kindai fujin mondai meicho senshū zoku hen,* vol. 10, edited by Nakajima Kuni et al. Tokyo: Nihon Tosho Sentā, 1982.

Keep, Christopher. "The Cultural Work of the Type-Writer Girl." *Victorian Studies* 40, no. 3 (Spring 1997): 401–26.

Keichō kenmon shū. Reprinted in *Nihon shomin seikatsu shiryō shūsei,* vol. 8, edited by Miyamoto Tsuneichi and Haraguchi Torao. Tokyo: San'ichi Shobō, 1969.

Keisatsu Kyōkai zasshi. 1900–1918.

Keishichō. *Kinrō gyōsei gaikyō.* Reprinted in *Nihon rōdō undō shiryō,* vol. 9, edited by Rōdō Undō Shiryō Iinkai, 354–536. Tokyo: Tokyo Daigaku Shuppankai, 1965.

Keishichō shi Hensan Iinkai, ed. *Keishichō shi Meiji hen.* Tokyo: Keishichō shi Hensan Iinkai, 1958.

————, ed. *Keishichō shi, Shōwa zenpen.* Tokyo: Keishichō shi Hensan Iinkai, 1962.

————, ed. *Keishichō shi Taishō hen.* Tokyo: Keishichō shi Hensan Iinkai, 1960.

Ketelaar, James Edward. *Of Heretics and Martyrs in Meiji Japan: Buddhism and Its Persecution.* Princeton, NJ: Princeton University Press, 1990.

Kimura Naoe, *"Seinen" no tanjō: Meiji Nihon ni okeru seijiteki jissen no tenkan.* Tokyo: Shinyōsha, 1998.

Kinmonth, Earl H. *The Self-Made Man in Meiji Japanese Thought: From Samurai to Salaryman.* Berkeley: University of California Press, 1981.

Kirihara Shigemi. *Rōdō to seinen.* Tokyo: Kagakushugi Kōgyōsha, 1940.

————. *Senji rōmu kanri.* Tokyo: Tōyō Shokan, 1942.

————. *Shokugyō shidō to rōmu hodō.* Tokyo: Chikura shobō, 1938.

Kitajima Masamoto. "Kabukimono: sono kōdō to ronri." In Kitajima Masamoto, *Kinseishi no gunzō,* 113–31. Tokyo: Yoshikawa Kōbunkan, 1977.

Kobayashi Hitomi, "Katei Gakkō to Koshio Juku ni kansuru kōsatsu: kanka kyōiku ni okeru 'katei' to 'gakkō'," *Kyōikugaku kenkyū* 58, no. 2 (June 1991): 22–31.

Kodama Kōta. *Genroku jidai.* Vol. 16 of *Nihon no rekishi.* Tokyo: Chūō Kōronsha, 1966.

Kojima Hideo. "Japanese Concepts of Child Development from the Mid-Seventeenth to the Mid-Nineteenth Century." *International Journal of Behavioral Development* 9, no. 3 (1986): 315–29.

Kokka Gakkai zasshi. 1895–1914.

Kōsei jigyō. 1940–44. Reprint edition. Tokyo: Ryūkei Shosha, 1982.

Kōsei mondai. 1942–44.

Kōseishō Seikatsukyoku. *Zenkoku yōkyōgo jidō chōsa hōkokusho.* 1943. Reprinted in *Senzen Nihon shakai jigyō chōsa shiryō shūsei,* vol. 5, edited by Shakai Fukushi Chōsa Kenkyūkai, 429–44. Tokyo: Keisō Shobō, 1990.

Kōseishō Shakaikyoku Jidōka, ed. *Jidō hogo kankei hōki.* 1938. Reprinted in *Senzenki shakai jigyō shiryō shūsei,* vol. 15, edited by Shakai Fukushi Chōsa Kenkyūkai. Tokyo: Nihon Tosho Sentā, 1985.

Kurata Yoshihiro. *Meiji Taishō no minshū goraku.* Tokyo: Iwanami Shoten, 1980.

Kusama Yasoo. *Furyōji.* 1936. Reprinted in Kusama Yasoo, *Furyōji, suijō rōdōsha, yoriko,* edited by Isomura Eiichi, with an introduction by Yasuoka Norihiko. Vol. 3 of *Kindai kasō minshū seikatsushi.* Tokyo: Akashi Shoten, 1987.

————. *Jokyū to baishōfu.* 1930. Reprinted in *Kindai fujin mondai meicho senshū zokuhen,* vol. 9, edited by Nakajima Kuni. Tokyo: Nihon Tosho Sentā, 1982.

————. *Kindai Nihon no donzoko shakai.* Edited by Isomura Eiichi, with an introduction by Yasuoka Norihiko. Tokyo: Akashi Shoten, 1992.

Kuwabara Saburō. *Shōnen kurabu no koro: Shōwa zenki no jidō bungaku.* Tokyo: Keiō Tsūshin, 1987.

Kuwabara Sanji. *Tōkyō-fu kōritsu chūgakkō kyōikushi.* Tokyo: Takayama Honten, 1981.

Kyōchōkai. *Senji rōdō jijō*. Tokyo: Kyōchōkai, 1944.

Kyōiku jiron. 1920–30.

Kyōsei Kyōkai, ed. *Shōnen kyōsei no kindaiteki tenkai*. Tokyo: Kyōsei Kyōkai, 1984.

Kyūsai kenkyū. 1913–22.

Lasch, Christopher. *Haven in a Heartless World: The Family Besieged*. New York: W. W. Norton and Company, 1995.

LeTendre, Gerald K. "Disruption and Reconnection: Counseling Young Adolescents in Japanese Schools." In *The Challenge of Eastern Asian Education: Implications for America*, edited by William K. Cummings and Philip G. Altbach, 101–14. Albany: State University of New York Press, 1997.

———. "Guiding Them On: Teaching, Hierarchy, and Social Organization in Japanese Middle Schools." *Journal of Japanese Studies* 20, no. 1 (Winter 1994): 37–59.

Leupp, Gary P. "The Five Men of Naniwa: Gang Violence and Popular Culture in Genroku Osaka." In *Osaka: The Merchants' Capital of Early Modern Japan*, edited by James L. McClain and Wakita Osamu, 125–57. Ithaca, NY: Cornell University Press, 1999.

———. *Servants, Shophands, and Laborers in the Cities of Tokugawa Japan*. Princeton, NJ: Princeton University Press, 1992.

Lincicome, Mark E. *Principle, Praxis, and the Politics of Educational Reform in Meiji Japan*. Honolulu: University of Hawai'i Press, 1995.

Maeda Ai. *Genkei no Meiji*. Vol. 4 of *Maeda Ai chosakushū*. Tokyo: Chikuma Shobō, 1989.

———. *Kindai dokusha no seiritsu*. Tokyo: Iwanami Shoten, 1993.

———. *Toshi kūkan no naka no bungaku*. Vol. 5 of *Maeda Ai chosakushū*. Tokyo: Chikuma Shobō, 1989.

Maeda Hajime. *Shokugyō fujin monogatari*. 1929. Reprinted in *Kindai josei bunken shiryō sōsho*, vol. 32, edited by Nakajima Kuni. Tokyo: Ōzorasha, 1993.

Marshall, Byron K. *Academic Freedom and the Japanese Imperial University, 1868–1939*. Berkeley: University of California Press, 1992.

———. *Learning to Be Modern: Japanese Political Discourse on Education*. Boulder, CO: Westview Press, 1994.

Maruyama Tsurukichi. *Gojūnen tokorodokoro*. Tokyo: Dai Nihon Yūben Kōdansha, 1934.

Matsubara Iwagorō. *Saiankoku no Tōkyō*. Tokyo: Iwanami Shoten, 1992.

———. *Shakai hyappōmen*. 1897. Reprinted in *Meiji bunka shiryō sōsho*, vol. 12, edited by Ōtō Tokihiko, 281–339. Tokyo: Kazama Shobō, 1960.

Matsumoto Kōjirō. *Katei ni okeru jidō kyōiku*. Tokyo: Kokkōsha, 1906.

Matsunaga Shōzō. "Shakai mondai no hassei." In *Iwanami kōza Nihon rekishi*, vol. 16, edited by Asao Naohiro et al., 241–80. Tokyo: Iwanami Shoten, 1976.

Matsuzaki Tenmin. *Ginza*. Tokyo: Ginbura Gaidosha, 1927.

Matza, David. "The Subterranean Traditions of Youth." *Annals of the American Academy of Political and Social Science* 228 (1961): 102–18.

McClain, James L., John M. Merriman, and Ugawa Kaoru, eds. *Edo and Paris: Urban Life and the State in the Early Modern Era*. Ithaca, NY: Cornell University Press, 1994.

Meiji nenkan hayari uta. Appendix to *Riyōshū shūi,* edited by Takano Tatsuyuki and Ōtake Shiyō. Tokyo: Rikugōkan, 1915.

Meiji Taishō Shōwa Shinbun Kenkyūkai, ed. *Shinbun shūsei Taishō hennenshi.* 44 vols. Tokyo: Meiji Taishō Shōwa Shinbun Kenkyūkai, 1966–88.

Meiji Taishō Shōwa Shinbun Kenkyūkai and Hirano Seisuke, eds. *Shinbun shūsei Shōwa hennenshi.* 27 vols. covering 1927–38. Tokyo: Meiji Taishō Shōwa Shinbun Kenkyūkai, 1955–.

Meyer, Stephen III. *The Five Dollar Day: Labor Management and Social Control in the Ford Motor Company, 1908–1921.* Albany: State University of New York Press, 1981.

Mimura Haruyo. "Furyō shōjo no kyōiku." In *Dai go kai kanka kyūsai kōenshū,* edited by Naimushō Chihōkyoku, 662–68. Tokyo: Naimushō Chihōkyoku, 1913.

Minami Hiroshi. *Shōwa bunka: 1925–1945.* Tokyo: Keisō Shobō, 1987.

———, ed. *Nihon modanizumu no kenkyū: shisō, seikatsu, bunka.* Tokyo: Bureen Shuppan, 1982.

Minami Hiroshi and Shakai Shinri Kenkyūjo. *Taishō bunka: 1905–1927.* Tokyo: Keisō Shobō, 1987.

Minami Hiroshi et al., eds. *Kindai shomin seikatsushi.* 20 vols. Tokyo: San'ichi Shobō, 1984–98.

Minami Kazuo. *Bakumatsu Edo shakai no kenkyū.* Tokyo: Yoshikawa Kōbunkan, 1978.

———. *Edo no shakai kōzō.* Tokyo: Hanawa Shobō, 1969.

Mitchell, Richard H. *Thought Control in Prewar Japan.* Ithaca, NY: Cornell University Press, 1976.

Miyachi Masato. *Nichi-Ro sengo seiji shi no kenkyū.* Tokyo: Tōkyō Daigaku Shuppankai, 1982.

Miyako shinbun. 1930–33.

Miyasaka Kōsaku. *Kindai Nihon no seinenki kyōiku.* Vol. 3 of *Miyasaka Kōsaku chosakushū.* Tokyo: Akashi Shoten, 1995.

Miyoshi Akira. *Arima Shirōsuke.* Tokyo: Yoshikawa Kōbunkan, 1967.

Monbushō Futsū Gakumukyoku. "Gakkō seito kōgai torishimari ni kansuru chōsa." *Teikoku kyōiku* 321 (April 10, 1909): 72–83.

———, ed. *Shokugyō shidō.* 2 vols. Tokyo: Shakai Kyōiku Kyōkai, 1924.

———. *Zenkoku chūgakkō ni kansuru shochōsa.* Tokyo: Monbushō, 1907 and June 1909 editions.

Mori Ogai. *Uita sekusuarisu.* 1909. In *Ōgai zenshū,* vol. 5, edited by Kinoshita Mokutarō et al., 83–179. Tokyo: Iwanami Shoten, 1971–75.

Morisue Yoshiaki et al., eds. *Seikatsushi 2.* Vol. 16 of *Taikei Nihonshi sōsho.* Tokyo: Yamakawa Shuppansha, 1966.

Morita Akira. "Taishō jūichinen shōnen hō no rippō katei: hikaku hōshiteki gaikan." In *Taishō shōnen hō,* vol. 1, edited by Morita Akira, 3–68. Vol. 18 of *Nihon rippō shiryō zenshū.* Tokyo: Shinzansha, 1993.

———, ed. *Taishō shōnen hō.* 2 vols. Vols. 18–19 of *Nihon rippō shiryō zenshū.* Tokyo: Shinzansha, 1993.

Moriya Katsuhiko. *Shōnen no hikō to kyōiku.* Tokyo: Keisō Shobō, 1977.

Morris-Suzuki, Tessa. *Re-Inventing Japan: Time, Space, Nation.* Armonk, NY: M.E. Sharpe, 1998.

Morrison, William Douglas. *Juvenile Offenders.* London: T. Fisher Unwin, 1896.

Murashima Yoriyuki. *Kanraku no ōkyū kafuee.* 1929. Reprinted in *Kyōraku, sei,* 317–79. Vol. 10 of *Kindai shomin seikatsushi,* edited by Minami Hiroshi et al. Tokyo: San'ichi Shobō, 1990.

Muta Kazue. "Images of the Family in Meiji Periodicals: The Paradox Underlying the Emergence of the 'Home'." *U.S.-Japan Women's Journal, English Supplement* 7 (1994): 53–71.

Nagai Kafū, "During the Rains." 1931. In *During the Rains and Flowers in the Shade: Two Novellas by Nagai Kafū,* 3–133. Translated by Lane Dunlop. Stanford, CA: Stanford University Press, 1994.

Nagy, Margit Maria. "'How Shall We Live?': Social Change, the Family Institution, and Feminism in Prewar Japan." Ph.D. diss., University of Washington, 1981.

Naigai rōdō shūhō. 1941–44.

Naigai shakai mondai chōsa shiryō. 1938–41.

Naikaku Tōkeikyoku. *Nihon teikoku tōkei nenkan.* Tokyo: Tōkeikyoku, 1882–1936.

Naikaku-fu, ed. *Seishōnen hakusho.* 2001 (Heisei 13) edition, *21 seiki o mukaete no seishōnen kenzen ikusei no arata na torikumi.* Tokyo: Naikaku-fu, 2001.

Naimushō Chihōkyoku, ed. *Dai go kai kanka kyūsai kōenshū.* Tokyo: Naimushō Chihōkyoku, 1913.

———. *Kanka kyūsai jigyō kōenshū.* Tokyo: Naimushō Chihōkyoku, 1909. 2 vols. Reprinted in *Senzenki shakai jigyō shiryō shūsei,* vols. 18–20, edited by Shakai Fukushi Chōsa Kenkyūkai. Tokyo: Nihon Tosho Sentā, 1985.

Naimushō Shakaikyoku, ed. *Kanka kyōiku shiryō (Musashino Gakuin kenkyū hōkoku).* 1921. Reprinted in *Senzen Nihon shakai jigyō chōsa shiryō shūsei,* vol. 5, edited by Shakai Fukushi Chōsa Kenkyūkai. Tokyo: Keisō Shobō, 1990.

———, ed. *Kankain shūyō jidō kanbetsu chōsa hōkoku.* 1925. Reprinted in *Senzen Nihon shakai jigyō chōsa shiryō shūsei,* vol. 5, edited by Shakai Fukushi Chōsa Kenkyūkai. Tokyo: Keisō Shobō, 1990.

Naimushō Shakaikyoku Shakaibu. *Kanka jigyō ni kansuru tōkei.* Tokyo: Naimushō, 1926 and 1927 editions.

Nakagawa Kiyoshi, ed. *Meiji Tōkyō kasō seikatsushi.* Tokyo: Iwanami Shoten, 1994.

———. "Senzen Nihon no hinkon no seikaku: sono jittai to ninshiki." In *Shakai fukushi no Nihonteki tokushitsu,* edited by Yoshida Kyūichi, 283–302. Tokyo: Kawashima Shoten, 1986.

———. "Senzen Tōkyō no toshi kasō." In *Toshi to gijutsu,* edited by Hayashi Takeshi and Koyano Seigo, 61–117. Tokyo: United Nations University Press, 1995.

———, ed. *Shōnen rōmusha.* Vol. 6 of *Rōdōsha seikatsu chōsa shiryō shūsei: kindai Nihon no rōdōsha zō, 1920–1930 nendai,* edited by Nakagawa Kiyoshi. Tokyo: Seishisha, 1995.

Nakamura Kokyō et al., eds. *Shōnen furyōka no keiro to sono kyōiku*. Tokyo: Nihon Seishin Igakkai, 1921.

Nakayama Tarō. *Nihon wakamonoshi*. Tokyo: Parutosusha, 1983.

Nakayama Yasumasa et al., eds. *Shinbun shūsei Meiji hennenshi*. 15 vols. Tokyo: Zaisei Keizai Gakkai, 1934–36.

Narita Ryūichi. "Kindai toshi to minshū." In *Toshi to minshū*, edited by Narita Ryūichi, 1–56. Vol. 9 of *Kindai Nihon no kiseki*. Tokyo: Yoshikawa Kōbunkan, 1993.

———. "Sei no chōryō: 1920 nendai no sekushuaritii." In *Shūkyō to minzoku, shintai to seiai*, 523–64. Vol. 1 of *Jendā no Nihonshi*, edited by Wakita Haruko and S. B. Hanley Tokyo: Tōkyō Daigaku Shuppankai, 1994.

———. "'Shōnen sekai' to dokusho suru shōnentachi: 1900 nen zengo, toshi kūkan no naka no kyōdōsei to sai." *Shisō* 845 (November 1994): 193–221.

———. "Teito Tōkyō." In *Iwanami Kōza Nihon tsūshi*, vol. 16, edited by Asao Naohiro et al., 175–214. Tokyo: Iwanami Shoten, 1993.

———, ed. *Toshi to minshū*. Vol. 9 of *Kindai Nihon no kiseki*. Tokyo: Yoshikawa Kōbunkan, 1993.

———. "Women and Views of Women within the Changing Hygiene Conditions of Late Nineteenth and Early Twentieth-Century Japan." *U.S.-Japan Women's Journal, English Supplement* 8 (1995): 64–86.

Nasaw, David. *Children of the City: At Work and Play*. New York: Oxford University Press, 1985.

Neuberger, Joan. *Hooliganism: Crime, Culture, and Power in St. Petersburg, 1900–1914*. Berkeley: University of California Press, 1993.

Nihon Gakudōkai, ed. *Akudō kenkyū*. Tokyo: Nanbokusha, 1916.

Nihon Shōnen Hogo Kyōkai. *Hogo tōkei zushū*. Osaka: Nihon Shōnen Hogo Kyōkai Osaka Shibu, 1932.

Nihon Shōnen Shidōkai Yōshōnen Kyōka Kenkyūbu, ed. *Shōnen furyōka to sono taisaku (shōhon), dai isshū*. Tokyo: Nihon Shōnen Shidōkai, 1937.

Nihonshi Kenkyūkai and Rekishigaku Kenkyūkai, ed. *Kōza Nihon rekishi*, vol. 5. Tokyo: Tōkyō Daigaku Shuppankai, 1985.

Ninsoku Yoseba Kenshōkai, ed. *Ninsoku yoseba shi: wagakuni jiyūkei, hoan shobun no genryū*. Tokyo: Sōbunsha, 1974.

Nishikawa Yūko. "The Changing Form of Dwellings and the Establishment of the Katei (Home) in Modern Japan." *U.S.-Japan Women's Journal, English Supplement* 8 (1995): 3–36.

Nishiyama Matsunosuke. *Edo Culture: Daily Life and Diversions in Early Japan, 1600–1868*. Translated by Gerald Groemer. Honolulu: University of Hawai'i Press, 1997.

———, ed. *Edo chōnin no kenkyū*. 5 vols. Tokyo: Yoshikawa Kōbunkan, 1972–78.

Nishiyama Matsunosuke et al., eds. *Edogaku jiten*. Tokyo: Kōbundō, 1984.

Nishizaka Yasushi. "Kinsei toshi to ōdana." In *Toshi no jidai*, edited by Yoshida Nobuyuki, 197–217. Vol. 9 of *Nihon no kinsei*. Tokyo: Chūō Kōronsha, 1992.

Noguchi Takehiko. *Edo wakamono kō*. Tokyo: Sanseidō, 1986.

Noguchi Yukio. *1940 nen taisei: saraba "senji keizai."* Tokyo: Tōyō Keizai Shinpōsha, 1995.

Nord, Deborah Epstein. "The Social Investigator as Anthropologist: Victorian Travellers among the Urban Poor." In *Visions of the Modern City: Essays in History, Art, and Literature,* edited by William Sharpe and Leonard Wallock, 122–34. Baltimore, MD: Johns Hopkins University Press, 1987.

———. *Walking the Victorian Streets: Women, Representation, and the City.* Ithaca, NY: Cornell University Press, 1995.

Notar, Ernest J. "Labor Unions and the Sangyō Hōkoku Movement, 1930–1945: A Japanese Model for Industrial Relations." Ph.D. diss., University of California, Berkeley, 1979.

Ōbinata Sumio. *Keisatsu no shakaishi.* Tokyo: Iwanami Shoten, 1993.

Odem, Mary E. *Delinquent Daughters: Protecting and Policing Adolescent Female Sexuality in the United States, 1885–1920.* Chapel Hill: University of North Carolina Press, 1995.

Ogawa Shigejirō. *Gokujidan.* Tokyo: Tōkyō Shoin, 1901.

———. *Ogawa Shigejirō chosaku senshū,* vol. 1. Edited by Ogawa Hakase Ibun Kankōkai. Tokyo: Nihon Hyōronsha, 1942.

———. *Ogawa Shigejirō shū.* Edited by Doi Yōichi and Endō Kōichi. Tokyo: Ōtori Shoin, 1980.

Ogawa Takeshi. *Ryūsenkei abekku.* 1935. Reprinted in *Kyōraku, sei,* 381–439. Vol. 10 of *Kindai shomin seikatsushi,* edited by Minami Hiroshi et al. Tokyo: San'ichi Shobō, 1990.

Ōhara Shakai Mondai Kenkyūjo, ed. *Nihon shakai jigyō nenkan.* Osaka: Ōhara Shakai Mondai Kenkyūjo Shuppanbu, 1920–26.

Oka Yoshitake. "General Conflict after the Russo-Japanese War." In *Conflict in Modern Japanese History: The Neglected Tradition,* edited by Tetsuo Najita and J. Victor Koschmann, 197–225. Princeton, NJ: Princeton University Press, 1982.

Ōkado Masakatsu. "Gakkō kyōiku to shakai idō: tokainetsu to seishōnen." In *Nihon no kindai to shihonshugi: kokusaika to chiiki,* edited by Nakamura Masanori, 157–87. Tokyo: Tōkyō Daigaku Shuppankai, 1992.

———. "Nōson kara toshi e: seishōnen no idō to 'kugaku,' 'dokugaku'." In *Toshi to minshū,* edited by Narita Ryūichi, 174–95. Vol. 9 of *Kindai Nihon no kiseki.* Tokyo: Yoshikawa Kōbunkan, 1993.

Okamoto Hōji, Fukutome Tsuyoshi, and Yahagi Misao, eds. *Gakkō, katei, chiiki to hikō bōshi: seishōnen kenzen ikusei no jissen kara.* Tokyo: Gyōsei, 1983.

Okanishi Shigesaburō, ed. *Tōkyō Kankain keiri ippan.* Tokyo: Tōkyō Kankain Hazawa Bunko, 1903.

Okano, Kaori. *School to Work Transition in Japan: An Ethnographic Study.* Clevedon, UK: Multilingual Matters Ltd., 1993.

Okuda Akiko. "Jochū no rekishi." In *Semegiau onna to otoko: kindai,* edited by Okuda Akiko, 376–401. Vol. 5 of *Onna to otoko no jikū,* edited by Tsurumi Kazuko et al. Tokyo: Fujiwara Shoten, 1995.

Ōmori Makoto. "Toshi shakai jigyō seiritsuki ni okeru chūkansō to minponshugi: Ōsaka-fu hōmen iin seido no seiritsu o megutte." *Hisutoria* 97 (December 1982): 58–77.

Ōmura Jintarō. *Jidō kyōhei ron.* 1900. Reprinted in *Nihon jidō mondai bunken senshū,* vol. 15, edited by Jidō Mondaishi Kenkyūkai. Tokyo: Nihon Tosho Sentā, 1984.

Ooms, Herman. *Charismatic Bureaucrat: A Political Biography of Matsudaira Sadanobu, 1758–1829.* Chicago: University of Chicago Press, 1975.

———. *Tokugawa Ideology: Early Constructs, 1570–1680.* Princeton, NJ: Princeton University Press, 1985.

———. *Tokugawa Village Practice: Class, Status, Power, Law.* Berkeley: University of California Press, 1996.

Osatake Takeki. *Bakuto to suri no kenkyū.* Tokyo: Shinsensha, 1969.

Ōsugi Sakae. *The Autobiography of Ōsugi Sakae.* Translated with an introduction by Byron K. Marshall. Berkeley: University of California Press, 1992.

Ōtani-ha Honganji Shakaika, ed. *Shōnen hogo ippan.* Kyoto: Ōtani-ha Shūmusho Shakaika, 1932.

Ototake Iwazō. *Furyōji kyōikuhō.* Tokyo: Meguro Shoten, 1910.

Otsubo, Sumiko. "Feminist Maternal Eugenics in Wartime Japan." *U.S.-Japan Women's Journal, English Supplement* 17 (1999): 39–76.

———. "Problematizing State Power: Eugenic Legislation in Wartime Japan." Paper presented to the annual meeting of the Association for Asian Studies. San Diego, California, March 9, 2000.

Peiss, Kathy. *Cheap Amusements: Working Women and Leisure in Turn-of-the-Century New York.* Philadelphia, PA: Temple University Press, 1987.

Perrot, Michelle. "Dans Paris de la Belle Epoque, les 'Apaches', Premières Bandes de Jeunes." In Michelle Perrot, *Les Ombres de l'Histoire: Crime et Châtiment au XIXe Siècle.* Paris: Flammarion, 2001.

Peukert, Detlev J.K. *Inside Nazi Germany: Conformity, Opposition, and Racism in Everyday Life.* Translated by Richard Deveson. New Haven, CT: Yale University Press, 1987.

Pflugfelder, Gregory M. *Cartographies of Desire: Male-Male Sexuality in Japanese Discourse, 1600–1950.* Berkeley: University of California Press, 1999.

Pierson, John D. *Tokutomi Sohō: A Journalist for Modern Japan.* Princeton, NJ: Princeton University Press, 1980.

Platt, Anthony M. *The Child Savers: The Invention of Delinquency.* Chicago: University of Chicago Press, 1977.

Pyle, Kenneth B. "The Advantages of Followership: German Economics and Japanese Bureaucrats, 1890–1925." *Journal of Japanese Studies* 1, no. 1 (Autumn 1974): 127–64.

———. *The New Generation in Meiji Japan: Problems of Cultural Identity, 1885–1895.* Stanford, CA: Stanford University Press, 1969.

———. "The Technology of Japanese Nationalism: The Local Improvement Movement 1900–1918." *Journal of Asian Studies* 33, no. 1 (November 1973): 51–65.

Robertson, Jennifer. *Takarazuka: Sexual Politics and Popular Culture in Modern Japan.* Berkeley: University of California Press, 1998.

Roden, Donald. *Schooldays in Imperial Japan: The Culture of a Student Elite.* Berkeley: University of California Press, 1980.

Rogers, Lawrence, ed. and trans. *Tokyo Stories: A Literary Stroll.* Berkeley: University of California Press, 2002.

Rohlen, Thomas P. *Japan's High Schools.* Berkeley: University of California Press, 1983.

———. "'Spiritual Education' in a Japanese Bank." *American Anthropologist,* New Series 75, no. 5 (1973): 1542–62.

Rose, Sonya O. "Cultural Analysis and Moral Discourses: Episodes, Continuities, and Transformations." In *Beyond the Cultural Turn: New Directions in the Study of Society and Culture,* edited by Victoria E. Bonnell and Lynn Hunt, 217–38. Berkeley: University of California Press, 1999.

Rosenhaft, Eve. "Organising the 'Lumpenproletariat'." in *The German Working Class, 1888–1933: The Politics of Everyday Life,* edited by Richard J. Evans, 174–219. London: Croom Helm, 1982.

Rothstein, Stanley William. *Schools and Society: New Perspectives in American Education.* Englewood Cliffs, NJ: Merrill, 1996.

Rueschemeyer, Dietrich, and Theda Skocpol, eds. *States, Social Knowledge, and the Origins of Modern Social Policies.* Princeton, NJ: Princeton University Press, 1996.

Saga Junichi. *Confessions of a Yakuza.* Translated by John Bester. Tokyo: Kodansha International, 1991.

Saguchi Kazurō. "Nihon no naibu rōdō shijō: 1960 nendaimatsu no henyō o chūshin toshite." In *Keizai riron e no rekishiteki paasupekutibu,* edited by Yoshikawa Hiroshi and Okazaki Tetsuji. Tokyo: Tōkyō Daigaku Shuppankai, 1990.

Saitō Toshihiko. *Kyōsō to kanri no gakkōshi: Meiji kōki chūgakkō kyōiku no tenkai.* Tokyo: Tōkyō Daigaku Shuppankai, 1995.

Sakaguchi Shizuo. *Furyō shōnen no kenkyū.* Tokyo: Nakamura Yasuke, distributed by Nihon Keisatsu Shinbunsha, 1917.

Sand, Jordan. "At Home in the Meiji Period: Inventing Japanese Domesticity." In *Mirror of Modernity: Invented Traditions of Modern Japan,* edited by Stephen Vlastos, 191–207. Berkeley: University of California Press, 1998.

Sanpō. 1942–44.

Santō Kyōden [Kitao Masanobu]. *Edo umare uwaki no kabayaki.* 1787. Reprinted in *Kibyōshi sharebon shū,* edited by Mizuno Minoru, 135–56. Vol. 58 of *Nihon koten bungaku taikei.* Tokyo: Iwanami Shoten, 1958.

Sato, Barbara. *The New Japanese Woman: Modernity, Media, and Women in Interwar Japan.* Durham, NC: Duke University Press, 2003.

Satō Hachirō. *Asakusa.* Tokyo: Seikōkan Shoten, 1932.

———. "Furyō shōjo no ryūkō." *Kaizō* 13, no. 5 (May 1931): 125–33.

Satō Hiromi. *Sōryokusen taisei to kyōiku kagaku: senzen Kyōiku Kagaku Kenkyūkai ni okeru "kyōiku kaikaku ron" no kenkyū.* Tokyo: Ōtsuki Shoten, 1997.

Satō, Ikuya. *Kamikaze Biker: Parody and Anomy in Affluent Japan.* Chicago: University of Chicago Press, 1991.

Satō Takeshi. "Modanizumu to Amerikaka: 1920 nendai o chūshin toshite," in *Nihon modanizumu no kenkyū: shisō, seikatsu, bunka,* edited by Minami Hiroshi, 1–56. Tokyo: Bureen Shuppan, 1982.

Sawayama Mikako. "Kosodate ni okeru otoko to onna." In *Nihon josei seikat-sushi*, vol. 4, edited by Joseishi Sōgō Kenkyūkai, 125–62. Tokyo: Tōkyō Daigaku Shuppankai, 1990.

———. "Kyōiku kazoku no seiritsu." In *Kyōiku: tanjō to shūen*, 108–31. Vol. 1 of *Sōsho umu, sodateru, oshieru: tokumei no kyōikushi*, edited by Henshū Iinkai. Tokyo: Fujiwara Shoten, 1990.

Schlossman, Steven L. *Love and the American Delinquent: The Theory and Practice of "Progressive" Juvenile Justice, 1825–1920*. Chicago: University of Chicago Press, 1977.

Schlossman, Steven, and Stephanie Wallach. "The Crime of Precocious Sexuality: Female Juvenile Delinquency in the Progressive Era." *Harvard Educational Review* 48, no. 1 (February 1978): 65–94.

Schneider, Eric C. *In the Web of Class: Delinquents and Reformers in Boston, 1810s–1930s*. New York: New York University Press, 1992.

Schoenbaum, David. *Hitler's Social Revolution: Class and Status in Nazi Germany, 1933–1939*. New York: W. W. Norton and Co., 1980.

Seidensticker, Edward. *Low City, High City: Tokyo from Edo to the Earthquake*. New York: Alfred A. Knopf, 1983.

———. *Tokyo Rising: The City since the Great Earthquake*. New York: Knopf, distributed by Random House, 1990.

Sen, Satadru. "A Separate Punishment: Juvenile Offenders in Colonial India." *Journal of Asian Studies* 63, no. 1 (February 2004): 81–104.

Serizawa Shunsuke. "Genkai toshite no kenryoku." In *Kaitai sareru kodomo-tachi: shōnen hanzai no seijigaku*, edited by Serizawa Shunsuke, 281–97. Tokyo: Seikyūsha, 1994.

———. "Hikō ga shōmetsu shita." In *Sedai no kōgengaku*, edited by Sanseidō Henshūbu, 149–57. Tokyo: Sanseidō, 1993.

Shakai. 1899–1901. Reprinted in *Meijiki shakaigaku kankei shiryō*, edited by Kawai Takao, vols. 3–8. Tokyo: Ryūkei Shosha, 1991.

Shakai fukuri. 1929–40. Reprint edition. Tokyo: Ryūkei Shosha, 1981–82.

Shakai Fukushi Chōsa Kenkyūkai, ed. *Senzen Nihon shakai jigyō chōsa shiryō shūsei*. 10 vols. Tokyo: Keisō Shobō, 1986–95.

———, ed. *Senzenki shakai jigyō shiryō shūsei*. 20 vols. Tokyo: Nihon Tosho Sentā, 1985.

Shakai jigyō. 1921–41.

Shakai jigyō kenkyū. 1922–42.

Shakai to kyūsai. 1917–21.

Shakai zasshi. 1897–98. Reprinted in *Meijiki shakaigaku kankei shiryō*, edited by Kawai Takao, vols. 1–2. Tokyo: Ryūkei Shosha, 1991.

Shakaigaku zasshi. 1902–1903. Reprinted in *Meijiki shakaigaku kankei shiryō*, edited by Kawai Takao, vols. 9–10. Tokyo: Ryūkei Shosha, 1991.

Shibusawa Seien Kinen Zaidan Ryūmonsha, ed. *Shibusawa Eiichi denki shiryō*, vol. 24. Tokyo: Shibusawa Eiichi denki shiryō Kankōkai, 1959.

Shibusawa Seika. *Asakusakko*. Tokyo: Mainichi Shuppansha, 1966.

Shigematsu Kazuyoshi. *Shōnen chōkai kyōikushi*. Tokyo: Daiichi Hōki Shuppan, 1976.

Shihō Daijin Kanbō Hogoka, ed. *Kaidō gijiroku: shōnen shinpanshochō hogo kansatsushochō kyōseiinchō, Shōwa 14 nen 6 gatsu 1–3 nichi. Shihō hogo shiryō*, no. 21. Tokyo: Shihō Daijin Kanbō Hogoka, 1939.

———, ed. *Kaidō gijiroku: shōnen shinpanshochō hogo kansatsushochō kyōseiinchō, Shōwa 15 nen 5 gatsu 15–18 nichi. Shihō hogo shiryō*, no. 22. Tokyo: Shihō Daijin Kanbō Hogoka, 1940.

———. *Shihō hogo tōkei shū*. Tokyo: Shihō Daijin Kanbō Hogoka, 1936.

Shihō hodō. 1944.

Shihō Hogo Kyōkai, ed. *Shihō hogo jigyō nenkan*, vol. 1. Tokyo: Shihō Hogo Kyōkai, 1940.

Shihōshō, ed. *Tokugawa kinreikō.* 12 vols. (1–6: *Tokugawa kinreikō;* 6–12: *Tokugawa kinrei kō goshū*). Tokyo: Yoshikawa Kōbunkan, 1931–32.

Shihōshō Hogokyoku, ed. *Kaidō gijiroku: shōnen shinpanshochō hogo kansatsushochō kyōseiinchō, Shōwa 16 nen 5 gatsu 19–21 nichi. Shihō hogo shiryō*, no. 27. Tokyo: Shihōshō Hogokyoku, 1942.

Shikita, Minoru, and Shinichi Tsuchiya. *Crime and Criminal Policy in Japan: Analysis and Evaluation of the Shōwa Era, 1926–1988.* New York and Berlin: Springer-Verlag, 1992.

Shin kōron. 1904–21.

Shinbori Tetsugaku. *Meian no Asakusa to furyō shōnen.* Tokyo: Hokutō Shobō, 1936.

Shively, Donald H. "*Bakufu* vs. *Kabuki.*" *Harvard Journal of Asiatic Studies* 18, nos. 3–4 (December 1955): 326–54.

———. "Sumptuary Regulation and Status in Early Tokugawa Japan." *Harvard Journal of Asiatic Studies* 25 (1964–65): 123–64.

Shokugyō shidō. 1937–46.

Shōnen hogo. 1936–43.

Silverberg, Miriam. "The Café Waitress Serving Modern Japan." In *Mirror of Modernity: Invented Traditions of Modern Japan*, edited by Stephen Vlastos, 208–25. Berkeley: University of California Press, 1998.

———. "Constructing the Japanese Ethnography of Modernity." *Journal of Asian Studies* 51, no. 1 (February 1992): 30–54.

Smelser, Ronald. *Robert Ley: Hitler's Labor Front Leader.* Oxford and New York: Berg Publishers, 1988.

Smethurst, Richard J. *A Social Basis for Prewar Japanese Militarism: The Army and the Rural Community.* Berkeley: University of California Press, 1974.

Smith, Henry D. "Tokyo as an Idea: An Exploration of Japanese Urban Thought until 1945." *Journal of Japanese Studies* 4, no. 1 (Winter 1978): 45–80.

Smith, Henry D. II. "The Edo-Tokyo Transition: In Search of Common Ground." In *Japan in Transition: From Tokugawa to Meiji*, edited by Marius B. Jansen and Gilbert Rozman, 347–74. Princeton, NJ: Princeton University Press, 1986.

———. "The Nonliberal Roots of Taishō Democracy." In *Japan Examined: Perspectives on Modern Japanese History*, edited by Harry Wray and Hilary Conroy, 191–98. Honolulu: University of Hawai'i Press, 1983.

Smith, Henry DeWitt II. *Japan's First Student Radicals.* Cambridge, MA: Harvard University Press, 1972.

Soeda Tomomichi. *Enka no Meiji Taishō shi*. Tokyo: Iwanami Shoten, 1970.

Sōmuchō Seishōnen Taisaku Honbu, ed. *Seishōnen hakusho*. 1996 (Heisei 8) edition, *Seishōnen mondai no genjō to taisaku*. Tokyo: Ōkurashō Insatsukyoku, 1997.

Stansell, Christine. *City of Women: Sex and Class in New York, 1789–1860*. Urbana and Chicago: University of Illinois Press, 1987.

Strange, Carolyn. *Toronto's Girl Problem: The Perils and Pleasures of the City, 1880–1930*. Toronto, Buffalo, and London: University of Toronto Press, 1995.

Sumiya Mikio. "Meiji nashonarizumu no kiseki." In *Tokutomi Sohō, Yamaji Aizan*, edited by Sumiya Mikio, 5–56. Vol. 40 of *Nihon no meicho*. Tokyo: Chūō Kōronsha, 1971.

———. *Nihon chinrōdō shiron*. Tokyo: Tōkyō Daigaku Shuppankai, 1974.

———. *Nihonteki yōsei seido no keisei*. Vol. 2 of *Nihon shokugyō kunren hatten shi*, edited by Sumiya Mikio and Koga Hiroshi. Tokyo: Nihon Rōdō Kyōkai, 1977.

Suzuki Kaichirō. *Furyō shōnen no kenkyū*. Tokyo: Daitōkaku, 1923.

———. *Ko no tame ni naku*. Tokyo: Shōkadō, 1934.

———, ed. *Tōkyō Shōnen Shinpanjo jūnenshi*. Tokyo: Nihon Shōnen Hogo Kyōkai Tōkyō Shibu, 1935.

Taeuber, Irene B. *The Population of Japan*. Princeton, NJ: Princeton University Press, 1958.

Tago Ichimin. *Shakai jigyō*. 1922. Reprinted in *Tago Ichimin, Yamasaki Iwao shū*, edited by Satō Susumu. Vol. 5 of *Shakai fukushi koten sōsho*. Tokyo: Koto Shoin, 1982.

Tajima Hajime. "Kyōdōtai no kaitai to 'seinen' no shutsugen." In *Kyōiku: tanjō to shūen*, 32–50. Vol. 1 of *Sōsho umu, sodateru, oshieru: tokumei no kyōikushi*, edited by Henshū Iinkai. Tokyo: Fujiwara Shoten, 1990.

Takano Yoshihiro. *Seinen gakkōshi*. Tokyo: San'ichi Shobō, 1992.

Takashima Heizaburō. "Jidō kenkyū." In *Kanka kyūsai jigyō kōenshū*, vol. 2, edited by Naimushō Chihōkyoku, 457–698. 1909. Reprinted in *Senzenki shakai jigyō shiryō shūsei*, vol. 20, edited by Shakai Fukushi Chōsa Kenkyūkai. Tokyo: Nihon Tosho Sentā, 1985.

———. *Jidō shinri kōwa*. Tokyo: Kōbundō Shoten, 1909.

Takayanagi Kaneyoshi. *Edo jidai hinin no seikatsu*. Vol. 21 of *Seikatsushi sōsho*. Tokyo: Yūzankaku, 1971.

Tamagawa Shinmei. *Boku wa Asakusa no furyō shōnen: jitsuroku Satō Hachirō den*. Tokyo: Sakuhinsha, 1991.

Tanaka Katsufumi. "Gimu kyōiku no rinen to hōsei." In *Kōza Nihon kyōikushi*, vol. 3, edited by Kōza Nihon kyōikushi Henshū Iinkai, 41–70. Tokyo: Daiichi Hōki Shuppankai, 1984.

Tanaka, Michiko. "Village Youth Organizations (Wakamono Nakama) in Late Tokugawa Politics and Society." Ph.D. diss., Princeton University, 1982.

Tanaka Tetsuo. *Keishichō monogatari: hiwa hyakunen*. Tokyo: Kasumigaseki Shuppankai N. T. Jigyōbu, 1974.

Tani Teruyuki. *Wakamono nakama no rekishi*. Tokyo: Nihon Seinenkan, 1984.

Tanioka, Ichiro, and Daniel Glaser. "School Uniforms, Routine Activities, and the Social Control of Delinquency in Japan." *Youth & Society* 23, no. 1 (September 1991): 50–75.

Tanizaki Jun'ichirō. *Chijin no ai.* 1924–25. In *Tanizaki Jun'ichirō zenshū,* vol. 10. Tokyo: Chūō Kōronsha, 1967.

———. *Naomi.* Translated by Anthony Chambers. New York: Alfred A. Knopf, 1985.

Tazaki Noriyoshi. "Josei rōdō no shoruikei." In *Nihon josei seikatsushi,* vol. 4, edited by Joseishi Sōgō Kenkyūkai, 164–90. Tokyo: Tōkyō Daigaku Shuppankai, 1990.

Teeters, Negley. *Deliberations of the International Penal and Penitentiary Congresses: Questions and Answers, 1872–1935.* Philadelphia, PA: Temple University Bookstore, 1949.

Teikoku kyōiku. 1905–44.

Terasaki Masao and Senjika Kyōiku Kenkyūkai, eds. *Sōryokusen taisei to kyōiku: kōkokumin "rensei" no rinen to jissen.* Tokyo: Tōkyō Daigaku Shuppankai, 1987.

Teruoka Gitō. "Kinrō seishōnen no dōkō ni tsuite." In *Shōnen hogo ronshū,* edited by Shihō Hogo Kenkyūjo, 645–70. Tokyo: Shihō Hogo kenkyūjo, 1943.

Thorne, Susan. "'The Conversion of Englishmen and the Conversion of the World Inseparable': Missionary Imperialism and the Language of Class in Early Industrial Britain." In *Tensions of Empire: Colonial Cultures in a Bourgeois World,* edited by Frederick Cooper and Ann Laura Stoler, 238–62. Berkeley: University of California Press, 1997.

Tipton, Elise K. "The Café: Contested Space of Modernity in Interwar Japan." In *Being Modern in Japan: Culture and Society from the 1910s to the 1930s,* edited by Elise K. Tipton and John Clark, 119–36. Honolulu: University of Hawai'i Press, 2000.

———. *The Japanese Police State: The Tokkō in Interwar Japan.* Honolulu: University of Hawai'i Press, 1990.

Tokufū. 1930–35.

Tokunaga Sunao. *Tokunaga Sunao shū (2).* Vol. 25 of *Nihon puroretaria bungakushū.* Tokyo: Shin Nihon Shuppansha, 1987.

Tokutomi Sohō. *Shin Nihon no seinen.* 1887. In *Tokutomi Sohō shū,* 3–53. Vol. 4 of *Gendai Nihon bungaku zenshū.* Tokyo: Kaizōsha, 1930.

———. *Shōrai no Nihon.* 1886. In *Tokutomi Sohō shū,* 54–128. Vol. 4 of *Gendai Nihon bungaku zenshū.* Tokyo: Kaizōsha, 1930.

Tōkyō hyakunenshi Henshū Iinkai, ed. *Tōkyō hyakunenshi.* 7 vols. Tokyo: Tōkyō-to, 1979–80.

Tōkyō Joshi Shūshoku Shidōkai, ed. *Tōkyō joshi shūshoku annai.* 1936. Reprinted in *Kindai josei bunken shiryō sōsho,* vol. 39, ed. Nakajima Kuni. Tokyo: Ōzorasha, 1994.

"Tōkyō no hinmin." Parts 1–6. *Jiji shinpō,* October 11, 18, and 25, and November 1, 22, and 29, 1896. Reprinted in *Meiji Tōkyō kasō seikatsushi,* edited by Nakagawa Kiyoshi, 90–153. Tokyo: Iwanami Shoten, 1994.

Tōkyō Shisei Chōsakai. *Toshi kyōiku no kenkyū.* Tokyo: Tōkyō Shisei Chōsakai, 1926.

Tōkyō Shiyakusho Shishi Hensan Kakari, ed. *Tōkyō annai.* 2 vols. Tokyo: Shōkadō, 1907.

Tōkyō Shōnen Shinpanjo. *Shōnen hogo tōkei: ji Taishō jūni nen shi Shōwa shichi nen.* Tokyo: Tōkyō Shōnen Shinpanjo, 1933.

Tōkyō Toritsu Kyōiku Kenkyūjo, ed. *Tōkyō kyōikushi shiryō taikei,* vol. 8. Tokyo: Tōkyō Toritsu Kyōiku Kenkyūjo, 1973.

Tōkyō-fu (Daiyō) Jidō Kenkyūjo. *Ippan jidō, furyōji, seishin hakujakuji ni kansuru tōkeiteki chōsa.* Tokyo: Takinokawa Gakuen, 1933.

Tōkyō-fu Gakumubu Shakai Kyōikuka. *Shōnen hogo no mondai ni tsuite. Kōgai seikatsu shidō sōsho,* no. 7. Tokyo: Tōkyō-fu Gakumubu Shakaika, 1940.

Tōkyō-fu Gakumubu Shakaika. *Honfu ni okeru jidō hogo jigyō no gaikyō. Shakai chōsa shiryō,* no. 10. Tokyo: Tōkyō-fu Gakumubu Shakaika, 1930.

———. ed. *Jidō kankei hōki shū. Shakai jigyō shiryō,* no. 23. 1935. Reprinted in *Senzenki shakai jigyō shiryō shūsei,* vol. 15, edited by Shakai Fukushi Chōsa Kenkyūkai. Tokyo: Nihon Tosho Sentā, 1985.

———. *Rōdō jidō chōsa, dai ni bu. Shakai chōsa shiryō,* no. 20. 1933. Reprinted in *Shōnen rōmusha.* Vol. 6 of *Rōdōsha seikatsu chōsa shiryō shūsei: kindai Nihon no rōdōsha zō, 1920–1930 nendai,* edited by Nakagawa Kiyoshi. Tokyo: Seishisha, 1995.

———. *Shōwa ninen honfu toriatsukai furyō jidō jōkyō. Shakai chōsa shiryō,* no. 8. Tokyo: Tōkyō-fu Gakumubu Shakaika, 1929.

Tōkyō-fu Jizen Kyōkai hō. 1917–20. Reprint edition. Tokyo: Ryūkei Shosha, 1981.

Tōkyō-fu Shakai Jigyō Kyōkai hō. 1920–29. Reprint edition. Tokyo: Ryūkei Shosha, 1981.

Tōkyō-fu Shakaika. "Honfu ni okeru jidō hogo jōkyō to sono keika: dai-ichi bu, furyō, furō jidō no bu." *Tōkyō-fu Shakai Jigyō Kyōkai hō* 27 (March 1926): 1–172.

Tōkyō-shi Asakusa Kuyakusho. *Asakusa-ku shi.* 2 vols. Tokyo: Bunkaidō Shoten, 1914.

Tōkyō-shi Kyōikukai zasshi. 1906–11.

Tōkyō-shi Shakaikyoku, ed. *Fujin jiritsu no michi.* 1925. Reprinted in *Kindai fujin mondai meicho senshū zokuhen,* vol. 7, edited by Nakajima Kuni. Tokyo: Nihon Tosho Sentā, 1982.

———. *Tōkyō-shi Yōshōnen Hogosho ni okeru hogo jidō jōkyō.* Tokyo: Tōkyō-shi Shakai Kyoku, 1924.

Tōkyō-shi Yōikuin. *Meiji 33 nendo Tōkyō-shi Yōikuin dai 29 kai hōkoku.* Tokyo: Tōkyō-shi Yōikuin, 1900.

———, ed. *Yōikuin rokujūnen shi.* Tokyo: Tōkyō-shi Yōikuin, 1933.

Tōkyō-to Shakai Fukushi Kyōgikai sanjūnenshi Kankō Iinkai, ed. *Tōkyō-to Shakai Fukushi Kyōgikai sanjūnenshi.* Tokyo: Tōkyō-to Shakai Fukushi Kyōgikai, 1983.

Tomeoka Kōsuke. *Jizen mondai.* Tokyo: Keiseisha Shoten, 1898.

———. "Kanka jigyō jisshi hōhō." 1912. In *Tomeoka Kōsuke Kun koki kinenshū,* edited by Makino Toraji, 421–99. 1933. Reprinted in vol. 21 of *Denki sōsho.* Tokyo: Ōzorasha, 1987.

———. *Kanka jigyō no hattatsu.* Tokyo: Keiseisha Shoten, 1897.

———. "Kanka jigyō to sono kanrihō." In *Kanka kyūsai jigyō kōenshū,* vol. 2, edited by Naimushō Chihōkyoku, 51–236. 1909. Reprinted in *Senzenki shakai jigyō shiryō shūsei,* vol. 19, edited by Shakai Fukushi Chōsa Kenkyūkai. Tokyo: Nihon Tosho Sentā, 1985.

———. *Katei Gakkō.* 1901. Reprinted in *Nihon jidō mondai bunken senshū,* vol. 1, edited by Jidō Mondaishi Kenkyūkai. Tokyo: Nihon Tosho Sentā, 1983.

———, ed. *Katei Gakkō dai ni hen.* 1902. Reprinted in *Nihon jidō mondai bunken senshū,* vol. 1, edited by Jidō Mondaishi Kenkyūkai. Tokyo: Nihon Tosho Sentā, 1983.

———. *Tomeoka Kōsuke chosakushū.* Edited by Dōshisha Daigaku Jinbun Kagaku Kenkyūjo. 5 vols. Kyoto: Dōmeisha, 1978.

———. *Tomeoka Kōsuke nikki.* Edited by Tomeoka Kōsuke nikki Henshū Iinkai. 5 vols. Tokyo: Kyōsei Kyōkai, 1979.

Toshi kyōiku. 1911–24.

Toshitani Nobuyoshi. "Oya to kyōshi no chōkaiken." In *Chiiki jūmin to kyōikuhō no sōzō,* 191–201. Vol. 4 of *Nihon Kyōikuhō Gakkai nenpō.* Tokyo: Yūhikaku, 1975.

———. "Senji taisei to kazoku: kokka sōdōin taisei ni okeru kazoku seisaku to kazoku hō." In *Kindai Nihon no kazoku seisaku to hō,* 255–362. Vol. 6 of *Kazoku: seisaku to hō,* edited by Fukushima Masao. Tokyo: Tōkyō Daigaku Shuppankai, 1984.

Tōyō Keizai Shinpōsha, ed. *Kanketsu Shōwa kokusei sōran.* 4 vols. Tokyo: Tōyō Keizai Shinpōsha, 1991.

———. *Meiji Taishō kokusei sōran.* Tokyo: Tōyō Keizai Shinpōsha, 1975.

Tsubouchi Shōyō. *Tōsei shosei katagi.* 1885–86. In *Tsubouchi Shōyō shū,* 59–163. Vol. 16 of *Meiji bungaku zenshū.* Tokyo: Chikuma Shobō, 1969.

Tsujimoto Yoshio and Nishimura Haruo. "Furoku: shōnen hogo no kagaku no tanjō: kagaku no shakaishiteki kokoromi." In *Kōza "shōnen hogo,"* vol. 3, edited by Hirano Ryūichi, 335–74. Tokyo: Taisei Shuppansha, 1983.

Tsukada Takashi. *Kinsei Nihon mibunsei no kenkyū.* Kōbe: Hyōgo Buraku Mondai Kenkyūjo, 1987.

———. *Mibunsei shakai to shimin shakai: kinsei Nihon no shakai to hō.* Tokyo: Kashiwa Shobō, 1992.

Ubukata Toshirō. *Meiji Taishō kenbunshi.* Tokyo: Chūō Kōronsha, 1978.

Ueda Kyūkichi. *Hogo kyōiku.* Tokyo and Osaka: Hōbunkan, 1911.

Ujiie Mikito. *Edo no Shōnen.* Tokyo: Heibonsha, 1994.

Uno, Kathleen S. *Passages to Modernity: Motherhood, Childhood, and Social Reform in Early Twentieth Century Japan.* Honolulu: University of Hawai'i Press, 1999.

Wada Atsuhiko. "Sei no sōchi to dokusho no sōchi: *Chūō kōron,* itsudatsu no kyōfu." *Bungei to hihyō* 70 (October 1994). http://fan.shinshu-u.ac.jp/~wada/report/tyuuouf.html (accessed January 29, 2003).

Wagatsuma, Hiroshi, and George A. De Vos. *Heritage of Endurance: Family Patterns and Delinquency Formation in Urban Japan.* Berkeley: University of California Press, 1984.

Walkowitz, Judith R. *City of Dreadful Delight: Narratives of Sexual Danger in Late-Victorian London.* Chicago: University of Chicago Press, 1992.

Weber, Eugen. *Peasants into Frenchmen: The Modernization of Rural France, 1870–1914.* Stanford, CA: Stanford University Press, 1976.

Weiner, Michael. *Race and Migration in Imperial Japan.* London: Routledge, 1994.

White, James B. "Internal Migration in Prewar Japan." *Journal of Japanese Studies* 4, no. 1 (1978): 81–123.

Yamamoto Akira. "Taishū seikatsu no henka to taishū bunka." In *Iwanami kōza Nihon rekishi,* vol. 19, edited by Asao Naohiro et al., 302–36. Tokyo: Iwanami Shoten, 1976.

Yamamoto Seikichi. *Gendai no furyō seinen tsuketari furyō joshi.* Tokyo: Shunyōdō, 1914.

Yamamoto Tsunehiko. *Kindai Nihon toshi kyōkashi kenkyū.* Tokyo: Reimei Shobō, 1972.

Yamanouchi, Yasushi, J. Victor Koschmann, and Ryūichi Narita, eds. *Total War and "Modernization."* Ithaca, NY: East Asia Program, Cornell University, 1998.

Yamazumi Masami and Nakae Kazue, eds. *Kosodate no sho.* 3 vols. Tokyo: Heibonsha, 1976.

Yasuda Seimei Shakai Jigyōdan, ed. *Nihon no jidō sōdan: Meiji, Taishō kara Shōwa e.* 2 vols. Tokyo: Kawashima Shoten, 1969.

Yasumaru Yoshio. "1850–70 nendai no Nihon: Ishin henkaku." In *Iwanami kōza Nihon tsūshi,* vol. 16, edited by Asao Naohiro et al., 1–64. Tokyo: Iwanami Shoten, 1993.

Yasuoka Shōtarō. "Bad Company." 1952. Translated by Kären Wigen Lewis. In *The Shōwa Anthology: Modern Japanese Short Stories, volume 1, 1929–1969,* edited by Van C. Gessel and Tomone Matsumoto, 76–99. Tokyo, New York, and San Francisco: Kodansha International, 1985.

Yatsuhama Tokusaburō. *Kasō shakai kenkyū.* Tokyo: Bungadō, 1920.

Yokoyama Gennosuke. *Kasō shakai tanpōshū.* Edited by Tachibana Yūichi. Tokyo: Shakai Shisōsha, 1990.

———. *Nihon no kasō shakai.* 1899. Tokyo: Iwanami Shoten, 1949.

Yorozu chōhō. 1900–1903.

Yoshida Kyūichi. *Gendai shakai jigyōshi kenkyū.* Tokyo: Kawashima Shoten, 1990.

———. *Nihon hinkonshi: seikatsushateki shiten ni yori mazushisa no keifu to sono jittai.* Tokyo: Kawashima Shoten, 1984.

———. *Nihon kindai Bukkyō shakaishi kenkyū.* Tokyo: Kawashima Shoten, 1991.

———, ed. *Shakai fukushi no Nihonteki tokushitsu.* Tokyo: Kawashima Shoten, 1986.

Yoshida Nobuyuki, ed. *"Kamiyui Shinza" no rekishi sekai.* Vol. 19 of *Asahi hyakka Nihon no rekishi bessatsu: rekishi o yominaosu.* Tokyo: Asahi Shinbunsha, 1994.

———. *Kinsei kyodai toshi no shakai kōzō.* Tokyo: Tōkyō Daigaku Shuppankai, 1991.

———. "Nihon kinsei toshi kasō shakai no sonzai kōzō." *Rekishigaku kenkyū* 534 (October 1984): 2–8.

———. *Seijuku suru Edo*. Vol. 17 of *Nihon no rekishi*. Tokyo: Kōdansha, 2002.

———. "Yatagorō Genshichi no shō: oyabun, tōrimono no isō." In *"Kamiyui Shinza" no rekishi sekai*, edited by Yoshida Nobuyuki, 48–56. Vol. 19 of *Asahi hyakka Nihon no rekishi bessatsu: rekishi o yominaosu*. Tokyo: Asahi Shinbunsha, 1994.

Yoshimi Shun'ya. "(Sōsetsu) Teito Tōkyō to modanitii no bunka seiji." In *Kakudai suru modanitii: 1920–30 nendai 2*, 1–62. Vol. 6 of *Iwanami kōza kindai Nihon no bunkashi*, edited by Komori Yōichi et al. Tokyo: Iwanami Shoten, 2002.

———. *Toshi no doramaturugii: Tōkyō, sakariba no shakaishi*. Tokyo: Kōbundo, 1987.

Young, Louise. "Imagined Empire: The Cultural Construction of Manchukuo." In *The Japanese Wartime Empire, 1931–1945*, edited by Peter Duus, Ramon H. Myers, and Mark R. Peattie, 71–96. Princeton, NJ: Princeton University Press, 1996.

———. *Japan's Total Empire: Manchuria and the Culture of Wartime Imperialism*. Berkeley: University of California Press, 1998.

Yutani, Eiji. "*Nihon no kasō shakai* of Yokoyama Gennosuke." Ph.D. diss., University of California, Berkeley, 1985.

Zakō Jun. *Asakusa Rokku wa itsumo modan data: opera, rebyū, sutorippu*. Tokyo: Asahi Shinbunsha, 1984.

Zen Nihon Shihō Hogo Jigyō Renmei, ed. *Jikyoku to shōnen hogo*. *Shihō hogo sōsho*, no. 8. Tokyo: Zen Nihon Shihō Hogo Jigyō Renmei, 1938.

Index

Text:	10/13 Sabon
Display:	Sabon
Compositor:	International Typesetting and Composition
Printer and binder:	Thomson-Shore, Inc.